Differentiated Instruction

Printed in the U.S.A.

ISBN   978-0-544-06564-2

2 3 4 5 6 7 8 9 10   0868   22 21 20 19 18 17 16 15 14 13
4500432942   A B C D E F G

Contents

Description of Contents x

Student Worksheets

Answers

Description of Contents

Using the Differentiated Instruction Worksheets	Integrating the ELPS
Practice and Problem Solving: A/B, C, D There are three worksheets for every lesson. All of these reinforce and practice the content of the lesson. Level A/B (slightly below/on level students) Level C (above level students) Level D (considerably below level students who require modified worksheets)	**c.4.C** develop basic sight vocabulary…used routinely in written…materials **c.4.E** …linguistically accommodated…material…with a decreasing need…for accommodations… **c.4.G** demonstrate comprehension of increasingly complex English…
Reteach (one worksheet per lesson) Provides an alternate way to teach or review the main concepts of the lesson, and for students to have further practice at a basic level.	**c.1.A** use prior knowledge… **c.1.F** use accessible language… **c.2.D** monitor understanding …seek clarification as needed **c.4.E** read linguistically accommodated…material…
Reading Strategies (one worksheet per lesson) Provides tools to help students master the math vocabulary or symbols, and comprehend word problems.	**c.3.D** speak using grade-level content…vocabulary in context **c.3.F** ask and give information using…key words…to using abstract and content-based vocabulary… **c.4.D** use…graphic organizers… pretaught…vocabulary and other prereading activities…
Success for English Learners (one worksheet per lesson) Provides teaching strategies for differentiated instruction and alternate practice. The worksheets use a visual approach with fewer words, which are ideal for English language learners as well as other students who are having difficulties with the lesson concepts.	**c.1.F** use accessible language…learn new and essential language… **c.2.C** learn…basic and academic vocabulary **c.2.E** use visual, contextual, and linguistic support to enhance and confirm understanding… **c.4.E** read linguistically accommodated…material…
Challenge (one worksheet per module) Provides extra non-routine problem solving opportunities, enhances critical thinking skills, and requires students to apply the math process skills.	**c.2.I** demonstrate…comprehension by following directions…responding to questions… **c.3.H**…explain with increasing specificity and detail…

Name _____ Date _____ Class_____

Identifying Integers and Their Opposites
Practice and Problem Solving: A/B

Name a positive or negative number to represent each situation.

1. depositing $85 in a bank account ____

2. riding an elevator down 3 floors ____

3. the foundation of a house sinking

    5 inches ____

4. a temperature of 98° above

    zero ____

Graph each integer and its opposite on the number line.

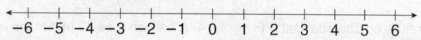

5. −2   6. +3   7. −5   8. +1

Write the correct answers.

9. The average temperature in Fairbanks, Alaska, in February is 4°F below zero. Write this temperature as an integer.

    _____

10. The average temperature in Fairbanks, Alaska, in November is 2°F above zero. Write this temperature as an integer.

    _____

11. The highest point in the state of Louisiana is Driskill Mountain. It rises 535 feet above sea level. Write the elevation of Driskill Mountain as an integer.

    _____

12. The lowest point in the state of Louisiana is New Orleans. The city's elevation is 8 feet below sea level. Write the elevation of New Orleans as an integer.

    _____

13. Death Valley, California, has the lowest elevation in the United States. Its elevation is 282 feet below sea level. Mount McKinley, Alaska, has the highest elevation in the United States. Its elevation is 20,320 feet above sea level. Use integers to describe these two locations in the United States.

    _____

14. Are there any integers between 0 and 1? Explain.

    _____

    _____

LESSON 1-1

Identifying Integers and Their Opposites
Practice and Problem Solving: C

Name a positive or negative number to represent each step in each situation.

1. Fabio is climbing a tree. He climbs up 7 feet.

   _____

   Then he falls back 3 feet.

   _____

2. Roya deposits $30 in her checking account.

   _____

   Then she writes a check for $12.

   _____

3. The temperature on Thursday fell 5°F.

   _____

   On Friday, it rose 11°F.

   _____

4. A balloon rose 32 feet in the air.

   _____

   Then it fell to the ground.

   _____

Graph the opposite of each integer on the number line. Label each correctly.

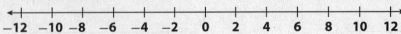

5. −7

6. −11

7. 3

8. 0

Write each temperature and its opposite.

9. The highest temperature ever recorded in Texas was 120°F in Seymour on August 12, 1936.

   _____

10. The lowest temperature ever recorded in Texas was −23°F in Seminole on February 8, 1933.

   _____

Solve.

11. The temperature at which water freezes on the Celsius scale is 0°C. It freezes at 32°F on the Fahrenheit scale. Write the opposites of these two temperatures as integers.

   _____

12. Water boils at 212°F on the Fahrenheit scale and 100°C on the Celsius scale, so these two temperatures are the same. Write the opposites of these temperatures as integers.

   _____

   Are the integers the same? _____

13. Describe an integer and its opposite on the number line. Give an example.

   _____

LESSON 1-1

Identifying Integers and Their Opposites
Practice and Problem Solving: D

Circle the letter that best represents each situation.

1. a gain of 5 yards in football

    A   −5

    B   +5

    C   +50

2. a bank withdrawal of $25

    A   +5

    B   −25

    C   +50

Write the integer that is graphed on each number line. The first one is done for you.

3.

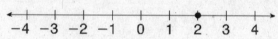

              2 or +2

4.

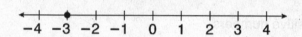

5. Jenny made a deposit of $20 into her bank account. Write this amount as an integer.

6. Mark withdrew $25 from his bank account. Write this amount as an integer.

Write the correct answer.

7. Mercury melts at 38°F below zero. Write this temperature as an integer.

   Solution:

   Think: Integers are whole numbers and their opposites.

   The temperature is 38, which is a whole number. The temperature is below zero, so use the opposite of 38. That integer is −38.

8. The lowest temperature recorded in San Francisco was 20°F. Buffalo's lowest recorded temperature was the opposite of San Francisco's. What was Buffalo's lowest temperature?

LESSON 1-1

Identifying Integers and Their Opposites
Reteach

Positive numbers are greater than 0. Use a positive number to represent a gain or increase. Include the positive sign (+).

an increase of 10 points	+10
a flower growth of 2 inches	+2
a gain of 15 yards in football	+15

Negative numbers are less than 0. Use a negative number to represent a loss or decrease. Also use a negative number to represent a value below or less than a certain value. Include the negative sign (−).

a bank withdrawal of $30	−30
a decrease of 9 points	−9
2° below zero	−2

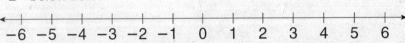

negative numbers   positive numbers

Opposites are the same distance from zero on the number line, but in different directions. −3 and 3 are opposites because each number is 3 units from zero on a number line.

Integers are the set of all whole numbers and their opposites.

Name a positive or negative number to represent each situation.

1. an increase of 3 points

2. spending $10

3. earning $25

4. a loss of 5 yards

Write each integer and its opposite. Then graph them on the number line.

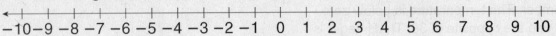

5. −1

6. 9

7. 6

8. −5

Name _____ Date _____ Class_____

Identifying Integers and Their Opposites
Reading Strategies: Use Context

We get information from the numbers we read.

A **positive number** is greater than zero. The plus sign (+) denotes a positive number. If no sign is shown, the number is positive.

- Our car travels 55 miles per hour. ⟶ 55 or +55
- The temperature climbed to 90°. ⟶ 90 or +90

Write the positive number for each of the following situations.

1. Alicia put $25 in her savings account. _____

2. Oklahoma City is 1,195 feet above sea level. _____

3. Our football team gained 12 yards on the last play.

   _____

A **negative number** is less than zero. A negative sign (−) is always used to denote a negative number.

- Death Valley is 282 feet below sea level. ⟶ −282
- The temperature dipped to 12° below zero. ⟶ −12

Write the negative number for each of the following situations.

4. Dave withdrew $50 from his savings account. _____

5. The coldest temperature recorded in Greenland was 87° below zero.

   _____

6. Oarfish live at 3,000 feet below sea level. _____

LESSON 1-1

Identifying Integers and Their Opposites

Success for English Learners

Problem 1

Is the number positive or negative?

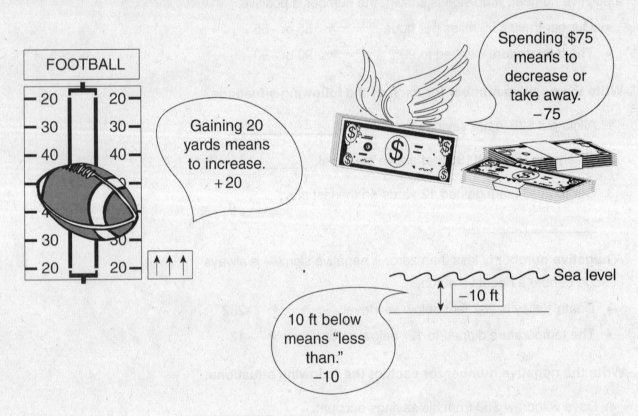

FOOTBALL

Gaining 20 yards means to increase. +20

Spending $75 means to decrease or take away. –75

Sea level

–10 ft

10 ft below means "less than." –10

Problem 2

The opposite of 7 is –7. They are the same distance from 0 on the number line.

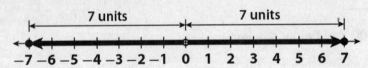

7 units   7 units

–7 –6 –5 –4 –3 –2 –1 0 1 2 3 4 5 6 7

1. If spending money is represented by negative numbers, what would represent positive numbers?

    _____

2. The integers are the set of all whole numbers and _____.

LESSON 1-2
Comparing and Ordering Integers
Practice and Problem Solving: A/B

Use the number line to compare each pair of integers. Write < or >.

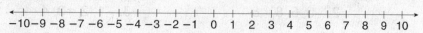

```
←──┼──┼──┼──┼──┼──┼──┼──┼──┼──┼──┼──┼──┼──┼──┼──┼──┼──┼──┼──┼──→
  −10−9 −8 −7 −6 −5 −4 −3 −2 −1  0  1  2  3  4  5  6  7  8  9 10
```

1. 10 ◯ −2

2. 0 ◯ 3

3. −5 ◯ 0

4. −7 ◯ 6

5. −6 ◯ −9

6. −8 ◯ −10

Order the integers in each set from least to greatest.

7. 5, −2, 6

8. 0, 9, −3,

9. −1, 6, 1

_____ _____ _____

Order the integers in each set from greatest to least.

10. −1, 1, 0

11. −12, 2, 1

12. −10, −12, −11

_____ _____ _____

13. 205, −20, −5, 50

14. −78, −89, 78, 9

15. −55, −2, −60, 0

_____ _____ _____

16. 28, −8, −8, 0

17. 37, −37, −38, 38

18. −111, −1, 1, 11

_____ _____ _____

Solve.

19. Four friends went scuba diving today. Ali dove 70 feet, Tim went down 50 feet, Carl dove 65 feet, and Brenda reached 48 feet below sea level. Write the 4 friends' names in order from the person whose depth was closest to the surface to the person whose depth was the farthest from the surface.

_____

20. Ted is comparing the temperatures of three days in January. The temperatures on Monday and Tuesday were opposites. The temperature on Wednesday was neither positive nor negative. The temperature dropped below zero on Monday. Write the 3 days in order from the highest to the lowest temperature.

_____

LESSON 1-2 Comparing and Ordering Integers
Practice and Problem Solving: C

Compare each group of integers. Write < or >.

1. 7, 10, −3, 0

   _____

2. −5, 5, 8, −8

   _____

3. −1, 2, −3, 4

   _____

4. 2, −1, −2, 0

   _____

5. −9, 6, −8, 7

   _____

6. 2, −1, 0, 1, −2

   _____

Order the integers in each set from least to greatest and then from greatest to least.

7. 9, 8, 0, −1

   _____

8. 3, −3, −2, 2, 0

   _____

9. 11, −11, 1, 0, −1

   _____

10. 13, −13, |−7|, 0, −5

    _____

11. |−8|, −8, 0, |7|, −7

    _____

12. |−15|, |16|, −13, 14, −15

    _____

Solve.

13. Five friends were flying kites. Abe's kite flew up to 15 feet, Beth's went to 23 feet, Casey's went to 11 feet, Davio's went to 31 feet, and Eric's never left the ground. Write the friend's names in order from the person whose kite flew the highest to the person whose kite flew the lowest.

    _____

14. An elevator made the following trips: up 5 floors, then down 3 floors, then up 7 floors, then down 2 floors, then up 2 floors, and finally down 4 floors.

    a. Write each of these trips as an integer.

       _____

    b. Which trip was the longest? _____

    c. Which, if any, trips were opposites?

       _____

    d. Was the elevator higher at the finish or at the start?

       _____

    e. If the elevator started on the 18th floor, on which floor did it end up?

       _____

LESSON 1-2 Comparing and Ordering Integers
Practice and Problem Solving: D

Use the number line to compare each pair of integers. Write < or >.
The first one is done for you.

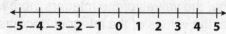

1. 4 ⟨ > ⟩ 3   2. −5 ◯ −1   3. −2 ◯ 5

Order the integers from least to greatest. The first one is done for you.

4. 2, −3, 4 _____**−3, 2, 4**_____   5. 2, −2, 3 _____

6. 3, −1, 0 _____   7. −1, −3, 1, 3, 0 _____

Circle the letter of the correct answer.

8. The Which set of integers is written from least to greatest?

   A   3, −1, 0, 8

   B   0, −1, 3, 8

   C   −1, 0, 3, 8

9. The Which set of integers is written from greatest to least?

   A   7, 4, −5, 2

   B   7, 4, 2, −5

   C   −5, 2, 4, 7

Use the table below to answer each question.

10. What is the lowest point on Earth? What is its elevation?

Look at the Elevation column. Two numbers

have four digits: _____ and

_____ .

Of those two numbers, the one
with the greater digit in the thousands

place is _____ .

The lowest point on Earth is _____ at an elevation of

_____ feet.

Location	Elevation (ft)
Lake Assal	−512
Bentley Subglacial Trench	−8,327
Dead Sea	−1,349
Lake Eyre	−52
Caspian Sea	−92

11. Which location on Earth is lower, the Caspian Sea or Lake Eyre?

_____

Name _____ Date _____ Class_____

Comparing and Ordering Integers
Reteach

You can use a number line to compare integers.

As you move *right* on a number line, the values of the integers *increase*.
As you move *left* on a number line, the values of the integers *decrease*.

Compare –4 and 2.

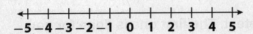

–4 is to the left of 2, so –4 < 2.

Use the number line above to compare the integers. Write < or >.

1. 1 ◯ –4   2. –5 ◯ –2   3. –3 ◯ 2

4. –1 ◯ –4   5. 5 ◯ 0   6. –2 ◯ 3

You can also use a number line to order integers.
Order –3, 4, and –1 from least to greatest.

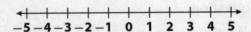

List the numbers in the order in which they appear from left to right.

The integers in order from least to greatest are –3, –1, 4.

Order the integers from least to greatest.

7. –2, –5, –1   8. 0, –5, 5   9. –5, 2, –3

_____   _____   _____

10. 3, –1, –4   11. 3, –5, 0   12. –2, –4, 1

_____   _____   _____

LESSON 1-2 Comparing and Ordering Integers
Reading Strategies: Use a Graphic Aid

Integers include all the **positive whole numbers** and **negative whole numbers** plus zero. Use a number line to help you picture and compare integers.

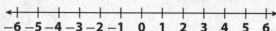

1. Start at the left and move to the right on the number line. As you move from left to right, do integers increase or decrease in value?

   _____

2. Now start at the right and move to the left along the number line. As you move from right to left, do integers increase or decrease in value?

   _____

Compare two numbers by checking their location on a number line.

Compare –4 and –2. –4 is to the left of –2.

   –4 < –2   ◄——— Read: "–4 is less than –2."

   –2 > –4   ◄——— Read: "–2 is greater than –4."

3. Start at –5. Move to –1. Did you move to the right or to the left?

   _____

4. Start at 3. Move to –2. Did you move to the right or to the left?

   _____

5. Compare the locations of –3 and 3 on the number line above.

   _____

6. Use < or > to compare –3 and 3.

   _____

7. Compare the locations of –1 and –4 on the number line above.

   _____

8. Use < or > to compare –1 and –4.

   _____

Comparing and Ordering Integers

LESSON 1-2

Success for English Learners

Problem 1

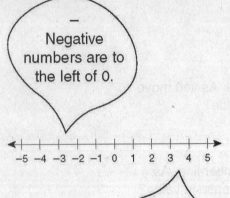

Negative numbers are to the left of 0.

Positive numbers are to the right of 0.

A number is less than all numbers to the right of it.

Is −4 < −3?   yes

Is −4 < 0?   yes

Is −4 < 2?   yes

Is −5 < −4?   yes

Is −5 < −3?   yes

Is −5 < 0?   yes

Is −5 < −2?   yes

How do you know?
The numbers are less than the numbers to the right of it on a number line.

Problem 2

Who won?

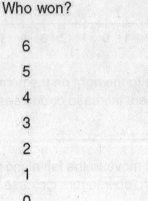

David Berganio

Golfers with more strokes than others lose.

Ernie Els

The golfer with the lowest number of strokes wins.

Sergio Garcia

1. How can −3 be greater than −5 if 3 is less than 5?

_____

Absolute Value

LESSON 1-3

Practice and Problem Solving: A/B

Graph each number on the number line.

1. −6   2. 3   3. −3   4. 5

−8 −7 −6 −5 −4 −3 −2 −1 0 1 2 3 4 5 6 7 8

Use the number line to find each absolute value.

5. |−6| _____   6. |3| _____   7. |8| _____

8. |6| _____   9. |−3| _____   10. |5| _____

11. What do you notice about the absolute values of 6 and −6?

_____

12. What do you call −6 and 6 or 3 and −3? _____

Use the table for exercises 13–19.

Andrea's Credit-Card Transactions				
Monday	**Tuesday**	**Wednesday**	**Thursday**	**Friday**
Bought $20 shirt	Bought $6 lunch	Made $15 payment	Paid $3 fee	Bought $8 app

Write a negative integer to show the amount spent on each purchase.

13. Monday ____   14. Tuesday ____   15. Friday ____

Find the absolute value of each transaction.

16. Monday ____   17. Tuesday ____   18. Wednesday ____

19. On which day did Andrea spend the most on her card? Explain.

_____

Solve.

20. Show that |3 + 10| = |3| + |10|.

_____

21. How many different integers can have the same absolute

value? _____ Give an example. _____

Name _____ Date _____ Class _____

Absolute Value
Practice and Problem Solving: C

Average Deviation from Daily Calorie Standard*				
Rob	**Jorge**	**Elan**	**Pietro**	**Bill**
+540	−125	+610	−220	+125

*Standard: An active 12-year-old male should consume about 2,300 calories a day.

Use the table above to answer the questions.

1. Which number acts like a base or 0 in this situation? _____

2. Whose calorie consumption is farthest from the standard?

   _____ How many calories does he consume?

   _____

3. Who consumes the fewest calories? _____

   How many calories does he consume? _____

4. Which two students' deviations from the standard are opposites?

   _____

5. Who consumes a number of calories closest to the standard?

   _____

6. Who consumes almost 3,000 calories? _____

7. What is the average deviation from the standard among these five

   students? _____

8. What is the average *absolute* deviation from the standard among these

   five students? _____

9. Find two calorie counts whose deviations from the standard are
   opposites. What can you say about their absolute values?

   _____

10. If the standard were reduced to 2,200 calories, how would that affect

    the deviations in the table? _____

    _____

LESSON 1-3

Absolute Value
Practice and Problem Solving: D

Graph each number on the number line. The first one is done for you.

1. –5   2. 4   3. –7   4. 5

Use the number line to find each absolute value. The first one is done for you.

5. |4| _____**4**_____   6. |–5| _____   7. |7| _____

8. |5| _____   9. |–4| _____   10. |6| _____

Complete.

11. The absolute values of –5 and 5 are the _____.

12. The integers –5 and 5 are called _____.

Use the table for exercises 13–22.

Temperatures at a Ski Resort				
Monday	**Tuesday**	**Wednesday**	**Thursday**	**Friday**
5°F below zero	2°F below zero	0°F	2°F above zero	3°F below zero

Write a negative integer to show the amount each temperature below zero. The first one is done for you.

13. 5°F below zero _–5_   14. 2°F below zero ____   15. 3°F below zero ____

16. Can 0°F be written as a negative integer? ____

Find the absolute value of each negative number for a temperature below zero. The first one is done for you.

17. |–5| = _5_   18. |–2| = ____   19. |–3| = ____

Complete.

20. On which day was the temperature the coldest? _____

21. On which day was the temperature the warmest? _____

22. When a number is negative, its opposite is also its

_____.

Name _____ Date _____ Class_____

Absolute Value

Reteach

> The absolute value of any number is its distance from 0 on the number line.
>
> Since distance is always positive or 0, absolute value is always positive or 0.
>
> Find the absolute value of –7 and 7.
>
>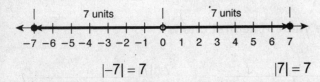
>
> $|-7| = 7$ $|7| = 7$

Match. You can use the letters more than once.

1. absolute value of 15 ____   a. –7

2. negative integer ____   b. 7

3. opposite of –7 ____   c. 15

4. opposite of 7 ____   d. –15

5. |–15| ____

Find each absolute value.

6. |–3| _____   7. |5| _____   8. |–7| _____

9. |6| _____   10. |0| _____   11. |–2| _____

12. |–10| _____   13. $\left|-\dfrac{3}{4}\right|$ _____   14. |0.8| _____

Answer the question.

15. Abby has been absent from class. How would you explain to her what absolute value is? Use the number line and an example in your explanation.

_____

_____

Absolute Value

Reading Strategies: Use Context Clues

In everyday speech, people describe certain situations by using absolute values instead of negative numbers.

When people use numbers with certain words or phrases, we know the numbers they are talking about are *positive numbers.*

> Jackie **deposited** $50 in her checking account.

> A mountain is 13,457 feet **above sea level**.

> The baseball team **scored** 7 runs in the last inning.

List the words or phrases above that refer to positive numbers.

1. deposited, _____ , _____

However, when people use numbers with certain other terms, we know the numbers they are talking about are actually *negative numbers.* In these contexts, people are using the **absolute value** of the number.

> The temperature was 5° **below zero**.

> A stock posted a **loss** of 5 points one week.

> New Orleans is about 8 feet **below sea level**.

List the words or phrases above that refer to absolute values.

2. below zero, _____ , _____

Underline each phrase that includes an amount. Then write the positive or negative integer that is being described.

3. a kite rising 17 feet into the air ____

4. drilling a foundation 5 feet below the surface ____

5. losing 6 points in a game ____

6. paying a fee of $35 on a checking account ____

7. a penalty of 5 yards in a football game ____

8. adding 32 MB of storage to a computer ____

9. an award of $50 for perfect attendance ____

10. crediting an account with a gift card of $60 ____

Name _____ Date _____ Class_____

Absolute Value
Success for English Learners

Problem 1

Compare the absolute values of –7 and 7.

The absolute value of a number is its distance from 0 on a number line.

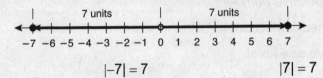

$$|-7| = 7 \qquad\qquad |7| = 7$$

The absolute values of –7 and 7 are equal: $|-7| = |7|$.

Problem 2

When people speak, they often use absolute values instead of negative numbers.

Complete the table.

1.

Situation	Numbers We Write	Absolute Value	Words We Say
bought $30 shoes	–30	$|-30| = 30$	"spent $30"
8-foot drop	–8	$|-8| = 8$	"dropped 8 feet"
5-point loss	____	$|-5| =$ ____	"lost 5 points"

Use the number line above to find the absolute values.

2. absolute value of –6 _____

3. $|-4| =$ _____

4. $|-3|$ _____

5. absolute value of 0 _____

6. absolute value of –2 _____

7. $|2| =$ _____

8. What do you notice about $|-2|$ and $|2|$?

_____

MODULE 1

Integers
Challenge

1. The table below shows in both degrees Celsius and degrees Fahrenheit the freezing and boiling points of pure ethanol.

Ethanol	Celsius (°C)	Fahrenheit (°F)
Freezing Point	–114	–173
Boiling Point	78	173

On a separate sheet of paper, draw two number lines without increments. On one, divide the line into even increments, then plot and label the two Celsius temperatures. On the other line, first plot and label the two Fahrenheit temperatures so that they align with the two Celsius temperatures on the first number line. Then divide the second number line into even increments. What do you notice about the size of the Fahrenheit and Celsius degrees?

_____

2. The following table shows average planting depths and flowering heights for several bulbs.

Bulb	Planting Depth (in.)	Height (in.)
Miniature Iris	3	5
Hyacinth	6	9
Trumpet Daffodil	6	18
Peacock Tulip	6	8
Perennial Tulip	7	21
Daffodil	6	12
Bluebell	4	12

a. Write the depths as integers._____

b. List those integers from least to greatest.

_____

c. Write the heights as integers._____

d. List those integers from least to greatest.

_____

e. Identify any opposites on your list.

_____

Name _____ Date _____ Class_____

Classifying Rational Numbers

Practice and Problem Solving: A/B

Write each rational number in the form $\frac{a}{b}$, where *a* and *b* are integers.

1. 0.3

2. $2\frac{7}{8}$

3. –5

4. 16

_____   _____   _____   _____

5. $-1\frac{3}{4}$

6. –4.5

7. 3

8. 0.11

_____   _____   _____   _____

Place each number in the correct place on the Venn diagram.
Then list all the set of numbers to which each number belongs.

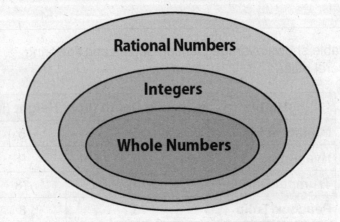

9. –13 _____

10. $\frac{1}{6}$ _____

11. 0 _____

12. 0.99 _____

13. –6.7 _____

14. 34 _____

15. $-14\frac{1}{2}$ _____

Name _____ Date _____ Class_____

Classifying Rational Numbers
Practice and Problem Solving: C

Write each rational number in the form $\frac{a}{b}$, where *a* and *b* are integers.

1. –4

2. 0

3. $5\frac{1}{3}$

4. 6.75

_____

_____

_____

_____

5. $2\frac{1}{8}$

6. –0.35

7. 7.8

8. $-9\frac{3}{5}$

_____

_____

_____

_____

Identify which of the following sets of numbers each number belongs to: rational numbers, integers, whole numbers.

9. $-1\frac{1}{2}$ _____

10. 7 _____

11. –6 _____

12. 4.25 _____

List two numbers that fit each description. Then write the numbers in the correct place on the Venn diagram.

13. Whole numbers greater than 5 _____

14. Integers that are not whole numbers _____

15. Rational numbers less than 0 that are not integers _____

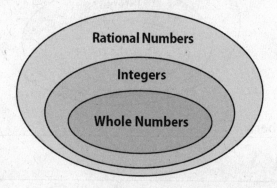

Name _____ Date _____ Class_____

Classifying Rational Numbers

Practice and Problem Solving: D

Write each rational number in the form $\frac{a}{b}$, where *a* and *b* are integers.
The first one is done for you.

1. $5\frac{1}{6}$

   $\frac{31}{6}$
   _____

2. –6

   _____

3. 0.97

   _____

4. 18

   _____

5. 3.3

   _____

6. $-2\frac{1}{8}$

   _____

Circle the number set(s) to which each number belongs. The first one
is done for you.

7. –9

   Whole Numbers   (Integers)   (Rational Numbers)

8. 0.16

   Whole Numbers   Integers   Rational Numbers

9. 146

   Whole Numbers   Integers   Rational Numbers

Place each number in the correct place on the Venn diagram.
Then list all the set of numbers to which each number belongs.
The first one is done for you.

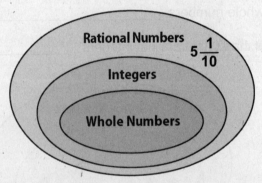

10. $5\frac{1}{10}$ rational numbers _____

11. –14 _____

12. 0 _____

LESSON 2-1 Classifying Rational Numbers
Reteach

A rational number is a number that can be written as $\frac{a}{b}$, where a and b

are integers and $b \neq 0$. Decimals, fractions, mixed numbers, and integers are all rational numbers.

You can demonstrate a number is rational by writing it in the form $\frac{a}{b}$.

A. $14 = \frac{14}{1}$ Write the whole number over 1.

B. $0.83 = \frac{83}{100}$ Write the decimal as a fraction. Simplify if possible.

C. $5\frac{1}{8} = \frac{41}{8}$ Change the mixed number to an improper fraction.

A Venn diagram is a graphical illustration used to show relationships between various sets of data or groups. Each set or group is represented by an oval, and the relationships among these sets are expressed by their areas of overlap.

- Integers contain the entire set of whole numbers.

- Rational numbers contain the entire sets of integers and whole numbers.

- If a number is a whole number, it is also an integer.

- If a number is an integer, it is to also a rational number.

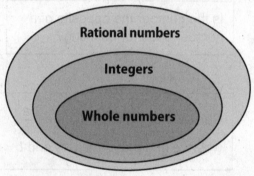

Rational numbers
Integers
Whole numbers

Write each rational number in the form $\frac{a}{b}$, where a and b are integers.

Then circle the name of each set to which the number belongs.

1. –12 _____   Whole Numbers   Integers   Rational Numbers

2. 7.3 _____   Whole Numbers   Integers   Rational Numbers

3. 0.41 _____   Whole Numbers   Integers   Rational Numbers

4. 6 _____   Whole Numbers   Integers   Rational Numbers

5. $3\frac{1}{2}$ _____   Whole Numbers   Integers   Rational Numbers

Name _____ Date _____ Class _____

 LESSON 2-1

Classifying Rational Numbers
Reading Strategies: Identify Relationships

You can classify rational numbers when you understand the relationships between number sets.

First, you need to understand the terms *whole numbers, integers* and *rational numbers*.

- A **whole number** is either 0 or a number used when counting.

- An **integer** is either a whole number or the opposite of a whole number.

- A **rational number** is a number that can be written as $\frac{a}{b}$, where a and b are integers and $b \neq 0$.

Use this flowchart to determine to which set(s) a number belongs:

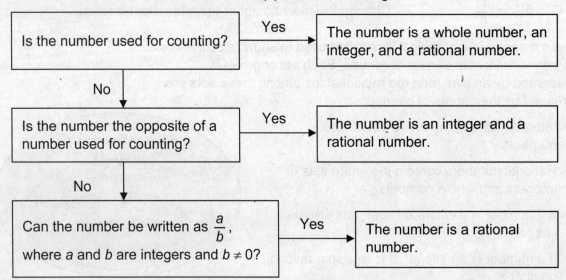

To which number sets does 85 belong?
Because 85 is used for counting, it is a whole number, an integer, and a rational number.

Write the number set(s) to which each number belongs.

1. 0.75

_____

2. −18

_____

3. $\frac{1}{3}$

_____

4. 37

_____

**LESSON
2-1**

Classifying Rational Numbers

Success for English Learners

Problem 1

Where does the number 15 belong in the diagram?

The Whole Numbers circle is inside the Integers circle. So, whole numbers are integers.

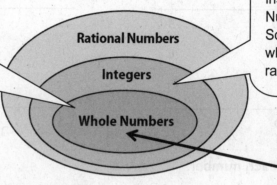

The Integers circle is inside the Rational Numbers circle. So, integers *and* whole numbers are rational numbers.

Rational Numbers

Integers

Whole Numbers

Write 15 **here**.

When you count by ones, you say the number 15.

So, 15 is a **whole number**.

Problem 2

To which set or sets of numbers does −0.71 belong?

When you count, do you say the number −0.71?

Is −0.71 the opposite of a number you count with?

No. So, it is not a whole number.

No. So, it is not an integer.

Can you write the number −0.71 as a fraction?

Yes: $-0.71 = -\dfrac{71}{100}$.

So, −0.71 *is* a rational number.

1. How do you write $5\dfrac{1}{5}$ in the form $\dfrac{a}{b}$?

_____

2. Explain why every whole number is a rational number.

_____

3. Is every integer a whole number? Explain why or why not.

_____

LESSON 2-2

Identifying Opposites and Absolute Value of Rational Numbers

Practice and Problem Solving: A/B

Graph each number and its opposite on a number line.

1. 3.5

2. –2.5

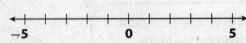

3. $2\frac{1}{2}$

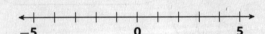

4. $-1\frac{1}{2}$

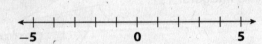

Name the opposite of each number.

5. 4.25 _____

6. $-5\frac{1}{4}$ _____

7. $\frac{1}{2}$ _____

Name the absolute value of each number.

8. $2\frac{1}{3}$ _____

9. –3.85 _____

10. –6.1 _____

The table shows elevations of checkpoints along a marathon route.
Use the table to answer problems 11–13.

Checkpoint	A	B	C	D	E
Elevation (ft)	15.6	17.1	5.2	–6.5	–18.5

11. Write the opposite value of each checkpoint elevation.

_____

12. Which checkpoint is closest to sea level? _____

13. Which checkpoint is furthest from sea level? Explain.

_____

_____

Name _____ Date _____ Class_____

LESSON 2-2 **Identifying Opposites and Absolute Value of Rational Numbers**
Practice and Problem Solving: C

Write the opposite and the absolute value of each rational number.

1. $-\dfrac{2}{3}$ 2. $1\dfrac{1}{7}$ 3. -0.89 4. 3.47

_____   _____   _____   _____

5. $\dfrac{7}{5}$ 6. $5\dfrac{2}{3}$ 7. -4.03 8. -1.11

_____   _____   _____   _____

9. When are the absolute value and the opposite of a rational number equal?

_____

Solve.

10. Ursula says the distance between −5.47 and 5.47 on a number line is equal to | − 5.47 |. Explain her error.

_____

_____

11. The table below shows temperatures of a mixture in a chemistry experiment over 5 days.

Day	Monday	Tuesday	Wednesday	Thursday	Friday
Temperature (°C)	−7.1	−3.4	−1.2	2.1	3.4

On which two days did the mixture's temperature have the same

absolute value? _____

12. Put the integers in the chart above in order from greatest to least and then from greatest to least absolute value.

_____

_____

Original content Copyright © by Houghton Mifflin Harcourt. Additions and changes to the original content are the responsibility of the instructor.

27

LESSON 2-2
Identifying Opposites and Absolute Value of Rational Numbers
Practice and Problem Solving: D

Plot each number and its opposite on a number line. The first one is done for you.

1. 1.0

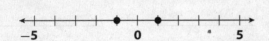

2. –2.0

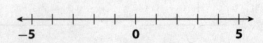

3. $2\frac{1}{2}$

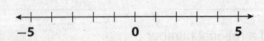

4. $-1\frac{1}{2}$

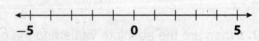

Find the opposite of each number. The first one is done for you.

5. 3 ___–3___

6. –4.5 _____

7. $\frac{1}{3}$_____

Find the absolute value of each number. The first one is done for you.

8. –4.0 ___4.0___

9. $-2\frac{1}{2}$_____

10. $\frac{2}{3}$ _____

Use the table to answer questions 11–14.

Lunch Account Balances					
Student	Aida	BJ	Camille	Darrin	Eric
Balance	–$1.50	$5.25	$9.00	$7.45	–$0.35

11. Who has the greatest balance? _____

12. What is the opposite of Darrin's balance? _____

13. How much money would Aida need to add to have a

    balance of $0.00? _____

14. How much money would BJ need to spend to have

    a balance of $0.00? _____

LESSON 2-2

Identifying Opposites and Absolute Values of Rational Numbers
Reteach

You can use charts to determine whether the opposites and absolute values of rational numbers are positive or negative.

For positive rational numbers:

Number	Opposite	Absolute Value
3.5	−3.5	3.5
number positive	opposite negative	absolute value always positive

For negative rational numbers:

Number	Opposite	Absolute Value
$-\dfrac{7}{8}$	$\dfrac{7}{8}$	$\dfrac{7}{8}$
number negative	opposite positive	absolute value always positive

Answer each question below.

1. Are the opposite of −6.5 and the absolute value of −6.5 the same?

   Give both. _____

2. Are the opposite of $3\dfrac{2}{5}$ and the absolute value of $3\dfrac{2}{5}$ the same?

   Give both. _____

3. Write a rational number whose opposite and absolute value are

   the same. _____

4. Write a rational number whose opposite and absolute value are

   opposites. _____

Name _____ Date _____ Class_____

LESSON 2-2 Identifying Opposites and Absolute Values of Rational Numbers

Reading Strategies: Use a Graphic Aid

Rational numbers can be decimals or fractions.
They can be positive or negative.

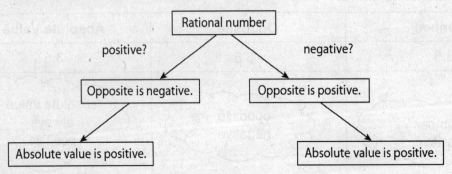

Use the flowchart to determine whether the opposites of the numbers in
questions 1 through 4 are positive or negative. Then give the opposite of
each number.

1. −2.7 _____ 2. $3\frac{1}{8}$ _____

3. $\frac{2}{7}$ _____ 4. − 0.9 _____

5. Do you need to use a flowchart to determine whether the absolute
value of a rational number is positive or negative? Explain.

_____

6. How can you define the absolute value of a rational number using the
number line?

_____

_____

LESSON 2-2 Identifying Opposites and Absolute Values of Rational Numbers

Success for English Learners

Problem 1

Use the number line below to answer the questions.

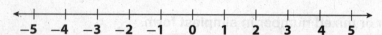

1. Place $-3\frac{2}{7}$ on the number line. What integers is it between? _____

2. Place the opposite of $-3\frac{2}{7}$ on the number line. What integers is it between? _____

3. What is the absolute value of $-3\frac{2}{7}$? _____

4. What is the absolute value of $3\frac{2}{7}$? _____

5. Why do $-3\frac{2}{7}$ and $3\frac{2}{7}$ have the same absolute value?

   _____

6. Place a decimal rational number on the number line. Then place its opposite. Give the absolute value for both numbers.

   _____

LESSON 2-3

Comparing and Ordering Rational Numbers
Practice and Problem Solving: A/B

Write each fraction as a decimal. Round to the nearest hundredth if necessary.

1. $\frac{3}{8}$ ____

2. $\frac{7}{5}$ ____

3. $\frac{21}{7}$ ____

4. $\frac{5}{3}$ ____

Write each decimal as a fraction or mixed number in simplest form.

5. 0.55 ____

6. 10.6 ____

7. −7.08 ____

Write the numbers in order from least to greatest.

8. 0.5, 0.05, $\frac{5}{8}$ _____

9. 1.3, $1\frac{1}{3}$, 1.34 _____

10. 2.07, $2\frac{7}{10}$, 2.67, −2.67 _____

Solve.

11. Out of 45 times at bat, Raul got 19 hits. Find Raul's batting average as

    a decimal rounded to the nearest thousandth. _____

12. Karen's batting average was 0.444. She was at bat 45 times. How

    many hits did she get? _____

13. To have batting averages over 0.500, how may hits in 45 times at bat

    would Raul and Karen need? _____

14. A car travels at 65 miles per hour. Going through construction, it

    travels at $\frac{3}{5}$ this speed. Write this fraction as a decimal and find the

    speed. _____

15. A city's sales tax is 0.07. Write this decimal as a fraction and tell how

    many cents of tax are on each dollar. _____

16. A ream of paper contains 500 sheets of paper. Norm has 373 sheets
    of paper left from a ream. Express the portion of a ream Norm has as a

    fraction and as a decimal. _____

LESSON 2-3

Comparing and Ordering Rational Numbers

Practice and Problem Solving: C

First, tell whether each fraction will be a decimal greater than, equal to, or less than 1. Then, write each fraction as a decimal. Round to the nearest hundredth, if necessary.

1. $\frac{5}{8}$ _____

2. $\frac{11}{5}$ _____

3. $\frac{17}{17}$ _____

4. $\frac{4}{7}$ _____

First, tell whether each decimal is a fraction or a mixed number. Then, write it in simplest form.

5. 0.85 _____

6. 3.8 _____

7. −11.16 _____

Write the score as a decimal rounded to the nearest thousandth. Then answer the question.

8. On her driver's test, Mrs. Lynch got 26 out of 30 questions correct. The passing grade was 0.85. Did Mrs. Lynch pass? _____

9. If she got 25 out of 30 questions correct, would she pass? _____

Write the numbers in order from least to greatest.

10. $5.78, -5\frac{7}{8}, -5.9$ _____

11. $\frac{3}{7}, 0.45, \frac{4}{9}$ _____

12. $-0.38, -\frac{3}{8}, -0.04$ _____

Solve.

13. In the 2008 election, there were 28 "blue" states and 22 "red" states. Express the "red" and "blue" states as fractions, in lowest terms, of the total number of states and also as decimals.

_____

14. A machine produces 75 widgets an hour. How many widgets does it produce in 6 minutes? _____

LESSON 2-3 Comparing and Ordering Rational Numbers

Practice and Problem Solving: D

Write each decimal as a fraction or mixed number. The first one is done for you.

1. 0.5 $\dfrac{5}{10}$ or $\dfrac{1}{2}$ _____

2. 0.25 _____

3. 0.75 _____

4. 0.4 _____

5. 0.8 _____

6. 1.2 _____

Write each fraction or mixed number as a decimal. The first one is done for you.

7. $\dfrac{3}{10}$ **0.3** _____

8. $\dfrac{3}{5}$ _____

9. $1\dfrac{2}{5}$ _____

Circle the letter of the best answer.

10. Which of the following sets is written in order from least to greatest?

  A. $0.4, \dfrac{7}{10}, 0.6$

  B. $\dfrac{1}{4}, 0.5, 0.75$

  C. $\dfrac{7}{10}, 0.4, 0.6$

11. Which of the following sets is written in order from greatest to least?

  A. $\dfrac{1}{3}, 1\dfrac{1}{2}, 1\dfrac{3}{4}$

  B. $\dfrac{2}{5}, 0.\overline{3}, 0.3$

  C. $0.3, 0.\overline{3}, \dfrac{2}{5}$

Solve.

12. At Franklin Elementary School, $\dfrac{2}{3}$ of all the students attended the chorus recital on Thursday. On Friday, $\dfrac{3}{4}$ of all the students attended the basketball game. Which event had the higher attendance?

_____

Comparing and Ordering Rational Numbers

LESSON 2-3

Reteach

You can write decimals as fractions or mixed numbers. A place value table will help you read the decimal. Remember the decimal point is read as the word "and."

To write 0.47 as a fraction, first think about the decimal in words.

Ones	Tenths	Hundredths	Thousandths	Ten Thousandths
0	4	7		

0.47 is read "forty-seven hundredths." The place value of the decimal tells you the denominator is 100.

$$0.47 = \frac{47}{100}$$

To write 8.3 as a mixed number, first think about the decimal in words.

Ones	Tenths	Hundredths	Thousandths	Ten Thousandths
8	3			

8.3 is read "eight and three tenths." The place value of the decimal tells you the denominator is 10. The decimal point is read as the word "and."

$$8.3 = 8\frac{3}{10}$$

Write each decimal as a fraction or mixed number.

1. 0.61 ____

2. 3.43 ____

3. 0.009 ____

4. 4.7 ____

5. 1.5 ____

6. 0.13 ____

7. 5.002 ____

8. 0.021 ____

Comparing and Ordering Rational Numbers

LESSON 2-3

Reading Strategies: Build Vocabulary

The word *repeating* means "something happening over and over." A town hall bell that chimes every hour is an example of a repeating sound.

The word *terminating* means "something that ends." The sixth-grade party will be terminating at 10:00 P.M.

When a fraction is rewritten as a decimal, the result can be a **repeating decimal** or a **terminating decimal**.

In a repeating decimal, sometimes one digit repeats and sometimes more than one digit repeats.

$\dfrac{1}{3}$ ⟶ means 1 ÷ 3 $\dfrac{1}{4}$ ⟶ means 1 ÷ 4

```
   0.333
3)1.000
  −9
  ──
   10
   −9
   ──
    10
    −9
    ──
     1
```

```
   0.25
4)1.00
  −8
  ──
   20
  −20
  ───
    0
```

$\dfrac{1}{3} = 0.\overline{3}$ $\dfrac{1}{4} = 0.25$

The bar over the 3 means the 3 keeps repeating.

0.25 is a decimal that terminates.

Write each fraction as a decimal. Then identify each decimal as *terminating* or *repeating*.

1. $\dfrac{1}{6}$

_____

2. $\dfrac{1}{8}$

_____

3. $\dfrac{1}{11}$

_____

4. $\dfrac{2}{9}$

_____

5. $\dfrac{4}{5}$

_____

6. $\dfrac{5}{9}$

_____

7. $\dfrac{1}{2}$

_____

8. $\dfrac{7}{9}$

_____

LESSON 2-3 Comparing and Ordering Rational Numbers
Success for English Learners

Problem 1

How do I write a decimal as a fraction?

Place the number in a place-value chart.

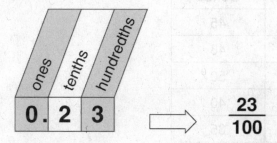 $\Rightarrow \dfrac{23}{100}$

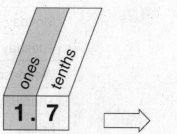 $\Rightarrow 1\dfrac{7}{10}$

Problem 2

How do I write a fraction as a decimal?

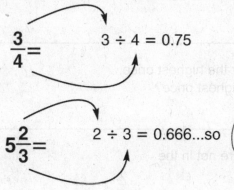

$\dfrac{3}{4} = \quad 3 \div 4 = 0.75$

$5\dfrac{2}{3} = \quad 2 \div 3 = 0.666...\text{so}$ $\quad 5\dfrac{2}{3} = 5.\overline{6}$

Use 3 dots or a bar over a number to show that it repeats.

1. How can you tell the difference between a terminating decimal and a repeating decimal?

_____

_____

2. Describe one method you can use to write a fraction as a decimal.

_____

Name _____ Date _____ Class_____

 MODULE 2

Rational Numbers
Challenge

1. A food processing plant packs oranges into boxes. The weight of the oranges to be packed and the number of boxes available on each day of a week are shown in the table below.

Day	Weight of Oranges (lb)	Number of Boxes
Monday	113	45
Tuesday	116	43
Wednesday	144	50
Thursday	129	40
Friday	109	35

The food processing plant will not ship a box if the weight of the box is greater than 3 pounds.

a. On which of the days in the five-day period shown will the boxes of oranges be too heavy to ship?

_____

b. Of the boxes that ship, the heaviest boxes sell for the highest price. On which day will the boxes packed sell for the highest price?

_____

2. The inequality below is incorrect. The five numbers are not in the correct order.

$$2 \le -\frac{1}{8} \le -10 \le -0.125 \le -\frac{15}{2}$$

You can correct the inequality by swapping the numbers. Each time you swap a pair of numbers, it counts as one "move."

What is the minimum number of "moves" that are required to make the above inequality correct?

_____

What is the correct inequality?

_____

LESSON
3-1

Multiplying Fractions

Practice and Problem Solving: A/B

Multiply. Write each answer in simplest form.

1. $4 \cdot \dfrac{1}{2}$

   _____

2. $8 \cdot \dfrac{1}{4}$

   _____

3. $10 \cdot \dfrac{1}{5}$

   _____

4. $\dfrac{1}{2} \cdot \dfrac{1}{4}$

   _____

5. $\dfrac{1}{4} \cdot \dfrac{2}{3}$

   _____

6. $\dfrac{3}{4} \cdot \dfrac{2}{3}$

   _____

7. $24 \cdot \dfrac{5}{6}$

   _____

8. $32 \cdot \dfrac{3}{8}$

   _____

9. $21 \cdot \dfrac{3}{8}$

   _____

Solve.

10. Louis spent 12 hours last week practicing guitar. If $\dfrac{1}{4}$ of the time was spent practicing chords, how much time did Louis spend practicing chords?

    _____

11. Rolf spent 15 hours last week practicing his saxophone. If $\dfrac{3}{10}$ of the time was spent practicing warm-up routines, how much time did he spend practicing warm-up routines?

    _____

12. A muffin recipe calls for $\dfrac{2}{5}$ tablespoon of vanilla extract to make 6 muffins. Arthur is making 18 muffins. How much vanilla extract does he need?

    _____

13. Angie and her friends ate $\dfrac{3}{4}$ of a pizza. Her brother Joe ate $\dfrac{2}{3}$ of what was left. How much did Joe eat?

    _____

LESSON 3-1

Multiplying Fractions
Practice and Problem Solving: C

Multiply. Write each answer in simplest form.

1. $7 \cdot \dfrac{3}{9}$

_____

2. $9 \cdot \dfrac{2}{5}$

_____

3. $11 \cdot \dfrac{2}{3}$

_____

4. $\dfrac{3}{7} \cdot \dfrac{4}{5}$

_____

5. $\dfrac{4}{9} \cdot \dfrac{3}{8}$

_____

6. $\dfrac{7}{9} \cdot \dfrac{4}{5}$

_____

7. $18 \cdot \dfrac{7}{9}$

_____

8. $13 \cdot \dfrac{3}{8}$

_____

9. $42 \cdot \dfrac{3}{16}$

_____

Solve.

10. Darius lifted weights for 15 minutes a day, every day, for the month of January. How many hours did he lift weights in January?

_____

11. Kim needed 9 inches of trim for every kitchen towel she was making. She made 25 towels. How many feet of trim did Kim use?

_____

12. A recipe calls for the following ingredients.

    3 c flour _____ $\dfrac{1}{2}$ t salt _____

    $\dfrac{3}{4}$ c sugar _____   4 c fruit _____

    2 T butter _____

    To make $\dfrac{2}{3}$ of the recipe, how much of each ingredient should you use? Write the revised amount on the line next to each ingredient.

13. Half of a pizza was broccoli and half was mushroom. George ate $\dfrac{1}{3}$ of the broccoli part and $\dfrac{1}{4}$ of the mushroom part. How much of the pizza did he eat?

_____

**LESSON
3-1**

Multiplying Fractions

Practice and Problem Solving: D

Multiply. Write each answer in simplest form. The first one is done for you.

1. $9 \cdot \dfrac{1}{3}$

    _____**3**_____

2. $6 \cdot \dfrac{1}{2}$

    _____

3. $8 \cdot \dfrac{1}{2}$

    _____

4. $\dfrac{1}{3} \cdot \dfrac{1}{2}$

    _____

5. $\dfrac{1}{3} \cdot \dfrac{2}{5}$

    _____

6. $\dfrac{2}{3} \cdot \dfrac{3}{4}$

    _____

7. $12 \cdot \dfrac{3}{4}$

    _____

8. $24 \cdot \dfrac{5}{8}$

    _____

9. $15 \cdot \dfrac{2}{7}$

    _____

Solve. The first one is done for you.

10. Lyza used 24 ounces of spaghetti to make a recipe. If she wanted to

    make $\dfrac{1}{4}$ as much, how much spaghetti should she use?

    $\dfrac{1}{4} \cdot 24 = 6;\ 6\ ounces$

11. Noah spent 25 hours working on his car. He spent $\dfrac{4}{5}$ of his time

    working on the transmission. How much time did Noah spend working
    on the transmission?

    _____

12. Professor Juwana spent $\dfrac{3}{5}$ of an hour correcting 6 papers. At this rate,

    how many hours will it take him to correct 30 papers?

    _____

13. Miguel baked 5 loaves of bread. Each loaf required $\dfrac{7}{8}$ cup of flour.

    How much flour did Miguel use?

    _____

Multiplying Fractions
Reteach

How to Multiply a Fraction by a Fraction

$\dfrac{2}{3} \cdot \dfrac{3}{8}$

$\dfrac{2}{3} \cdot \dfrac{3}{8} = \dfrac{6}{}$ Multiply numerators.

$\dfrac{2}{3} \cdot \dfrac{3}{8} = \dfrac{6}{24}$ Multiply denominators.

$= \dfrac{1}{4}$ Write in simplest form.

How to Multiply a Fraction by a Whole Number

$7 \cdot \dfrac{3}{4}$

$\dfrac{7}{1} \cdot \dfrac{3}{4}$ Rewrite the whole number as a fraction over 1.

$\dfrac{7}{1} \cdot \dfrac{3}{4} = \dfrac{21}{}$ Multiply numerators.

$\dfrac{7}{1} \cdot \dfrac{3}{4} = \dfrac{21}{4}$ Multiply denominators.

$= 5\dfrac{1}{4}$ Write in simplest form.

Multiply.

1. $\dfrac{3}{4} \cdot \dfrac{7}{8}$

        2. $\dfrac{2}{7} \cdot \dfrac{7}{9}$

        3. $\dfrac{7}{11} \cdot \dfrac{22}{28}$

_____

        _____

        _____

4. $\dfrac{2}{3} \cdot 5$

        5. $8 \cdot \dfrac{3}{10}$

        6. $7 \cdot \dfrac{5}{6}$

_____

        _____

        _____

7. $\dfrac{4}{9} \cdot \dfrac{2}{3}$

        8. $3 \cdot \dfrac{5}{8}$

        9. $\dfrac{3}{7} \cdot \dfrac{2}{3}$

_____

        _____

        _____

LESSON
3-1

Multiplying Fractions
Reading Strategies: Use Graphic Aids

You can find the answer to $4 \cdot \dfrac{2}{3}$ using fraction strips and multiplication.

$$4 \cdot \frac{2}{3} = \frac{8}{3}$$

1. What fractional part of each fraction strip is shaded? _____

2. How many of these fraction strips are there? _____

3. Write a multiplication equation for this picture. _____

Multiply to find $3 \cdot \dfrac{3}{5}$.

$$\frac{3}{5} \quad + \quad \frac{3}{5} \quad + \quad \frac{3}{5}$$

4. What fractional part of each fraction strip is shaded? _____

5. How many of these fraction strips are there? _____

6. Write a multiplication problem for this picture. _____

Find the products. Write each answer in simplest form.

7. $2 \cdot \dfrac{4}{7}$ _____

8. $5 \cdot \dfrac{3}{4}$ _____

9. $6 \cdot \dfrac{1}{9}$ _____

10. $4 \cdot \dfrac{3}{7}$ _____

11. $3 \cdot \dfrac{5}{9}$ _____

12. $2 \cdot \dfrac{11}{13}$ _____

13. Explain why using fraction strips would be more difficult for problems
    with larger whole numbers.

_____

Multiplying Fractions
Success for English Learners

Problem 1

How do you multiply a fraction by a whole number?

Remember:

$$5 = \frac{5}{1}$$

$$\frac{5}{1} \cdot \frac{1}{8} = \frac{5}{8}$$

Problem 2

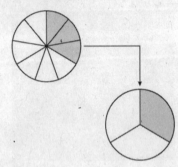

$$\frac{3}{1} \cdot \frac{1}{9} = \frac{3}{9}$$

$$\frac{3}{9} = \frac{1}{3}$$

1. What is the first step in multiplying a whole number by a fraction?

_____

2. Compare the steps you do to multiply fractions with the steps you do to add fractions.

_____

_____

_____

LESSON 3-2

Multiplying Mixed Numbers
Practice and Problem Solving: A/B

Multiply. Write each answer in simplest form.

1. $\dfrac{1}{2} \bullet 1\dfrac{1}{3}$

_____

2. $1\dfrac{1}{5} \bullet \dfrac{4}{5}$

_____

3. $1\dfrac{1}{4} \bullet \dfrac{2}{3}$

_____

4. $1\dfrac{1}{8} \bullet \dfrac{2}{5}$

_____

5. $\dfrac{2}{5} \bullet 1\dfrac{1}{2}$

_____

6. $1\dfrac{3}{5} \bullet \dfrac{1}{3}$

_____

7. $\dfrac{2}{7} \bullet 1\dfrac{1}{4}$

_____

8. $\dfrac{2}{3} \bullet 1\dfrac{1}{10}$

_____

9. $\dfrac{1}{8} \bullet 1\dfrac{1}{2}$

_____

10. $\dfrac{4}{5} \bullet 1\dfrac{1}{6}$

_____

11. $\dfrac{3}{5} \bullet 1\dfrac{1}{4}$

_____

12. $1\dfrac{3}{4} \bullet \dfrac{1}{3}$

_____

13. $1\dfrac{3}{10} \bullet 1\dfrac{1}{3}$

_____

14. $2\dfrac{1}{2} \bullet 2\dfrac{1}{2}$

_____

15. $1\dfrac{2}{3} \bullet 3\dfrac{1}{2}$

_____

Solve.

16. Dominick lives $1\dfrac{3}{4}$ miles from his school. His mother drives him half

way there. How much farther does Dominick have to walk to school?

_____

17. Katoni bought $2\dfrac{1}{2}$ dozen pencils. There are 12 pencils in a dozen.

How many pencils did Katoni buy?

_____

18. A train travels at 110 miles per hour. At this rate, how far will the train

travel in $2\dfrac{1}{2}$ hours?

_____

19. A sandbox is $1\dfrac{1}{3}$ feet tall, $1\dfrac{5}{8}$ feet wide, and $4\dfrac{1}{2}$ feet long. How many

cubic feet of sand will it hold? (Volume = length • width • height)

_____

LESSON 3-2

Multiplying Mixed Numbers

Practice and Problem Solving: C

Tell whether each answer will be greater than 1. Then, multiply and write each answer in simplest form.

1. $1\frac{1}{5} \cdot \frac{1}{3}$

2. $1\frac{5}{8} \cdot \frac{1}{8}$

3. $1\frac{4}{5} \cdot \frac{2}{3}$

_____   _____   _____

Find each product. Write the answer in simplest form.

4. $1\frac{1}{3} \cdot 2\frac{1}{2}$

5. $1\frac{2}{3} \cdot 2\frac{4}{5}$

6. $2\frac{1}{3} \cdot 3\frac{1}{2}$

_____   _____   _____

Answer each question.

7. When you multiply a fraction and a mixed number, will the product always be greater than 1?

_____

8. When you multiply two mixed numbers, will the product always be greater than 1?

_____

Solve.

9. A plane travels at $550\frac{1}{5}$ miles per hour. Will it be able to travel 1,900 miles between city A and city B in $3\frac{1}{2}$ hours? _____

10. A room is $20\frac{1}{2}$ feet by $15\frac{3}{5}$ feet. Carpeting covers $\frac{1}{2}$ of the floor. How many square feet of the floor are carpeted?

_____

11. The following recipe serves 6 people. Tell how much of each ingredient you need to serve 9 people. Then tell how much of each ingredient you need to serve only 3 people.

$3\frac{1}{2}$ c flour	$6\frac{2}{3}$ T butter	2 eggs	$1\frac{1}{3}$ c cocoa

a. flour _____   b. eggs _____

c. butter _____   d. cocoa _____

LESSON 3-2

Multiplying Mixed Numbers

Practice and Problem Solving: D

Rewrite each mixed number as an improper fraction by filling in the correct numerator. Then find the product. Write each answer in simplest form. The first one is done for you.

1. $\frac{1}{3} \cdot 1\frac{1}{2}$

$= \frac{1}{3} \cdot \frac{3}{2}$

$= \underline{\quad\frac{1}{2}\quad}$

2. $1\frac{1}{4} \cdot \frac{4}{5}$

$= \frac{\quad}{4} \cdot \frac{4}{5}$

$= \underline{\qquad}$

3. $2\frac{1}{3} \cdot \frac{3}{5}$

$= \frac{\quad}{3} \cdot \frac{3}{5}$

$= \underline{\qquad}$

4. $1\frac{2}{7} \cdot \frac{4}{9}$

$= \frac{\quad}{7} \cdot \frac{4}{9}$

$= \underline{\qquad}$

5. $1\frac{1}{3} \cdot \frac{2}{9}$

$= \frac{\quad}{3} \cdot \frac{2}{9}$

$= \underline{\qquad}$

6. $\frac{2}{7} \cdot 1\frac{1}{6}$

$= \frac{2}{7} \cdot \frac{\quad}{6}$

$= \underline{\qquad}$

Find each product. Write each answer in simplest form. The first one is done for you.

7. $\frac{3}{4} \cdot 1\frac{1}{5}$

$\underline{\quad\frac{9}{10}\quad}$

8. $\frac{2}{5} \cdot 1\frac{2}{3}$

$\underline{\qquad}$

9. $1\frac{3}{4} \cdot \frac{2}{7}$

$\underline{\qquad}$

10. $1\frac{1}{3} \cdot 2\frac{3}{10}$

$\underline{\qquad}$

11. $2\frac{2}{3} \cdot 3\frac{1}{4}$

$\underline{\qquad}$

12. $2\frac{1}{2} \cdot \frac{3}{5}$

$\underline{\qquad}$

Solve.

13. Dwayne plans to spend $1\frac{2}{3}$ hours doing his homework. He has already put in half that time. How many more hours does he have left?

_____

14. Maria reads at a speed of about $25\frac{2}{10}$ pages per hour. She reads for $1\frac{1}{2}$ hours. About how many pages does Maria read?

_____

LESSON 3-2

Multiplying Mixed Numbers
Reteach

Find $\frac{1}{10}$ of $2\frac{1}{2}$.

First change the mixed number to an improper fraction: $2\frac{1}{2} = \frac{5}{2}$.

$$\frac{1}{10} \cdot \frac{5}{2}$$

Before you multiply, check to see if you can simplify the problem.

$\frac{1}{10} \cdot \frac{5}{2}$ The GCF of 10 and 5 is 5.

$\frac{1}{2} \cdot \frac{1}{2}$ Divide both 10 and 5 by the GCF.

Finally, multiply the numerators and multiply the denominators.

$$\frac{1 \cdot 1}{2 \cdot 2} = \frac{1}{4}$$

So, $\frac{1}{10} \cdot 2\frac{1}{2} = \frac{1}{4}$.

Find the product. First, rewrite each mixed number as an improper fraction. Then, write *yes* or *no* to tell whether you can simplify the improper fraction before you multiply. If so, name the GCF.

1. $\frac{1}{4} \cdot 1\frac{1}{3}$

_____

2. $\frac{1}{6} \cdot 2\frac{1}{2}$

_____

3. $\frac{1}{8} \cdot 1\frac{1}{2}$

_____

4. $\frac{1}{3} \cdot 1\frac{2}{5}$

_____

5. $1\frac{1}{3} \cdot 1\frac{2}{3}$

_____

6. $1\frac{1}{2} \cdot 1\frac{1}{3}$

_____

7. $1\frac{3}{4} \cdot 2\frac{1}{2}$

_____

8. $1\frac{1}{6} \cdot 2\frac{2}{3}$

_____

Multiply.

9. $3\frac{1}{3} \cdot \frac{2}{5}$ _____

10. $2\frac{1}{2} \cdot \frac{1}{5}$ _____

Name _____ Date _____ Class_____

Multiplying Mixed Numbers
Reading Strategies: Use a Flowchart

A **mixed number** includes both a whole number part and a fraction part.

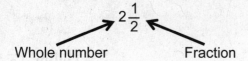

Whole number   Fraction

An **improper fraction** has a numerator that is greater than its denominator.

$$\frac{5}{2} \longrightarrow 5 > 2$$

You can change mixed numbers to improper fractions.

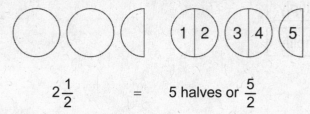

$2\frac{1}{2}$ =   5 halves or $\frac{5}{2}$

Answer each question.

1. What is the mixed number in the above example? _____

2. What is the improper fraction? _____

3. How many halves are in $2\frac{1}{2}$? _____

Change $3\frac{2}{5}$ to an improper fraction. Use the flowchart to help you.

| Multiply the denominator by the whole number. | → | Add the numerator. | → | The denominator stays the same. |

4. What is the first step? What is the result?

   _____

5. What is the next step? What is the result?

   _____

6. The improper fraction is _____.

Multiplying Mixed Numbers
Success for English Learners

Problem 1

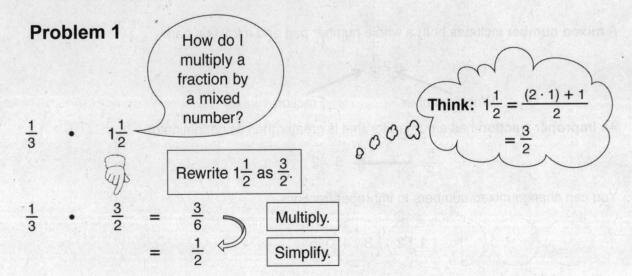

How do I multiply a fraction by a mixed number?

$\frac{1}{3}$ • $1\frac{1}{2}$

Think: $1\frac{1}{2} = \frac{(2 \cdot 1) + 1}{2}$

$= \frac{3}{2}$

Rewrite $1\frac{1}{2}$ as $\frac{3}{2}$.

$\frac{1}{3}$ • $\frac{3}{2}$ $=$ $\frac{3}{6}$ → Multiply.

$= \frac{1}{2}$ → Simplify.

Problem 2

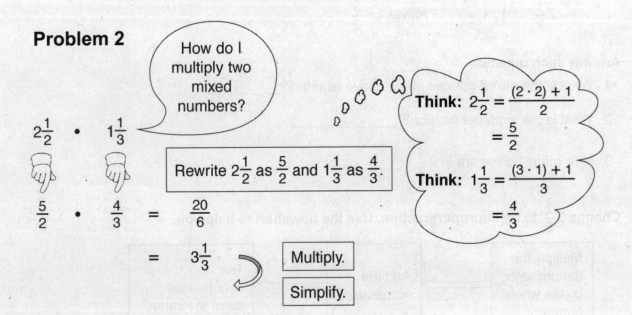

How do I multiply two mixed numbers?

$2\frac{1}{2}$ • $1\frac{1}{3}$

Rewrite $2\frac{1}{2}$ as $\frac{5}{2}$ and $1\frac{1}{3}$ as $\frac{4}{3}$.

Think: $2\frac{1}{2} = \frac{(2 \cdot 2) + 1}{2}$

$= \frac{5}{2}$

Think: $1\frac{1}{3} = \frac{(3 \cdot 1) + 1}{3}$

$= \frac{4}{3}$

$\frac{5}{2}$ • $\frac{4}{3}$ $=$ $\frac{20}{6}$

$= 3\frac{1}{3}$ → Multiply.

Simplify.

1. Why is the product for the numbers in Problem 1 **not** $1\frac{1}{6}$?

_____

2. When you need to multiply two mixed numbers, what is the first thing you should do?

_____

LESSON 3-3 Dividing Fractions
Practice and Problem Solving: A/B

Find the reciprocal.

1. $\frac{5}{7}$ _____

2. $\frac{3}{4}$ _____

3. $\frac{3}{5}$ _____

4. $\frac{1}{10}$ _____

5. $\frac{4}{9}$ _____

6. $\frac{13}{14}$ _____

7. $\frac{7}{12}$ _____

8. $\frac{3}{10}$ _____

9. $\frac{5}{8}$ _____

Divide. Write each answer in simplest form.

10. $\frac{5}{6} \div \frac{1}{2}$ _____

11. $\frac{7}{8} \div \frac{2}{3}$ _____

12. $\frac{9}{10} \div \frac{3}{4}$ _____

13. $\frac{3}{4} \div 9$ _____

14. $\frac{6}{9} \div \frac{6}{7}$ _____

15. $\frac{5}{6} \div \frac{3}{10}$ _____

16. $\frac{5}{6} \div \frac{3}{4}$ _____

17. $\frac{5}{8} \div \frac{3}{5}$ _____

18. $\frac{21}{32} \div \frac{7}{8}$ _____

Solve.

19. Mrs. Marks has $\frac{3}{4}$ pound of cheese to use making sandwiches.

    She uses about $\frac{1}{32}$ pound of cheese on each sandwich. How many

    sandwiches can she make with the cheese she has?

    _____

20. In England, mass is measured in units called *stones*. One pound

    equals $\frac{1}{14}$ of a stone. A cat weighs $\frac{3}{4}$ stone. How many pounds does

    the cat weigh?

    _____

21. Typographers measure font sizes in units called *points*. One point is

    equal to $\frac{1}{72}$ inch. Esmeralda is typing a research paper on her

    computer. She wants the text on the title page to be $\frac{1}{2}$ inch tall. What

    font size should she use?

    _____

LESSON
3-3

Dividing Fractions
Practice and Problem Solving: C

Find the reciprocal. Tell whether it is greater or less than 1.

1. $\frac{3}{7}$

2. $\frac{3}{4}$

3. $\frac{8}{5}$

_____

_____

_____

4. $\frac{1}{11}$

5. $\frac{8}{9}$

6. $\frac{13}{4}$

_____

_____

_____

7. If a fraction is less than 1, what do you know about its reciprocal?

_____

8. If a fraction is greater than 1, what do you know about its reciprocal?

_____

_____

9. What is the product of a number and its reciprocal? _____

Divide. Write each answer in simplest form.

10. $\frac{5}{6} \div \frac{2}{3}$ _____

11. $\frac{7}{8} \div \frac{3}{5}$ _____

12. $\frac{8}{9} \div \frac{2}{5}$ _____

13. $\frac{2}{3} \div \frac{4}{5}$ _____

14. $\frac{5}{7} \div \frac{7}{9}$ _____

15. $\frac{3}{5} \div \frac{9}{11}$ _____

Answer each question.

16. In problems 10–12, the dividend is greater than the divisor. What do you know about the quotients?

_____

17. In questions 13–15, the divisor is greater than the dividend. What do you know about the quotients?

_____

18. A fraction is less than 1. Is its reciprocal greater or less than 1?

_____

19. Jonathan has $1\frac{3}{4}$ hours to practice guitar. If he spends $\frac{1}{8}$ hour on each song, how many songs can Jonathan practice? For how many minutes does he practice each song?

_____

LESSON 3-3

Dividing Fractions

Practice and Problem Solving: D

Find the reciprocal. The first one is done for you.

1. $\frac{2}{3}$ ___$\frac{3}{2}$___

2. $\frac{7}{9}$ _____

3. $\frac{8}{5}$ _____

4. $\frac{1}{9}$ _____

5. $\frac{9}{10}$ _____

6. $\frac{3}{10}$ _____

7. $\frac{4}{7}$ _____

8. $\frac{8}{1}$ _____

9. $\frac{6}{7}$ _____

Divide. Write each answer in simplest form. The first one is done for you.

10. $\frac{3}{4} \div \frac{1}{2}$

$$\frac{3}{4} \cdot \frac{2}{1} = \frac{6}{4} = 1\frac{1}{2}$$

11. $\frac{7}{10} \div \frac{2}{3}$

_____

12. $\frac{5}{6} \div \frac{3}{4}$

_____

13. $\frac{3}{10} \div \frac{5}{6}$

_____

14. $\frac{5}{9} \div \frac{5}{7}$

_____

15. $\frac{7}{10} \div \frac{5}{6}$

_____

16. $\frac{7}{8} \div \frac{3}{4}$

_____

17. $\frac{11}{12} \div \frac{2}{3}$

_____

18. $\frac{5}{7} \div \frac{10}{13}$

_____

Solve. The first one has been started for you.

19. Each package of dried fruit contains $\frac{3}{16}$ of a pound. Mr. Lopez has
    4 pounds of dried fruit. How many packages can he fill?

$$4 \div \frac{3}{16} = 4 \cdot \underline{\quad\quad} = \frac{\quad\quad}{3} = \underline{\quad\quad} \text{ packages}$$

20. One inch is $\frac{1}{12}$ of a foot. Eunice has a puppy that is $\frac{3}{4}$ of a foot tall.
    How many inches tall is her puppy?

    _____

21. One minute is $\frac{1}{60}$ of an hour. What part of an hour is 12 minutes?

    _____

Name _____ Date _____ Class_____

Dividing Fractions
Reteach

Two numbers are reciprocals if their product is 1.

$\frac{2}{3}$ and $\frac{3}{2}$ are reciprocals because $\frac{2}{3} \cdot \frac{3}{2} = \frac{6}{6} = 1$.

Dividing by a number is the same as multiplying by its reciprocal.

$$\frac{1}{4} \div \frac{1}{2} = \frac{1}{2} \qquad \longrightarrow \qquad \frac{1}{4} \cdot \frac{2}{1} = \frac{1}{2}$$

So, you can use reciprocals to divide by fractions.

Find $\frac{2}{3} \div \frac{1}{4}$.

First, rewrite the expression as a multiplication expression.

Use the reciprocal of the divisor: $\frac{1}{4} \cdot \frac{4}{1} = 1$.

$$\frac{2}{3} \div \frac{1}{4} = \frac{2}{3} \cdot \frac{4}{1}$$
$$= \frac{8}{3}$$
$$= 2\frac{2}{3}$$

Think: 6 thirds is 2, and 2 of the 8 thirds are left over.

Rewrite each division expression as a multiplication expression. Then find the value of the expression. Write each answer in simplest form.

1. $\frac{1}{4} \div \frac{1}{3}$

2. $\frac{1}{2} \div \frac{1}{4}$

3. $\frac{3}{8} \div \frac{1}{2}$

4. $\frac{1}{3} \div \frac{3}{4}$

_____ _____ _____ _____

Divide. Write each answer in simplest form.

5. $\frac{1}{5} \div \frac{1}{2}$

6. $\frac{1}{6} \div \frac{2}{3}$

7. $\frac{1}{8} \div \frac{2}{5}$

8. $\frac{1}{8} \div \frac{1}{2}$

_____ _____ _____ _____

**LESSON
3-3**

Dividing Fractions
Reading Strategies: Use Models

Bar models can help you picture dividing by fractions.

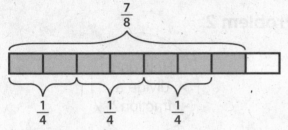

What is $\frac{7}{8} \div \frac{1}{4}$? Think: How many one-fourths are in $\frac{7}{8}$?

Use the picture to answer each question.

1. How many whole groups of $\frac{1}{4}$ are in $\frac{7}{8}$? _____

   What fraction of a group of $\frac{1}{4}$ is left? _____

2. $\frac{7}{8} \div \frac{1}{4}$ = _____

Instead of dividing, multiply by the reciprocal. Think: $\frac{7}{8}$ four times.

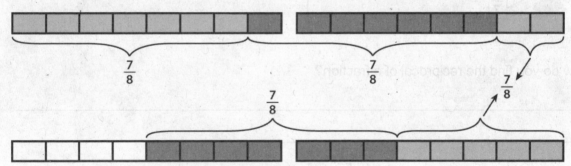

Use the picture to answer each question.

3. How many whole bars are shaded? _____

4. How many additional eighths of a bar are shaded? _____

   What is this fraction in simplest form? _____

5. All together, how many bars are shaded? _____

6. Compare the multiplication and division examples. What do you notice

   about the answer you get when you divide by $\frac{1}{4}$ or multiply by 4?

_____

LESSON 3-3

Dividing Fractions
Success for English Learners

Problem 1

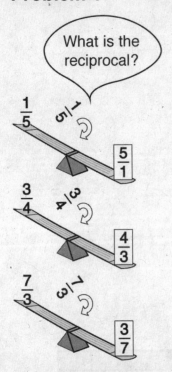

What is the reciprocal?

$\frac{1}{5}$ $\frac{5}{1}$

$\frac{3}{4}$ $\frac{4}{3}$

$\frac{7}{3}$ $\frac{3}{7}$

Problem 2

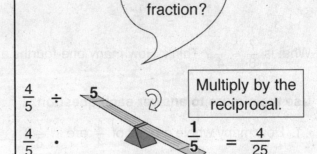

How do I divide a fraction?

$\frac{4}{5} \div 5$

Multiply by the reciprocal.

$\frac{4}{5} \cdot \frac{1}{5} = \frac{4}{25}$

1. How do you find the reciprocal of a fraction?

_____

_____

2. Explain the steps you follow to divide $\frac{5}{8}$ by $\frac{1}{3}$.

_____

_____

3. You multiply any fraction times its reciprocal. What is the product? Give an example.

_____

_____

LESSON 3-4

Dividing Mixed Numbers
Practice and Problem Solving: A/B

Find the reciprocal. Show that the product of the mixed number and its reciprocal is 1.

1. $10\frac{1}{2}$

2. $6\frac{3}{7}$

3. $2\frac{8}{9}$

_____

4. $15\frac{1}{4}$

5. $9\frac{2}{3}$

6. $7\frac{5}{8}$

_____

Divide. Write each answer in simplest form.

7. $\frac{8}{10} \div 1\frac{5}{6}$

8. $2 \div 1\frac{6}{7}$

9. $3\frac{3}{5} \div 2\frac{1}{4}$

_____

10. $4\frac{1}{2} \div 2\frac{3}{8}$

11. $5\frac{5}{6} \div 3\frac{1}{6}$

12. $\frac{11}{12} \div 2\frac{5}{8}$

_____

13. $1\frac{9}{13} \div \frac{3}{8}$

14. $6\frac{4}{5} \div 3\frac{2}{9}$

15. $9\frac{2}{3} \div 6\frac{8}{9}$

_____

Write each situation as a division problem. Then solve.

16. A concrete patio is $5\frac{2}{3}$ feet wide. It has an area of $36\frac{5}{6}$ square feet.

    Is the concrete slab long enough to fit a 7-foot picnic table without placing the table along the diagonal of the patio?

_____

17. The area of a mirror is 225 square inches, and its width is $13\frac{3}{4}$ inches.

    Will the mirror fit in a space that is 15 inches by 16 inches?

_____

18. Barney has $16\frac{1}{5}$ yards of fabric. To make an elf costume, he needs

    $5\frac{2}{5}$ yards of fabric. How many costumes can Barney make?

LESSON
3-4
Dividing Mixed Numbers
Practice and Problem Solving: C

Solve.

1. Vanessa buys a strip of 25 postage stamps. The strip of stamps is
   $21\frac{7}{8}$ inches long. How long is a strip after Vanessa uses 1 stamp?

   _____

2. Hasan has $18\frac{3}{4}$ yards of fabric. It take $3\frac{1}{6}$ yards to make a
   pillowcase. Hasan plans to make as many pillowcases as he can.
   How many yards of fabric will be left over?

   _____

3. Takafumi is hiking on a path that is $5\frac{7}{8}$ miles long. There are

   6 markers evenly posted along the path. Takafumi arrives at the
   4th marker. How many miles has he hiked so far?

   _____

4. Yuki has a ribbon that is $12\frac{1}{4}$ feet long. She divides it into pieces that

   are each $1\frac{7}{8}$ feet long. She uses three pieces to make a bow. How

   many bows can she make in all?

   _____

5. Mrs. Lemke has $10\frac{2}{3}$ ounces of fertilizer for her plants. She plans to

   use $\frac{3}{4}$ ounce of fertilizer on each plant. After she puts fertilizer on as

   many plants as she can, how much fertilizer will be left over?

   _____

6. Gabriel has $15\frac{5}{8}$ pounds of clay. He will use $\frac{7}{10}$ pound to make each

   bowl. After making 8 bowls, Gabriel wonders how many more bowls he
   can make. How many more bowls can he make? Explain how you
   know.

   _____

   _____

   _____

LESSON 3-4

Dividing Mixed Numbers

Practice and Problem Solving: D

Show how to write each mixed number as an improper fraction. Then find the reciprocal. The first one is done for you.

1. $9\dfrac{1}{2}$

   $$\dfrac{(9 \times 2) + 1}{2} = \dfrac{19}{2}$$

   The reciprocal is $\dfrac{2}{19}$.

2. $5\dfrac{3}{7}$

3. $1\dfrac{8}{9}$

4. $14\dfrac{1}{4}$

5. $8\dfrac{2}{3}$

6. $6\dfrac{5}{8}$

Divide. Write each answer in simplest form. The first one is done for you.

7. $\dfrac{7}{10} \div 1\dfrac{2}{6}$

   $$\dfrac{7}{10} \div \dfrac{8}{6} = \dfrac{7}{10} \times \dfrac{6}{8} = \dfrac{42}{80} = \dfrac{21}{40}$$

8. $2 \div 1\dfrac{5}{7}$

9. $4\dfrac{3}{5} \div 2\dfrac{2}{5}$

10. $\dfrac{11}{12} \div 1\dfrac{3}{4}$

Write a division expression for each problem. Then solve.

11. Larry has $9\dfrac{3}{5}$ yards of fabric. He will use $2\dfrac{2}{5}$ yards to make each vest. How many vests can Larry make?

    $$9\dfrac{3}{5} \div 2\dfrac{2}{5} = \dfrac{48}{5} \div \dfrac{12}{5} = \dfrac{48}{5} \times \dfrac{5}{12} = \dfrac{48}{12} = 4$$

    Larry can make __4__ vests.

12. A patio has an area of $20\dfrac{5}{6}$ ft², and the width is $3\dfrac{1}{2}$ feet. What is the length of the patio?

    _____ The patio is _____ feet long.

Dividing Mixed Numbers
Reteach

Two numbers are **reciprocals** if their product is 1.

$\dfrac{7}{3}$ and $\dfrac{3}{7}$ are reciprocals because $\dfrac{7}{3} \times \dfrac{3}{7} = 1$.

Write a mixed number as an improper fraction to find its reciprocal.

$2\dfrac{3}{4}$ and $\dfrac{4}{11}$ are reciprocals because $2\dfrac{3}{4} = \dfrac{11}{4}$ and $\dfrac{11}{4} \times \dfrac{4}{11} = 1$.

To find $2\dfrac{3}{4} \div 1\dfrac{3}{4}$, first rewrite the mixed numbers as improper fractions.

$\dfrac{11}{4} \div \dfrac{7}{4}$

Next, rewrite the expression as a multiplication expression and replace the divisor with its reciprocal.

$\dfrac{11}{4} \times \dfrac{4}{7}$

Solve. Write your answer in simplest form.

$2\dfrac{3}{4} \div 1\dfrac{3}{4} = \dfrac{11}{4} \div \dfrac{7}{4} = \dfrac{11}{4} \times \dfrac{4}{7} = \dfrac{11}{7} = 1\dfrac{4}{7}$

Find the reciprocal.

1. $\dfrac{9}{14}$

2. $3\dfrac{1}{2}$

3. $10\dfrac{2}{3}$

_____   _____   _____

Complete the division. Write each answer in simplest form.

4. $3\dfrac{3}{5} \div 2\dfrac{1}{4}$

    $= \dfrac{18}{5} \div \dfrac{}{4}$

    $= \dfrac{}{5} \times \dfrac{}{9}$

    _____

5. $1\dfrac{1}{2} \div 1\dfrac{1}{4}$

    $= \dfrac{3}{2} \div \dfrac{}{4}$

    $= \dfrac{}{} \times \dfrac{}{}$

    _____

6. $\dfrac{5}{12} \div 1\dfrac{7}{8}$

    $= \dfrac{}{12} \div \dfrac{}{8}$

    $= \dfrac{}{} \times \dfrac{}{}$

    _____

7. $3\dfrac{1}{8} \div \dfrac{1}{2}$

    _____

8. $1\dfrac{1}{6} \div 2\dfrac{2}{3}$

    _____

9. $2 \div 1\dfrac{1}{5}$

    _____

Name _____ Date _____ Class_____

LESSON 3-4

Dividing Mixed Numbers

Reading Strategies: Use a Model

A model is useful for dividing mixed numbers.

The Smith family has a $2\frac{1}{2}$-foot-long sandwich to share. Each $\frac{1}{2}$-foot of the sandwich serves one person. How many $\frac{1}{2}$-foot servings are in this sandwich?

Find $2\frac{1}{2} \div \frac{1}{2}$.

Step 1: Draw a square and label it $\frac{1}{2}$.

$\frac{1}{2}$

Step 2: Draw a row of these squares until they add up to $2\frac{1}{2}$.

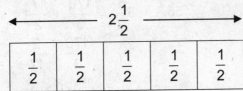

Step 3: Count the number of squares needed to reach $2\frac{1}{2}$.

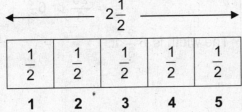

1. How do you represent a single serving?

   _____

2. Why draw a row of servings until they add up to $2\frac{1}{2}$?

   _____

   _____

3. How many $\frac{1}{2}$-foot servings does the Smith family have?

   _____

4. What is $2\frac{1}{2} \div \frac{1}{2}$? _____

Original content Copyright © by Houghton Mifflin Harcourt. Additions and changes to the original content are the responsibility of the instructor.

LESSON 3-4

Dividing Mixed Numbers
Success for English Learners

Problem 1

What is the reciprocal of $2\frac{3}{4}$?

Write the mixed number as an improper fraction.

$$2\frac{3}{4} = 2 + \frac{3}{4}$$
$$= \frac{8}{4} + \frac{3}{4}$$
$$= \frac{11}{4}$$

What is the reciprocal of $\frac{11}{4}$?

Flip it!

How can I tell this is right?

$\frac{11}{4} \times \frac{4}{11} = \frac{44}{44} = 1$

Wow! The product is 1.

Problem 2

How wide is the rectangle?

$A = 56\frac{2}{3}\text{ft}^2$ $W = ?$

$l = 8\frac{1}{2}\text{ft}$

What is the area? $56\frac{2}{3}\text{ft}^2$

What is the length? $8\frac{1}{2}\text{ft}$

How can I find the width?

Divide the area by the length.

$$56\frac{2}{3} \div 8\frac{1}{2} = \frac{170}{3} \div \frac{17}{2}$$
$$= \frac{170}{3} \times \frac{2}{17}$$
$$= \frac{^{10}\cancel{170} \times 3}{3 \times \cancel{17}_1}$$
$$= \frac{20}{3} \text{ or } 6\frac{2}{3}$$

The width is $6\frac{2}{3}$ ft.

---

1. How is dividing mixed numbers different from multiplying mixed numbers?

_____

_____

2. What is the first step to divide mixed numbers?

_____

3. Why would you expect the width of the rectangle to be about 7 ft?

_____

_____

Multiplying and Dividing Fractions
Challenge

The table shows the length and width of 4 rug designs that
a carpet store stocks. Use the table to answer problems 1–2.

Rug Design	Length (ft)	Width (ft)
Classic	$8\frac{1}{2}$	$10\frac{3}{4}$
Deco	$10\frac{3}{4}$	$9\frac{3}{8}$
Solid	$7\frac{2}{5}$	$8\frac{3}{5}$
Modern	$10\frac{3}{5}$	$9\frac{1}{2}$

1. The price of each rug is found by multiplying the area of the rug
   (length times width) by the price per square foot. The price for all 4
   rug designs listed above is $8 per square foot. Which rug is the most
   expensive? How much does it cost?

   _____

2. Pauline orders a custom rug. She wants a rug that is the same final
   price as the Deco but the same width as the Modern. What is the
   length of the rug Pauline wants to purchase? Explain.

   _____

   _____

Solve.

3. $\frac{1}{2}, \frac{2}{3}, \frac{3}{4}, \frac{4}{5}, \frac{5}{6}, \cdots \frac{99}{100}$

   In the list above, each fraction after the first is obtained by adding
   1 to both the numerator and denominator of the fraction before it.

   For example, the first fraction is $\frac{1}{2}$. To get the second fraction, add

   1 to 1 and to 2: $\frac{1+1}{2+1} = \frac{2}{3}$. This pattern continues to $\frac{99}{100}$. What is

   the product of the fractions in the list above? What pattern can help
   you find the product quickly?

   _____

   _____

Name _____ Date _____ Class_____

Multiplying Decimals
Practice and Problem Solving: A/B

Show the decimal multiplication on the grids. Find the product.

1. 0.2 × 0.6 _____

2. 0.3 × 0.7 _____

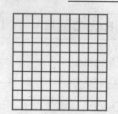

Draw an area model to represent the multiplication problems below. Find the product.

3. 1.2 × 3.3 = _____

4. 4.1 × 2.1 = _____

Multiply.

5. 0.1
    × 0.2
    _____

6. 0.9
    × 6
    _____

7. 0.3
    × 0.8
    _____

8. 1.6
    × 2.9
    _____

9. 1.5 × 0.41 =

10. 0.24 × 2.68 =

11. 3.13 × 4.69 =

12. 5.48 × 15.12 =

_____

Solve.

13. Each basket can hold 2.5 pounds of apples. How many pounds can 7 baskets hold?

_____

14. Canvas cloth costs $7.50 per square meter. How much will 3.5 square meters of canvas cost?

_____

LESSON 4-1

Multiplying Decimals

Practice and Problem Solving: C

Estimate each product to the nearest whole number. Then, find the product.

1. 0.7×0.85

2. 3.05×1.95

3. 0.45×2.3

_____

_____

_____

4. 4.699×1.74

5. 10.37×5.086

6. 5.593×19.71

_____

_____

_____

Compare using < or > without calculating the product.

7. 2.4×3.8 ◯ 3.5×2.8

8. 6.28×3.82 ◯ 3.3×6.84

Solve.

9. A forestry service biologist has time to study insect infestation in an area of 50 square kilometers. On the forest service map, the scale is 1 centimeter equals 1 kilometer. The four possible sectors available for study appear as rectangles on the map. Complete the table by calculating the map area of each sector.

Sector	Map Dimensions (cm)	Map Area (cm²)
A	2.5×5.8	
B	3.7×2.1	
C	4.7×3.5	
D	4.2×2.8	

a. How can you calculate the actual area of each sector?

_____

b. Does the biologist have time to study all four areas? Explain why or why not?

_____

_____

c. What combinations of three sectors could the scientist study?

_____

d. Which combination of sectors maximizes the area to be studied? Explain why.

_____

LESSON 4-1

Multiplying Decimals

Practice and Problem Solving: D

Multiply. The first one is done for you.

1. 0.5
    × 3
    ‾‾‾‾
    1.5

2. 4
    × 0.8
    ‾‾‾‾

3. 9
    × 0.7
    ‾‾‾‾

4. 0.25
    × 3
    ‾‾‾‾

Show the decimal multiplication on the grids. Do not solve.

5. 0.1 × 0.7

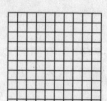

6. 0.4 × 0.8

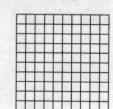

7. 0.3 × 0.7

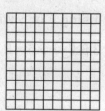

Name the number of decimal places.

8.   2.4 ← _____ decimal places
    × 0.83 ← _____ decimal places
    ‾‾‾‾‾‾‾
    Answer ← _____ total decimal places

9. 0.456 ← _____ decimal places
    × 2.5 ← _____ decimal places
    ‾‾‾‾‾
    Answer ← _____ total decimal places

Multiply. The first one is done for you.

10. 7.1 5
     × 2.5
     ‾‾‾‾‾
     3575
     1420
     ‾‾‾‾‾
     17.775

11. 4.36
     ×1.2
     ‾‾‾‾

Solve.

12. A cabinetmaker buys 3.5 liters of oak varnish. The varnish costs
    $4.95 per liter.

    a. Write a multiplication expression for this purchase.

    _____

    b. How much does 3 liters of varnish cost? _____

    c. How much does 0.5 liters of varnish cost? _____

    d. What is the total cost of 3.5 liters of varnish? _____

Multiplying Decimals

Reteach

You can use a model to help you multiply a decimal by a whole number.

Find the product of 0.12 and 4.

Use a 10-by-10 grid. Shade 4 groups of 12 squares.

Count the number of shaded squares. Since you have shaded 48 of the 100 squares, $0.12 \times 4 = 0.48$.

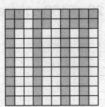

Find each product.

1. 0.23×3　　　　2. 0.41×2　　　　3. 0.01×5　　　　4. 0.32×2

_____　_____　_____　_____

5. 0.15×3　　　　6. 0.42×2　　　　7. 0.04×8　　　　8. 0.22×4

_____　_____　_____　_____

You can also use a model to help you multiply a decimal by a decimal.

Find the product of 0.8 and 0.4.

Step 1　Shade 8 tenths of the figure.

Step 2　Shade darker 4 tenths of the shaded area.

Step 3　How many squares have you shaded twice?

You have twice shaded 32 of the squares.

So, $0.8 \times 0.4 = 0.32$.

Find each product.

9. 0.2×0.8　　　　10. 0.7×0.9　　　　11. 0.5×0.5　　　　12. 0.3×0.6

_____　_____　_____　_____

13. 0.5×0.2　　　　14. 0.4×0.4　　　　15. 0.1×0.9　　　　16. 0.4×0.7

_____　_____　_____　_____

LESSON 4-1

Multiplying Decimals

Reading Strategies: Use Graphic Aids

Each grid has 26 of 100 squares shaded to represent 0.26.

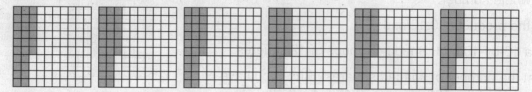

You can add the decimals to find out how much of the grids are shaded.

⟵ $0.26 + 0.26 + 0.26 + 0.26 + 0.26 + 0.26 = 1.56$

Or, you can multiply the shading of one grid by 6.

⟵ $0.26 \times 6 = 1.56$

Use the grids for problems 1 to 5.

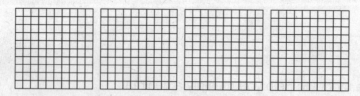

1. Shade the grids so that each one represents 0.89.

2. Write an addition expression to represent the shaded grids.

   _____

3. Evaluate your addition expression to find the sum.

   _____

4. Write a multiplication expression to represent the shaded grids.

   _____

5. Evaluate your multiplication expression to find the product.

   _____

Multiplying Decimals
Success for English Learners

Problem 1

How many decimal places are in each number?

2.7   1.25   23

Start at the decimal point. Count the digits to its right.

one decimal place

two decimal places

no decimal place

Problem 2

Multiply: 1.2×1.6

1.2 $\longrightarrow$	1 decimal place	1.2
1.6 $\longrightarrow$	1 decimal place	$\times$ 1.6
		72
		+ 120
$1 + 1 = 2$ decimal places $\longrightarrow$		1.92

1. How do you find the decimal place in the product of two decimals?

   _____

2. To place the decimal point in the product of two decimals, do you move the decimal point to the left or to the right?

   _____

3. After you place the decimal point in a product of two decimals, how do you tell if the answer is reasonable?

   _____

Is each product reasonable? Write *yes* or *no*. If no, give a reasonable estimate.

4. $0.8 \times 3 = 0.12$ 5. $5.2 \times 6.7 = 34.84$ 6. $2.4 \times 3 = 72$

   _____   _____   _____

Name _____ Date _____ Class_____

Dividing Decimals
Practice and Problem Solving: A/B

Use decimal grids to find each quotient. First, shade the grid.
Then, separate the model to show the correct number of equal parts.

1. 3.6 ÷ 1.2

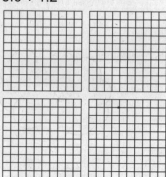

_____

2. 3.27 ÷ 3

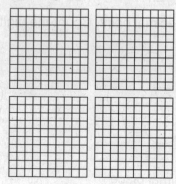

_____

Find each quotient.

3. $9.5\overline{)142.5}$

_____

4. $3\overline{)39.6}$

_____

5. $2\overline{)10.88}$

_____

6. 10.5 ÷ 1.5

_____

7. 9.75 ÷ 1.3

_____

8. 37.5 ÷ 2.5

_____

Estimate each quotient to the nearest whole number. Then, find the actual quotient

9. $0.9\overline{)3.78}$

_____

10. $2.5\overline{)36}$

_____

11. $0.25\overline{)7}$

_____

12. $9.5\overline{)142.5}$

_____

Solve.

13. A camera attached to a telescope photographs a star's image once
every 0.045 seconds. How many complete images can the camera
capture in 3 seconds?

_____

14. A geologist noticed that land along a fault line moved 24.8 centimeters
over the past 175 years. On average, how much did the land move
each year?

_____

Dividing Decimals

Practice and Problem Solving: C

Estimate the quotient. Then find the exact quotient.

1. $8.4 \div 2.4$

2. $13.75 \div 2.25$

3. $5.45 \div 0.5$

Estimate:

Estimate:

Estimate:

_____

_____

_____

Exact Quotient:

Exact Quotient:

Exact Quotient:

_____

_____

_____

Compare using <, >, or = without calculating the quotient.

4. $0.05\overline{)3}$ ◯ $0.005\overline{)3}$

5. $1.9\overline{)4.7}$ ◯ $19\overline{)4.7}$

6. $0.35\overline{)0.78}$ ◯ $0.35\overline{)7.8}$

7. $1.2\overline{)34}$ ◯ $0.12\overline{)3.4}$

Solve.

8. Acme Hardware is introducing a new product called Greener Cleaner. Complete the table by finding the cost per milliliter for each size based on the sales price. One liter is 1,000 milliliters.

Size	Amount of Liquid	Sale Price	Price per Milliliter
Small	250 milliliters	$4.50	
Medium	500 milliliters	$9.95	
Large	1 liter	$16.95	

a. Write an expression using < or > to compare the three containers by price per milliliter.

_____

b. What is the least expensive way to buy 1,500 milliliters of Green Cleaner? Write an expression to represent your choice and evaluate.

_____

c. What is the most expensive way to buy 1,500 milliliters of Green Cleaner? Write an expression to represent your choice and evaluate?

_____

LESSON 4-2

Dividing Decimals

Practice and Problem Solving: D

Find each quotient. The first one is done for you.

1. $2.8 \div 4$

 _____**0.7**_____

2. $1.8 \div 2$

 _____

3. $3.6 \div 6$

 _____

4. $7.2 \div 9$

 _____

5. $0.15 \div 3$

 _____

6. $4.8 \div 8$

 _____

Find each quotient. The first one is done for you.

7. $2.4 \div 0.4$

 _____**6**_____

8. $1.4 \div 0.2$

 _____

9. $4.8 \div 0.6$

 _____

10. $3.3 \div 0.3$

 _____

11. $2.6 \div 1.3$

 _____

12. $7.2 \div 1.2$

 _____

Solve.

13. At the grocery store, a six-pack of bottled water costs $2.88.
 How much does each bottle cost?

 _____

14. It rained 2.79 inches in July. What was the average daily rainfall in
 July? (Hint: July has 31 days.)

 _____

15. Over several months, a meteorologist recorded a total snowfall of
 8.6 centimeters. During this period, the average monthly snowfall was
 4.3 centimeters. For how many months did the meteorologist collect
 measurements of the snowfalls?

 _____

16. Almonds cost $3.49 per pound. A bag of almonds costs $6.95.
 To the nearest whole pound, about how many pounds of almonds
 are in the bag?

 _____

LESSON 4-2

Dividing Decimals

Reteach

You can use decimal grids to help you divide by whole numbers.

To divide 0.35 by 7, first shade in a decimal grid to show thirty-five hundredths.

0.35 ÷ 7 means "divide 0.35 into 7 equal groups." Show this on the decimal grid.

 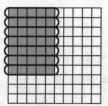

The number of units in each group is the quotient.

So, 0.35 ÷ 7 = 0.05.

Find each quotient.

1. 0.6 ÷ 5

2. 0.78 ÷ 6

3. 0.32 ÷ 4

4. 0.99 ÷ 0.0033

_____ _____ _____ _____

You can use powers of 10 to help you divide a decimal by a decimal.

Divide 0.048 by 0.12.

Notice that 0.12 has two decimal places.
To make this a whole number, multiply by 100.

0.048 ÷ 0.12 ⟶ 0.12 • 100 = 12   0.048 • 100 = 4.8

Then divide.

$$\begin{array}{r} 0.4 \\ 12\overline{)4.8} \\ \underline{4\,8} \\ 0 \end{array}$$

4.8 ÷ 12

Step 1: Divide as you would with a whole number.

Step 2: Think 48 ÷ 12 = 4.

Step 3: Place the decimal point in the quotient.
Add a zero as necessary.

So, 0.048 ÷ 0.12 = 0.4.

Find each quotient.

5. 0.4)0.08

6. 0.9)0.63

7. 0.008)0.4

8. 0.04)0.032

_____ _____ _____ _____

LESSON 4-2
Dividing Decimals
Reading Strategies: Use Graphic Aids

You can use a hundreds grid to show division with decimals.

The grid shows 0.15. ➜

0.15 ÷ 3 means "separate
0.15 into 3 equal groups." ➜

0.15 ÷ 3 makes 3 equal
groups of 0.05. ➜
0.15 ÷ 3 = 0.05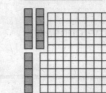

Use the grids to complete 1–8.

1. Shade 0.60 of the grid at right.

2. Divide the shaded area into 3 equal sections.

3. Write a decimal that represents each section. _____

4. Write a division problem for your model.

   _____

5. Shade 0.72 of the grid at right.

6. Divide the shaded area into 8 equal sections.

7. Write a decimal that represents each section. _____

8. Write a division problem for your model.

   _____

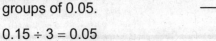

Dividing Decimals
Success for English Learners

Problem 1

Find $3.6 \div 1.2$.

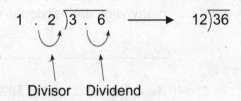

Remember: To multiply by 10, move the decimal point 1 place to the right.

Problem 2

Sari's car goes 17.5 miles for every gallon of gas.
How many gallons of gas does Sari's car use to go 227.5 miles?

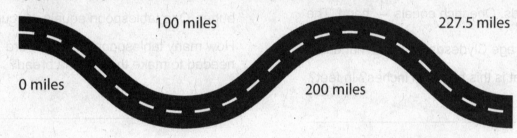

$$17.5\overline{)227.5} \quad \frac{13.0}{}$$

1. What is the quotient in Problem 1?

_____

2. Does the quotient in Problem 1 have a remainder? How do you know?

_____

3. Write another question to go with Problem 2. Solve.

_____

_____

LESSON 4-3

Applying Multiplication and Division of Rational Numbers

Practice and Problem Solving: A/B

Solve.

1. Four friends equally shared the cost of supplies for a picnic. The supplies cost $12.40. How much did each pay?

   _____

2. Twenty people are going by van to a movie. Each van seats 8 people. How many vans are needed to take everyone?

   _____

3. Plastic forks come in packs of 6. You need 40 forks a party. How many packs of forks should you buy?

   _____

4. Kesha spent a total of $9.60 on new shoelaces. Each pair cost $1.20. How many pairs of shoelaces did she buy?

   _____

5. Horses are measured in units called hands. One inch equals $\frac{1}{4}$ hand. The average Clydesdale is $17\frac{1}{5}$ hands tall. What is this height in inches? In feet?

   _____

6. A banana bread recipe calls for $\frac{3}{4}$ cup butter. One tablespoon equals $\frac{1}{16}$ cup. How many tablespoons of butter are needed to make the banana bread?

   _____

7. Cindy works part-time and earns $5.75 an hour. One year she worked 50 weeks and averaged 12.4 hours of work per week. About how much money did she earn that year?

   _____

8. At a gymnastics competition, Joey scored 9.4, 9.7, 9.9, and 9.8. Carlos scored 9.5, 9.2, 9.7, and 9.6. Who had the greater average score? By how many points was his score greater?

   _____

9. A granola recipe calls for $2\frac{1}{3}$ cups of almonds. A bag of almonds contains 2 cups. To make $2\frac{1}{2}$ batches of granola, Ali buys 5 bags of almonds. How many cups of almonds will he have left over?

   _____

10. At a zoo, 3 pandas eat a total of $181\frac{1}{2}$ pounds of bamboo shoots each day. The male panda eats 3 times as much as the baby. The female eats twice as much as the baby. How many pounds of bamboo shoots does the female panda eat?

   _____

Applying Multiplication and Division of Rational Numbers

Practice and Problem Solving: C

Solve.

1. Sandy makes linen scarves that are $\frac{7}{8}$ of a yard long. How many scarves can she make from 156 feet of fabric?

   _____

2. A small rug is 36 inches long. Its width is $\frac{2}{3}$ of its length. What is the width of the rug in feet?

   _____

3. Four friends split equally a lunch bill of $36.96 plus 20% tip. How much did each person pay?

   _____

4. Jade spent $37.60 on groceries. $\frac{4}{5}$ of that total was spent on vegetables. How much was spent on other items?

   _____

5. In January, Gene watched 5 movies. Their lengths are shown in the table. How many hours did Gene spend watching movies? _____

   What was the average length of a movie in hours?

   _____

   Which movies were longer than the average?_____

Movie	Length (min)
A	147.8
B	119.7
C	156.4
D	158.3
E	112.9

6. Derrick's garden is $18\frac{1}{2}$ feet long. He plants bulbs $\frac{3}{8}$ of a foot apart. How many bulbs can Derrick plant in one row?

   _____

   Derrick plants three rows of bulbs that cost $0.79 each.

   How much does he spend on bulbs? _____

7. Yin's cellphone plan costs $30 a month. She used 22.5 hours in May.

   What was her cost per minute? _____

   Yin's average call lasted 3.4 minutes. How much did an average

   call cost? _____

   About how many calls did Yin make in May? _____

LESSON 4-3

Applying Multiplication and Division of Rational Numbers

Practice and Problem Solving: D

Solve each problem. The first one has been done for you.

1. A hiking trail is $\frac{9}{10}$ mile long. There are 6 markers evenly posted along the trail to direct hikers. How far apart are the markers?

   $\frac{3}{20}$ **of a mile**

2. Tomas is saving $17.00 each week to buy a new sewing machine that costs $175.50. How many weeks will he have to save to have enough money to buy the sewing machine?

3. Sequins come in packs of 75. Agnes uses 12 sequins on each costume. If she has one pack of sequins, how many costumes can she make?

4. Jessie pays $2.19 each month for an annual subscription to *Sewing* magazine. She receives 12 magazines annually. How much does Jessie pay for an annual subscription?

5. Lisa's family drove 830.76 miles to visit her grandparents. Lisa calculated that they used 30.1 gallons of gas. How many miles per gallon did the car average?

6. Jamal spent $6.75 on wire. Wire costs $0.45 per foot. How many feet of wire did Jamal buy?

7. In England, mass is measured in units called stones. One pound equals $\frac{1}{14}$ of a stone. A cat has a mass of $\frac{3}{4}$ stone. What is its mass in pounds?

8. Dan uses $6\frac{1}{4}$ cups of flour to make pita bread for his family. The recipe calls for $2\frac{1}{2}$ cups. How many batches of the pita bread recipe did he make?

9. Shari used a total of 67.5 yards of cotton material to make costumes for the play. Each costume used 11.25 yards of cloth. How many costumes did Shari make?

10. Mike earned $11.76 per hour for working 23.5 hours last week. How much money did Mike earn last week?

LESSON 4-3 Applying Multiplication and Division of Rational Numbers
Reteach

When a word problem involves fractions or decimals, use these four steps to help you decide which operation to use.

Tanya has $13\frac{1}{2}$ feet of ribbon. To giftwrap boxes, she needs to cut it into $\frac{7}{8}$-foot lengths. How many lengths can Tanya cut?

Step 1	Read the problem carefully. What is asked for?	The number of lengths is asked for.
Step 2	Think of a simpler problem that includes only whole numbers.	Tanya has 12 feet of ribbon. She wants to cut it into 2-foot lengths. How many lengths can she cut?
Step 3	How would you solve the simpler problem?	Divide 12 by 2. Tanya can cut 6 lengths.
Step 4	Use the same reasoning with the original problem.	Divide $13\frac{1}{2}$ by $\frac{7}{8}$. Tanya can cut 15 lengths.

Tell whether you should multiply or divide. Then solve the problem.

1. Jan has $37.50. Tickets to a concert cost $5.25 each. How many tickets can Jan buy?

   _____

2. Jon has $45.00. He plans to spend $\frac{4}{5}$ of his money on sports equipment. How much will he spend?

   _____

3. Ricki has 76.8 feet of cable. She plans to cut it into 7 pieces. How long will each piece be?

   _____

4. Roger has $2\frac{1}{2}$ cups of butter. A recipe for a loaf of bread requires $\frac{3}{4}$ cup of butter. How many loaves can Roger bake?

   _____

Name _____ Date _____ Class _____

Applying Multiplication and Division of Rational Numbers
Reading Strategies: Analyze Information

Word problems contain information that helps you choose which operation to use. Look for clues to help you decide whether to multiply or divide.

Read the problem carefully.

What is given? What are you asked to find?

Given	Asked to Find	Operation
a whole	a fractional part	Multiply by the fraction.
a whole *and* the **number** of parts	the **size** of the parts	Divide.
a whole *and* the **size** of a part	the **number** of parts	Divide.

Identify the information given and what you are asked to find.
Tell whether to multiply or divide. Then solve the problem.

1. A pumpkin weighs 31.3 pounds. It is split into 3 equal pieces. What does each part weigh?

   Given: _____

   Find: _____

   Operation and solution: _____

2. A pumpkin weighs $22\frac{2}{3}$ pounds. What does $\frac{1}{6}$ of it weigh?

   Given: _____

   Find: _____

   Operation and solution: _____

3. A pumpkin weighs $42\frac{1}{3}$ pounds. A grocer wants to cut it into pieces

   weighing $2\frac{1}{2}$ pounds each. How many pieces can he cut?

   Given: _____

   Find: _____

   Operation and solution: _____

**LESSON
4-3**

Applying Multiplication and Division of Rational Numbers
Success for English Learners

Problem 1

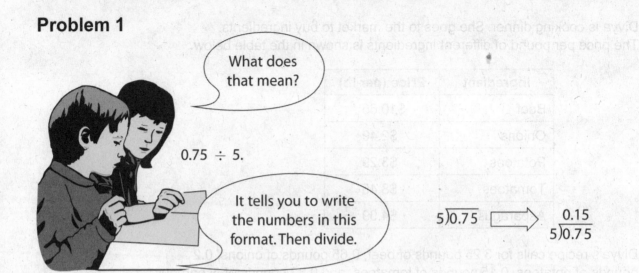

Problem 2

Total Cost: $11.61

1. How do you know where to place the decimal point in the quotient in
   Problem 1?

   _____

2. How can you determine if your answer to Problem 2 is correct?

   _____

   _____

MODULE 4

Multiplying and Dividing Decimals
Challenge

Divya is cooking dinner. She goes to the market to buy ingredients.
The price per pound of different ingredients is shown in the table below.

Ingredient	Price (per lb)
Beef	$10.65
Onions	$2.49
Potatoes	$3.29
Tomatoes	$8.45
Asparagus	$4.99

Divya's recipe calls for 3.25 pounds of beef, 0.65 pounds of onions, 0.2
pounds of potatoes, 0.15 pounds of tomatoes, and 0.33 pounds of asparagus.

1. How much will Divya pay for all the ingredients in the recipe? Show
   your work.

   _____

   _____

   _____

   _____

2. Divya decides to make a vegetarian version of the recipe. To do this
   she replaces beef with 2.5 pounds of chickpeas and 1.75 pounds of
   lentils. At the market, chickpeas cost $2.49 per pound and lentils cost
   $3.59 per pound. How much money does Divya save by making the
   vegetarian version of her meal? Show your work.

   _____

   _____

   _____

   _____

3. Divya also wants to make fruit smoothies for dessert. She purchases
   a container of rice milk for $3.49, two pounds of strawberries at $4.99
   per pound, and six bananas at $0.75 each. How much did Divya spend
   on dessert? Show your work.

   _____

   _____

LESSON
5-1

Adding Integers with the Same Sign

Practice and Problem Solving: A/B

Find each sum. White counters are positive. Black counters are negative.

1. $-5 + (-3)$

   ⬤ ⬤ ⬤ ⬤ ⬤
   ⬤ ⬤ ⬤

   a. How many counters are there? _____

   b. Do the counters represent positive

      or negative integers? _____

   c. $-5 + (-3) =$ _____

2. $-4 + (-7)$

   ⬤ ⬤ ⬤ ⬤
   ⬤ ⬤ ⬤ ⬤ ⬤ ⬤ ⬤

   a. How many counters are there? _____

   b. Do the counters represent positive

      or negative integers? _____

   c. $-4 + (-7) =$ _____

Model each addition problem on the number line to find each sum.

3. $-4 + (-2) =$ _____

   ← + + + + + + + + + →
   $-8\ -7\ -6\ -5\ -4\ -3\ -2\ -1\ \ 0$

4. $-5 + (-5) =$ _____

   ← + + + + + + + + →
   $-20\ \ -16\ \ -12\ \ \ -8\ \ \ -4$

5. $-3 + (-6) =$ _____

   ← + + + + + + + + + →
   $-11\ -10\ -9\ -8\ -7\ -6\ -5\ -4\ -3$

6. $-7 + (-5) =$ _____

   ← + + + + + + + + + →
   $-13\ -12\ -11\ -10\ -9\ \ -8\ \ -7\ \ -6\ \ -5$

Find each sum.

7. $-7 + (-1) =$ _____

8. $-5 + (-4) =$ _____

9. $-36 + (-17) =$ _____

10. $-51 + (-42) =$ _____

11. $98 + 126 =$ _____

12. $-20 + (-75) =$ _____

13. $-350 + (-250) =$ _____

14. $-110 + (-1200) =$ _____

Solve.

15. A construction crew is digging a hole. On the first day, they dug a hole
    3 feet deep. On the second day, they dug 2 more feet. On the third
    day, they dug 4 more feet. Write a sum of negative numbers to
    represent this situation. Find the total number of feet the construction
    crew dug. Write your answer as a negative integer.

_____

Name _____ Date _____ Class_____

LESSON
5-1

Adding Integers with the Same Sign
Practice and Problem Solving: C

Solve.

1. A grocery sells green apples and red apples. On Monday, the store put
500 of each kind of apple on display. That day, the store sold 42 red
apples and 57 green apples. On Tuesday, the store sold 87 red apples
and 75 green apples. On Wednesday, the store sold 29 red apples and
38 green apples.

   a. Write an addition expression using negative integers to show the
   number of red apples the store sold.

   _____

   b. Write an addition expression using negative integers to show the
   number of green apples the store sold.

   _____

   c. Did the store have more red apples or green apples left over?
   Explain.

   _____

   _____

2. A hotel has 18 floors. The hotel owner believes the number 13 is
unlucky. The first 12 floors are numbered from 1 to 12. Floor 13 is
numbered 14, and the remaining floors are numbered from 15 to 19.
The hotel manager starts on the top floor of the apartment building. He
rides the elevator two floors down. The doors open and a hotel guest
gets in. They ride the elevator three floors down. The hotel guest gets
off the elevator. The hotel manager rides the elevator the remaining
floors down to the first floor.

   a. Write an addition expression using negative integers to show the
   number of floors the hotel manager rode down in the elevator.

   _____

   b. On what floor did the hotel guest get off the elevator? Explain.

   _____

   _____

Adding Integers with the Same Sign

Practice and Problem Solving: D

Find each sum. White counters are positive. Black counters are negative. The first one is done for you.

1. 5 + 2 =

   ⚪⚪⚪⚪⚪
   ⚪⚪

   a. How many counters are there? __7__

   b. Do the counters represent positive

      or negative numbers? __positive__

   c. 5 + 2 = ___+7___

2. –4 + (–6) =

   ⚫⚫⚫⚫
   ⚫⚫⚫⚫⚫⚫

   a. How many counters are there? _____

   b. Do the counters represent positive

      or negative numbers? _____

   c. –4 + (–6) = _____

Model each addition problem on the number line to find each sum. The first one is done for you.

3. –3 + (–2) = __–5__

   ←————•——————→
   –7 –6 –5 –4 –3 –2 –1

4. –5 + (–1) = _____

   ←——————————————→
   –7 –6 –5 –4 –3 –2 –1

5. –4 + (–3) = _____

   ←——————————————→
   –7 –6 –5 –4 –3 –2 –1

6. –1 + (–6) = _____

   ←——————————————→
   –7 –6 –5 –4 –3 –2 –1

Find each sum. The first one is done for you.

7. –3 + (–1) = __–4__

8. –6 + (–2) = _____

9. –12 + (–7) = _____

10. –20 + (–15) = _____

Solve.

11. The table shows how much money Hannah withdrew in 3 days.

Day	Day 1	Day 2	Day 3
Dollars	–5	–1	–2

Find the total amount Hannah withdrew. _____

LESSON 5-1

Adding Integers with the Same Sign
Reteach

How do you add integers with the same sign?

Add $4 + 5$.

Step 1 Check the signs. Are the integers both positive or negative?

4 and 5 are both positive.

Step 2 Add the integers.
$4 + 5 = 9$

Step 3 Write the sum as a positive number.
$4 + 5 = 9$

Add $-3 + (-4)$.

Step 1 Check the signs. Are the integers both positive or negative?

−3 and −4 are both negative.

Step 2 Ignore the negative signs for now. Add the integers.
$3 + 4 = 7$

Step 3 Write the sum as a negative number.
$-3 + (-4) = -7$

Find each sum.

1. $3 + 6$
   a. Are the integers both positive or negative? _____
   b. Add the integers. _____
   c. Write the sum. $3 + 6 = $_____

2. $-7 + (-1)$
   a. Are the integers both positive or negative? _____
   b. Add the integers. _____
   c. Write the sum. $-7 + (-1) = $_____

3. $-5 + (-2)$
   a. Are the integers both positive or negative? _____
   b. Add the integers. _____
   c. Write the sum. $-5 + (-2) = $_____

4. $6 + 4$
   a. Are the integers both positive or negative? _____
   b. Add the integers. _____
   c. Write the sum. $6 + 4 = $_____

Find each sum.

5. $-10 + (-3) = $_____

6. $-4 + (-12) = $_____

7. $22 + 15 = $_____

8. $-10 + (-31) = $_____

9. $-18 + (-6) = $_____

10. $35 + 17 = $_____

Adding Integers with the Same Sign
Reading Strategies: Use a Model

Sarah withdraws the following amounts from her bank account in 4 days.

Day	1	2	3	4
Withdrawal	−3	−5	−4	−1

Write a sum of negative integers to represent this situation.
Find the sum and explain how it is related to the problem.

You can use counters to model this problem.

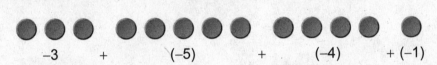

$$-3 \qquad + \qquad (-5) \qquad + \qquad (-4) \qquad + (-1)$$

KEY
● = 1
● = −1

To represent this situation, write: $-3 + (-5) + (-4) + (-1)$

The total number of counters is 13.

Since the counters are negative, the sum is −13.

Over the four days, Sarah withdrew a total of $13 from her bank account.

Answer each question.

1. What does each counter represent?

   _____

2. How do the counters help you represent the information in the table?

   _____

   _____

3. How do the counters help you find the sum?

   _____

   _____

4. Write an equation to show the total amount Sarah withdrew from her
   bank account.

   _____

Name _____ Date _____ Class_____

LESSON 5-1

Adding Integers with the Same Sign
Success for English Learners

Problem 1

7 + 5

Use counters.

7 + 5 = 12

KEY

⬤ = 1

⬤ = −1

Problem 2

−5 + (−4)

Use a number line.

Start at − 5.

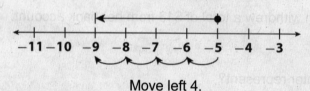

−11 −10 −9 −8 −7 −6 −5 −4 −3

Move left 4.

1. What kind of counters are used in Problem 1, positive or negative?

_____

2. Why do you move left in Problem 2?

_____

3. Write a word problem about adding integers with the same sign.

_____

_____

_____

LESSON 5-2

Adding Integers with Different Signs

Practice and Problem Solving: A/B

Show the addition on the number line. Find the sum.

1. 2 + (–3) _____

$$-5\ -4\ -3\ -2\ -1\ \ 0\ \ 1\ \ 2\ \ 3\ \ 4\ \ 5$$

2. –3 + 4 _____

$$-5\ -4\ -3\ -2\ -1\ \ 0\ \ 1\ \ 2\ \ 3\ \ 4\ \ 5$$

Find each sum.

3. – 4 + 9

4. 7 + (–8)

5. –2 + 1

6. 6 + (–9)

_____

7. 5 + (–7)

8. 9 + (–5)

9. (–1) + 9

10. 9 + (–7)

_____

11. 50 + (–7)

12. 27 + (–6)

13. 1 + (–30)

14. 15 + (–25)

_____

Solve.

15. The temperature outside dropped 13°F in 7 hours. The final temperature was –2°F. What was the starting temperature?

_____

16. A football team gains 8 yards in one play, then loses 5 yards in the next. What is the team's total yardage for the two plays?

_____

17. Matt is playing a game. He gains 7 points, loses 10 points, gains 2 points, and then loses 8 points. What is his final score?

_____

18. A stock gained 2 points on Monday, lost 5 points on Tuesday, lost 1 point on Wednesday, gained 4 points on Thursday, and lost 6 points on Friday.

   a. Was the net change for the week positive or negative? _____

   b. How much was the gain or loss? _____

LESSON 5-2 Adding Integers with Different Signs
Practice and Problem Solving: C

Tell whether each sum will be positive or negative. Then find each sum.

1. $-3 + (-7)$

2. $14 + (-9)$

3. $-12 + 5$

4. $-3 + 8$

_____   _____   _____   _____

5. $11 + (-5)$

6. $7 + 8$

7. $-8 + 7$

8. $-2 + 3$

_____   _____   _____   _____

9. If two integers have the same sign, what is the sign of their sum?

_____

10. When adding two integers with different signs, how do you find the sign?

_____

Evaluate $a + b$ for the given values.

11. $a = 9, b = -24$

12. $a = -17, b = -7$

13. $a = 32, b = -19$

_____   _____   _____

14. $a = -15, b = -15$

15. $a = -20, b = 20$

16. $a = -30, b = 12$

_____   _____   _____

Solve.

17. The high temperature for the day dropped 7°F between Monday and Tuesday, rose 9°F on Wednesday, dropped 2°F on Thursday, and dropped 5°F on Friday. What was the total change in the daily high temperature from Monday to Friday?

_____

18. Karen deposited $25 in the bank on Monday, $50 on Wednesday and $15 on Friday. On Saturday, she took out $40. Karen's original balance was $100. What is her balance now?

_____

19. Lance and Rita were tied in a game. Then Lance got these scores: 19, −7, 3, −11, 5. Rita got these scores: 25, −9, 5, −9, 8. Who had the higher score? How much higher was that higher score?

_____

Name _____ Date _____ Class _____

Adding Integers with Different Signs
Practice and Problem Solving: D

Show the addition on the number line. Then write the sum. The first one is done for you.

1. $2 + (-3)$

2. $-3 + (-4)$

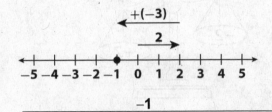

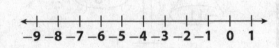

_____ -1 _____   _____

Find each sum. The first one is done for you.

3. $4 + (-9)$ 4. $7 + (-8)$ 5. $-2 + 1$

_____ -5 _____   _____   _____

6. $5 + 7$ 7. $9 + (-5)$ 8. $-1 + 9$

_____   _____   _____

9. $2 + (-7)$ 10. $-6 + (-4)$ 11. $-15 + 9$

_____   _____   _____

Solve. The first one is done for you.

12. The temperature dropped 12°F in 8 hours. If the final temperature was −7°F, what was the starting temperature?

    _____ **5°F** _____

13. At 3 P.M., the temperature was 9°F. By 11 P.M., it had dropped 31°F. What was the temperature at 11 P.M.?

    _____

14. A submarine submerged at a depth of −40 feet dives 57 feet more. What is the new depth of the submarine?

    _____

15. An airplane cruising at 20,000 feet drops 2,500 feet in altitude. What is the airplane's new altitude?

    _____

LESSON 5-2

Adding Integers with Different Signs
Reteach

This balance scale "weighs" positive and negative numbers. Negative numbers go on the left of the balance, and positive numbers go on the right.

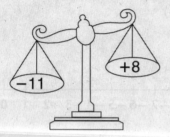   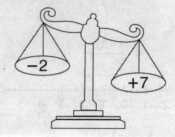

Find −11 + 8.
The scale will tip to the left side because the sum of −11 and +8 is negative.
−11 + 8 = −3

Find −2 + 7.
The scale will tip to the right side because the sum of −2 and +7 is positive.
−2 + 7 = 5

Find 3 + (−9).

1. Should you add or subtract 3 and 9? Why?

   _____

2. Is the sum positive or negative? _____

   3 + (−9) = −6

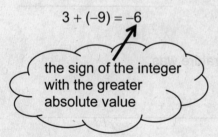

   the sign of the integer with the greater absolute value

Find the sum.

3. 7 + (−3) = _____   4. −2 + (−3) = _____   5. −5 + 4 = _____

6. −3 + (−1) = _____   7. −7 + 9 = _____   8. 4 + (−9) = _____

9. 16 + (−7) = _____   10. −21 + 11 = _____   11. −12 + (−4) = _____

12. When adding 3 and −9, how do you know that the sum is negative?

    _____

Adding Integers with Different Signs
Reading Strategies: Use Graphic Aids

Randy's football team had the ball on its own zero yard line. On their first play they gained 6 yards. On the second play they lost 4 yards. On what yard line is the ball now?

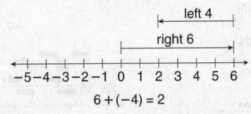

$$6 + (-4) = 2$$

Use the number line to help you answer the questions.

1. On which number do you begin? _____

2. In which direction do you move first? How many places do you move?

   _____

3. In which direction do you move next? How many places do you move?

   _____

4. At which number do you end up? _____

The temperature was zero degrees. Two hours later, the temperature went down 5 degrees. Then, the temperature went down another 3 degrees. What was the final temperature?

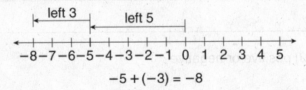

$$-5 + (-3) = -8$$

Use the number line to help you answer the questions.

5. On which number do you begin? _____

6. In which direction do you move first? How many spaces?

   _____

7. In which direction do you move next? How many spaces?

   _____

8. At which number do you end up? _____

LESSON 5-2

Adding Integers with Different Signs

Success for English Learners

Problem 1

6 + (−5)

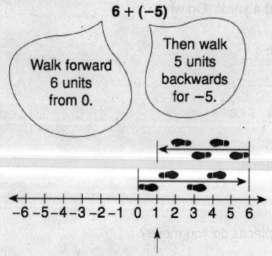

Walk forward 6 units from 0.

Then walk 5 units backwards for −5.

You stop at 1. This is the sum.

Problem 2

−7 + (4)

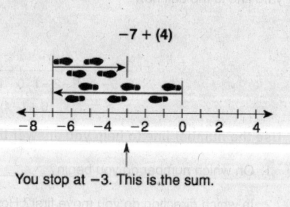

You stop at −3. This is the sum.

1. The sum of *x* + *y* is to the left of *x* on a number line. Is *y* a positive number or a negative number?

_____

2. Based on Problems 1 and 2, does the addition of integers always mean the sum is positive? Explain.

_____

_____

3. Is the sum of 3 + (−9) positive or negative?

_____

4. Is the sum of 13 + (−11) positive or negative?

_____

Name _____ Date _____ Class_____

LESSON 5-3

Subtracting Integers

Practice and Problem Solving: A/B

Show the subtraction on the number line. Find the difference.

1. –2 – 3

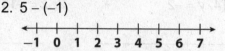

$$\begin{array}{c}\longleftarrow\!\!\mid\!\!\mid\!\!\mid\!\!\mid\!\!\mid\!\!\mid\!\!\mid\!\!\mid\!\!\mid\!\!\mid\longrightarrow\\ -6\ -5\ -4\ -3\ -2\ -1\ \ 0\ \ 1\ \ 2\end{array}$$

2. 5 – (–1)

$$\begin{array}{c}\longleftarrow\!\!\mid\!\!\mid\!\!\mid\!\!\mid\!\!\mid\!\!\mid\!\!\mid\!\!\mid\!\!\mid\longrightarrow\\ -1\ \ 0\ \ 1\ \ 2\ \ 3\ \ 4\ \ 5\ \ 6\ \ 7\end{array}$$

_____

Find the difference.

3. –6 – 4   4. –7 – (–12)   5. 12 – 16   6. 5 – (–19)

_____   _____   _____   _____

7. –18 – (–18)   8. 23 – (–23)   9. –10 – (–9)   10. 29 – (–13)

_____   _____   _____   _____

11. 9 – 15   12. –12 –14   13. 22 – (–8)   14. –16 – (–11)

_____   _____   _____   _____

Solve.

15. Monday's high temperature was 6°C. The low temperature was –3°C.
    What was the difference between the high and low temperatures?

_____

16. The temperature in Minneapolis changed from –7°F at 6 A.M. to 7°F at
    noon. How much did the temperature increase?

_____

17. Friday's high temperature was –1°C. The low temperature was –5°F.
    What was the difference between the high and low temperatures?

_____

18. The temperature changed from 5°C at 6 P.M. to –2°C at midnight. How
    much did the temperature decrease?

_____

19. The daytime high temperature on the moon can reach 130°C. The
    nighttime low temperature can get as low as –110°C. What is the
    difference between the high and low temperature?

_____

Original content Copyright © by Houghton Mifflin Harcourt. Additions and changes to the original content are the responsibility of the instructor.

95

Subtracting Integers
Practice and Problem Solving: C

For each set of values find *x – y*. Answer the questions that follow.

1. $x = 14$, $y = -2$

2. $x = -11$, $y = 11$

3. $x = -8$, $y = -15$

_____   _____   _____

4. $x = -9$, $y = -9$

5. $x = 9$, $y = -20$

6. $x = 0$, $y = -9$

_____   _____   _____

7. $x = 9$, $y = 11$

8. $x = -1$, $y = -1$

9. $x = -5$, $y = 5$

_____   _____   _____

10. If *x* and *y* are both positive, when is *x – y* negative? _____

11. If *x* and *y* are both negative, when is *x – y* positive? _____

Solve.

12. The temperature changed from 7°F at 6 P.M. to –5°F at midnight. What was the difference between the high and low temperatures? What was the average change in temperature per hour?

_____

13. The lowest point in the Pacific Ocean is about –11,000 meters. The lowest point in the Atlantic Ocean is about –8,600 meters. Which ocean has the lower point? How much lower?

_____

14. At 11,560 feet above sea level, Climax, Colorado is the highest town in the United States. The lowest town is Calipatria, California at 185 feet below sea level. Express both of these distances as integers and tell which is closer to sea level. How much closer to sea level is the town that is closer?

_____

Use the table for 15–16.

Temperatures at a Ski Resort

Day	High	Low
Saturday	8°F	–3°F
Sunday	6°F	–2°F

15. On which day was the difference in temperature greater? _____

16. How much greater was the difference one day than the other? _____

**LESSON
5-3**
Subtracting Integers
Practice and Problem Solving: D

**Show the subtraction on the number line. Then write the difference.
The first one is done for you.**

1. 3 – 8   2. –5 – (–1)

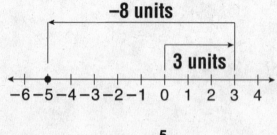

−5
_____   _____

Find each difference. The first one is done for you.

3. –3 – 4   4. –7 – (–2)   5. 12 – 6

          –7
_____   _____   _____

6. –8 – 8   7. –5 – (–5)   8. –1 – (–2)

_____   _____   _____

9. 8 – 1   10. 7 – (–9)   11. –3 – 8

_____   _____   _____

Solve. The first one is done for you.

12. The daytime temperature on the planet Mercury can reach 430°C.
    The nighttime temperature can drop to –180°C. What is the difference
    between these temperatures?

          610°C
_____

13. An ice cream company made a profit of $24,000 in 2011. The same
    company had a loss of $11,000 in 2012. What is the difference
    between the company's financial results for 2011 and 2012?

_____

14. The high temperature on Saturday day was 6°F. The low temperature
    was –3°F. What was the difference between the high and low
    temperatures for the day?

_____

LESSON 5-3 Subtracting Integers
Reteach

The total value of the three cards shown is –6.

$$3 + (-4) + (-5) = -6$$

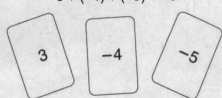

What if you take away the 3 card?

Cards –4 and –5 are left. The new value is –9.

$$-6 + -(3) = -9$$

What if you take away the –4 card?

Cards 3 and –5 are left. The new value is –2.

$$-6 - (-4) = -2$$

Answer each question.

1. Suppose you have the cards shown.
   The total value of the cards is 12.

   a. What if you take away the 7 card? $12 - 7 = $ _____

   b. What if you take away the 13 card? $12 - 13 = $ _____

   c. What if you take away the –8 card? $12 - (-8) = $ _____

2. Subtract. $-4 - (-2)$.

   a. $-4 < -2$. Will the answer be positive or negative? _____

   b. $|4| - |2| = $ _____

   c. $-4 - (-2) = $ _____

Find the difference.

3. $31 - (-9) = $ _____   4. $15 - 18 = $ _____   5. $-9 - 17 = $ _____

6. $-8 - (-8) = $ _____   7. $29 - (-2) = $ _____   8. $13 - 18 = $ _____

LESSON 5-3 Subtracting Integers
Reading Strategies: Use Graphic Aids

Brett borrowed $7 from his father to buy a cap. He paid back $3.
How much money does Brett have now?

A number line can help you picture this situation.

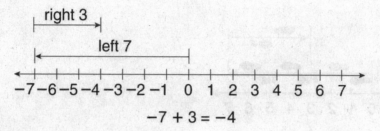

$$-7 + 3 = -4$$

1. Beginning at 0, in which direction will you move first? _____

2. How many places? _____

3. In which direction do you move next? _____

4. How many places? _____

5. On what number do you end? _____

Brett does not have any more money. He owes his dad $4. He has negative $4.

Sally and her friends made up a game with points. You can either win or lose up to ten points on each round of the game. After the first round, Sally's team had 2 points. In the second round, they lost 6 points. By how many points was Sally's team down after the second round?

The number line will help you picture the problem.

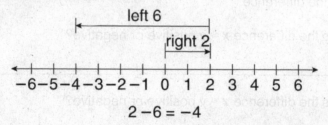

$$2 - 6 = -4$$

6. Beginning at 0, in which direction will you move first? How many places?

_____

7. Which direction will you move next? How many places?

_____

8. On what number do you end? _____

LESSON 5-3

Subtracting Integers
Success for English Learners

Problem 1

What is the difference?

$$7 - 4$$

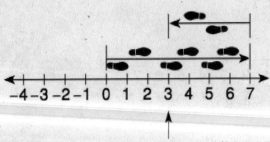

You stop at 3. This is the difference.

Problem 2

What is the difference?

$$-8 - (-2)$$

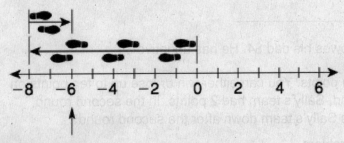

You stop at −6. This is the difference.

1. If $x > 0$ and $x > y$, is the difference $x - y$ positive or negative?

_____

2. If $x > 0$ and $y > x$, is the difference $x - y$ positive or negative?

_____

Name _____ Date _____ Class_____

Applying Addition and Subtraction of Integers

Practice and Problem Solving: A/B

Write an expression to represent the situation. Then solve by finding the value of the expression.

1. Owen is fishing from a dock. He starts with the bait 2 feet below the surface of the water. He reels out the bait 19 feet, then reels it back in 7 feet. What is the final position of the bait relative to the surface of the water?

   _____

2. Rita earned 45 points on a test. She lost 8 points, earned 53 points, then lost 6 more points. What is Rita's final score on the test?

   _____

Find the value of each expression.

3. $-7 + 12 + 15$

   _____

5. $40 - 33 + 11$

   _____

7. $-21 - 17 + 25 + 65$

   _____

4. $-5 - 9 - 13$

   _____

6. $57 + 63 - 10$

   _____

8. $12 + 19 + 5 - 2$

   _____

Compare the expressions. Write <, > or =.

9. $-15 + 3 - 7$ ◯ $-9 - 1 + 16$

10. $31 - 4 + 6$ ◯ $-17 + 22 - 5$

Solve.

11. Anna and Maya are competing in a dance tournament where dance moves are worth a certain number of points. If a dance move is done correctly, the dancer earns points. If a dance move is done incorrectly, the dancer loses points. Anna currently has 225 points.

   a. Before her dance routine ends, Anna earns 75 points and loses 30 points. Write and solve an expression to find Anna's final score.

      _____

   b. Maya's final score is 298. Which dancer has the greater final score?

      _____

LESSON
5-4

Applying Addition and Subtraction of Integers

Practice and Problem Solving: C

Write an expression to represent the situation. Then solve by finding the value of the expression.

1. Jana is doing an experiment. She is on a dock that is 10 feet above the surface of the water. Jana drops the weighted end of a fishing line 35 feet below the surface of the water. She reels out the line 29 feet, and then reels it back in 7 feet. What is the final distance between Jana and the end of the fishing line?

   _____

2. Kirsten and Gigi are riding in hot air balloons. They start 500 feet above the ground. Kirsten's balloon rises 225 feet, falls 105 feet, and then rises 445 feet. Every time Kirsten's balloon travels up or down, Gigi's balloon travels 15 feet farther in the same direction. Then both balloons stop moving so a photographer on the ground can take a picture.

   a. Find Kirsten's final position relative to the ground.

   _____

   b. Is Kirsten or Gigi closer to the ground when the photographer takes the picture?

   _____

3. In a ring-toss game, players get points for the number of rings they can toss and land on a colored stake. They earn 20 points for landing on a red stake and 30 points for landing on a blue stake. They lose 10 points each time they miss. The table shows the number of rings tossed by David and Jon during the game.

   a. Write and evaluate an expression that represents David's total score.

Player	Red	Blue	Miss
David	2	3	3
Jon	3	2	2

   _____

   b. Who scored more points during the game?

   _____

LESSON 5-4

Applying Addition and Subtraction of Integers
Practice and Problem Solving: D

Write an expression to represent the situation. Then solve by finding the value of the expression. The first one is done for you.

1. Jeremy is fishing from a dock. He starts with the bait 2 feet below the surface of the water. He lowers the bait 9 feet, then raises it 3 feet. What is the final position of the bait relative to the surface of the water?

   −2 − 9 + 3 = −8; 8 feet below the surface of the water

2. Rita earned 20 points on a quiz. She lost 5 points for poor penmanship, then earned 10 points of extra credit. What is Rita's final score on the quiz?

   _____

Find the value of each expression. The first one is done for you.

3. −7 + 1 + 5

   _____ **−1** _____

4. −5 − 9 − 10

   _____

5. 40 − 30 + 10

   _____

6. 2 + 8 − 19

   _____

7. −12 + 14 + 6

   _____

8. 50 + 60 − 10

   _____

Compare the expressions. Write <, >, or =.

9. −20 + 5 − 10 ◯ −10 − 11 + 30

10. −10 + 40 − 5 ◯ 25 − 15 + 3

Solve.

11. Angela is competing in a dance competition. If a dance move is done correctly, the dancer earns points. If a dance move is done incorrectly, the dancer loses points. Angela currently has 200 points. Angela then loses 30 points and earns 70 points. Write and evaluate an expression to find Angela's final score.

   _____

LESSON 5-4

Applying Addition and Subtraction of Integers
Reteach

How do you find the value of expressions involving addition and subtraction of integers?

Find the value of $17 - 40 + 5$.

$(17 + 5) - 40$	Regroup the integers with the same sign.
$22 - 40$	Add inside the parentheses.
$22 - 40 = -18$	Subtract.

So, $17 - 40 + 5 = -18$.

Find the value of each expression.

1. $10 - 19 + 5$

   a. Regroup the integers.

   _____

   b. Add and subtract.

   _____

   c. Write the sum. $10 - 19 + 5 = $ _____

2. $-15 + 14 - 3$

   a. Regroup the integers.

   _____

   b. Add and subtract.

   _____

   c. Write the sum. $-15 + 14 - 3 = $ _____

3. $-80 + 10 - 6$

   a. Regroup the integers.

   _____

   b. Add and subtract.

   _____

   c. Write the sum. $-80 + 10 - 6 = $ _____

4. $7 - 21 + 13$

   a. Regroup the integers.

   _____

   b. Add and subtract.

   _____

   c. Write the sum. $7 - 21 + 13 = $ _____

5. $-5 + 13 - 6 + 2$

   a. Regroup the integers.

   _____

   b. Add and subtract.

   _____

   c. Write the sum. $-5 + 13 - 6 + 2 = $ ____

6. $18 - 4 + 6 - 30$

   a. Regroup the integers.

   _____

   b. Add and subtract.

   _____

   c. Write the sum. $18 - 4 + 6 - 30 = $ ____

Name _____ Date _____ Class_____

LESSON 5-4

Applying Addition and Subtraction of Integers
Reading Strategies: Analyze Information

Read the problem below.

Angelo is riding in a hot air balloon. The balloon begins at 700 feet above the ground. It drops 200 feet, rises 500 feet, and then drops 100 feet. Write and evaluate an expression to find Angelo's position relative to the ground.

To solve this problem, look at the meanings of words to help you:

- decide what integer starts the expression.
- decide when to add.
- decide when to subtract.

Answer each question.

1. What integer starts the expression? What word tells you if it is positive or negative?

_____

2. When do you add? What word tells you when to add?

_____

3. When do you subtract? What word tells you when to subtract?

_____

4. Write and find the value of the expression to solve the problem.

_____

5. Where is Angelo's hot air balloon in relation to the ground?

_____

6. Is Angelo higher or lower than where he started? Explain.

_____

_____

_____

Applying Addition and Subtraction of Integers
LESSON 5-4

Success for English Learners

Problem

Casey starts with $180 in her bank account. She withdraws $90, and then she deposits $50. Mitchell starts with $120 in his bank account. He deposits $75, and then he withdraws $45. Who has more money in the bank at the end?

Draw a diagram and evaluate.

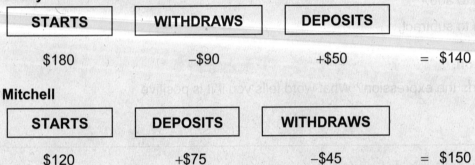

Casey

STARTS	WITHDRAWS	DEPOSITS	
$180	−$90	+$50	= $140

Mitchell

STARTS	DEPOSITS	WITHDRAWS	
$120	+$75	−$45	= $150

Now, compare.

	Casey		Mitchell
	$140	<	$150

At the end, Mitchell has more money in his account.

1. Why do you subtract when money is withdrawn?

_____

2. Why do you add when money is deposited?

_____

3. Write a word problem adding and subtracting integers. Solve.

_____

_____

_____

Adding and Subtracting Integers
Challenge

Maria wants to compare the difficulty of different bicycle paths in her town. She recorded the elevation of the trail at each mile marker. She also calculated the difference in the elevation at each mile marker with the elevation at the previous mile marker. The difficulty score she assigned to each trail is the sum of these differences.

Trail	Elevation (ft)					
	Start	Mile 1	Mile 2	Mile 3	Mile 4	Mile 5
Easy Rider	1	–2	10	–1	120	–5
Breakneck	–2	100	–2	150	–8	250
Lake Shore	–10	0	6	55	–1	60
Mountain View	40	–2	120	35	200	180

For example, to find the difficulty of the Easy Rider trail, Maria first calculated the differences in elevation at each mile marker.

	Mile 1	Mile 2	Mile 3	Mile 4	Mile 5
Difference in Elevation	–2 – 1 = –3	10 – (–2) = 12	–1 – 10 = –11	120 – (–1) =121	–5 – 120 = –125

The difficulty score of the Easy Rider is the sum of these differences.

$$-3 + 12 + (-11) + 121 + (-125) = -6$$

1. Which trail has the highest difficulty rating? Show your work in a table.

_____

_____

Solve.

2. –3 ☐ 5 ☐ –4 ☐ –10 ☐ 18

   Each of the boxes in the expression above can be filled with + or – .

   What is the greatest possible value of the expression? Explain.

_____

Name _____ Date _____ Class_____

 LESSON 6-1

Multiplying Integers

Practice and Problem Solving: A/B

Find each product.

1. 4(−20)

_____

2. −6(12)

_____

3. (−8)(−5)

_____

4. (13)(−3)

_____

5. (−10)(0)

_____

6. (−5)(16)

_____

7. (−9)(−21)

_____

8. 11(−1)

_____

9. 18(−4)

_____

10. 10(8)

_____

11. 9(−6)

_____

12. −7(−7)

_____

Write a mathematical expression to represent each situation. Then find the value of the expression to solve the problem.

13. You play a game where you score −6 points on the first turn and on each of the next 3 turns. What is your score after those 4 turns?

_____

14. The outdoor temperature declines 3 degrees each hour for 5 hours. What is the change in temperature at the end of those 5 hours?

_____

15. You have $200 in a savings account. Each week for 8 weeks, you take out $18 for spending money. How much money is in your account at the end of 8 weeks?

_____

16. The outdoor temperature was 8 degrees at midnight. The temperature declined 5 degrees during each of the next 3 hours. What was the temperature at 3 A.M.?

_____

17. The price of a stock was $325 a share. The price of the stock went down $25 each week for 6 weeks. What was the price of that stock at the end of 6 weeks?

_____

Name _____ Date _____ Class _____

LESSON 6-1

Multiplying Integers
Practice and Problem Solving: C

Find each product.

1. (–14)(7)

_____

2. (–24)(–5)

_____

3. 12(–12)

_____

4. 15(–9)(–1)

_____

5. 2(–3)(4)

_____

6. –3(–6)(–2)

_____

7. 40(–78)(0)

_____

8. –6(–60)(–4)

_____

9. –24(7)(–7)

_____

Write a mathematical expression to represent each situation. Then find the value of the expression to solve the problem.

10. A football team loses 4 yards on each of three plays. Then they complete a pass for 9 yards. What is the change in yardage after those four plays?

_____

11. You have $220 in your savings account. You take $35 from your account each week for four weeks. How much is left in your account at the end of the four weeks?

_____

12. A submarine is at –125 feet in the ocean. The submarine makes three dives of 50 feet each. At what level is the submarine after the three dives?

_____

Find each product. Use a pattern to complete the sentences.

13. –1(–1) _____

14. –1(–1)(–1) _____

15. –1(–1)(–1)(–1) _____

16. –1(–1) (–1)(–1)(–1) _____

17. –1(–1)(–1)(–1)(–1)(–1) _____

18. When multiplying integers, if there is an odd number of negative factors, then the product is _____.

If there is an even number of negative factors, then the product is

_____.

Original content Copyright © by Houghton Mifflin Harcourt. Additions and changes to the original content are the responsibility of the instructor.

109

LESSON 6-1

Multiplying Integers
Practice and Problem Solving: D

Find each product. The first one is done for you.

1. 3(–2)

    _____ **–6** _____

2. 5(0)

    _____

3. (–1)(–8)

    _____

4. (–4)(7)

    _____

5. (–3)(–4)

    _____

6. (6)(–6)

    _____

7. 10(–5)

    _____

8. –2(9)

    _____

9. 7(–10)

    _____

10. –1(–1)

    _____

11. 2(–6)

    _____

12. –2(–2)

    _____

Write a mathematical expression to represent each situation. Then find the value of the expression to solve the problem. The first one is done for you.

13. You play a game where you score –3 points on the first 5 turns. What is your score after those 5 turns?

    5(–3) = –15; –15 points

14. The outdoor temperature gets 1 degree colder each hour for 3 hours. What is the change in temperature at the end of those 3 hours?

    _____

15. A football team loses 4 yards on each of 2 plays. What is the change in yardage after those 2 plays?

    _____

16. You take $9 out of your savings account each week for 7 weeks. At the end of 7 weeks, what is the change in the amount in your savings account?

    _____

17. The price of a stock went down $5 each week for 5 weeks. What was the change in the price of that stock at the end of 5 weeks?

    _____

LESSON 6-1 Multiplying Integers

Reteach

You can use patterns to learn about multiplying integers.

$6(2) = 12$
$6(1) = 6$ $\quad$ –6
$6(0) = 0$ $\quad$ –6
$6(–1) = –6$ $\quad$ –6
$6(–2) = –12$ $\quad$ –6

Each product is 6 less than the previous product.

The product of two positive integers is positive.

The product of a positive integer and a negative integer is negative.

Here is another pattern.

$–6(2) = –12$
$–6(1) = –6$ $\quad$ +6
$–6(0) = 0$ $\quad$ +6
$–6(–1) = 6$ $\quad$ +6
$–6(–2) = 12$ $\quad$ +6

Each product is 6 more than the previous product.

The product of a negative integer and a positive integer is negative.

The product of two negative integers is positive.

Find each product.

1. $1(–2)$

   Think: $1 \times 2 = 2$. A negative and a positive integer have a negative product.

2. $–6(–3)$

   Think: $6 \times 3 = 18$. Two negative integers have a positive product.

_____

3. $(5)(–1)$

4. $(–9)(–6)$

5. $11(4)$

_____

Write a mathematical expression to represent each situation. Then find the value of the expression to solve the problem.

6. You are playing a game. You start at 0. Then you score –8 points on each of 4 turns. What is your score after those 4 turns?

_____

7. A mountaineer descends a mountain for 5 hours. On average, she climbs down 500 feet each hour. What is her change in elevation after 5 hours?

_____

Multiplying Integers

LESSON 6-1

Reading Strategies: Use Graphic Aids

The opposite of 6 is –6.

Losing points is the opposite of gaining points.

Losing 6 points is the opposite of gaining 6 points.

Answer each question.

1. What is the opposite of losing 10 points? _____

2. What is the opposite of gaining 17 points? _____

You start a game with a score of 0. You lose 4 points on each of the first three turns. How many points will you lose in all on those three turns? What will your score be after the third turn?

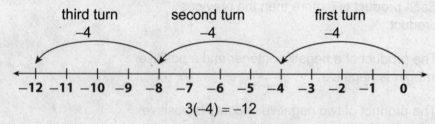

Use the number line to help you answer the questions.

3. Starting at zero, which direction do you move first? _____

4. How many places do you move? _____

5. Which direction do you move next? _____

6. How many places do you move? _____

7. Which direction do you move next? _____

8. How many places do you move? _____

9. How did your score change from the beginning of the game to the end of the third move?

_____

10. What was your score at the end of the third move? _____

11. Suppose you lose another 4 points on your next move.
    What would your score be at the end of that move?

_____

Multiplying Integers
Success for English Learners

Problem 1

Multiply: -8×5.

Use the absolute values of the numbers.

$|-8| = 8$ $|5| = 5$

Think about multiplying integers.

Since $8 \times 5 = 40$, $(-8)(5) = -40$

> $(1)(-1) = -1$ $(-1)(1) = -1$
> Multiply numbers with *different* signs, and get a *negative* product.

Problem 2

Multiply: -6×-4.

Use the absolute values of the numbers.

$|-6| = 6$ $|-4| = 4$

Think about multiplying integers.

Since, $6 \times 4 = 24$, $(-6)(-4) = 24$

> $(1)(1) = 1$ $(-1)(-1) = 1$
> Multiply numbers with *the same* sign, and get a *positive* product.

You have money in a bank account. You take out $20 each week for three weeks. After the three weeks, what is the change in the amount of money in your account?

1. What integer shows the money you take out each week? _____

2. What integer shows the number of weeks you take money out?

   _____

3. What expression can you use to solve the problem? _____

4. What is the change in your account after three weeks? _____

Answer each question.

5. You know $50 \times 8 = 400$. Explain how that helps you find $(-50)(-8)$.

   _____

   _____

6. Are the products of 4×-8 and -4×8 the same? Explain.

   _____

   _____

LESSON
6-2

Dividing Integers
Practice and Problem Solving: A/B

Find each quotient.

1. $7\overline{)-84}$

2. $-38 \div -2$

3. $-27\overline{)81}$

_____

_____

_____

4. $-28 \div 7$

5. $-121 \div -11$

6. $-35 \div 4$

_____

_____

_____

Simplify.

7. $(-6 - 4) \div 2$

8. $5(-8) \div 4$

9. $-6(-2) \div 4(-3)$

_____

_____

_____

Write a mathematical expression for each phrase.

10. thirty-two divided by the opposite of 4

_____

11. the quotient of the opposite of 30 and 6, plus the opposite of 8

_____

12. the quotient of 12 and the opposite of 3 plus the product of the
    opposite of 14 and 4

_____

Solve. Show your work.

13. A high school athletic department bought 40 soccer uniforms at a cost
    of $3,000. After soccer season, they returned some of the uniforms but
    only received $40 per uniform. What was the difference between what
    they paid for the uniforms and what they got for returns?

_____

14. A commuter has $245 in his commuter savings account. This account
    charges –$15 each week he buys a ticket. In one time period, the
    account changed by –$240.

    a. For how many weeks did the commuter buy tickets?

    _____

    b. How much must he add to his account if he wants to buy 20 weeks
       of tickets?

    _____

Dividing Integers

Practice and Problem Solving: C

Simplify.

1. $-\dfrac{-8}{-2} + (-12)$

2. $\dfrac{6}{-3} - \dfrac{15-7}{-2}$

3. $3 - 2(4-7) \div 9$

_____   _____   _____

The integers from −3 to +3 can be used in the blanks below. Which of these integers produces a positive, even integer for the expression? Show your work for those that do.

4. $-\dfrac{8}{2} + 4\,(\underline{\hspace{1cm}}) - 2$

5. $\dfrac{(\underline{\hspace{0.6cm}})}{4} + \dfrac{3}{2}$

_____   _____

6. $\underline{\hspace{1cm}} \div \dfrac{2}{-3}$

7. $\left(\dfrac{-1}{\underline{\hspace{0.6cm}}}\right) \div -\dfrac{1}{2}$

_____   _____

Solve. Show your work.

8. In a sports competition, Alyssa received −16 points. She got these points evenly in 4 events. How many points was she penalized for each event?

_____

9. The surface temperature of a deep, spring-fed lake is 70°F. The lake temperature drops 2°F for each yard below the lake surface until a depth of 6 yards is reached. From 6 yards to 15 yards deep, the temperature is constant. From 15 yards down to the spring source, the temperature *increases* 3°F per *foot* until the spring source is reached at 20 yards below the surface.

   a. What is the temperature at 10 yards below the surface?

   _____

   b. What is the temperature at 50 feet below the surface?

   _____

   _____

   c. Write an expression for finding the lake temperature at the spring source.

   _____

LESSON 6-2

Dividing Decimals
Practice and Problem Solving: D

Find the quotient. The first one is done for you.

1. $-3\overline{)-15}$

    _____5_____

2. $27 \div -3$

    _____

3. $\dfrac{28}{-7}$

    _____

Compare the quotients. Write >, <, or =.

4. $-4\overline{)-16}$ ◯ $-16\overline{)-4}$

5. $11 \div 77$ ◯ $77 \div 11$

6. $\dfrac{48}{-6}$ ◯ $\dfrac{-48}{6}$

Write a mathematical expression for the written expression. Then solve. The first one is done for you.

7. the opposite of 45 divided by 5

    $-45 \div 5 = -9$

8. fifty-five over negative eleven

    _____

9. negative 38 divided by positive 19

    _____

10. negative four divided by negative two

    _____

Solve. Show your work. The first one is done for you.

11. Four investors lost 24 percent of their combined investment in a company. On average, how much did each investor lose?

    $-24 \div 4 = -6$; On average, each investor lost 6%.

    _____

12. The temperature in the potter's kiln dropped 760 degrees in 4 hours. On average, how much did the temperature drop per hour?

    _____

    _____

13. The value of a car decreased by $5,100 over 3 years. On average, how much did its value decrease each year?

    _____

    _____

LESSON
6-2

Dividing Integers

Reteach

You can use a number line to divide a negative integer by a positive integer.

$$-8 \div 4$$

Step 1 Draw the number line.

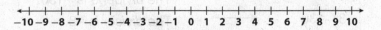

Step 2 Draw an arrow to the left from 0 to the value of the dividend, −8.

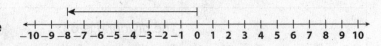

Step 3 Divide the arrow into the same number of small parts as the divisor, 4.

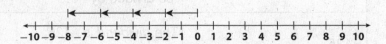

Step 4 How long is each small arrow? When a negative is divided by a positive the quotient is negative, so the sign is negative.

⟵ Each arrow is −2.

So, $-8 \div 4 = -2$.

On a number line, in which direction will an arrow that represents the dividend point? What is the sign of the divisor? Of the quotient?

1. $54 \div -9$

   Dividend: _____

   Sign of
   Divisor: _____

   Sign of
   Quotient: _____

2. $-4\overline{)-52}$

   Dividend: _____

   Sign of
   Divisor: _____

   Sign of
   Quotient: _____

3. $\dfrac{-39}{3}$

   Dividend: _____

   Sign of
   Divisor: _____

   Sign of
   Quotient: _____

Complete the table.

4.

Divisor	Dividend	Quotient
+	+	
	+	
	−	−
		+

Name _____ Date _____ Class_____

LESSON 6-2

Dividing Integers

Reading Strategies: Understand Symbols

Different symbols can be used to show division with integers.
Each symbol can also be described with words.

$-8\overline{)-136}$ ←	The *dividend* is −136. The *divisor* is −8. "−8 goes into −136."
$63 \div -3$ ←	The *dividend* is 63. The *divisor* is −3. "63 divided by −3."
$\dfrac{-125}{5}$ ←	The *dividend* is −125. The *divisor* is 5. "−125 over 5."

Name the dividend and the divisor. Then find the quotient.

1. The total distance is 3,600 kilometers. The average speed is
   225 kilometers per hour. How long did it take to drive that distance?

   dividend: _____ divisor: _____ quotient: _____

2. The temperature dropped 35 degrees in 7 hours. What was the
   average drop in temperature per hour?

   dividend: _____ divisor: _____ quotient: _____

3. A beverage company produced 1,600 liters of fruit punch, which will be
   bottled in 2-liter bottles. How many bottles can be filled?

   dividend: _____ divisor: _____ quotient: _____

Use words to describe each division problem two ways.

4. $-6\overline{)102}$ _____

   _____

5. $\dfrac{-221}{-17}$ _____

   _____

Dividing Integers
Success for English Learners

Problem 1

Words help you find the dividend, the divisor, and the quotient.
They also tell the sign of the numbers.

"45 *divided by* negative 5 *is* the opposite of 9."

dividend   divisor   quotient

$$-5\overline{)45} = -9$$

OR $\dfrac{45}{-5} = -9$

OR $45 \div -5 = -9$

Write a math expression for the words. Then solve.

1. the opposite of 210 over 70 _____

2. negative 4,200 divided by 300 _____

3. negative 50 divided by positive 10 _____

4. 54 divided by 27 _____

Problem 2

Find the sign of the quotient before dividing.

$\dfrac{-720}{-8}$ ⟵ Negative (−) divided by negative (−) gives positive (+).

Negative (−) divided by positive (+) gives negative (−).

Positive (+) divided by negative (−) gives negative (−).

Positive (+) divided by positive (+) gives positive (+).

Write the sign of the quotient, + or −. Then find the quotient.

5. $\dfrac{33}{33}$

6. $\dfrac{128}{-4}$

7. $\dfrac{-100}{25}$

8. $\dfrac{-75}{-15}$

Sign: _____   Sign: _____   Sign: _____   Sign: _____

Quotient: _____   Quotient: _____   Quotient: _____   Quotient: _____

_____   _____   _____   _____

Name _____ Date _____ Class _____

Applying Integer Operations

Practice and Problem Solving: A/B

Find the value of each expression.

1. $(-3)(-2) + 8$

2. $(-18) \div 3 + (5)(-2)$

3. $7(-3) - 6$

_____

_____

_____

4. $24 \div (-6)(-2) + 7$

5. $4(-8) + 3$

6. $(-9)(0) + (8)(-5)$

_____

_____

_____

Compare. Write <, =, or >.

7. $(-5)(8) + 3$ ◯ $(-6)(7) + 1$

8. $(-8)(-4) + 16 \div (-4)$ ◯ $(-9)(-3) + 15 \div (-3)$

Write an expression to represent each situation. Then find the value of the expression to solve the problem.

9. Dave owns 15 shares of ABC Mining stock. On Monday, the value of each share rose $2, but on Tuesday the value fell $5. What is the change in the value of Dave's shares?

_____

10. To travel the Erie Canal, a boat must go through locks that raise or lower the boat. Traveling east, a boat would have to be lowered 12 feet at Amsterdam, 11 feet at Tribes Hill, and 8 feet at Randall. By how much does the elevation of the boat change between Amsterdam and Randall?

_____

11. The Gazelle football team made 5 plays in a row where they gained 3 yards on each play. Then they had 2 plays in a row where they lost 12 yards on each play. What is the total change in their position from where they started?

_____

12. On Saturday, Mrs. Armour bought 7 pairs of socks for $3 each, and a sweater for her dog for $12. Then she found a $5 bill on the sidewalk. Over the course of Saturday, what was the change in the amount of money Mrs. Armour had?

_____

LESSON 6-3

Applying Integer Operations
Practice and Problem Solving: C

Complete the table to answer questions 1–4.

	You Own	Company	Monday	Tuesday	Wednesday	Net Gain or Loss
1.	5 shares	ABC	–$2	+$5	–$1	
2.	2 shares	DEF	+$8	–$7	–$10	
3.	8 shares	GHI	–$2	+$9	+$6	
4.	7 shares	JKL	+$5	–$12	+$3	

5. What expression shows your net gain or loss on GHI Company?

_____

6. How much value did you gain or lose overall? _____

Write an expression to represent each situation. Then, find the value of the expression to solve the problem.

7. A submarine cruised below the surface of the water. During a training exercise, it made 4 dives, each time descending 45 feet more. Then it rose 112 feet. What is the change in the submarine's position?

_____

8. A teacher wanted to prevent students from guessing answers on a multiple-choice test. The teacher graded 5 points for a correct answer, 0 points for no answer, and –2 points for a wrong answer. Giselle answered 17 questions correctly, left 3 blank, and had 5 wrong answers. She also got 8 out of 10 possible points for extra credit. What was her final score?

_____

9. Hugh wrote six checks from his account in the following amounts: $20, $20, $12, $20, $12, and $42. He also made a deposit of $57 and was charged a $15 service fee by the bank. What is the change in Hugh's account balance?

_____

10. a. Without finding the product, what is the sign of this product? Explain how you know.

$$(-4)(-1)(-2)(-6)(-3)(-5)(-2)(-2)$$

_____

b. Find the product. _____

LESSON 6-3

Applying Integer Operations

Practice and Problem Solving: D

Find the value of each expression. Show your work. The first one is done for you.

1. $15 + (-6)(2)$

    $= 15 + (-12)$ **Multiply**
    _____
    $= 3$ **Add.**
    _____

2. $(-5)(-3) + 18$

    _____

    _____

3. $42 \div (-6) + 23$

    _____

    _____

4. $52 + 45 \div (-9)$

    _____

    _____

Write an expression to represent each situation. Then find the value of the expression to solve the problem. The first one is done for you.

5. Mr. Carlisle paid his utility bills last weekend. He paid $50 to the phone company, $112 to the power company, and $46 to the water company. After he paid those bills, what was the change in the total amount of money that Mr. Carlisle had?

    $(-50) + (-112) + (-46) = -208$; He had $208 less.
    _____

6. Over 5 straight plays, a football team gained 8 yards, lost 4 yards, gained 7 yards, gained 3 yards, and lost 11 yards. What is the team's position now compared to their starting position?

    _____

7. At the grocery store, Mrs. Knight bought 4 pounds of apples for $2 per pound and 2 heads of lettuce for $1 each. She had a coupon for $3 off the price of the apples. After her purchases, what was the change in the amount of money that Mrs. Knight had?

    _____

8. The depth of the water in a water tank changes every time someone in the Harrison family takes a bath or does laundry. A bath lowers the water level by 4 inches. Washing a load of laundry lowers the level by 2 inches. On Monday the Harrisons took 3 baths and washed 4 loads of laundry. By how much did the water level in the water tank change?

    _____

LESSON 6-3

Applying Integer Operations
Reteach

To evaluate an expression, follow the order of operations.

1. Multiply and divide in order from left to right. $(-5)(6) + 3 + (-20) \div 4 + 12$

$-30 + 3 + (-20) \div 4 + 12$

$-30 + 3 + \textbf{(-20)} \div \textbf{4} + 12$

$-30 + 3 + (-5) + 12$

2. Add and subtract in order from left to right. $\textbf{-30} + \textbf{3} + (-5) + 12$

$\textbf{-27} + \textbf{(-5)} + 12$

$\textbf{-32} + \textbf{12} = -20$

Name the operation you would do first.

1. $-4 + (3)(-8) + 7$

_____

2. $-3 + (-8) - 6$

_____

3. $16 + 72 \div (-8) + 6(-2)$

_____

4. $17 + 8 + (-16) - 34$

_____

5. $-8 + 13 + (-24) + 6(-4)$

_____

6. $12 \div (-3) + 7(-7)$

_____

7. $(-5)6 + (-12) - 6(9)$

_____

8. $14 - (-9) - 6 - 5$

_____

Find the value of each expression.

9. $(-6) + 5(-2) + 15$

_____

10. $(-8) + (-19) - 4$

_____

11. $3 + 28 \div (-7) + 5(-6)$

_____

12. $15 + 32 + (-8) - 6$

_____

13. $(-5) + 22 + (-7) + 8(-9)$

_____

14. $21 \div (-7) + 5(-9)$

_____

Applying Integer Operations
Reading Strategies: Use Context

Someone mentions an amount when describing a mathematical situation.

Should you represent that number with a positive integer or a negative integer?

Use key words to help you decide.

Mrs. Adams **paid** Dan $10 to mow her grass. Mrs. Adams has less money. −$10	→ $10 →	Dan **earned** $10 by mowing Mrs. Adams' grass. Dan has more money. +$10

Words That Show Negative Numbers	Words That Show Positive Numbers
He **spent** $20. −20	He **found** $5. +5
They **lost** 8 yards. −8	120 feet **above** sea level. +120
15° **below** zero. −15	They **gained** 38 yards. +38

Write an expression to represent each situation. Underline the words you used to decide whether each number in your expression should be positive or negative. Find the value of the expression to solve the problem.

1. Antoine went to the store. He paid $3 each for 4 pounds of grapefruit. When he got home, his mother gave him $7 for some of the grapefruit. What is the change in the amount of money Antoine has?

   _____

2. Matt went scuba diving. He dove to a depth of 48 feet below the surface. Elena dove one-fourth as deep as Matt. What number describes the depth Elena dove?

   _____

3. The Cougars football team had 3 straight plays where they lost 5 yards on each play. On the fourth play they gained 32 yards. How many yards did they gain or lose for those 4 plays?

   _____

LESSON 6-3

Applying Integer Operations
Success for English Learners

Problem 1

What is the value?

$$(-3)(2) + 4 + (-16) \div 4 + 3$$

1. First, **multiply and divide** $(-3)(2) + 4 + (-16) \div 4 + 3$
   from left to right. $-6 + 4 + (-4) + 3$

2. Then **add and subtract** $-6 + 4 + (-4) + 3$
   from left to right. $-2 + (-4) + 3$
                                  $-6 + 3 = -3$

Problem 2

To solve the problem, write a math expression.

> Manny bought 8 gallons of gas. He paid $4 for each gallon.
> What is the change in the amount of money Manny has?

Manny *paid* $4 for each gallon, so the 4 is negative.

Manny bought 8 gallons. So, multiply by the cost of one gallon by 8.

$$8(-4) = -32$$

Manny has $32 less now.

Find the value.

1. $(-4)(-5) + 19$ 2. $(-9)(4) + 31$ 3. $(-36) \div 9 + 4 + (-2)(-3)$

_____   _____   _____

4. a. Write a problem that could be shown by this expression.

   $$3(-20) + 5$$

   _____

   _____

   _____

   b. Find the value of the expression to answer your question.

   _____

Name _____ Date _____ Class_____

MODULE 6

Multiplying and Dividing Integers
Challenge

1. Write an expression with integers that uses all four operations, includes at least 5 terms, and that, when simplified, is −17. Use the rules for the order of operations. Show your work.

_____

_____

_____

_____

2. You have two sets of integer cards −15 to 15, and four sets of operation cards (+, −, ×, and ÷). Make up a game that could be played using these cards. Write the rules for your game.

_____

_____

_____

_____

_____

3. Explain to a new student how to simplify the expression below. Show the updated expression after each step you take.

$$(-8) + (-3) + (-4)(7) \div 14 + 9 \, (-2)$$

_____

_____

_____

_____

_____

_____

Original content Copyright © by Houghton Mifflin Harcourt. Additions and changes to the original content are the responsibility of the instructor.

126

Ratios
Practice and Problem Solving: A/B

LESSON 7-1

The number of animals at the zoo is shown in the table. Write each ratio in three different ways.

1. lions to elephants

   _____

2. giraffes to otters

   _____

3. lions to seals

   _____

4. seals to elephants

   _____

5. elephants to lions

   _____

Animals in the Zoo	
Elephants	12
Giraffes	8
Lions	9
Seals	10
Otters	16

Write three equivalent ratios for the given ratio.

6. $\dfrac{4}{3}$ _____

7. $\dfrac{12}{14}$ _____

8. $\dfrac{6}{9}$ _____

Find three ratios equivalent to the ratio described in each situation.

9. The ratio of cats to dogs in a park is 3 to 4. _____

10. The ratio of rainy days to sunny days is $\dfrac{5}{7}$. _____

11. The ratio of protein to fiber in a granola bar is $\dfrac{9}{2}$. _____

12. The ratio of clown fish to angel fish at a pet store is 5:4. The ratio of angel fish to goldfish is 4:3. There are 60 clown fish at the pet store.

    a. How many angel fish are there? _____

    b. How many goldfish are there? _____

Ratios

LESSON 7-1

Practice and Problem Solving: C

For centuries, people all over the world have considered a certain rectangle to be one of the most beautiful shapes. Which of these rectangles do you find the most attractive?

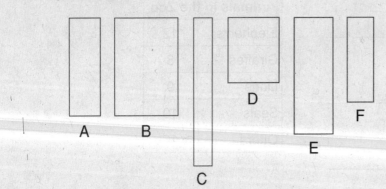

If you are like most people, you chose rectangle B. Why? It's a golden rectangle, of course! In a golden rectangle, the ratio of the length to the width is called the **golden ratio**—about 1.6 to 1.

The golden ratio pops up all over the place—in music, sculptures, the Egyptian pyramids, seashells, paintings, pinecones, and of course in rectangles.

To create your own golden rectangle, just write a ratio equivalent to the golden ratio. This will give you the length and width of another golden rectangle.

Use a ruler to draw a new golden rectangle in the space below. Then draw several non-golden rectangles around it. Now conduct a survey of your family and friends to see if they choose the golden rectangle as their favorite.

Golden Ratio

$$\frac{\ell}{w} = \frac{1.6}{1}$$

$w = 1$ in.

$\ell = 1.6$ in.

Ratios
Practice and Problem Solving: D

The number of square patches compared to circle patches on a quilt is represented by the model below.

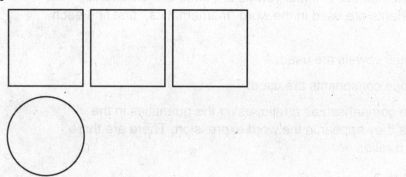

Complete. The first one is done for you.

1. Write a ratio that compares the number of circle patches to the number of square patches.

   1 circle patch to 3 square patches; 1 to 3

2. If there are 9 square patches on the quilt, how many circle patches are there?

   9 ÷ _____ = _____ circle patches

3. How many square patches are there if there are 4 circle patches on a quilt?

   4 × _____ = _____ square patches

The number of Caroline's pet fish is shown in the table. Write each ratio in three different ways. The first one is done for you.

4. tiger barbs to catfish

   5 to 1, 5:1, $\dfrac{5}{1}$

5. catfish to angel fish

   _____

6. angel fish to tiger barbs

   _____

Caroline's Pet Fish	
Tiger Barbs	5
Catfish	1
Angel fish	4

Write three equivalent ratios for the given ratio. The first one is done for you.

7. $\dfrac{2}{3}$ $\dfrac{4}{6}, \dfrac{6}{9}, \dfrac{8}{12}$

8. $\dfrac{3}{4}$ _____

9. $\dfrac{1}{6}$ _____

LESSON 7-1

Ratios

Reteach

A ratio is a comparison of two quantities by division.

To compare the number of times vowels are used to the number of time consonants are used in the word "mathematics," first find each quantity.

Number of times vowels are used: 4

Number of times consonants are used: 7

Then write the comparison as a ratio, using the quantities in the same order as they appear in the word expression. There are three ways to write a ratio.

$$\frac{4}{7} \qquad 4 \text{ to } 7 \qquad 4{:}7$$

Write each ratio.

1. days in May to days in a year

_____

2. sides of a triangle to sides of a square

_____

Equivalent ratios are ratios that name the same comparison.

The ratio of inches in a foot to inches in a yard is $\frac{12}{36}$. To find equivalent ratios, divide or multiply the numerator and denominator by the same number.

$$\frac{12}{36} = \frac{12 \div 3}{36 \div 3} = \frac{4}{12} \qquad \frac{12}{36} = \frac{12 \cdot 2}{36 \cdot 2} = \frac{24}{72}$$

So, $\frac{12}{36}$, $\frac{4}{12}$, and $\frac{24}{72}$ are equivalent ratios.

Write three equivalent ratios to compare each of the following.

3. 8 triangles to 12 circles

_____

4. 20 pencils to 25 erasers

_____

5. 5 girls to 6 boys

_____

6. 10 pants to 14 shirts

_____

Name _____ Date _____ Class_____

Ratios

Reading Strategies: Use the Context

A **ratio** is a comparison between two similar quantities. The picture below shows geometric figures. You can write ratios to compare the figures.

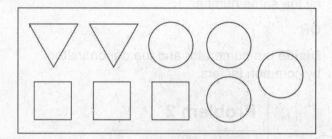

Compare the number of triangles to the total number of figures. This comparison can be written as a ratio in three different ways.

$$\frac{\text{number of triangles}}{\text{total figures}} \longrightarrow \frac{2}{9} \qquad \text{Read: "two to nine."}$$

$$2 \text{ to } 9$$

$$2:9 \qquad \text{Read: "two to nine."}$$

Compare the number of squares to the number of circles.

1. Write the ratio that compares the number of squares to the number of circles in three different ways.

_____

A **rate** compares two different kinds of quantities. Rates can be shown in different ways.

You can buy 3 cans of juice for $4. The comparison of juice to money can be written:

$$\frac{3 \text{ cans}}{\$4} \longrightarrow \frac{3}{4} \qquad 3 \text{ to } 4 \qquad 3{:}4$$

Julie can jog eight miles in two hours. Use this information to complete Exercises 2–4.

2. Write the rate using words. _____

3. Write the rate with numbers in three different ways.

_____

4. Compare ratios and rates. How are they alike?

_____

Name _____ Date _____ Class_____

 Ratios

Success for English Learners

Ways to write ratios

Word form: 3 to 2

Fraction form: $\dfrac{3}{2}$

Ratio form: 3 : 2

To read all forms, say "3 to 2."

Ways to find equivalent ratios

Multiply the numerator and the denominator by the same number.

OR

Divide the numerator and the denominator by common factors.

Problem 1

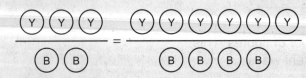

Y	3	6	9	12
B	2	4	6	8

What is happening to the numerator and denominator?

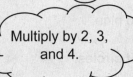
Multiply by 2, 3, and 4.

Equivalent ratios for $\dfrac{3}{2}$:

Multiply by 2 = $\dfrac{3 \bullet 2 = 6}{2 \bullet 2 = 4} = \dfrac{6}{4}$

Multiply by 3 = $\dfrac{3 \bullet 3 = 9}{2 \bullet 3 = 6} = \dfrac{9}{6}$

Multiply by 4 = $\dfrac{3 \bullet 4 = 12}{2 \bullet 4 = 8} = \dfrac{12}{8}$

Equivalent ratios for $\dfrac{3}{2}$ **are** $\dfrac{6}{4}$, $\dfrac{9}{6}$, **and** $\dfrac{12}{8}$.

Problem 2

40	20	10	5
16	8	4	2

40 : 16 = $\dfrac{40}{16}$

Divide by 2 = $\dfrac{40 \div 2 = 20}{16 \div 2 = 8}$

Divide by 2 = $\dfrac{20 \div 2 = 10}{8 \div 2 = 4}$

Divide by 2 = $\dfrac{10 \div 2 = 5}{4 \div 2 = 2}$

So, **equivalent ratios** for $\dfrac{40}{16}$ are $\dfrac{20}{8}$, $\dfrac{10}{4}$, and $\dfrac{5}{2}$.

1. Complete the ratio in the table. Did you multiply or divide to find the equivalent ratio?

Y	3	6	9	12	☐
B	2	4	6	8	10

_____

2. Write a sentence explaining how to find an equivalent ratio for $\dfrac{5}{2}$.

_____

LESSON 7-2
Rates
Practice and Problem Solving: A/B

Find the unit rate.

1. David drove 135 miles in 3 hours. _____

2. Three medium apples have about 285 calories. _____

3. A 13-ounce package of pistachios costs $5.99. _____

Use the information in the table to solve Exercises 4–6.

Morgan's favorite spaghetti sauce is available in two sizes: pint and quart. Each size and its price are shown in the table.

Size	Quantity (oz)	Price ($)
pint	16	3.98
quart	32	5.98

4. What is the unit rate to the nearest cent for each size?

   a. pint: _____   b. quart: _____

5. Which size is the better buy? _____

6. A coupon offers $1.00 off the 16-ounce size. Which size is the better buy then?

   _____

Find the unit rate. Compare.

7. a. A 24-ounce box of cornflakes costs $4.59. _____

   b. A 36-ounce box of cornflakes costs $5.79. _____

   c. Which is the better buy? _____

Solve.

8. Karyn proofreads 15 pages in 2 hours for $40.

   a. What is her proofreading rate in pages per hour?

   _____

   b. How much does she receive on average for a page?

   _____

LESSON 7-2

Rates

Practice and Problem Solving: C

Find the unit rate. Compare.

1. Jason drives 180 miles in 4 hours and Ali drives 90 miles in 1.7 hours.

   Jason: _____   Ali: _____

   _____ is the faster driver.

2. Five medium apples have about 475 calories. Three medium oranges have about 186 calories.

   apple: _____   orange: _____

   _____ have fewer calories.

Use the information in the table to solve Exercises 3–5.

Paint is available in 3 sizes. Each size and its price are shown in the table.

Size	Quantity (oz)	Price ($)
pint	16	$12.29
quart	32	$19.98
gallon	128	$34.99

3. What is the unit rate to the nearest cent for each size?

   a. pint: _____   b. quart: _____   c. gallon: _____

4. Per ounce, which size paint container costs about three times as much as another size paint container?

   _____

   _____

5. How much larger is a gallon than a quart? _____

Find the unit costs. Solve.

6. a. A 15-inch link of silver chain costs $82.99. _____

   b. A 15-inch link of gold chain costs $112.59. _____

LESSON
7-2

Rates
Practice and Problem Solving: D

Find the unit rate. The first one is done for you.

1. Carrie biked 75 miles in 3 days. _____**25 mi per day**_____

2. Twenty emails in 5 minutes. _____

3. A quart (32-ounce) bottle of milk costs $1.19. _____

Use the information in the table to solve the problems. The first one is done for you.

Rob's favorite shampoo is available in two sizes: regular and economy. Each size and its price are shown in the table.

Size	Quantity (oz)	Price ($)
regular	20	$8.00
economy	40	$10.00

4. What is the unit rate to the nearest cent for each size?

   a. regular: _____**$0.40**_____   b. economy: _____**$0.25**_____

5. Which size is the better buy? _____

6. A coupon offers $1.00 off the regular size. Which size is the better buy then?

   _____

Find the unit rate. The first one is done for you

7. a. A pound (16 ounces) of cheddar cheese costs $8.00 ___**$0.50 per oz**___

   b. A half-pound of Swiss cheese costs $8.00 _____

Solve. The first one is done for you.

8. Eric paints 8 rooms in 3 days for $600.

   a. What is his painting rate in dollars per day? ___**$200 per day**___

   b. How much does he receive on average for a room? _____

   c. About how many rooms could Eric paint in 6 days? _____

Name _____ Date _____ Class_____

Rates
Reteach

You can divide to find a unit rate or to determine a best buy.

A. Find the unit rate.
Karin bikes 35 miles in 7 hours.
$35 \div 7 = 5$ mph

B. Find the best buy.

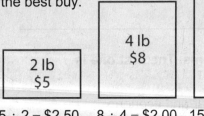
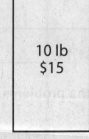

2 lb
$5

4 lb
$8

10 lb
$15

BEST BUY!

$5 \div 2 = \$2.50$ $8 \div 4 = \$2.00$ $15 \div 10 = \$1.50$
per lb   per lb   per lb

Divide to find each unit rate. Show your work.

1. Jack shells 315 peanuts in 15 minutes. _____

2. Sharmila received 81 texts in 9 minutes. _____

3. Karim read 56 pages in 2 hours. _____

Find the best buy. Show your work.

4.

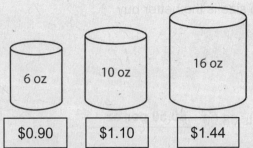

6 oz   10 oz   16 oz

$0.90 $1.10 $1.44

_____

_____

5.

Bread	Weight (oz)	Cost ($)
Whole wheat	16	2.24
Pita	20	3.60
7-grain	16	2.56

_____

_____

_____

_____

Name _____ Date _____ Class _____

LESSON 7-2

Rates

Reading Strategies: Read a Table

A table organizes data in rows and columns.

> Column headings tell you what data is below.

> The title tells you what the whole table is about.

> Columns are read up and down.

Rice Prices at Grandee Supermarket

Bag Size	Quantity (lb)	Bag Price ($)	Unit Price ($)
mini	1	1.50	1.50 per lb
small	2	3.40	1.70 per lb
medium	5	7.00	1.40 per lb
large	10	12.50	
extra large	25	26.25	

> Rows are read back and forth.

Find the unit price. Round to the nearest cent. Answer the questions.

1. What is the unit price of the large bag? _____

2. What is the unit price of the extra large bag? _____

3. Which size bag has the highest unit price? _____

4. Which size bag is the best buy? _____

5. How do you know? _____

This table shows the hours three carpenters worked, the number of chairs each made, and how much money each made.

Carpenter	Time worked (h)	Chairs made	Money earned ($)
Dan	38	7	459.80
Flora	35	6	903.00
Chandra	32	5	680.00

6. Which carpenter makes the most money per hour? _____

7. Which makes the least money per hour? _____

8. Based on labor costs alone, which carpenter makes the most

   expensive chairs? _____

LESSON 7-2

Rates
Success for English Learners

Problem 1

Mr. Jackson corrects 56 tests in 3 hours. About how many tests does he correct per hour?

> Find the unit rate.
> Divide 56 by 3.

$56 \div 3 = 18.7$

Mr. Jackson corrects about 19 tests per hour.

Problem 2

Find the best buy for different size boxes of breakfast bars.

Size	Weight (oz)	Cost ($)
small	8	5.99
medium	16	8.99
large	32	18.99

> Divide the cost by the number of ounces.

Small $5.99 \div 8 = \$0.75$
Medium $8.99 \div 16 = \$0.56$
Large $18.99 \div 32 = \$0.59$

> To the nearest cent

Compare. $0.56 < 0.59 < 0.75$.

The unit cost of the medium box of breakfast bars is lowest, so the medium size is the best buy.

1. How would you find the number of miles per hour Mrs. Rodriguez drives if you know she drives 300 miles in 5.2 hours?

   _____

2. Is the best buy always the largest size? Explain.

   _____

3. Should you always buy the largest size? Explain.

   _____

   _____

4. Write your own "best buy" problem.

   _____

   _____

LESSON 7-3   Using Ratios and Rates to Solve Problems
Practice and Problem Solving: A/B

Solve using ratios.

1. Mark is using the ratio of 3 tablespoons of sugar to 2 tablespoons of milk in a recipe. Complete the table to show equivalent ratios if Mark decides to increase the recipe.

sugar	3	6		18	
milk	2		8		20

2. Mark's ratio is 3 tablespoons sugar to 2 tablespoons milk. Sharri is using 4 tablespoons of sugar to 3 tablespoons of milk. Eve is using 9 tablespoons of sugar to 6 tablespoons of milk. Which girl's ratio is equivalent to Mark's? _____

3. A school cafeteria makes cheese sauce for macaroni using 15 cups of Swiss cheese and 17 cups of cheddar cheese. Perry tries to make the sauce for a family party using 5 cups of Swiss and 7 cups of cheddar.

   Is Perry using the correct ratio? Explain. _____

   _____

4. The chess club members bought 6 tickets to a tournament for $15. How much would they have paid if all 9 members wanted to go?

   _____

5. The Khan's car averages 22 miles per gallon of gas. Predict how far

   they can travel on 5 gallons of gas. _____

6. Cafe A offers 2 free bottled waters or juices for every 20 purchased. Cafe B offers 3 free bottled waters or juices for every 25 purchased.

   a. What is Cafe A's ratio of free drinks to purchased drinks?

      _____

   b. What is Cafe B's ratio of free drinks to purchased drinks?

      _____

   c. If you purchased 50 drinks at each café, how many free drinks would you get?

      _____

LESSON 7-3

Using Ratios and Rates to Solve Problems
Practice and Problem Solving: C

Solve using ratios.

1. A water molecule is formed from two hydrogen atoms and one oxygen atom. Fill in the table for 2, 5, 10 and 20 water molecules.

water molecule				
hydrogen atoms				
oxygen atoms				

2. Hydrogen peroxide has two hydrogen atoms and two oxygen atoms.

   How would a table for this compound differ? _____

3. Ammonia has three hydrogen (H) atoms and one nitrogen (N) atom. How many of each atom are in five molecules of ammonia?

   _____

4. Tickets to a science exposition cost $5.75 each for students and $7.00 for adults. How many students and adults went if the ticket charge was

   $42.75? _____

5. The bus to the exposition averaged 18 miles to a gallon of gas. How far away was the exposition if they used 8 gallons of gas for the round trip?

   _____

6. Flyaway airline program offers 5 points for every mile flown, plus a bonus of 20 points for every trip over 500 miles. My Sky airline program offers 7 points for every mile flown plus a bonus of 30 points for each trip. Which program gives more points for this itinerary?

Trip A 600 mi	Trip D 825 mi	Trip G 1,000 mi
Trip B 450 mi	Trip E 300 mi	Trip H 545 mi
Trip C 710 mi	Trip F 300 mi	

   _____

7. An appliance store sells lamps at $95.00 for two. A department store sells similar lamps at five for $250.00. Which store sells at a better

   rate? How much better? _____

Using Ratios and Rates to Solve Problems

Practice and Problem Solving: D

Solve using ratios. The first one is done for you.

1. Pam is making fruit punch for a party using the ratio of 2 cups of club soda to 5 cups of juice. Complete the table to show equivalent ratios for increasing numbers of guests.

club soda	2	4	8	10	
juice	5	10			50

2. Pam's ratio is 2 cups club soda to 5 cups juice. Barry is making punch with 3 cups club soda to 8 cups juice. Erin is also making punch with 4 cups of club soda to 10 cups of juice. Whose ratio is the same as Pam's?

   _____

3. A restaurant makes vegetable soup using 22 cups of mixed vegetables and 15 cups of stock. Henri tries to make this at home with 5 cups of mixed vegetables and 10 cups of stock. Is Henri using the correct ratio? Explain.

   _____

4. Barbara bought 5 amusement park tickets at a cost of $30. If she bought 7 tickets, how much would it cost?

   _____

5. Tony bikes 7 miles in one hour. Predict how far he would bike in 4 hours.

   _____

6. A sports store sells bicycle baskets at $40.00 for two. Another sports store sells bicycle baskets at $110 for five. Which store sells at the better rate?

   _____

7. Gobbler Stuffing mix has 3 cups of cubed bread and 1 cup of dried vegetables. Perfect Poultry mix has 5 cups of cubed bread to 2 cups of dried vegetables. Which mix has the greater vegetable to bread ratio?

   _____

LESSON 7-3
Using Ratios and Rates to Solve Problems
Reteach

You can write a ratio and make a list of equivalent ratios to compare ratios.

Find out who uses more detergent.

Terri's recipe for soap bubble liquid uses 1 cup of dishwashing detergent to 4 cups of water.

Torri's recipe for soap bubble liquid uses 1 cup of dishwashing detergent to 12 cups of water (plus some glycerin drops).

Terri's ratio of detergent to water: 1 to 4 or $\dfrac{1}{4}$

Torri's ratio of detergent to water: 1 to 12 or $\dfrac{1}{12}$

List of fraction equivalent to $\dfrac{1}{4}$: $\dfrac{1}{4}$, $\dfrac{2}{8}$, $\left(\dfrac{3}{12}\right)$, $\dfrac{4}{16}$, $\dfrac{5}{20}$ ...

List of fraction equivalent to $\dfrac{1}{12}$: $\left(\dfrac{1}{12}\right)$, $\dfrac{2}{24}$, $\dfrac{3}{36}$, $\dfrac{4}{48}$, $\dfrac{5}{60}$ ...

You can compare $\dfrac{3}{12}$ to $\dfrac{1}{12}$, $\dfrac{3}{12} > \dfrac{1}{12}$.

Terri uses much more detergent.

Use the list to compare the ratios. Circle ratios with the same denominator and compare.

1. $\dfrac{2}{3}$ and $\dfrac{3}{4}$

_____

_____

2. $\dfrac{4}{5}$ and $\dfrac{3}{7}$

_____

_____

3. Jack's recipe for oatmeal uses 3 cups of oats to 5 cups of water. Evan's recipe uses 4 cups of oats to 6 cups of water. Compare the ratios of oatmeal to water to see who makes the thicker oatmeal. Show your work.

_____

_____

Name _____ Date _____ Class_____

 LESSON 7-3

Using Ratios and Rates to Solve Problems
Reading Strategies: Identify Relationships

To identify a relationship between different units, you can use a table to find a rate. You know that a salad has 6 cups of mixed vegetables.

The Greens Salad Bar provides 3 cups of greens to 2 cups of mixed fresh vegetables.

The Veggie Salad Bar provides 3 cups of mixed fresh vegetables to 2 cups of greens.

The tables below show rates for each salad bar.

Greens (cups)	3	6	9	12	15
Veggies (cups)	2	4	6	8	10

Greens Salad Bar

Greens (cups)	2	4	6	8	10
Veggies (cups)	3	6	9	12	15

Veggie Salad Bar

1. At which salad bar would you get more vegetables in your salad?

   _____

2. Marge really likes lettuce and spinach. To which salad bar should she go?

   _____

3. Rich bought salad for a tailgate party. He had 18 cups of greens and 12 cups of veggies. At which salad bar did he buy the salad?

   _____

4. You know that a salad has 10 cups of mixed vegetables. Can you tell which salad bar it came from? Explain.

   _____

   _____

5. You have 20 cups of veggies in a salad for a large picnic.

   a. How many cups of greens do you have if you bought it at Greens

      Salad Bar? _____

   b. How many cups of greens do you have if you bought it at Veggie

      Salad Bar? _____

LESSON 7-3 Using Ratios and Rates to Solve Problems

Success for English Learners

Problem 1

Mrs. O'Hara frames 5 pictures in 3 hours. Use a table to predict how many pictures she will frame in her workweek of 30 hours.

pictures framed	5	10	15	20	25	. . .	50
hours	3	6	9	12	15	. . .	30

Mrs. O'Hara probably frames about 50 pictures in her workweek.

Problem 2

Mr. Suarez plants 6 large trees in 8 hours. Use a double number line to predict how many large trees he will plant in his workweek of 40 hours.

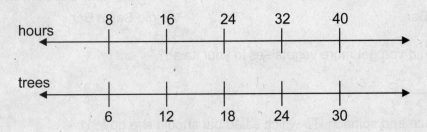

Mr. Suarez will plant 30 large trees in 40 hours.

You can use a table or a double number line. Predict how many sit ups each person can do in 12 seconds.

1. Janet does 3 sit ups in 2 seconds. _____

2. Paulo does 5 sit ups in 6 seconds. _____

3. Shah does 3 sit ups in 4 seconds. _____

4. Which method do you prefer to predict: table or a number line?
   Explain.

_____

_____

Name _____ Date _____ Class_____

MODULE 7

Representing Ratios and Rates
Challenge

Arabella, Bettina, Chandra, and Divya are runners on the track team. The distance and time for each runner are shown in the table below.

Runner	Distance	Time
Arabella	7,229 feet	561 seconds
Bettina	3,425 yards	13 minutes, 12 seconds
Chandra	8,214 feet	0.195 hours
Divya	1.62 miles	732 seconds

1. Find the rate for each runner in miles per hour.

   _____

   _____

2. Which runner ran the fastest? Which runner ran the slowest?

   _____

   _____

3. Why is it helpful to convert the rates above, as in Exercise 1, when comparing the runners?

   _____

   _____

4. Suppose each runner ran at the rate given in the table above for 3.1 miles. How much time will elapse between the first place finisher and the last place finisher? Show your work.

   _____

   _____

LESSON 8-1 Comparing Additive and Multiplicative Relationships

Practice and Problem Solving: A/B

Complete each table. Tell whether the relationship is additive or multiplicative and give the rule. Write the ordered pairs and graph them on the coordinate plane.

1. Jeff rents 6 movies per month.

Months	1	2	5	17	32
Movies	6	12			

_____

_____

_____

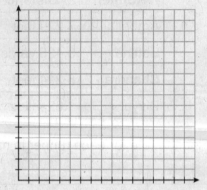

2. Maria has 3 ceramic cats. She plans to buy some more.

New cats	1	2	3		5
Total cats	4	5		7	

_____

_____

_____

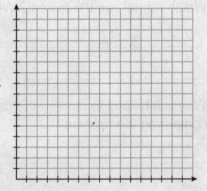

3. a. Rewrite one of the problems above to change it to the other kind of relationship. Predict how the graph will change.

   b. Complete the problem by filling out the table, writing ordered pairs, and drawing the graph.

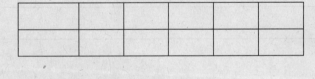

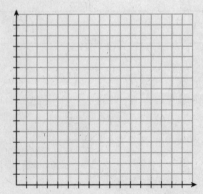

LESSON 8-1

Comparing Additive and Multiplicative Relationships

Practice and Problem Solving: C

Solve.

1. a. Complete each table. Show an additive relationship in the first table and a multiplicative relationship in the second table.

A	1	2	3	4	5
B	5				

A	1	2	3	4	5
B	5				

    b. Describe the graphs that could be made from the two tables.

    _____

    _____

    c. Name a real-life situation that could be described by the data in each table.

    _____

    _____

2. Describe a real-world additive situation and a real-world multiplicative situation that both include the ordered pair (4, 12). Make a table for each situation and plot both sets of points on the same graph.

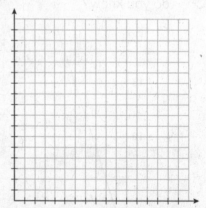

3. Without making a table or graph, determine this relationship:

    > Della made 2 pans of vegetable lasagna. She makes 2 pans of her lasagna every week.

    What relationship is described? Explain how you know.

    _____

    _____

LESSON
8-1
Comparing Additive and Multiplicative Relationships
Practice and Problem Solving: D

Find each solution. The first one is done for you.

1. Lashonda has 6 pairs of shoes. She plans to go shopping and buy more shoes.

   Complete the table to show the total number of pairs of shoes she will have. Then describe the rule for the table.

Pairs of shoes bought	1	2	3	4	5
Total pairs of shoes	7	8	9	10	11

The total pairs of shoes is equal to the number of pairs bought plus 6.

2. Ta'ama has football practice 4 days every week.

   Complete the table to show the number of practices. Then describe the rule for the table.

Weeks	1	2	3	4	5
Number of practices	4				

3. Does each graph show an additive or multiplicative relationship? How do you know?

a.

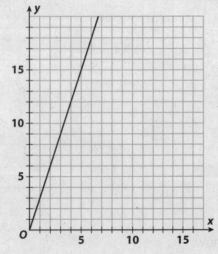

b.

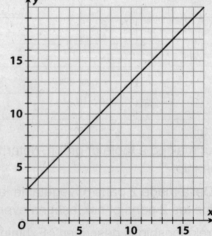

LESSON 8-1

Comparing Additive and Multiplicative Relationships
Reteach

This table and graph show an **additive** relationship.

A	1	2	3	4	5
B	4	5	6	7	8

In each column, $A + 3 = B$.

The line of the graph starts at (0, 3).

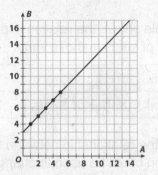

This table and graph show a **multiplicative** relationship.

A	1	2	3	4	5
B	3	6	9	12	15

In each column, $A \times 3 = B$.

The line of the graph starts at (0, 0).

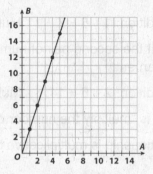

Describe the relationship shown in each table. Write the rule.

1.

A	1	2	3	4	5
B	6	7	8	9	10

_____

2.

A	1	2	3	4	5
B	2	4	6	8	10

_____

3.

A	1	2	3	4	5
B	4	8	12	16	20

_____

LESSON 8-1 Comparing Additive and Multiplicative Relationships

Reading Strategy: Identify Relationships

This table shows the relationship between a number of vans and the number of seats in those vans.

Vans	1	2	3	4	5
Total Number of Seats	7	14	21	28	35

To find the relationship between the vans and the seats, think of what operation could be used to change the number of vans into the number of seats.

Addition: $1 + 6 = 7$ Multiplication: $1 \times 7 = 7$

Then test the second pair of numbers to see if the same rule will make a true statement.

Addition: $2 + 6 \neq 14$ Multiplication: $2 \times 7 = 14$

The rule is "multiply the number of vans by 7 to find the number of seats."

The relationship is multiplicative because the rule uses multiplication.

Write the rule and complete the table. Tell if the relationship is additive or multiplicative.

1.

Tables	1	2	3	4	5
Chairs	6	12			

_____

2.

Number of dogs	1	2	3	4	5
Total number of pets	4	5			

_____

3.

Number of guests		1	2	3		8
Total number people served		5	6		9	

_____

4.

Number of books	1	2	3	6	13
Number of pages	204	408			

_____

Name _____ Date _____ Class _____

LESSON 8-1

Comparing Additive and Multiplicative Relationships
Success for English Learners

Problem 1

What kind of relationship is shown?

A	1	2	4	7	15
B	6	7	9	12	20

The rule for this table is "add 5." A + 5 = B
The relationship is **additive**.

Problem 2

What kind of relationship is shown?

A	1	2	3	6	9
B	4	8	12	24	36

The rule for this table is "multiply by 4."
A × 4 = B
The relationship is **multiplicative**.

Write the rule for each table and tell what kind of relationship it shows.

1.

A	1	2	3	4	5
B	5	6	7	8	9

_____

2.

A	1	2	3	4	5
B	7	14	21	28	35

_____

3.

A	1	2	3	4	5
B	3.5	7	10.5	14	17.5

_____

4.

A	1	2	3	4	5
B	3.8	4.8	5.8	6.8	7.8

_____

Write one additive relationship and one multiplicative relationship.
Complete each table and write the rule.

5. a.

A					
B					

_____

b.

A					
B					

_____

LESSON 8-2

Ratios, Rates, Tables, and Graphs
Practice and Problem Solving: A/B

Use the table to complete Exercises 1–7.

The table shows information about the packets of flavoring added to an amount of water to make soup.

Packets of Flavoring	2	5		10	
Ounces of Water	24		84		144

1. Find the rate of ounces of water needed for each packet of flavoring. Show your work.

$$\frac{\text{ounces of water}}{\text{packets of flavoring}} = \underline{\hspace{6cm}}$$

2. Use the unit rate to help you complete the table.
3. Graph the information in the table.
4. How much water should be added to 23 packets of flavoring?

   _____

5. Does the point (9.5, 114) make sense in this context? Explain.

   _____

   _____

   _____

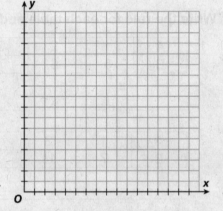

6. What are the equivalent ratios shown in the table? Complete the statement.

$$\frac{24}{2} = \frac{}{3} = \frac{}{5.5} = \frac{108}{} = \frac{}{15}$$

7. Is the relationship shown additive or multiplicative? Explain.

   _____

   _____

Name _____ Date _____ Class_____

LESSON 8-2

Ratios, Rates, Tables, and Graphs

Practice and Problem Solving: C

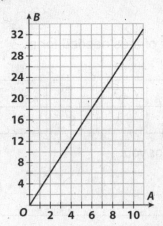

1. Choose several points from the graph and make a table of the ordered pairs.

A					
B					

2. Find the unit rate from the information in the table.

_____

3. Write a problem whose solution could be described by the table, rate, ratios, and graph above.

_____

_____

_____

4. Is the relationship in your problem additive or multiplicative?

_____

5. Does the point (6.5, 19.5) make sense in the context of your problem? Why or why not?

_____

LESSON 8-2

Ratios, Rates, Tables, and Graphs
Practice and Problem Solving: D

Use the table to complete Exercises 1–6.

The table shows information about the number of tires needed for a number of cars.

Number of Tires	8	12		20		
Number of Cars	2	3	4		6	7

1. Complete the table. The first one is done for you.

2. Write the rule for the table.

   _____

3. Find the rate of tires needed for one car. Start with a ratio from the table.

   $\dfrac{\text{tires}}{\text{cars}}$ = ——— = ——— = _____ tires for every _____ car

4. Write the information in the table as ordered pairs.

   _____

5. Plot the ordered pairs on the graph and draw the line.

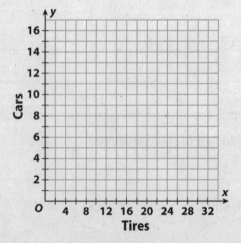

6. Write some equivalent ratios shown by the line of the graph.

   $\dfrac{8}{2}$ = ——— = ——— = ——— = $\dfrac{40}{10}$

LESSON 8-2 Ratios, Rates, Tables, and Graphs
Reteach

A **ratio** shows a relationship between two quantities.

Ratios are **equivalent** if they can be written as the same fraction in lowest terms.

A **rate** is a ratio that shows the relationship between two different units of measure in lowest terms.

You can make a table of equivalent ratios. You can graph the equivalent ratios.

A	4	6	10	12
B	2	3	5	6

$$\frac{4}{2} = \frac{2}{1} \qquad \frac{6}{3} = \frac{2}{1}$$

$$\frac{10}{5} = \frac{2}{1} \qquad \frac{12}{6} = \frac{2}{1}$$

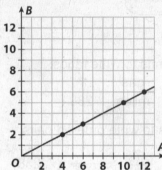

1. Use equivalent ratios to complete the table.

A	6	9			18		
B	2		4	5		7	8

2. Show the ratios are equivalent by simplifying any 4 of them.

_____

3. Find the rate of $\frac{A}{B}$ and complete the equivalent ratio: $\dfrac{69}{\rule{1.5em}{0.4pt}}$.

_____

4. Use the rate to find how many As are needed for 63 Bs, then write the ratio.

_____

LESSON 8-2

Ratios, Rates, Tables, and Graphs
Reading Strategy: Read a Table

Tables help us organize information.

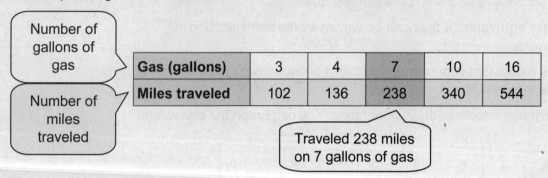

Number of gallons of gas

Number of miles traveled

Gas (gallons)	3	4	7	10	16
Miles traveled	102	136	238	340	544

Traveled 238 miles on 7 gallons of gas

Use the columns to write ratios.

$$\frac{\text{gas}}{\text{miles}} = \frac{7}{238} \qquad \frac{\text{miles}}{\text{gas}} = \frac{238}{7}$$

Use the ratios to write ordered pairs.

$$\frac{7}{238} \longrightarrow (7, 238) \qquad \frac{238}{7} \longrightarrow (238, 7)$$

1. Read the table. Write all the ordered pairs of cost to pounds. Then write the ordered pairs of pounds to cost.

Cost	$4.50	$7.50	$10.50	$13.50	$16.50
Pounds of Oranges	3	5	7	9	11

_____

_____

2. Find the unit rate. What is the cost of 1 pound of oranges?

_____

3. Read the table. Write all of the ordered pairs in the order you choose.

Cups of Flour	6	8	10	12	18	24
Teaspoons of Baking Soda	3	4	5	6	9	12

_____

_____

4. Write the unit rate of baking soda to flour.

_____

Ratios, Rates, Tables, and Graphs

LESSON 8-2

Success for English Learners

Problem 1

The table shows the cost of cereal and the amount of cereal for each amount of money. Write the ratios of ounces to cost.

Cereal (oz)	8	32	48	64	96
Cost	$1	$4	$6	$8	$12

$$\frac{\text{ounces}}{\text{cost}} = \frac{8}{\$1} = \frac{32}{\$4} = \frac{48}{\$6} = \frac{64}{\$8} = \frac{96}{\$12}$$

Problem 2

Write the ratios as ordered pairs. Graph the ordered pairs and draw the line.

(8, 1), (32, 4), (48, 6), (64, 8), (96, 12)

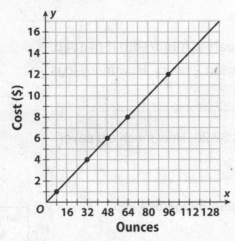

1. How would the ratios change if the problem asked for the ratios of cost to ounces?

   _____

2. How would the graph change?

   _____

3. Make your own table of ratios of gallons of gas used to the miles traveled. Write the ratios as ordered pairs.

Gas (gal)				
Miles				

   _____

LESSON 8-3 Solving Problems with Proportions

Practice and Problem Solving: A/B

Find the unknown value in each proportion. Round to the nearest tenth if needed.

1. $\dfrac{4}{5} = \dfrac{}{20}$

2. $\dfrac{3}{7} = \dfrac{}{35}$

3. $\dfrac{4}{3} = \dfrac{12}{}$

4. $\dfrac{13}{15} = \dfrac{52}{}$

Solve using equivalent ratios.

5. Wayne has a recipe on a 3-inch-by-5-inch index card that he wants to enlarge to 15 inches long. How wide will the enlargement be?

_____

6. Sharon is decreasing the size of a diagram of a leaf that is 30 centimeters long by 10 centimeters wide. If the reduced diagram is 4 centimeters wide, how long will it be?

_____

Solve using unit rates. Round to the nearest hundredth if needed.

7. A wood stove burns 4 same-sized logs in 2 hours. How many logs

does the stove burn in 8 hours? _____

8. In 2012, five U.S. postal stamps cost $2.20. How much did seven

stamps cost? _____

9. a. What is the actual distance between Saugerties and

Kingston? _____

b. Catskill is 15 miles from Saugerties. What would the

distance on the map be? _____

c. On another map, the distance between Saugerties and
Kingston is 2 inches. What would the distance from

Saugerties to Catskill be on this map? _____

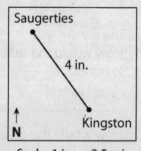

Scale: 1 in. = 2.5 mi.

10. The scale of a map is 1 in. : 250 miles. City A is 378 miles from City B. To the nearest tenth, how far is its distance on the map?

_____

LESSON 8-3

Solving Problems with Proportions

Practice and Problem Solving: C

Find the unknown value in each proportion. Round to the nearest tenth if needed.

1. $\dfrac{2}{3} = \dfrac{}{7.5}$

2. $\dfrac{7}{100} = \dfrac{3.5}{}$

3. $\dfrac{9}{5} = \dfrac{}{16}$

4. $\dfrac{2}{7} = \dfrac{}{20}$

Solve using equivalent ratios.

5. Suki has a 9 foot by 12 foot oriental rug. She is making a scale drawing of the rug that is 1 foot long. How many inches wide should

   the diagram be? _____

6. Another rug is 6 feet by 8 feet. For this one, Suki makes a diagram that

   is $1\dfrac{1}{3}$ feet long. How many inches should its width be? _____

Solve using unit rates. Round to the nearest hundredth if needed.

7. You can buy 4 pounds of peaches for $5.96. What do $4\dfrac{1}{2}$ pounds of

   peaches cost? _____

8. The table shows the number of miles that Dave, Raul, and Sinead drove on their last trips, as well as the time it took for each drive.

Driver	Distance (mi)	Time (min)
Dave	15	20 min
Raul	15	15 min
Sinead	20	30 min

   a. What is Sinead's unit rate in miles per minutes? _____

   b. Whose speed was the slowest? _____

   c. If all three drivers drove for 2.5 hours at the same speed as their last drive, how many total miles will all three drivers have driven?

   _____

9. The scale of a scientific drawing is 1 cm = 2 in. If the actual length of an object in the drawing was 4.5 inches, how long would it be in the

   drawing? _____

Name _____ Date _____ Class_____

LESSON
8-3

Solving Problems with Proportions

Practice and Problem Solving: D

Find the unknown value in each proportion. The first one has been done for you.

1. $\dfrac{2}{5} = \dfrac{8}{20}$

2. $\dfrac{2}{7} = \dfrac{}{28}$

3. $\dfrac{5}{4} = \dfrac{}{16}$

4. $\dfrac{11}{15} = \dfrac{}{45}$

Solve using equivalent ratios. The first one has been done for you.

5. Jackie has a poster that is 8 inches by 11 inches. She wants to enlarge it so that its length is 33 inches. What should the width be?

   $\dfrac{8}{11} = \dfrac{x}{33}$, **x = 24; The width should be 24 in.**

6. Tom has a large photo he wants to shrink to wallet-sized. Its width is 20 centimeters and its length is 30 centimeters. If he wants the width to be 5 centimeters what should the length be? _____

Solve using equivalent ratios. The first one has been done for you.

7. Mr. Sanchez drives 120 miles in 3 hours. At the same rate, how far will

   he drive in 5 hours? _____ **200 mi.** _____

8. Six pounds of apples cost $12.00. How much do 8 pounds cost?

   _____

9. a. What is the actual distance between River City and Pine Bluff?

      _____

   b. White Oak is 15 miles from River City. What would its distance

      be on the map? _____

   c. On another map, the distance between River City and Pine Bluff is 6 inches. What is the scale of the map?

      _____

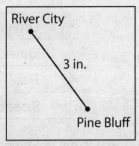

Scale: 1 in. = 3 mi.

10. The scale of a map is 1 in : 500 miles. City A is 650 miles from City C.

    How far is its distance on the map? _____

Name _____ Date _____ Class _____

LESSON 8-3

Solving Problems with Proportions
Reteach

You can solve problems with proportions in two ways.

A. Use equivalent ratios.

Hanna can wrap 3 boxes in 15 minutes.
How many boxes can she wrap in 45 minutes?

$$\frac{3}{15} = \frac{}{45}$$

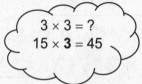

$$3 \times 3 = ?$$
$$15 \times 3 = 45$$

$$\frac{3 \cdot 3}{15 \cdot 3} = \frac{9}{45}$$

Hanna can wrap 9 boxes in 45 minutes.

B. Use unit rates.

Dan can cycle 7 miles in 28 minutes.
How long will it take him to cycle 9 miles?

$$\frac{28 \text{ min}}{7 \text{ mi}} = \frac{}{1 \text{ mi}}$$

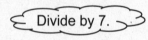

Divide by 7.

$$\frac{28}{7} = \frac{28 \div 7}{1} = \frac{4}{1}, \text{ or 4 minutes per mile}$$

To cycle 9 miles, it will take Dan 9 × 4, or 36 minutes.

Solve each proportion. Use equivalent ratios or unit rates. Round to the nearest hundredth if needed.

1. Twelve eggs cost $2.09. How much would 18 eggs cost?

   _____

2. Seven pounds of grapes cost $10.43. How much would 3 pounds

   cost? _____

3. Roberto wants to reduce a drawing that is 12 inches long by 9 inches
   wide. If his new drawing is 8 inches long, how wide will it be?

   _____

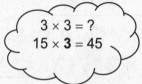

Solving Problems with Proportions

LESSON 8-3

Reading Strategies: Read a Table

This table shows the prices for different-sized bottles of fruit juices.

Column headings tell you what data is below.

Size	Capacity (oz.)	Cost ($)
Small	8	2.80
Medium	12	3.96
Large	16	4.80

Rows are read left to right.

Columns are read up and down.

1. What is the unit cost for each bottle?

   a. Small (8 oz): _____

   b. Medium (12 oz): _____

   c. Large (16 oz): _____

2. Cara drank a 6-ounce glass from the 12-ounce bottle. How much did her drink cost?

   _____

3. Sean drank an 8-ounce glass from the 16-ounce bottle. How much did his drink cost?

   _____

4. Luca had a 4-ounce glass from the 16-ounce bottle. How much did his drink cost?

   _____

This table shows the time three delivery people worked, the miles they drove, and the amount each earned.

Driver	Miles Driven	Hours Driven	Earnings ($)
Jeff	65	7	158.75
Alicia	82	8	180.80
LeShawn	56	6	118.50

5. a. How much did Alicia earn per hour? _____

   b. How much would she earn for 5 hours of work? _____

6. a. On average, how far did LeShawn drive in an hour? _____

   b. On average, how far would she drive in 2 hours? _____

7. Who had the highest earnings per hour? _____

LESSON 8-3

Solving Problems with Proportions
Success for English Learners

Problem 1

Mrs. O'Neill tiles 24 square feet in 3 hours. How many square feet can she tile in 9 hours?

Use a proportion.

$$\frac{24}{3} = \frac{}{9}$$ $3 \times 3 = 9$

$$\frac{24}{3} = \frac{72}{9}$$ $24 \times 3 =$

She can tile 72 square feet in 9 hours.

Problem 2

Which is the better buy: an 18-ounce box of cereal for \$4.50 or a 30-ounce box of cereal for \$9.00?

Use a unit rate.

$$\frac{4.50}{18} = 0.25$$ $0.25 < 0.30$

$$\frac{9.00}{30} = 0.30$$

The 18-ounce box has a lower unit rate, so it is the better buy.

1. Can you use a unit rate to solve Problem 1? Explain. _____

_____

_____

2. Can you use a proportion to solve Problem 2? Explain. _____

_____

_____

LESSON 8-4

Converting Measurements
Practice and Problem Solving: A/B

Use proportions to convert.

1. 4 feet to inches

_____

2. 6 quarts to gallons

_____

3. 5 kilometers to meters

_____

4. 2,000 grams to kilograms

_____

Use conversion factors to convert. Write the factor you used.

5. 5 quarts to cups

_____

6. 600 centimeters to meters

_____

Solve.

7. Denver is called the Mile-High City because it is at an altitude of 1 mile.

How many feet is this? _____

8. The distance from the library to the park is 0.7 kilometers.

How many meters is this? _____

9. Marcus has three dowels with the lengths shown in the table.
Complete the table to give each length in inches, feet, and yards.

Dowel	in.	ft	yd
A	36		
B		$5\frac{1}{2}$	
C			$2\frac{1}{2}$

10. Cameron wants to measure a poster frame, but he only has a sheet of

paper that is $8\frac{1}{2}$ by 11 inches.

a. He lays the long edge of the paper along the long edge of the frame several times
and finds the frame is 4 papers long. How long is this in inches?

_____ In feet? _____

b. He lays the short edge of the paper along the short edge of the frame several times
and finds the frame is 3 papers wide. How long is this in inches?

_____ In feet? _____

11. How would you convert 3 yards 2 feet to inches?

_____

_____

Name _____ Date _____ Class_____

LESSON 8-4

Converting Measurements
Practice and Problem Solving: C

Use proportions to convert.

1. 4.5 feet to inches

   _____

2. 4.5 inches to feet

   _____

3. 543 centimeters to meters

   _____

4. 5.1 kilometers to meters and centimeters

   _____

Use conversion factors to convert.

5. 6.5 quarts to cups

   _____

6. 3.9 meters to centimeters

   _____

Solve.

7. Denver is the Mile-High City. How high is this in feet? _____

   In yards?_____

8. The distance from the porch to the flagpole is 736 centimeters. How far is this in meters?

   _____

9. Tammy has 3 chains of different lengths as shown in the table. Complete the table. Find the length of the longest and shortest chains and the difference between them. Show the difference in inches, feet, and yards.

Chain	yd	ft	in.
gold	$3\frac{1}{2}$		
silver		12.5	
bronze			148

10. a. Pat has a 10-centimeter length of string she is going to use to measure a small square table. The length she measures is 5 strings. What are the dimensions of the table?

    _____

    b. What is the area of the table? _____

    c. Is that as large as a square meter? Explain.

    _____

LESSON	**Converting Measurements**
8-4	

Practice and Problem Solving: D

Use proportions to convert. The first one is done for you.

1. 48 inches to feet

   $\dfrac{12 \text{ in}}{1 \text{ ft}} = \dfrac{48}{x} = 4 \text{ ft}$

2. 2 gallons to quarts

   _____

3. 3,000 meters to kilometers

   _____

4. 1,500 grams to kilograms

   _____

Use conversion factors to convert. Write the factor you used. The first one is done for you.

5. 7 quarts to cups

   4c = 1 qt; 28 c

6. 500 centimeters to meters

   _____

Solve.

7. A bike race takes place over a 3 mile course. How many feet is it?

   _____

8. The distance from the school to the corner is 0.9 kilometers.
   How many meters is this?

   _____

9. Christina has two pieces of lace trim with lengths as shown in
   the table. Complete the table to give each length in inches,
   feet, and yards.

Trim	In.	Ft.	Yd.
A	24		
B			6

10. a. Lyza has a 9-inch board. She wants to measure the length of a
       small rug in feet. How can she do this?

    _____

    b. She finds that the 9-inch board fits 4 times along the rug length.

       How many inches is this? _____

       How many feet? _____

11. How would you convert 4 meters 20 centimeters to

    centimeters?_____

Name _____ Date _____ Class_____

LESSON 8-4

Converting Measurements
Reteach

You can use a bar model to convert measurements.

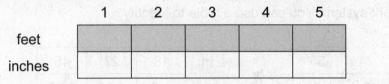

	1	2	3	4	5
feet					
inches					

$\dfrac{1}{12} = \dfrac{3}{36}$ so 3 feet = 36 inches

	1,000	2,000	3,000	4,000
grams				
kilograms				

$\dfrac{1,000}{1} = \dfrac{4,000}{4}$ so 4,000 g = 4 kg

1. Draw a bar model for converting feet to yards.

2. Draw a bar model for converting cups to fluid ounces.

3. Do you think a bar model would be a good model for converting miles to feet? Explain.

_____

_____

_____

Name _____ Date _____ Class_____

LESSON
8-4

Converting Measurements
Reading Strategies: Identify Relationships

You can use relationships between customary and metric units to convert within the same measurement system. You can use a table to identify a relationship.

in.	12	24	36
ft	1	2	3

or

in.	18	27	45
ft	1.5	2.25	3.75

1. a. A foot is _____ inches.

   b. An inch is _____ foot.

2. a. To convert feet to inches, _____.

   b. To convert inches to feet, _____.

3. If you wanted to show the relationship between meters and centimeters, what would differ in your table?

   _____

   _____

4. Choose a customary and a metric relationship and make a table to show the relationship for each.

Name _____ Date _____ Class_____

Converting Measurements
Success for English Learners

The two most common systems of measurement used around the world are the **metric system** and the **customary system.** The United States uses the customary system of measurements. Some examples of **customary measurements** are yards (yd), feet (ft), ounces (oz), and pounds (lb).

Problem 1

Nicole bought <u>2 pounds</u> of grapes. <u>How many ounces</u> is this?

How do you **convert,** or change, pounds to ounces?

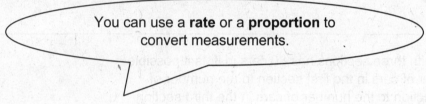

You can use a **rate** or a **proportion** to convert measurements.

1 pound (lb) = 16 ounces (oz)

$$\frac{1 \text{ lb}}{16 \text{ oz}} = \frac{1 \text{ lb} \times 2}{16 \text{ oz} \times 2} = \frac{2 \text{ lb}}{32 \text{ oz}}$$

Two pounds is equal to 32 ounces. So, Nicole bought 32 ounces of grapes.

Problem 2

Joel bought 42 inches of wire. How many yards is that?

Conversion factor: $\frac{1 \text{ yd}}{36 \text{ in.}}$

$$\frac{1 \text{ yd}}{36 \text{ in.}} = \frac{\frac{7}{6} \times 1}{42 \text{ in.}} = \frac{7}{6} \text{ or } 1\frac{1}{6} \text{ yd}$$

42 inches is $1\frac{1}{6}$ yards. Joel bought $1\frac{1}{6}$ yards of wire.

1. Convert 5.5 yards to inches. _____

2. Convert 450 inches to yards. _____

Applying Ratios and Rates
Challenge

A parking lot has three sections. The ratio of the number of cars in the first section to the number of cars in the second section to the number of cars in the third section is 1 : 2 : 3. There are 36 cars in all three sections of the parking lot.

1. How many cars are in each section of the parking lot?

_____

_____

2. What is one way in which you can move some of the cars between sections so the ratio of cars between sections of the parking lot is 1 : 1 : 1?

_____

_____

3. Another parking lot with three sections has 80 cars in it. Is it possible for ratio of the number of cars in the first section to the number of cars in the second section to the number of cars in the third section to 1 : 2 : 3? Explain why or why not.

_____

_____

_____

4. Suppose 18 cars are added to the original parking lot of 36 cars in which the ratio of the number cars in the first section to the number of cars in the second section to the number of cars in the third section is 1 : 2 : 3. If all 18 cars are placed in the third section, what will be the new ratio of the number of cars in each section?

_____

_____

_____

LESSON 9-1
Understanding Percent
Practice and Problem Solving: A/B

Write each percent as a fraction in simplest form and as a decimal to the nearest hundredth.

1. 30% _____

2. 42% _____

3. 18% _____

4. 35% _____

5. 100% _____

6. 29% _____

7. 56% _____

8. $66\frac{2}{3}$% _____

9. 25% _____

Write each decimal or fraction as a percent.

10. 0.03 _____

11. 0.92 _____

12. 0.18 _____

13. $\frac{2}{5}$ _____

14. $\frac{23}{25}$ _____

15. $\frac{7}{10}$ _____

Solve.

16. Bradley completed $\frac{3}{5}$ of his homework. What percent of his homework

    does he still need to complete? _____

17. After reading a book for English class, 100 students were asked
    whether or not they enjoyed it. Nine twenty-fifths of the class did not
    like the book. How many students liked the book?

    _____

18. At a concert, 20% of the people are wearing black dresses or suits,

    $\frac{1}{4}$ are wearing navy, 0.35 are wearing brown, and the rest are wearing

    a variety of colors (other). Write the percent, fraction, and decimal for
    each color clothing.

    black _____

    navy _____

    brown _____

    other _____

LESSON 9-1

Understanding Percent

Practice and Problem Solving: C

Write each percent as a fraction in simplest form and as a decimal to the nearest thousandth.

1. 4.5% _____

2. 119% _____

3. 200% _____

_____

_____

_____

4. 0.7% _____

5. 307% _____

6. $5\frac{1}{2}$% _____

_____

_____

_____

Write each decimal or fraction as a percent.

7. $7\frac{1}{7}$ _____

8. $\frac{3}{400}$ _____

9. 0.0054 _____

10. How could you use grids to model percents greater than 100%, such as 217%?

_____

_____

11. How could you use grids to model percents less than 1%, such as 0.7%?

_____

_____

12. In Jeffrey's class, 30% of the students are wearing blue shirts, $\frac{1}{4}$ of the students are wearing green shirts, 0.15 of the students are wearing red shirts and the rest are wearing white shirts. Write the percent, fraction, and decimal for each color shirt.

blue: _____

green: _____

red: _____

white: _____

13. Annabelle's homework is 75% complete. It took her 3 hours. How long should she estimate it will take her to complete her homework?

_____

14. Explain what percent of a dollar a quarter, 2 nickels, a dime and 3 pennies are.

LESSON
9-1

Understanding Percent
Practice and Problem Solving: D

Use the 10-by-10 square grids to model each percent. The first one is done for you.

67% means
67 out of 100.

1. 12%

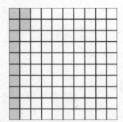

2. 67%

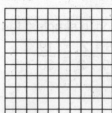

Write each percent as a fraction in simplest form and as a decimal. The first is done for you.

3. 50% **50%** $= \dfrac{50}{100} = \dfrac{1}{2}$

   50 hundredths = 0.50

4. 1% _____

5. 11% _____

_____

_____

6. 10% _____

7. 99% _____

8. 17% _____

_____

_____

_____

9. 73% _____

10. 47% _____

11. 11.5% _____

_____

_____

_____

Write each decimal or fraction as a percent. The first one is done for you.

12. 0.1 $\dfrac{1}{10} = \dfrac{10}{100}$ 10%

13. 0.6 _____

14. 0.02 _____

15. $\dfrac{1}{2}$ _____

16. $\dfrac{7}{10}$ _____

17. $\dfrac{97}{100}$ _____

Solve.

18. A math workbook has 100 pages. Each chapter of the book is 10 pages long. What percent of the book does each chapter make up?

_____

Understanding Percent

LESSON 9-1

Reteach

A. A percent is a ratio of a number to 100. Percent means "per hundred."
To write 38% as a fraction, write a fraction with a denominator of 100.

$$\frac{38}{100}$$

Then write the fraction in simplest form.

$$\frac{38}{100} = \frac{38 \div 2}{100 \div 2} = \frac{19}{50}$$

So, $38\% = \frac{19}{50}$.

B. To write 38% as a decimal, first write it as fraction.

$$38\% = \frac{38}{100}$$

$\frac{38}{100}$ means "38 divided by 100."

$$\begin{array}{r} 0.38 \\ 100\overline{)38.00} \\ -300 \\ \hline 800 \\ -800 \\ \hline 0 \end{array}$$

So, $38\% = 0.38$.

Write each percent as a fraction in simplest form.

1. 43%   2. 72%   3. 88%   4. 35%

_____   _____   _____   _____

Write each percent as a decimal.

5. 64%   6. 92%   7. 73%   8. 33%

_____   _____   _____   _____

**LESSON
9-1**

Understanding Percent

Reading Strategies: Use Graphic Aids

The word **percent** means "per hundred." It is a ratio that compares a number to 100. A grid with 100 squares is used to picture percents.

Twelve percent is pictured on the grid below.

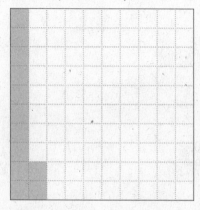

12 percent is a ratio, and means per hundred. $\rightarrow \dfrac{12}{100}$

12 percent can be written with symbols. $\rightarrow$ 12%

Use this figure to complete Exercises 1–4.

1. What is the ratio of shaded squares to total

   squares? _____

2. Write the shaded amount using the %

   symbol._____

3. What is the ratio of unshaded squares to

   total squares? _____

4. Use the % symbol to write the unshaded

   amount. _____

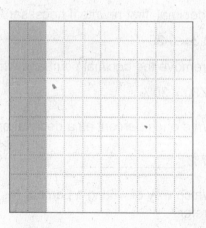

LESSON 9-1 Understanding Percent
Success for English Learners

Problem 1

A percent compares numbers to 100 with the symbol %.

You can rewrite a percent as a decimal or fraction.

$$27\% = \frac{27}{100} = 0.27$$

Problem 2

You can also rewrite a fraction or a decimal as a percent.

For a fraction, first rewrite it as a fraction with a denominator of 100.

$$\frac{3}{4} \quad \times 25 \quad \frac{75}{100}$$
$$\times 25$$

Then write it as a percent.

$$\frac{75}{100} = 75\%$$

For a decimal, first rewrite if necessary as a decimal in hundredths.

$$0.3 = 0.30$$

Then remove the decimal point and write the number as a percent.

$$0.30 = 30\%$$

1. Write each percent as a decimal and as a fraction.

   37% _____   6% _____

2. Which way of writing a percent (as a decimal or as a fraction) do you prefer?

   _____

   _____

Name _____ Date _____ Class_____

LESSON 9-2

Percents, Fractions, and Decimals
Practice and Problem Solving: A/B

Find the percent of each number.

1. 25% of 56

2. 10% of 110

3. 5% of 150

4. 90% of 180

_____ _____ _____ _____

5. 125% of 48

6. 225% of 88

7. 2% of 350

8. 285% of 200

_____ _____ _____ _____

Find the percent of each number. Check whether your answer is reasonable.

9. 55% of 900

10. 140% of 50

11. 75% of 128

12. 3% of 600

_____ _____ _____ _____

13. 16% of 85

14. 22% of 105

15. 0.7% of 110

16. 95% of 500

_____ _____ _____ _____

Solve.

The world population is estimated to be nearly 9 billion by the year 2050. Use the circle graph to solve Exercises 17–19.

17. What is the estimated population of Africa in

the year 2050? _____

18. Which continent is estimated to have more than 5.31 billion people by the year 2050?

_____

19. What is the combined estimated population for North and South America in the year 2050?

_____

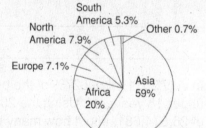

Estimated 2050 World Population

South America 5.3%
North America 7.9%
Other 0.7%
Europe 7.1%
Asia 59%
Africa 20%

20. In the year 2002, the world population was estimated at 6 billion people. Based on research from the World Bank, about 20% lived on less than $1 per day. How many people lived on less than $1 per day?

_____

21. The largest frog in the world is the goliath, found in West Africa. It can grow to be 12 inches long. The smallest frog in the world is about 2.5% as long as the goliath. About how long is the smallest frog in the

world?_____

Name _____ Date _____ Class_____ .

Percents, Fractions, and Decimals
Practice and Problem Solving: C

Tell whether the percent of the number will be greater than, less than, or equal to the number. Explain your reasoning.

1. 25% of 56

_____

_____

2. 220% of 35

_____

_____

Solve.

3. The price of a shirt was $38. It was reduced by 20% and then again by 10%.

   a. What is the final price of the shirt? _____

   b. What would the price of the shirt be if it were reduced by 30% from

      the original? _____

   c. Explain why the two prices in a. and b. differ.

_____

_____

4. In July 2011, about 27% of the population of Texas was under 18 years old. Using the 2011 population figure of 25,674,681, about how many people who lived in Texas were under 18? _____

5. The circle graph shows how the Chinn family spends its monthly budget of $5,000.

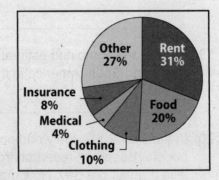

   a. How much greater is the family's spending on rent than it is on food? Give your answer as a percent and in dollars.

_____

   b. How much does the family spend on insurance and medical?

_____

LESSON 9-2

Percents, Fractions, and Decimals
Practice and Problem Solving: D

Find the percent of each number. Check whether your answer is reasonable. The first one is done for you.

1. 20% of 75

$$\frac{20}{100} = \frac{x}{75}$$

$$\frac{1}{5} = \frac{x}{75}$$

$$x = 15$$

2. 25% of 64

$$\frac{25}{100} = \frac{x}{64}$$

$$\underline{\quad\quad} = \frac{x}{64}$$

$$x = \underline{\quad\quad}$$

3. 4% of 75

_____

4. 2% of 400

_____

5. 160% of 80

_____

6. 12% of 50

_____

7. 87% of 500

_____

8. 28% of 250

_____

9. 500% of 25

_____

Solve.

10. Frank's Sports Store discounts all sports equipment by 20%. What is the cost of a baseball mitt that originally cost $45?

_____

11. In a science experiment, two tomato seeds were planted and watered. After six weeks, the plant that was fertilized was 26 centimeters tall. The plant that was not fertilized was only 74% as tall. What was the height of the shorter plant?_____

12. Jackie made $28 babysitting last week. Her brother Joe made only 86% as much as she did. How much did Joe make?

_____

13. Meredith bought a book that cost $18 at a discount of 16%. What did she pay for the book?_____

14. Tomás bought a book that cost $18. It was on sale for 84% of its original price. How much did Tomás pay?

_____

15. Explain why the prices were the same in 13 and 14.

_____

_____

LESSON 9-2
Percents, Fractions, and Decimals
Reteach

Percent is a ratio whose second term is 100. The ratio of 27 to 100 is 27%.

To write a fraction as a percent, convert the fraction to an equivalent fraction with a denominator of 100. Then, write it as a percent.

$$\frac{3}{4} \overset{\times 25}{\underset{\times 25}{=}} \frac{75}{100} = 75\%$$

To write a decimal as a percent, move the decimal point two places to the right and write a percent sign.

$$0.89 = 89\%$$

Use the methods above to find the percents.

1. Write the ratio of 41 to 100 as a percent. _____

2. Write 0.23 as a percent. _____

3. Write $\frac{3}{8}$ as a percent. _____

4. How did you change $\frac{3}{8}$ to an equivalent fraction with a denominator of 100?

_____

_____

5. Which do you find easier to work with: percents, fractions, or decimals?

_____

_____

LESSON 9-2	**Percents, Fractions, and Decimals**

Reading Strategies: Find a Pattern

You can use decimals to find the percent of a number.

Find 35% of 80.

35% of 80 means 35% times 80.

Step 1: Change the percent to a decimal by using place values.

$$35\% = \frac{35}{100}$$

$$= 0.35$$

Step 2: Multiply the decimal times the number. → 0.35×80

The answer is 28, so 35% of 80 is 28.

Answer each question.

1. What decimal is equal to 35%? _____

2. How do you change a percent to a decimal?

    _____

3. After the percent is changed to a decimal, what is the next step in

    finding the percent of a number? _____

4. Write 10% as a decimal. _____

5. What is 10% of 60? _____

6. What is 20% of 60? _____

7. What is 30% of 60? _____

8. What is 40% of 60? _____

9. What pattern did you notice in the answers to 10%, 20%, 30%,
    and 40% of 60?

    _____

10. Suppose you know that 10% of 250 is 25. How could you use
    that information to find 30% of 250?

    _____

    _____

Percents, Fractions, and Decimals

LESSON 9-2

Success for English Learners

Problem 1

How much more time will the download take?

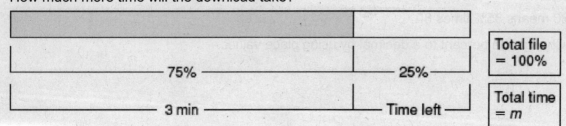

$$\frac{75}{100} = \frac{3}{m}$$
$$m = 4$$

It will take 4 minutes for the entire file.

It will take 1 more minute to download the file.

Total time − time passed = time left.
4 min − 3 min = 1 min

Problem 2

What is 20% of 150?

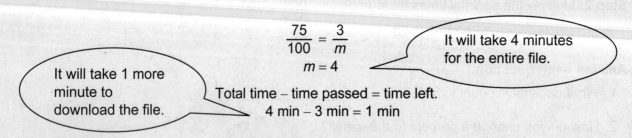

First, write the percent as a decimal.
20% = 20 hundredths
   = 0.20

Then multiply the decimal by the number given, 150.

0.20 · 150 = 30

20% of 150 is 30.

1. What is 15% of 84? _____

2. Explain why you represent 75% as $\frac{75}{100}$ in Problem 1.

_____

_____

3. What are two methods of finding the percent of a number?

_____

_____

LESSON 9-3

Solving Percent Problems

Practice and Problem Solving: A/B

Solve.

1. 22 students is ____% of 55.

2. 24 red marbles is 40% of ____ marbles.

3. 15% of $9 is $_____.

4. 12 is ____ % of 200.

5. Yesterday, Bethany sent 60 text messages. She said that 15% of those messages were to her best friend. How many text messages did Bethany send to her friend yesterday?

   _____

6. In a survey, 27% of the people chose salads over a meat dish. In all, 81 people chose salads. How many people were in the survey?

   _____

7. The sales tax on a $350 computer is $22.75. Find the sale tax rate?

   _____

Use the circle graph to complete Exercises 8–12.

8. If 6,000 people voted in the election, how many were from 18 to 29 years old?

   _____

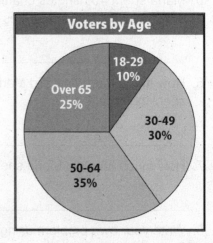

Voters by Age

18-29 10%

30-49 30%

50-64 35%

Over 65 25%

9. If 12,000 people voted in the election, how many were from 50 to 64 years old?

   _____

10. If 596 people voted in the election, how many were over 65 years old?

    _____

11. Suppose that Sahil knows that 45 people with ages of 18 to 29 voted. Without using a calculator, he quickly says then 135 people with ages of 30 to 49 voted. Is he correct? How might Sahil have come up with his answer so quickly?

    _____

    _____

    _____

LESSON
9-3

Solving Percent Problems

Practice and Problem Solving: C

Solve.

1. Selina earns 8% commission on sales. On one sale, her commission was $20.40. What was the amount of that sale?

   _____

2. Bryan bought two shirts for $14.50 each and a pair of shoes for $29.99. The sales tax was 6%. How much did Bryan spend?

   _____

3. Josh created a pattern by using tiles. Twenty tiles were blue. For the rest of the pattern he used equal numbers of red and white tiles. Forty percent of the pattern was made with blue tiles. How many red tiles were used to make the pattern?

   _____

4. Suppose you have a coupon for a 20% discount. You buy a game that costs $38. The sales tax rate is 5.5%. Sales tax applies to the cost after the discount. What is the total cost of the game?

   _____

Use the circle graph to complete Exercises 5–8.

5. Maria spent 40 minutes chatting online. How many minutes did she spend playing games?

   _____

6. How much more time did Maria spend doing research than checking email?

   _____

7. How much time did Maria spend online on Saturday?

   _____

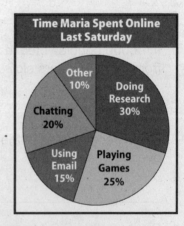

8. Write your own problem using the data from the graph. Your problem should need more than one-step in the solution. Then show how to solve your problem and give the answer.

   Problem: _____

   _____

   Solution: _____

   _____

**LESSON
9-3**

Solving Percent Problems
Practice and Problem Solving: D

Solve each problem. The first one is done for you.

The world population is estimated to exceed 9 billion by the
year 2050. Use the circle graph to solve Exercises 1–2.

1. What is the estimated population of Africa in 2050?

   Solution:

   The graph shows in 2050, Africa will have 20%
   of the world population. Find 20% of 9 billion.

   Write 20% as a decimal.   20% = 0.2

   Multiply 9 by 0.2. $9 \cdot 0.2 = 1.8$

   The estimated population of Africa in 2050

   is about _____**1.8 billion**_____

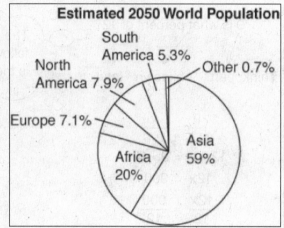

Estimated 2050 World Population

2. Which continent is estimated to have more
   than 5.31 billion people by 2050?

   To solve, find what percent 5.31 billion is of 9 billion.

   Write a ratio of part to whole. $\dfrac{?}{100} = \dfrac{5.31}{9}$

   Solve for?. Change $\dfrac{\text{your answer for?}}{100}$ to a decimal and then to a percent._____ %

   Use the graph to complete: In 2050, _____ will have _____ %
   of the population on the graph.

3. A half-cup of pancake mix has 5% of the total daily allowance of
   cholesterol. The total daily allowance of cholesterol is 300 mg.
   How much cholesterol does a half-cup of pancake mix have?

   _____

4. The student population at King Middle School is 52% female.
   There are 637 girls at King Middle School. What is the total student
   population King Middle School? How many boys go to King Middle
   School?

   _____

5. Carey needs $45 to buy her mother a gift. She has saved 22% of
   that amount so far. How much more money does she need?

   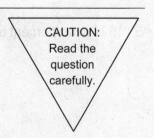

   CAUTION:
   Read the
   question
   carefully.

   _____

LESSON 9-3 Solving Percent Problems
Reteach

You can use this proportion to solve percent problems.

$$\frac{\text{part}}{\text{total}} = \frac{\text{percent}}{100}$$

9 is what percent of 12?

Think: part   unknown   total

> The number following "of" is the total.

30% of what number is 24?

Think: percent unknown part

$$\frac{9}{12} = \frac{x}{100}$$

$12 \cdot x = 9 \cdot 100$

$12x = 900$

$$\frac{12x}{12} = \frac{900}{12}$$

$x = 75$

So, 9 is 75% of 12.

$$\frac{24}{x} = \frac{30}{100}$$

$30 \cdot x = 24 \cdot 100$

$30x = 2,400$

$$\frac{30x}{30} = \frac{2,400}{30}$$

$x = 80$

So, 30% of 80 is 24.

Solve.

1. What percent of 25 is 14?

   a. part = _____

   b. total = _____

   c. percent = _____

   d. Write and solve the proportion.

   Answer: _____ % of 25 is 14.

2. 80% of what number is 16?

   a. part = _____

   b. total = _____

   c. percent = _____

   d. Write and solve the proportion.

   Answer: 80% of _____ is 16.

3. What percent of 20 is 11? _____

4. 18 is 45% of what number? _____

5. 15 is what percent of 5? _____

6. 75% of what number is 105? _____

Solving Percent Problems

LESSON 9-3
Reading Strategies: Connecting Words and Symbols

You can connect words and symbols to write equations for percent problems.

Ten percent of 190 students are in the band. How many students are in the band?

Use what you know: *n* is 10% of 190

Use symbols: *n* = 10% • 190

Jessica has saved $38. That is 20% of what she wants to save this year. How much does she want to save this year?

Use what you know: $38 is 20% of what number

Use symbols: 38 = 20% • *n*

Bart answered 18 questions correctly. What percent of the 20 questions on the test did he get correct?

Use what you know: 18 is what percent of 20

Use symbols: 18 = *n* • 20

> *Remember*: When finding a percent, your answer will be a decimal that needs to be rewritten as a percent.

Answer each question.

1. What is the symbol for the word "of"? _____

2. What symbol means "is"? _____

3. What symbol in the above examples stands for the unknown

   number? _____

Write an equation for each problem.

4. Mika has completed 5 birdhouses. That is 25% of the number of birdhouses she wants to build. How many birdhouses does she want to build?

   _____

5. A baker made 40 loaves of wheat bread. In all, 160 loaves of bread were made. What percent of the loaves of bread made was wheat bread?

   _____

Name _____ Date _____ Class_____

Solving Percent Problems

Success for English Learners

Problem 1

For Sale $39,500

Just to inform you, I get a 4% commission if I sell a car.

Commission	is	Commission Rate	of	Total Sales
⇩	⇩	⇩	⇩	⇩
c	=	4%	•	$39,500

$c = 4\% \cdot \$39,500$ Write the equation.

$c = 0.04 \cdot \$39,500$ Change the percent to a decimal.

$c = \$1,580$ Multiply.

The salesperson will be paid $1,580 for selling the car.

Problem 2

```
        HH Mart
   Welcome to our store

1@ 145.80      $145.80
2@ 15.99        $31.98

Subtotal       $177.78
- - - - - - - - - - - - - -
Tax (7.75%)     $13.78
```

Add the cost of total purchases to get a subtotal.

Multiply the subtotal by the tax rate.

Find the tax on the sale.

$t = 7.75\% \cdot \$177.78$

$t = 0.0775 \cdot \$177.78$

$t \approx \$13.78$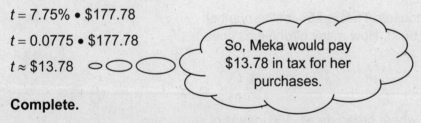

So, Meka would pay $13.78 in tax for her purchases.

Complete.

1. In Problem 2, what is the total cost, including tax? _____

2. How much is a 6% commission on a sale of $24,000? _____

3. What is the total cost, including tax, of a $48 coat

   with 8% sales tax? _____

MODULE 9

Percents
Challenge

1. Anthony found a number that is 20% of 30% of 400. What percent of 45 is the number that Anthony found?

_____

2.   Book A: 120 pages

         Book B: 170 pages

         Book C: 90 pages

Kevin and Dashawn were both assigned reading from books A, B and C above. Kevin completed 40% of Book A, 30% of Book B, and 10% of Book C. Dashawn completed 50% of Book A, 20% of Book B, and 30% of Book C. How many pages did each student read?

_____

Food	Calories	Fat (grams)
Whole Milk	150	8
Egg	80	6
Hamburger	220	15
Pizza	160	3

3. The table above shows calories and fat grams for different foods. Fat grams contain 9 calories each. Find the percent of calories from fat for each of the foods above.

_____

_____

_____

4. Suppose a food has 300 calories per serving. What is the maximum number of grams of fat that the food can contain in order for the percent of calories from fat to be 40% or less?

_____

Name _____ Date _____ Class_____

LESSON 10-1

Exponents

Practice and Problem Solving: A/B

Write each expression in exponential form and find its value.

1. $2 \times 2 \times 2 \times 2$

2. $-3 \times -3 \times -3$

3. $\dfrac{3}{5} \times \dfrac{3}{5}$

_____

_____

_____

4. -10×-10

5. $-\dfrac{1}{6} \times -\dfrac{1}{6} \times -\dfrac{1}{6} \times -\dfrac{1}{6}$

6. $0.5 \times 0.5 \times 0.5$

_____

_____

_____

Find each value.

7. $(1.2)^3$

8. $\left(-\dfrac{1}{4}\right)^4$

9. $(-2)^6$

10. -2^6

_____

_____

_____

_____

Solve.

11. The volume of a cubic box is 10^6 cubic millimeters.
Write the volume of the box in standard form.

_____

How long is each side of the box? (*Hint*: The length, width, and height of a cube are equal.)

_____

12. The voltage in an electrical circuit is multiplied by itself each time it is

reduced. The voltage is $\dfrac{27}{125}$ of a volt and it has been reduced three

times. Write the voltage in exponential form. _____

What was the original voltage in the circuit? _____

Compare using >, <, or =.

13. $\left(\dfrac{1}{3}\right)^4$ _____ $\left(\dfrac{1}{3}\right)^0$

14. $(-2.5)^5$ _____ $-(2.5)^5$

15. 5^0 _____ -5^0

16. Use exponents to write 81 three different ways.

$81 =$ _____ ; $81 =$ _____ ; $81 =$ _____

LESSON
10-1

Exponents

Practice and Problem Solving: C

Use the definitions of exponents to show that each statement is true.

1. $-3^5 = (-3)^5$

2. $\left(\dfrac{2}{3}\right)^3 < \left(\dfrac{2}{3}\right)^1$

3. $(0.72)^7 > (-7.2)^7$

_____   _____   _____

4. A halogen-lighting manufacturer packs 64 halogen lamps in a cube-shaped container. The manufacturer has been asked by his distributors to package the lamps in a smaller container that holds 8 lamps.

a. Write the number of lamps in the larger package in exponential form. _____

b. Use the answer to part a. to indicate how many lamps wide, deep, and high the larger shipping container is.

_____

c. Write the number of lamps in the smaller package in exponential form. _____

d. How many of the smaller cubic packages fit into the larger cubic package? Explain how you get your answer.

_____

Simplify each exponential number. Then, multiply the numbers.

5. $\left(\dfrac{2}{3}\right)^4 = $ _____

$\left(\dfrac{3}{2}\right)^4 = $ _____

$\left(\dfrac{2}{3}\right)^4 \times \left(\dfrac{3}{2}\right)^4 = $ _____

6. $(-0.5)^3 = $ _____ $(-2)^3 = $ _____

$(-0.5)^3 \times (-2)^3 = $ _____

Use the answers to the third parts of Exercises 5 and 6 to supply the missing number in each problem.

7. $\left(\dfrac{7}{5}\right)^2 \times$ _____ $= 1$

8. $(-4)^3 \times$ _____ $= 1$

9. $(0.3)^6 \times$ _____ $= 1$

LESSON 10-1

Exponents

Practice and Problem Solving: D

Name the *base* and *exponent*. The first one is done for you.

1. 2^7

Base: ___2___

Exponent: ___7___

2. $\left(\dfrac{5}{6}\right)^4$

Base: _____

Exponent: _____

3. $(-5)^{10}$

Base: _____

Exponent: _____

Write using exponents. The first one is done for you.

4. $10,000 = 10 \times 10 \times 10 \times 10 =$

___10^4___

5. $\dfrac{8}{27} = \underline{} \times \underline{} \times \underline{} =$

_____

6. $-64 = \underline{} \times \underline{} \times \underline{} =$

_____

Write as repeated multiplication. The first one is done for you.

7. $(-2)^2 =$

___$(-2) \times (-2)$___

8. $(0.25)^3 =$

_____

9. $\left(\dfrac{1}{9}\right)^3 =$

_____

Solve. The first one is done for you.

10. The temperature inside the glazing oven is about 1,000 degrees Fahrenheit. Write 1,000 using exponents.

   Count the number of places from the decimal point on the right to

   the comma between the "1" and the "0" next to it. That number of

   places is the exponent. The base is 10. The answer is $1,000 = 10^3$.

11. A sports memorabilia collector has 3^3 1980 baseball cards and 4^3 1990 football cards. Write the number of baseball cards and football cards in standard form.

   _____

12. A long-distance runner ran $4 \times 4 \times 4 \times 4 \times 4 \times 4$ miles last year. How many miles is this?

   _____

LESSON 10-1

Exponents
Reteach

You can write a number in exponential form to show repeated multiplication. A number written in exponential form has a **base** and an **exponent**. The exponent tells you how many times a number, the base, is used as a factor.

8^4 ◄——— exponent

base

Write the expression in exponential form.

$(-0.7) \times (-0.7) \times (-0.7) \times (-0.7)$

−0.7 is used as a factor 4 times.

$(-0.7) \times (-0.7) \times (-0.7) \times (-0.7) = (-0.7)^4$

Write each expression in exponential form.

1. $\dfrac{1}{20} \times \dfrac{1}{20} \times \dfrac{1}{20} \times \dfrac{1}{20}$ 2. 8×8

3. $7.5 \times 7.5 \times 7.5$ 4. (-0.4)

_____   _____   _____   _____

You can find the value of expressions in exponential form.
Find the value.
5^6

Step 1 Write the expression as repeated multiplication.
$5 \times 5 \times 5 \times 5 \times 5 \times 5$

Step 2 Multiply.
$5 \times 5 \times 5 \times 5 \times 5 \times 5 = 15{,}625$

$5^6 = 15{,}625$

Simplify.

5. $\left(-\dfrac{1}{2}\right)^3$ 6. $(1.2)^5$ 7. 3^6 8. $\left(\dfrac{4}{3}\right)^2$

_____   _____   _____   _____

LESSON 10-1

Exponents

Reading Strategies: Synthesize Information

Exponents are an efficient way to write repeated multiplication.

Read 2^4 $\longrightarrow$ *2 to the fourth power*

2^4 means **2 is a factor 4 times**, or

$2 \times 2 \times 2 \times 2$

Read $2^4 = 16$ $\longrightarrow$ *2 to the fourth power equals 16.*

Exponent	Meaning	Value
10^3 *10 to the third power*	10 is a factor 3 times: $10 \times 10 \times 10$	$10^3 = 1{,}000$
6^5 *6 to the fifth power*	6 is a factor 5 times: $6 \times 6 \times 6 \times 6 \times 6$	$6^5 = 7{,}776$

Answer each question.

1. Write in words how you would read $(-2)^5$.

   _____

2. What does $(-2)^5$ mean?

   _____

3. What is the value of $(-2)^5$?

   _____

4. Write in words how you would read $\left(\dfrac{3}{5}\right)^4$.

   _____

5. Write $\left(\dfrac{3}{5}\right)^4$ as repeated multiplication.

   _____

6. Is the value of $\left(\dfrac{3}{5}\right)^4$ equal to $\dfrac{3}{5}$ times four? Explain your answer.

   _____

LESSON 10-1

Exponents

Success for English Learners

Problem 1

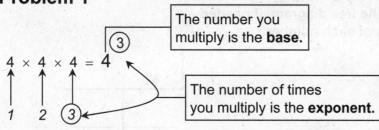

Problem 2

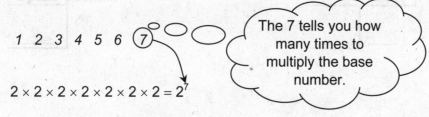

1. In Problem 2, what is the base? _____

2. In Problem 2, what is the exponent? _____

3. How do you read the number in Problem 1?

_____

4. How do you read the number in Problem 2?

_____

5. a. Write the number 7 raised to the third power. _____

   b. What is the exponent? _____

   c. What is the base? _____

6. a. Write the number 5 raised to the sixth power. _____

   b. What number do you multiply? _____

   c. How many times do you multiply it? _____

Name _____ Date _____ Class _____

LESSON
10-2

Prime Factorization

Practice and Problem Solving: A/B

Fill in the missing information. Add more "steps" to the ladder
diagram and more "branches" to the tree diagram, if needed.
Then, write the prime factorization of each number.

1.

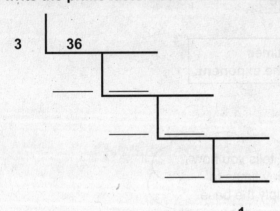

2.

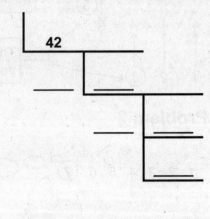

3.

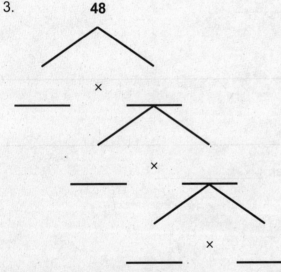

4.

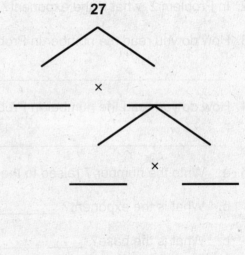

Write the prime factorizations.

5. 44   6. 125   7. 85   8. 39

_____   _____   _____   _____

LESSON 10-2 — Prime Factorization

Practice and Problem Solving: C

If 9 is divisible by 3 and 14 is divisible by 2, then 9 × 14 is divisible by 3 × 2. Use this rule to complete Exercises 1–3. Simplify the numbers to prove the result.

1. Twenty-one is divisible by 3. Fifteen is divisible by 5. Therefore,

   _____ times _____ is divisible by _____ times _____

   _____

2. Eighteen is divisible by 2. Twelve is divisible by 3. Therefore,

   _____ times _____ is divisible by _____ times _____

   _____

3. Ten is divisible by 5. Fourteen is divisible by 7. Therefore,

   _____ times _____ is divisible by _____ times _____

   _____

Unit fractions are fractions of the form $\dfrac{1}{n}$. Give the prime factorization of each unit fraction into fractions that cannot be reduced.

4. $\dfrac{1}{100}$ 5. $\dfrac{1}{24}$

   _____   _____

Any integer *n* that is greater than 1 is either prime or a product of primes. List the different prime numbers that make up the prime factorization of these composite numbers.

6. 24   7. 105   8. 924

   _____   _____   _____

Solve.

9. There are 126 different combinations of soups, salads, and sandwiches available at a café. If there are more choices of sandwiches than choices of salads and fewer choices of soups than salads, how many of each type of food is available at the café?

   _____

Name _____ Date _____ Class_____

LESSON 10-2

Prime Factorization

Practice and Problem Solving: D

List all of the factors of each number. Circle the prime factors. The first one is done for you.

1. 6

   1; (2); (3); 6

2. 9

   _____

3. 10

   _____

4. 12

   _____

5. 21

   _____

6. 31

   _____

Write the prime factorization of each number. The first one is done for you.

7. 9

   3^2

8. 25

   _____

9. 8

   _____

10. 14

    _____

11. 12

    _____

12. 15

    _____

13. There are 12 chairs in the meeting hall and an odd number of tables. Each table has the same number of chairs. How many tables are there?

    _____

14. What are two different ways that 9 can be written as a product of two numbers?

    _____

15. Find the prime factorization of 63 with the factor ladder. The first step is done for you.

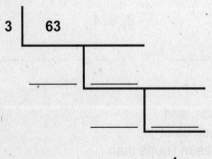

    Prime factorization: _____

LESSON 10-2 Prime Factorization
Reteach

Factors of a product are the numbers that are multiplied to give that product.

A factor is also a whole number that divides the product with no remainder.

To find all of the factors of 32, make a list of multiplication facts.

$1 \cdot 32 = 32$

$2 \cdot 16 = 32$

$4 \cdot 8 = 32$

The factors of 32 are 1, 2, 4, 8, 16, and 32.

Write multiplication facts to find the factors of each number.

1. 28

2. 15

_____

3. 36

4. 29

_____

A number written as the product of prime factors is called the **prime factorization** of the number.

To write the prime factorization of 32, first write it as the product of two numbers. Then, rewrite each factor as the product of two numbers until all of the factors are prime numbers.

$32 = 2 \cdot \mathbf{16}$ (Write 32 as the product of 2 numbers.)

   $= 2 \cdot \mathbf{4} \cdot \mathbf{4}$ (Rewrite 16 as the product of 2 numbers.)

      $\downarrow$ $\downarrow$

   $= 2 \cdot 2 \cdot 2 \cdot 2 \cdot 2$ (Rewrite the 4's as the product 2 prime numbers.)

So, the prime factorization of 32 is $2 \cdot 2 \cdot 2 \cdot 2 \cdot 2$ or 2^5.

Find the prime factorization of each number.

5. 28   6. 45   7. 50   8. 72

_____   _____   _____   _____

LESSON 10-2

Prime Factorization

Reading Strategies: Use a Graphic Organizer

A graphic organizer can help you "see" how to factor numbers. One of the organizers used in this lesson is the **factor tree**.

Example

Factor 75 using a factor tree.

Start by writing 75 at the top of the tree. Then, think of a prime number that divides 75 evenly.

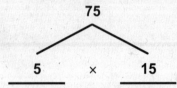

Then, think of a prime number that divides 15 evenly. Add two new "branches" to the tree below 15 as shown.

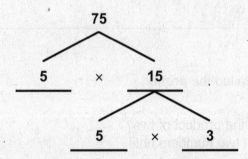

Continue adding "branches" as needed. When the numbers on the last "branch" of the tree are prime numbers, write the prime factorization of the number: $75 = 3 \times 5 \times 5 = 3 \times 5^2$.

Draw a factor tree for each number on the back of this page or on another sheet of paper. Then, write the prime factorization of the number.

1. $360 =$

2. $378 =$

_____ _____

LESSON 10-2 Prime Factorization
Success for English Learners

Problem 1

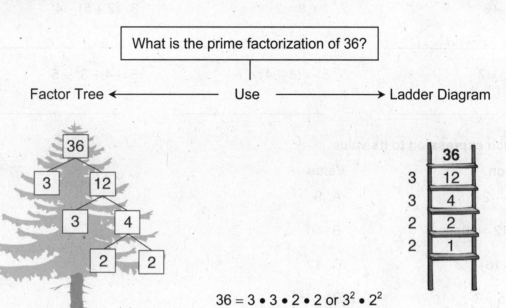

What is the prime factorization of 36?

Factor Tree ←——————— Use ——————→ Ladder Diagram

$36 = 3 \bullet 3 \bullet 2 \bullet 2$ or $3^2 \bullet 2^2$

Complete each diagram. Then, write the prime factorization.

1.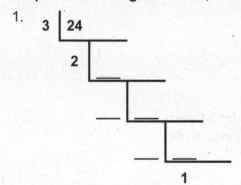

   3 | 24
   2
   1

2.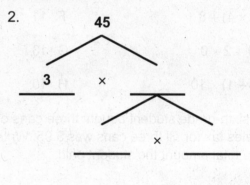

   45
   3   ×
        ×

_____

Order of Operations

Practice and Problem Solving: A/B

Name the operation you should perform first.

1. $4 \times 6 - 3$ 2. $1 + 8 \div 2$ 3. $(2 + 5) - 4^2$

_____   _____   _____

4. $7 \div 7^3 \times 7$ 5. $8^2 \div (8 - 4)^2$ 6. $-4 + 3^3 \div 5$

_____   _____   _____

Match each expression to its value.

Expression	Value
7. $7 + 8 - 2$	A. 9
8. $9 + (12 - 10)$	B. 40
9. $(20 - 15) \times 2$	C. 12
10. $10 \div 5 + 7$	D. 14
11. $6 + 2 \times 3$	E. 16
12. $(2 \times 4) + 8$	F. 11
13. $14 + 2 \times 0$	G. 13
14. $(5 - 1) \times 10$	H. 10

15. A sixth-grade student bought three cans of tennis balls for $4 each. Sales tax for all three cans was $.95. Write an expression to show the total amount the student paid.

_____

16. The middle-school camera club sold 240 tulip bulbs and 360 daffodil bulbs. Students divided the bulbs into 100 bags to sell at the school fair. Write an expression to show how many bulbs went into each of the 100 bags if students put the same number of each kind of bulb in each bag.

_____

LESSON 10-3

Order of Operations

Practice and Problem Solving: C

Insert +, −, ×, and/or a ÷ signs to make each statement true.

1. 1 ◯ 2 < 3 ◯ 4

2. (5 ◯ 6) + 7 = 6 ◯ (5 − 4)

3. 8 + 9 ◯ 10 > (6 × 7) ◯ 5

Evaluate each expression.

4. $(5 + 0) \div 4$

5. $5 + (0 \div 4)$

_____

_____

6. $7 \div (6 + 0)$

7. $(7 + 6) \div 0$

_____

_____

8. $(1 \times 2) \div 3$

9. $1 \div (2 \times 3)$

_____

_____

Write the consecutive integers that make the statements true.

10. _____ < $(15 \div 7) \times 4$ < _____

11. _____ > $7 \times (6 \div 4)^2$ > _____

The Pythagorean Theorem states that sum of the squares of the two legs of a right triangle, *a* and *b*, is equal to the square of the hypotenuse, *c*, of the right triangle: $a^2 + b^2 = c^2$. Use the theorem to complete Exercises 12–14.

12. One leg of a right triangle is 4 less than the other leg. The square of the hypotenuse of the right triangle is 80. How long are the legs of the right triangle? Show your work.

_____

_____

13. Find the square of the leg *b* of this right triangle: $a = 2b$, $c = 10$

14. Find the square of the hypotenuse of a right triangle with *a* and *b* related by the statement $a = b - 5$.

_____

_____

LESSON 10-3

Order of Operations

Practice and Problem Solving: D

Name the operation you should perform first. The first one is done for you.

		Order of Operations
1. $5 + 6 \times 2$	2. $18 \div 3 - 1$	1. Parentheses
Multiplication	_____	2. Exponents
3. $3^2 + 6$	4. $(15 + 38) \times 6$	3. Multiplication
_____	_____	4. Division
		5. Addition
		6. Subtraction

Match each expression to its value. The first one is done for you.

	Expression	Value
____E____	5. $7 + 8 - 2$	A. 9
_____	6. $9 + (12 - 10)$	B. 12
_____	7. $(20 - 15) \times 2$	C. 16
_____	8. $10 \div 5 + 7$	D. 11
_____	9. $6 + 2 \times 3$	E. 13
_____	10. $(2 \times 4) + 8$	F. 10

11. a. Sam bought two CDs for $13 each. Sales tax for both CDs was $3. Write an expression to show how much Sam paid in all.

_____

  b. How much did Sam pay?

_____

12. Write an expression using multiplication and addition with a sum of 16.

_____

13. Write an expression using division and subtraction with a difference of 3.

_____

Order of Operations

LESSON 10-3

Reteach

A mathematical phrase that includes only numbers and operations is called a *numerical expression*.

$9 + 8 \times 3 \div 6$ is a numerical expression.

When you evaluate a numerical expression, you find its value.

You can use the order of operations to evaluate a numerical expression.

<u>Order of operations:</u>

1. Do all operations within *parentheses*.
2. Find the values of numbers with *exponents*.
3. *Multiply* and *divide* in order from left to right.
4. *Add* and *subtract* in order from left to right.

Evaluate the expression.

$60 \div (7 + 3) + 3^2$

$60 \div 10 + 3^2$	Do all operations within parentheses.
$60 \div 10 + 9$	Find the values of numbers with exponents.
$6 + 9$	Multiply and divide in order from left to right.
15	Add and subtract in order from left to right.

Simplify each numerical expression.

1. $7 \times (12 + 8) - 6$

   $7 \times$ _____ $- 6$

   _____ $- 6$

   _____

2. $10 \times (12 + 34) + 3$

   $10 \times$ _____ $+ 3$

   _____ $+ 3$

   _____

3. $10 + (6 \times 5) - 7$

   $10 +$ _____ $- 7$

   _____ $- 7$

   _____

4. $2^3 + (10 - 4)$

5. $7 + 3 \times (8 + 5)$

6. $36 \div 4 + 11 \times 8$

7. $5^2 - (2 \times 8) + 9$

8. $3 \times (12 \div 4) - 2^2$

9. $(3^3 + 10) - 2$

Solve.

10. Write and evaluate your own numerical expression. Use parentheses, exponents, and at least two operations.

   _____

LESSON 10-3 Order of Operations
Reading Strategies: Use a Memory Aid

A memory aid can help you recall the order of operations in simplifying
a numerical expression. Just remember the first letter of each operation.

P $\longrightarrow$ **Parentheses**

E $\longrightarrow$ **Exponents**

M $\longrightarrow$ **Multiply**

D $\longrightarrow$ **Divide**

A $\longrightarrow$ **Add**

S $\longrightarrow$ **Subtract**

The six letters form the "word" **PEMDAS**, pronounced "Pem-das". "Pem"
rhymes with "Tim", and "das" sounds like "does."

Another way to recall the order of operation is in a sentence.

"Please Excuse My Dear Aunt Sally."

You can come up with your own sentence using the first letters of the
operations, too.

Fill in the steps in each simplification.

1. $4 + (9 \div 3)^2 \times 5 - 1$

   P: _____

   E: _____

   M: _____

   D: _____

   A: _____

   S: _____

2. $(3 \times 2) + 5^2 - 8 \div 2$

   P: _____

   E: _____

   M: _____

   D: _____

   A: _____

   S: _____

Simplify.

3. $12 \times 4 \div 2 + (7 - 5)^4$

   _____

4. $1 + 2^3 - (4 \times 5) \div 10$

   _____

**LESSON
10-3**

Order of Operations
Success for English Learners

Problem 1

What did Regina spend on both glass and wooden beads?

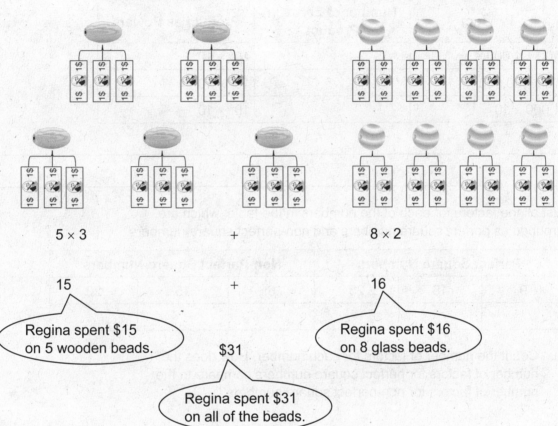

Wooden beads   **Glass beads**

5×3 + 8×2

15   +   16

Regina spent $15 on 5 wooden beads.

Regina spent $16 on 8 glass beads.

$31

Regina spent $31 on all of the beads.

1. Why do you have to multiply the number of beads by the price before adding?

_____

_____

2. When would you add the number of beads first and then multiply by the price?

_____

_____

Generating Equivalent Numerical Expressions
Challenge

1. Complete the table using the fact that the exponent in a power of 10 is the same as the number of zeros when the number is written out. Then use your observations to explain how you can find the product of any two powers of 10, $10^a \times 10^b$.

Product	Number of Zeros in Product	Product as Powers
$100 \times 1{,}000 =$		$10^2 \times 10^3 =$
$10 \times 100{,}000 =$		$10^1 \times 10^5 =$
$1{,}000 \times 10 =$		$10^3 \times 10^1 =$

_____

_____

2. List all the factors for each of the numbers in the table, which are grouped as perfect square numbers and non-perfect square numbers.

Perfect Square Numbers			Non-Perfect Square Numbers		
9	16	25	6	15	20

   a. Count the number of factors for each number. How does the number of factors for perfect square numbers compare to the number of factors for non-perfect square numbers?

   _____

   b. Use your observation to answer this question: What is the least whole number that has exactly 9 factors, including 1 and itself?

   _____

3. Insert parentheses to make each statement true. If parentheses are not needed, then say so.

   $28 \div 4 + 3 \times 48 \div 6 - 2 = 29$ _____

   $28 \div 4 + 3 \times 48 \div 6 - 2 = 30$ _____

   $28 \div 4 + 3 \times 48 \div 6 - 2 = 43$ _____

Modeling Equivalent Expressions

Practice and Problem Solving: A/B

Solve.

1. Jessica rode 9 miles farther than Roger rode. Let *r* represent the number of miles Roger rode. Write an expression for the number of miles Jessica rode.

   _____

2. Let *m* represent the number of children playing soccer. Those children are separated into 4 equal teams. Write an expression for the number of children on each team.

   _____

3. Glenda bought some apps for her tablet. Each app cost $5. Let *n* represent the number of apps she bought. Write an expression to show the total amount she spent.

   _____

Write each phrase as a numerical or algebraic expression.

4. 25 multiplied by 3

   _____

5. 3 added to *n*

   _____

6. *r* divided by 8

   _____

7. the product of 7 and *m*

   _____

8. the difference between 48 and 13

   _____

9. the quotient of 18 and 3

   _____

10. 189 subtracted from *t*

    _____

11. the sum of *w* and 253

    _____

Write two word phrases for each expression.

12. $t + 23$ _____

13. $45 - n$ _____

Solve.

14. Write an expression that has two terms. Your expression should have a variable and a constant.

    _____

LESSON 11-1
Modeling Equivalent Expressions
Practice and Problem Solving: C

Solve.

1. Cal bought 2 packs of 100 paper plates and 1 pack of 60 paper plates. Write an expression for the total number of plates that he bought.

   _____

2. The temperature dropped 25°. Then the temperature went up 17°. Let *t* represent the beginning temperature. Write an expression to show the ending temperature.

   _____

3. Jill purchased fruit juice boxes for a party. She purchased 1 case of 44 boxes and several packs containing 4 boxes each. Let *p* represent the number of 4-box packs she purchased. Write an expression for the total number of juice boxes Jill purchased.

   _____

Use the figures at the right for Exercises 4–6.

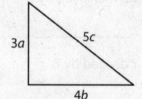

4. Write an expression for the perimeter of the triangle at the right.

   _____

5. Write an expression for the perimeter of the square.

   _____

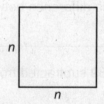

6. Write an expression for the area of the square.

   _____

Solve.

7. Write an expression that has four terms. Your expression should have three different variables and a constant.

   _____

8. Josef said that he could represent the amount of money he made last week with the expression: $24d + 8n$. Write problem about the money Josef made last week.

   _____

   _____

LESSON 11-1

Modeling Equivalent Expressions

Practice and Problem Solving: D

Circle the letter of the correct answer. The first one is done for you.

solution: result: answer

1. Which of the following is the **solution** to an addition problem?

   (A) sum

   B plus

   C add

2. Which word phrase represents the following expression $n - 3$?

   A the quotient of n and 3

   B 3 less than n

   C n less than 3

3. Which word phrase represents the following expression $5m$?

   A 5 fewer than m

   B m groups of 5

   C m divided by 5

4. Which of the following is the **solution** to a multiplication problem?

   A quotient

   B factor

   C product

5. Which word phrase represents the following expression $r \div 6$?

   A the product of r and 6

   B the quotient of r and 6

   C take away 6 from r

6. Which word phrase represents the following expression $3 + p$?

   A 3 increased by p

   B 3 decreased by p

   C the difference of 3 and p

Match the algebraic expressions A–E to Exercises 5–10. Some letters may be used more than once. Some letters may not be used at all. The first one is done for you.

A. $9x$	B. $9 + x$	C. $x - 9$	D. $x \div 9$	E. $9 - x$

7. 9 less than x   **C**

8. the quotient of 9 and x ____

9. the sum of 9 and x ____

10. the product of 9 and x ____

11. x more than 9   ____

12. x decreased by 9   ____

Solve.

13. Nicole had 38 beads. She lost some of them. This can be modeled by the expression $38 - x$. What does x represent?

   _____

14. Wilhelm bought some shirts. He paid $12 for each shirt. This can be modeled by the expression $12x$. What does x represent?

   _____

LESSON 11-1

Modeling Equivalent Expressions
Reteach

Write an expression that shows how much longer the Nile River is than the Amazon River.

NILE RIVER

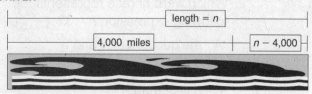

The expression is **_n_ – 4,000**.

AMAZON RIVER

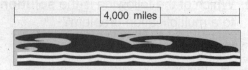

Each state gets the same number of senators. Write an expression for the number of senators there are in the United States Congress.

There are 50 states.

There are *s* senators from each state.

50s

The total number of senators is **50 times s**.

Solve.

1. Why does the first problem above use subtraction?

   _____

2. Why does the second problem above use multiplication?

   _____

3. Jackson had *n* autographs in his autograph book. Yesterday he got 3 more autographs. Write an expression to show how many autographs are in his autograph book now.

   _____

4. Miranda earned $*c* for working 8 hours. Write an expression to show how much Miranda earned for each hour worked.

   _____

Modeling Equivalent Expressions
Reading Strategies: Use a Visual Map

Identifying word phrases for different operations can help you understand and write algebraic expressions. This visual map shows the four different operations with key word phrases in boldface.

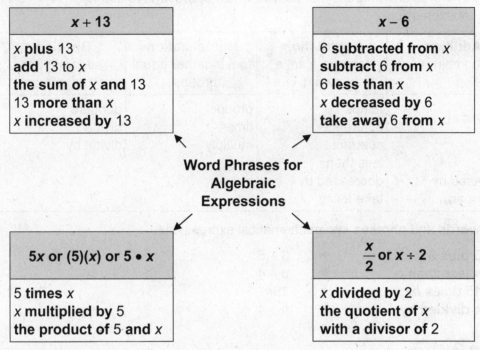

Write a word phrase for each algebraic expression.

1. $t - 8$ _____

2. $\dfrac{n}{6}$ _____

3. $4w$ _____

4. $z + 8$ _____

5. $9 \bullet m$ _____

Write an algebraic expression for each word phrase.

6. the sum of p and 12   _____

7. i decreased by 7   _____

8. the quotient of r with a divisor of 3   _____

9. z decreased by 1   _____

10. the product of y and 19   _____

Name _____ Date _____ Class_____

LESSON
11-1

Modeling Equivalent Expressions
Success for English Learners

Problem 1

There are key words and phrases that tell you which operations to use for mathematical expressions.

Addition (combine)	Subtraction (compare, take away)	Multiplication (put together equal groups)	Division (separate into equal groups)
add plus sum total increased by more than	minus difference subtract less than decreased by take away	product times multiply	quotient divide divide by

Translate **words** and **phrases** into mathematical expressions:

3 **plus** 5	$\longrightarrow$	$3 + 5$
4 **less than** p	$\longrightarrow$	$p - 4$
15 **times** n	$\longrightarrow$	$15n$
h **divided by** 4	$\longrightarrow$	$h \div 4$

Problem 2

You can use key words to write word phrases for mathematical expressions. You can write different word phrases for the same expression.

$7k \rightarrow$ the **product of** 7 and k $8 - 2 \rightarrow 2$ **less than** 8 $n + 10 \rightarrow 10$ **more than** n

$\rightarrow 7$ **times** k $\rightarrow 8$ **minus** 2 $\rightarrow$ the **sum of** n and 10

Write each phrase as a numerical or algebraic expression.

1. m increased by 5   2. 18 divided by 2   3. the difference between t and 7

_____   _____   _____

4. r multiplied by 4   5. x decreased by 9   6. the quotient of 21 and 7

_____   _____   _____

Write a phrase for each expression.

7. $a - 2$ 8. $8 \cdot 6$

_____   _____

9. $p \div 8$ 10. $v + 10$

_____   _____

LESSON 11-2 Evaluating Expressions

Practice and Problem Solving: A/B

Evaluate each expression for the given value(s) of the variable(s).

1. $a - 4$ when $a = 16$

   _____

2. $2b + 9$ when $b = 3$

   _____

3. $c \div 2$ when $c = 26$

   _____

4. $5(9 + d) - 6$ when $d = 3$

   _____

5. $g^2 + 23$ when $g = 6$

   _____

6. $3h - j$ when $h = 8$ and $j = 11$

   _____

7. $(n - 2) \bullet m$ when $n = 5$ and $m = 9$

   _____

8. $r(s^2)(t)$ when $r = 2$, $s = 3$, and $t = 5$

   _____

Use the given values to complete each table.

9.

p	$2(13 - p)$
2	
3	
4	

10.

v	w	$3v + w$
4	2	
6	3	
8	4	

11.

x	y	$x^2 \div y$
2	1	
6	2	
8	4	

Solve.

12. The sales tax in one town is 8%. So, the total cost of an item can be written as $c + 0.08c$. What is the total cost of an item that sells for $12?

    _____

13. To change knots per hour to miles per hour, use the expression $1.15k$, where k is the speed in knots per hour. A plane is flying at 300 knots per hour. How fast is that plane flying in miles per hour?

    _____

14. Lurinda ordered some boxes of greeting cards online. The cost of the cards is $6.50n + $3 where n is the number of boxes ordered and $3 is the shipping and handling charge. How much will Lurinda pay if she orders 8 boxes of cards?

    _____

LESSON 11-2

Evaluating Expressions

Practice and Problem Solving: C

Use the given values to complete each table.

1.

r	$3.14 \bullet r^2$
2	
3	
4	

2.

z	a	$2z - a$
–4	2	
0	2	
4	2	

3.

x	y	$10x^2 \div (y + 1)$
2	1	
–1	3	
–4	4	

Solve.

4. Melinda is hauling water in her pickup truck. An old bridge has a maximum weight limit of 6,000 pounds. To find the weight of her truck, Melinda uses the expression $5,275 + 8.36g$, where g is the number of gallons of water she is hauling. Can Melinda safely drive her pickup across the bridge if she is hauling 120 gallons of water? Explain.

_____

5. A certain machine produces parts that are rectangular prisms. The surface area of each part is found by using the expression $2s^2 + 4sh$, where s is the length of a side of the base and h is the height. What is the surface area of that part when s is 0.5 mm and h is 2 mm? _____ mm^2

Three students incorrectly evaluated $4x^2 + 2y$ for $x = 3$ and $y = -2$. Use the table below to complete Exercises 6–9.

Grayson	Emily	Pat
$4x^2 + 2y = 4(3)^2 + 2(-2)$ $= 144 + (-4)$ $= 140$	$4x^2 + 2y = 4(3)^2 + 2(-2)$ $= 36 + 2(-2)$ $= 38(-2)$ $= -76$	$4x^2 + 2y = 4(3)^2 + 2(2)$ $= 36 + 4$ $= 40$

6. What error did Grayson make?

_____

7. What error did Emily make?

_____

8. What error did Pat make?

_____

9. Show the correct way to complete the evaluation of $4x^2 + 2y$ for $x = 3$ and $y = -2$.

_____

_____

LESSON
11-2

Evaluating Expressions
Practice and Problem Solving: D

Evaluate each expression for the given value of the variable.
Show each step you used. The first one is done for you.

1. $3n + 4^2$ when $n = 2$

   $3 \times \mathbf{2} + 4^2$ → Substitute 2 for n. _____

   $3 \times 2 + \mathbf{16}$ → Evaluate exponents. _____

   $\mathbf{6} + 16$ → Multiply. _____

   $\mathbf{22}$ → Add. _____

2. $2 \times (a + 3)$ when $a = 5$

   $2 \times (5 + 3)$ → Substitute values.

   $2 \times$ ____ → Clear the parentheses.

   ____ → Multiply.

3. $r + r \div 2 \times 4$ when $r = 8$

   $8 + 8 \div 2 \times 4$ → Substitute values.

   $8 +$ ____ $\times 4$ → Multiply or divide from left to right, so divide first.

   $8 +$ ____ → Multiply.

   ____ → Add.

Use the given values to complete each table. The first one is done for you.

4.

w	$6(3 + w)$
2	30
3	36
4	42

5.

c	$2c + 7$
4	
6	
8	

6.

w	$w^2 - 3$
2	
3	
4	

Solve. Show your work.

7. The height of horses is measured in *hands*. To find the height of a horse in inches, use the expression $4h$, where h is the number of hands. Rosa has a horse that is 15 hands tall. How tall is Rosa's horse in inches?

   Rosa's horse is ____ inches tall. _____

LESSON 11-2

Evaluating Expressions
Reteach

A **variable** is a letter that represents a number that can change in an expression. When you **evaluate** an algebraic expression, you substitute the value given for the variable in the expression.

- Algebraic expression: $x - 3$

  The value of the expression depends on the value of the variable x.

  If $x = 7$ → $7 - 3 = 4$

  If $x = 11$ → $11 - 3 = 8$

  If $x = 25$ → $25 - 3 = 22$

- Evaluate $4n + 5$ for $n = 7$.

  Replace the variable n with 7. → $4(7) + 5$

  Evaluate, following the order of operations. → $4(7) + 5 → 28 + 5 → 33$

Evaluate each expression for the given value. Show your work.

1. $a + 7$ when $a = 3$

   $a + 7 = 3 + 7 =$ ____

2. $y \div 3$ when $y = 6$

   $y \div 3 =$ ____ $\div 3 =$ ____

3. $n - 5$ when $n = 15$

   $n - 5 =$ ____ $- 5 =$ ____

4. $(6 + d) \cdot 2$ when $d = 3$

   $(6 + d) \cdot 2 = (6 +$ ____ $) \cdot 2$

   $=$ _____ $\cdot 2 =$ ____

5. $3n - 2$ when $n = 5$

   $3n - 2 = 3($ ____ $) - 2 =$ ____

6. $6b$ when $b = 7$

   _____

7. $12 - f$ when $f = 3$

   _____

8. $\dfrac{m}{5}$ when $m = 35$

   _____

9. $2k + 5$ when $k = 8$

   _____

10. $10 - (p + 3)$ when $p = 7$

   _____

LESSON 11-2

Evaluating Expressions

Reading Strategies: Use a Flowchart

A flowchart gives you a plan. You can use a flowchart to evaluate expressions.

1 Substitute for each variable.	⇨	**2** Evaluate exponents.	⇨	**3** Eliminate parentheses.	⇨	**4** Multiply and divide from left to right.	⇨	**5** Add and subtract from left to right.

Evaluate $x^2 - 3(4 + 1)$ when $x = 7$.

$7^2 - 3(4 + 1)$

$49 - 3(4 + 1)$

$49 - 3(5)$

$49 - 15$

34

Plan
1 Substitute for each variable.
2 Evaluate exponents.
3 Eliminate parentheses.
4 Multiply and divide from left to right.
5 Add and subtract from left to right.

Evaluate $(2n + 8) \div t - 2$ when $n = 6$ and $t = 5$.

$(2 \bullet 6 + 8) \div 5 - 2$

There are no exponents.

$(12 + 8) \div 5 - 2$
$20 \div 5 - 2$

$4 - 2$

2

Use the flowchart to evaluate each expression.

1.

Plan	Evaluate $(5 + y) - 3^2$ when $y = 14$.
1 Substitute for each variable.	
2 Evaluate exponents.	
3 Eliminate parentheses.	
4 Multiply and divide from left to right.	
5 Add and subtract from left to right.	

2.

Plan	Evaluate $m^2 - 2(3p + 6)$ when $m = 10$ and $p = 4$.
1 Substitute for each variable.	
2 Evaluate exponents.	
3 Eliminate parentheses.	
4 Multiply and divide from left to right.	
5 Add and subtract from left to right.	

LESSON 11-2 Evaluating Expressions

Success for English Learners

Problem 1

Find the missing values in the table.

Step 1: Substitute for the variables.

Step 2: Compute. Follow the order of operations.

Evaluate $4 \times n + 6^2$ for each value of n.

n	$4 \times n + 6^2$	
2	$4 \times \mathbf{2} + 6^2 \rightarrow$ $4 \times \mathbf{2} + \mathbf{36} \rightarrow$ $\mathbf{8} + 36 \rightarrow$ $44 \rightarrow$	Substitute 2 for n. Evaluate exponents. Multiply. Add.
5	$4 \times \mathbf{5} + 6^2 \rightarrow$ $4 \times 5 + \mathbf{36} \rightarrow$ ____ $+ 36 \rightarrow$ ____ $\rightarrow$	Substitute 5 for n. Evaluate exponents. Multiply. Add.
9	$4 \times \mathbf{9} + 6^2 \rightarrow$ $4 \times 9 + \mathbf{36} \rightarrow$ ____ $+ 36 \rightarrow$ ____ $\rightarrow$	Substitute 9 for n. Evaluate exponents. Multiply. Add.

Fill in the missing values in the table above.

Check your work.

Did you get a result of 56 when $n = 5$?

Did you get a result of 72 when $n = 9$?

Problem 2

Find the missing values in the table.

Step 1: Substitute for the variables.

Step 2: Compute. Follow the order of operations.

Evaluate $2l + 2w$ for the given values.

l	w	$2l + 2w$	
4	3	$2 \times \mathbf{4} + 2 \times \mathbf{3} \rightarrow$ $\mathbf{8} + \mathbf{6} \rightarrow$ $14 \rightarrow$	Substitute values. Multiply first. Add.
5	2	$2 \times \mathbf{5} + 2 \times \mathbf{2} \rightarrow$ ____ $+$ ____ $\rightarrow$ ____ $\rightarrow$	Substitute values. Multiply first. Add.
9	6	$2 \times$ ____ $+ 2 \times$ ____ $\rightarrow$ ____ $+$ ____ $\rightarrow$ ____ $\rightarrow$	Substitute. Multiply first. Add.

Fill in the missing values in the table above.

Check your work.

Did you get a result of 14 when $l = 5$ and $w = 2$?

Did you get a result of 30 when $l = 9$ and $w = 6$?

Use the given values to complete each table.

1.

r	$2(3 + r)$
2	
3	
4	

2.

c	t	$2c + t$
4	2	
6	3	
8	4	

3.

w	k	$w^2 - k$
2	1	
5	2	
8	3	

LESSON
11-3

Generating Equivalent Expressions

Practice and Problem Solving: A/B

Justify each step used to simplify the expression.

1. $3x + 2y - 2x + 2 = 3x - 2x + 2y + 2$ _____

2. $= (3x - 2x) + 2y + 2$ _____

3. $= (3 - 2)x + 2y + 2$ _____

4. $= x + 2y + 2$ _____

Simplify.

5. $3r + n^2 - r + 5 - 2n + 2$ _____

6. $8v + w + 7 - 8v + 2w$ _____

7. $4c^2 + 6c - 3c^2 - 2c - 3$ _____

8. $z^3 + 5z + 3z^2 + 1 - 4 - 2z^2$ _____

Write and simplify an expression for the perimeter of each figure.

9.
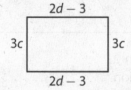

10.
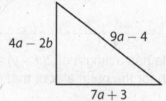

_____   _____

11. A square has sides of $10x$. Write and simplify an expression for the perimeter of that square.

_____

12. A rectangle has a length of $2x + 7$ and a width of $3x + 8y$. Write and simplify an expression for the perimeter of that rectangle.

_____

13. In the space at the right, draw a triangle. Use an algebraic expression to label the length of each side. Write an expression for the perimeter of your triangle. Then simplify that expression.

_____

LESSON 11-3

Generating Equivalent Expressions

Practice and Problem Solving: C

Simplify.

1. $3a + a^2 + 5(a - 2)$ _____

2. $8(v + w) - 7(v + 2w)$ _____

3. $4c^2 + 6(c - c^2) - 2c$ _____

4. $z^3 + 5(z + 3) - 4(2 - 2z^2)$ _____

Write and simplify an expression for the perimeter of each figure.

5.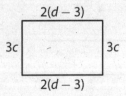

6.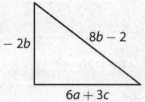

_____ _____

7. A square has sides of $x - 0.4$. Write an expression for the perimeter of that square. Simplify the expression.

_____

8. A rectangle has a length of $2(x + y)$ and a width of $3(x - y)$. Write an expression for the perimeter of that rectangle. Simplify the expression.

_____

Solve.

9. Peter collected soup for the food pantry. He packed 6 small boxes with n cans of soup in each box. He packed 4 boxes with twice as many cans as in the small boxes. Write and simplify an expression for the number of cans that Peter packed.

_____

10. Netta faxed n pages from the library. The library charges $1.50 per page. Later the same day, Netta faxed n more pages from a local copy shop. The copy shop charges $1.25 per page plus a $2 convenience fee. Write and simplify an expression for the amount Netta spent on faxes that day.

_____

Name _____ Date _____ Class_____

LESSON 11-3

Generating Equivalent Expressions

Practice and Problem Solving: D

Identify like terms in each list. The first one is done for you.

1. $5a$ b 43 $2a$ b^2 $2b$ 4 $\underline{5a \text{ and } 2a;\ b \text{ and } 2b;\ 43 \text{ and } 4}$

2. n $4n^3$ $2m$ $6m$ $5n$ $2n$ _____

3. $2d$ $5f$ $2g$ 7 $3g$ g _____

4. $7x^2$ x $3x^2$ 2 y^2 3 $3x$ _____

Combine like terms to simplify. The first one is done for you.

5. $4r + 5n^2 - 3r + 9 - 2n - 2$ $\underline{r + 5n^2 + 7 - 2n}$

6. $3v + w + 8 - 2v + 2$ _____

7. $8c^2 + 6c - 2c^2 - 5c$ _____

8. $z + 5e + 3z + 13 - 8 - 2e$ _____

Perimeter is the distance around a figure. Write an expression for the perimeter of each figure. Be sure to combine like terms. The first one is done for you.

9.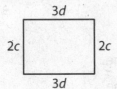

10.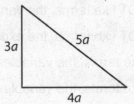

 $6d + 4c$

Circle the letter of the correct answer.

11. A square has sides of $6x$. Which expression shows the perimeter of that square?

    A $6x$

    B $12x$

    C $24x$

    D $36x$

12. A rectangle has a length of $4x + 5$ and a width of $8x - 4$. Which expression shows the perimeter of that rectangle?

    A $4x + 1$

    B $12x - 2$

    C $12x + 1$

    D $24x + 2$

Generating Equivalent Expressions
Reteach

Look at the following expressions: $x = 1x$
$$x + x = 2x$$
$$x + x + x = 3x$$

The numbers 1, 2, and 3 are called **coefficients** of x.

Identify each coefficient.

1. $8x$ ____

2. $3m$ ____

3. y ____

4. $14t$ ____

An algebraic expression has terms that are separated by $+$ and $-$.
In the expression $2x + 5y$, the **terms** are $2x$ and $5y$.

Expression	Terms
$8x + 4y$	$8x$ and $4y$
$5m - 2m + 9$	$5m$, $2m$, and 9
$4a^2 - 2b + c - 2a^2$	$4a^2$, $2b$, c, and $2a^2$

Sometimes the terms of an expression can be combined.
Only **like terms** can be combined.

$2x + 2y$ NOT like terms, the variables are different.

$4a^2 - 2a$ NOT like terms, the exponents are different.

$5m - 2m$ Like terms, the variables and exponents are both the same.

$n^3 + 2n^3$ Like terms, the variables and exponents are both the same.

To **simplify** an expression, combine like terms by adding or subtracting
the coefficients of the variable.

$5m - 2m = 3m$

$4a^2 + 5a + a + 3 = 4a^2 + 6a + 3$ Note that the coefficient of a is 1.

Simplify.

5. $8x + 2x$

6. $3m - m$

7. $6y + 6y$

8. $14t - 3t$

_____

_____

_____

_____

9. $3b + b + 6$

10. $9a - 3a + 4$

11. $n + 5n - 3c$

12. $12d - 2d + e$

_____

_____

_____

_____

Generating Equivalent Expressions

LESSON 11-3

Reading Strategies: Organization Patterns

An algebraic expression is made up of parts called **terms**.

constants	variables	constants and variables
$3.2 \quad \frac{1}{2} \quad 12$	$m \quad s \quad x$	$4x \quad \frac{n}{2} \quad 3m^2 \quad \frac{2}{3}y$

A **coefficient** is a value multiplied by a variable.

Term	Value of Coefficient	Meaning
$7x$	7	$7 \bullet x$
y	1	$1 \bullet y$
$\frac{n}{2}$	$\frac{1}{2}$	$\frac{1}{2} \bullet n$

The expression below has 6 terms. Terms are separated by + and −.

Term	Term	Term	Term	Term	Term
↓	↓	↓	↓	↓	↓
$2x \quad +$	$5b \quad +$	$7 \quad -$	$b \quad +$	$3x \quad +$	$2x^2$

Like terms have **both** the same variable **and** the same exponent.
Like terms can have different coefficients.

Like Terms	Unlike Terms
$2y$ and $3y$ $\quad$ $4b$ and b $\quad$ $4n^2$ and $2n^2$	$3x$ and $2x^2$ $\quad$ $4x$ and b $\quad$ $7n$ and $7m$

You can **simplify** an algebraic expression. To do that, you **combine** like terms.

First, reorganize the terms so like terms are together: $\quad 2x + 3x + 5b - b + 7 + 2x^2$

Then add or subtract coefficients to combine like terms: $\quad 5x \quad + \quad 4b \quad + 7 + 2x^2$

Solve.

1. How many terms are there in this expression: $6b + b^2 + 5 + 2b - 3f$? ____ terms

2. $6b$ and b^2 are unlike terms. Explain why.

_____

Use $5a^2 + 6b + a^2 - 3b - 2 + 4c$ for Exercises 3–5.

3. How many terms are there in the expression? ____ terms

4. Reorganize the terms so like terms are together. _____

5. Combine like terms to rewrite the expression. _____

Generating Equivalent Expressions
Success for English Learners

Problem 1

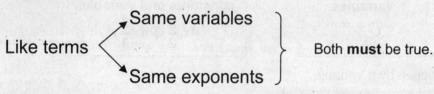

Like terms
- Same variables
- Same exponents

Both **must** be true.

$6x^2$ and $2x^3$ ⟶ Same variables, different exponents, so **NOT like terms**

$4x^4$ and $5y^4$ ⟶ Different variables, same exponents, so **NOT like terms**

$3a^3$ and $6a^3$ ⟶ Same variables, same exponents, so **like terms**

Problem 2

Combining like terms

$8w + 9w$	Like terms
$8w + 9w$	Identify coefficients.
$17w$	Add ONLY the coefficients.

$7n^3 - n^3$	Like terms
$7n^3 - 1n^3$	Identify coefficients.
$6n^3$	Subtract ONLY the coefficients.

Answer the questions below.

1. Can you combine the terms $6x^2$ and $2x^3$ shown in Problem 1? If you can, then combine the terms. If you cannot, explain why not.

   _____

2. Can you combine the terms $4x^4$ and $5y^4$ shown in Problem 1? If you can, then combine the terms. If you cannot, explain why not.

   _____

3. Can you combine the terms $3a^3$ and $6a^3$ shown in Problem 1? If you can, then combine the terms. If you cannot, explain why not.

   _____

4. When a term has no number in front of the variable, what is the coefficient of that variable?

   _____

Name _____ Date _____ Class _____

 Generating Equivalent Algebraic Expressions
MODULE 11 *Challenge*

Areas of Regular Figures

Regular polygons have equal side lengths and angle measures. Regular polyhedra are three-dimensional. Each regular polyhedron has congruent regular polygons for its faces. Four of these shapes are shown in the figures.

Identify each regular polygon. Then evaluate the area expression to find its area for a side length *s* of 5 centimeters.

	Number of Sides	Name	Area Expression	Area for *s* = 5 cm
1.	3		$\frac{s^2}{4}\sqrt{3}$	
2.	4		s^2	
3.	5		$\frac{s^2}{4}\sqrt{25 + 10\sqrt{5}}$	
4.	6		$\frac{3s^2}{2}\sqrt{3}$	
5.	8		$2s^2(\sqrt{2} + 1)$	
6.	10		$\frac{5s^2}{2}\sqrt{5 + 2\sqrt{5}}$	

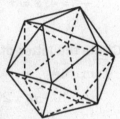
icosahedron

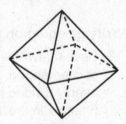
octahedron

Use the figures to identify each regular polyhedra. Then write an expression for its surface area for an edge length *s*.

	Number of Faces	Name	Surface Area for Edge Length *s*
7.	4 triangles		
8.	6 squares		
9.	8 triangles		
10.	12 pentagons		
11.	20 triangles		

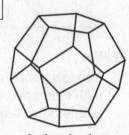
dodecahedron

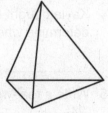
tetrahedron

LESSON 12-1

Writing Equations to Represent Situations
Practice and Problem Solving: A/B

Determine whether the given value is a solution of the equation. Write *yes* or *no*.

1. $x + 11 = 15$; $x = 4$ _____

2. $36 - w = 10$; $w = 20$ _____

3. $0.2v = 1.2$; $v = 10$ _____

4. $15 = 6 + d$; $d = 8$ _____

5. $28 - w = 25$; $w = 3$ _____

6. $4t = 32$; $t = 8$ _____

7. $\dfrac{12}{s} = 4$; $s = 3$ _____

8. $\dfrac{33}{p} = 3$; $p = 11$ _____

Circle the letter of the equation that each given solution makes true.

9. $m = 19$

   A $10 + m = 20$ C $7m = 26$

   B $m - 4 = 15$ D $\dfrac{18}{m} = 2$

10. $a = 16$

   A $2a = 18$ C $24 - a = 6$

   B $a + 12 = 24$ D $\dfrac{a}{4} = 4$

Write an equation to represent each situation.

11. Seventy-two people signed up for the soccer league. After the players were evenly divided into teams, there were 6 teams in the league and x people on each team.

_____

12. Mary covered her kitchen floor with 10 tiles. The floor measures 6 feet long by 5 feet wide. The tiles are each 3 feet long and w feet wide.

_____

Solve.

13. The low temperature was 35°F. This was 13°F lower than the daytime high temperature. Write an equation to determine whether the high temperature was 48°F or 42°F.

_____

14. Kayla bought 16 bagels. She paid a total of $20. Write an equation to determine whether each bagel cost $1.50 or $1.25.

_____

15. Write a real-world situation that could be modeled by the equation $\dfrac{24}{y} = 3$. Then solve the problem.

_____

LESSON
12-1

Writing Equations to Represent Situations
Practice and Problem Solving: C

Circle the letter of the value that makes each equation true.

1. $\dfrac{18}{m} = 15 - 12$

    A $m = 6$ C $m = 9$

    B $m = 3$ D $m = 2$

2. $6d = 8(12 - 6)$

    A $d = 18$ C $d = 8$

    B $d = 48$ D $d = 4$

3. $x = \dfrac{14 - 6}{2}$

    A $x = 6$ C $x = 16$

    B $x = 8$ D $x = 4$

4. $\dfrac{a}{4} = 3(10 \div 2)$

    A $a = 15$ C $a = 40$

    B $a = 60$ D $a = 20$

For Exercises 5–7, use the table at the right that shows how many minutes certain mammals can stay underwater.

Animal	Min
Hippopotamus	15
Platypus	10
Sea Cow	
Seal	22
Sperm Whale	112

5. A sperm whale can stay under water 7 times longer than *x* minutes more than a platypus can. Write an equation that states the relationship of the minutes these two mammals can stay under water.

_____

6. A sea cow can stay under water *y* minutes. This is 11 minutes longer than one-third the time a hippopotamus can. Write an equation that states the relationship of the minutes these two mammals can stay under water. Complete the table with 16 or 56.

_____

7. Write an equation that includes division that relates the number of minutes a seal can stay under water to the number of minutes a sperm whale can stay under water.

_____

Solve.

8. Mr. Sosha teaches 4 math classes, with the same number of students in each class. Of those students, 80 are sixth graders and 40 are fifth graders. Write an equation to determine whether there are 22, 25, or 30 students in each class. How many are in each class?

_____

9. Write an equation that involves multiplication, addition, contains a variable, and has a solution of 8.

_____

Writing Equations to Represent Situations

Practice and Problem Solving: D

Is the given value of the variable a solution of the equation?
Write *yes* or *no*. The first one is done for you.

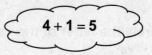

$4 + 1 = 5$

1. $x + 1 = 5; x = 4$ _____**yes**_____

2. $13 - w = 10; w = 2$ _____

3. $2v = 12; v = 10$ _____

4. $\dfrac{14}{p} = 2; p = 7$ _____

5. $8 + w = 11; w = 3$ _____

6. $4t = 20; t = 5$ _____

Circle the letter of the equation that each given solution makes true.
The first one is done for you.

7. $x = 5$
   Ⓐ $2 + x = 7$
   B $9 - x = 3$
   C $3x = 18$

$2 + 5 = 7$

8. $g = 7$
   A $9g = 16$
   B $8 - g = 1$
   C $11 + g = 17$

9. $y = 2$
   A $7 - y = 1$
   B $3y = 6$
   C $\dfrac{10}{y} = 20$

10. $m = 9$
   A $m - 4 = 13$
   B $7m = 36$
   C $\dfrac{18}{m} = 2$

11. $z = 4$
   A $5z = 20$
   B $\dfrac{12}{z} = 4$
   C $z - 3 = 7$

12. $a = 8$
   A $2a = 10$
   B $a + 12 = 20$
   C $\dfrac{a}{4} = 4$

13. Rhonda has $13. She has one $5 bill, three $1 bills, and one
    other bill. Is the other bill a $1 bill or a $5 bill? Explain.

    __(1)$5__ + (3)_____ + Other bill = $ _____

_____

_____

LESSON 12-1 Writing Equations to Represent Situations
Reteach

An **equation** is a mathematical sentence that says that two quantities are equal.

Some equations contain variables. A **solution** for an equation is a value for a variable that makes the statement true.

You can write related facts using addition and subtraction.
$7 + 6 = 13$ $13 - 6 = 7$

You can write related facts using multiplication and division.
$3 \bullet 4 = 12$ $\frac{12}{4} = 3$

You can use related facts to find solutions for equations. If the related fact matches the value for the variable, then that value is a solution.

A. $x + 5 = 9$; $x = 3$
   Think: $9 - 5 = x$
              $4 = x$
              $4 \neq 3$
   3 is **not** a solution of $x + 5 = 9$.

B. $x - 7 = 5$; $x = 12$
   Think: $5 + 7 = x$
              $12 = x$
              $12 = 12$
   12 is a solution of $x - 7 = 5$.

C. $2x = 14$; $x = 9$
   Think: $14 \div 2 = x$
              $7 = x$
              $7 \neq 9$
   9 is **not** a solution of $2x = 14$.

D. $\frac{x}{5} = 3$; $x = 15$
   Think: $3 \bullet 5 = x$
              $15 = x$
              $15 = 15$
   15 is a solution of $x \div 5 = 3$.

Use related facts to determine whether the given value is a solution for each equation.

1. $x + 6 = 14$; $x = 8$

2. $\frac{s}{4} = 5$; $s = 24$

3. $g - 3 = 7$; $g = 11$

_____

4. $3a = 18$; $a = 6$

5. $26 = y - 9$; $y = 35$

6. $b \bullet 5 = 20$; $b = 3$

_____

7. $15 = \frac{v}{3}$; $v = 45$

8. $11 = p + 6$; $p = 5$

9. $6k = 78$; $k = 12$

_____

LESSON 12-1

Writing Equations to Represent Situations

Reading Strategies: Build Vocabulary

You can see part of the word **equal** in **equation**. In math, an equation indicates that two expressions have the same value, or are equal. The = **sign** in an equation separates one expression from the other. The value on each side of the = sign is the same.

Look at the equations below. Notice how the value on each side of the = sign is the same for each equation:

$$5 + 7 = 8 + 4 \qquad 19 - 7 = 12 \qquad 42 = 3 \bullet 14$$

If an equation contains a variable, and the variable is replaced by a value that keeps the equation equal, that value is called a **solution** of the equation.

Determine whether 80 or 60 is a solution to $\frac{y}{4} = 15$

$$\frac{y}{4} = 15 \qquad\qquad\qquad \frac{y}{4} = 15$$

$$\frac{80}{4} \overset{?}{=} 15 \qquad\qquad\qquad \frac{60}{4} \overset{?}{=} 15$$

$$20 \overset{?}{=} 15 \qquad\qquad\qquad 15 \overset{?}{=} 15$$

"20 is **not** equal to 15."   "15 is equal to 15."

Which are equations? Write *yes* or *no*.

1. $7 + 23 \overset{?}{=} 9 + 21$ _____

2. $35 + 15 \overset{?}{=} 45$ _____

3. $28 - 7 \overset{?}{=} 15 + 6$ _____

Replace the given value for the variable. Is it a solution? Write *yes* or *no*.

4. $d + 28 = 45$; $d = 17$

_____

5. $\frac{84}{s} = 28$; $s = 3$

6. $17 = 56 - t$; $t = 40$

_____

7. $86 = 4w$; $w = 24$

Solve.

8. Use the numbers 2, 11, 13, and 15 to write an equation.

_____

9. Replace one of the numbers in your equation in Exercise 8 with the variable *y*. Determine whether 2, 11, 13, or 15 is a solution of your equation.

_____

_____

LESSON 12-1
Writing Equations to Represent Situations
Success for English Learners

Problem

Determine whether 61 or 59 is a solution of the equation $a + 23 = 82$.

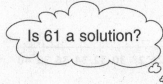 Is 61 a solution?

$a + 23 = 82$

$61 + 23 \overset{?}{=} 82$ Replace a with 61.

$84 \neq 82$

These are NOT equal.
61 is NOT a solution.

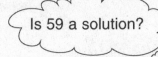 Is 59 a solution?

$a + 23 = 82$

$59 + 23 \overset{?}{=} 82$ Replace a with 59.

$82 = 82$

These are equal.
59 is a solution.

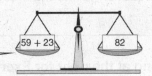

1. How do you know that 61 is not a solution of $a + 23 = 82$?

_____

_____

2. How can you find out whether 65 is a solution of $a + 23 = 82$?

_____

_____

3. Write a real-world situation that could be modeled by $a + 23 = 82$.

_____

_____

_____

LESSON 12-2

Addition and Subtraction Equations

Practice and Problem Solving: A/B

Solve each equation. Graph the solution on the number line.

1. $6 = r + 2$ $r =$ _____
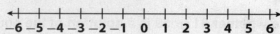

2. $26 = w - 12$ $w =$ _____

3. $\dfrac{1}{2} = m - \dfrac{1}{8}$ $m =$ _____

4. $t + 1 = -3$ $t =$ _____

Use the drawing at the right for Exercises 5–6.

5. Write an equation to represent the measures of the angles.

   _____

6. Solve the equation to find the measure of the unknown angle.

   _____

Use the drawing at the right for Exercises 7–8.

7. Write an equation to represent the measures of the angles.

   _____

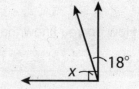

8. Solve the equation to find the measure of the unknown angle.

   _____

Write a problem for the equation $3 + x = 8$. Then solve the equation and write the answer to your problem.

9. _____

   _____

   _____

LESSON 12-2

Addition and Subtraction Equations

Practice and Problem Solving: C

Solve each equation.

1. $b + 2.3 = 5.7$ $b =$ ____

2. $s - \dfrac{1}{3} = \dfrac{4}{9}$ $s =$ ____

3. $6\dfrac{1}{2} + n = 12$ $n =$ ____

4. $15.35 = z - 1.84$ $z =$ ____

5. $d + (-3) = -7$ $d =$ ____

6. $12 = g + 52$ $g =$ ____

Use the drawing at the right for Exercises 7–8.

7. Write an equation to represent the measures of the angles.

   _____

8. Solve the equation to find the measure of the unknown angle.

   _____

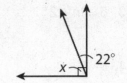

Write and solve an equation to answer each question.

9. Kayla is 13 years old. Her uncle says that his age minus 22 is equal to Kayla's age. How old is Kayla's uncle?

   _____

10. Gavin wants to buy a jacket that sells for $38.95. An advertisement says that next week that jacket will be on sale for $22.50. How much will Gavin save if he waits until next week to buy the jacket?

   _____

11. Sierra sawed $10\dfrac{1}{2}$ inches off the end of a board. The remaining board

   was $37\dfrac{1}{2}$ inches long. How long was the board that Sierra started with?

   _____

Write a problem for the equation $4.65 = x - 2.35$. Then solve the equation and write the answer to your problem.

12. _____

   _____

   _____

   _____

LESSON 12-2

Addition and Subtraction Equations

Practice and Problem Solving: D

**Solve each equation. Graph the solution on the number line.
The first one is done for you.**

1. $5 = r - 1$ $r = \underline{\ 6\ }$

   $5 = r - 1$

   $\underline{+1 \quad +1}$

   $6 = r$

   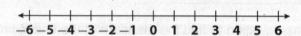

2. $2 = w + 3$ $w = \underline{\quad}$

3. $5 = m + 2$ $m = \underline{\quad}$

4. $t - 5 = 0$ $t = \underline{\quad}$

Use the drawings at the right for Exercises 5–8. The first one has been done for you.

5. Write an equation to represent the measures of the angles.

   $\underline{\quad\quad x + 100 = 180 \quad\quad}$

   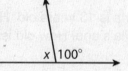

6. Solve the equation to find the measure of the unknown angle.

   _____

7. Mayumi has the boxes shown at the right. The total number of objects in two of the boxes is the same as the number of objects in the third box. Write an equation to show the relationship of the number of objects in the boxes.

   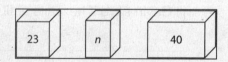

   _____

8. How many objects are in the box marked n? ____ objects

Write a problem for the equation $x - 5 = 2$. Then solve the equation and write the answer to your problem.

9. _____

   _____

   _____

Addition and Subtraction Equations

LESSON 12-2

Reteach

To solve an equation, you need to get the variable alone on one side of the equal sign.

You can use tiles to help you solve subtraction equations.

Variable	**+1** add 1	**−1** subtract 1

Addition undoes subtraction, so you can use addition to solve subtraction equations.

One positive tile and one negative tile make a **zero pair**.

Zero pair: $+1 + (-1) = 0$

add 1 → **+1**
subtract 1 → **−1** make zero

To solve $x - 4 = 2$, first use tiles to model the equation.

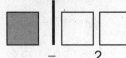

$x \quad - \quad 4 \quad = \quad 2$

To get the variable alone, you have to add positive tiles. Remember to add the same number of positive tiles to each side of the equation.

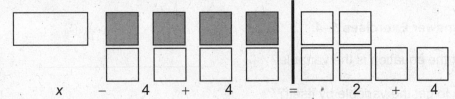

$x \quad - \quad 4 \quad + \quad 4 \quad = \quad 2 \quad + \quad 4$

Then remove the greatest possible number of zero pairs from each side of the equal sign.

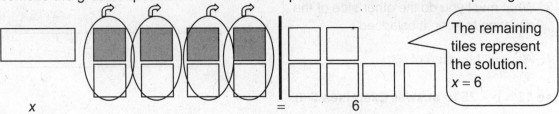

$x \quad = \quad 6$

The remaining tiles represent the solution. $x = 6$

Use tiles to solve each equation.

1. $x - 5 = 3$ $x = $____

2. $x - 2 = 7$ $x = $____

3. $x - 1 = 4$ $x = $____

4. $x - 8 = 1$ $x = $____

4. $x - 3 = 3$ $x = $____

6. $x - 6 = 2$ $x = $____

Name _____ Date _____ Class_____

Addition and Subtraction Equations
Reading Strategies: Use a Visual Clue

You can picture balanced scales to solve subtraction equations.
Picture balanced scales for this equation.

Step 1: To find the value of b, get b by itself on the left side of the equation. So, add 17 to the left side of the equation.

$$b - 17 = 65$$

Step 2: To keep the equation balanced, add 17 to the right side of the equation as well.

$$b - 17 + 17 = 65 + 17$$

Step 3: Check to verify that $b = 82$ is the solution.

$$b - 17 = 65$$
$$82 - 17 \overset{?}{=} 65$$
$$65 \overset{?}{=} 65 \checkmark$$

$$b = 82$$

To get the variable by itself in a subtraction equation, add the same value to both sides of the equation.

Use $n - 21 = 32$ to answer Exercises 1–4.

1. On which side of the equation is the variable? _____

2. What will you do to get the variable by itself? _____

3. What must you do the other side of the equation to keep it balanced? _____

4. What is the value of n? _____

Use $12 = p - 25$ to answer Exercises 5–8.

5. On which side of the equation is the variable? _____

6. What will you do to get the variable by itself? _____

7. What must you do the other side of the equation to keep it balanced? _____

8. What is the value of p? _____

Original content Copyright © by Houghton Mifflin Harcourt. Additions and changes to the original content are the responsibility of the instructor.

LESSON 12-2 Addition and Subtraction Equations
Success for English Learners

Problem 1

The surfboard is 14 inches
taller than the person.
How tall is the person?

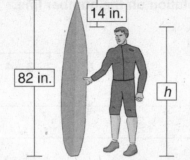

14 in.

82 in.

h

Height of person

Surfboard height

Think: This is
an addition
equation.
I subtract to
undo the
addition.

$h + 14 = 82$

$\underline{-14 \quad -14}$

$h = 68$

Subtract 14 from both sides.

The person is
68 inches tall.

$68 + 14 = 82$ ✓ Check your answer.

Problem 2

Think: This is a
subtraction equation.
I add to undo the
subtraction.

$x - 21 = 36$

$\underline{+21 \quad +21}$

$x = 57$

Add 21 to both sides.

1. Why do you use an addition equation to find the surfer's height?

_____

_____

2. How can you check the answer to Problem 2?

_____

_____

3. Write an addition or a subtraction equation. Explain how to solve your
   equation. Give the solution to your equation.

_____

_____

Name _____ Date _____ Class _____

Multiplication and Division Equations

Practice and Problem Solving: A/B

Solve each equation. Graph the solution on the number line.
Check your work.

1. $\frac{e}{2} = 3$ $e =$ ___

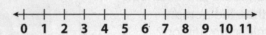

_____

_____

2. $20 = 2w$ $w =$ ___

_____

_____

3. $\frac{1}{2} = 2m$ $m =$ ___

_____

_____

4. $\frac{k}{5} = 2$ $k =$ ___

_____

_____

Use the drawing at the right for Exercises 5–6.

5. Write an equation you can use to find the length of the rectangle.

_____

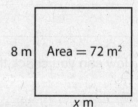

8 m   Area = 72 m²

x m

6. Solve the equation. Give the length of the rectangle.

_____

Solve.

7. Alise separated her pictures into 3 piles. Each pile contained
9 pictures. How many pictures did she have in all? Write and solve an
equation to represent the problem. State the answer to the problem.

_____

_____

LESSON 12-3

Multiplication and Division Equations

Practice and Problem Solving: C

Solve each equation.

1. $8b = 5.6$ $b = $ ____

2. $9 = \dfrac{s}{3}$ $s = $ ____

3. $2\dfrac{1}{2} = 5n$ $n = $ ____

4. $15 = 0.2z$ $z = $ ____

5. $3.5d = 70$ $d = $ ____

6. $\dfrac{t}{3} = \dfrac{4}{9}$ $t = $ ____

Use the drawing at the right for Exercises 7.

7. The perimeter of the square at the right is 48 inches. What is the area of the square at the right? Explain how you found your answer.

s perimeter $= 48$ in.

s

_____

_____

_____

Write and solve an equation to answer each question.

8. Jose is making model SUVs. Each SUV takes 5 tires. He used 85 tires for the models. How many model SUVs did Jose make?

_____

9. Renee talked for 6 minutes on the phone. Nathan talked for n minutes. Nathan talked three times as long as Renee. How long did Nathan talk?

_____

10. Sylvia rented a boat for $16.50 per hour. Her total rental fee was $49.50. For how many hours did Sylvia rent the boat?

_____

Write a problem for the equation $0.5n = 12.5$. Then solve the equation and write the answer to your problem.

11. _____

_____

_____

_____

Name _____ Date _____ Class_____

 LESSON 12-3

Multiplication and Division Equations
Practice and Problem Solving: D

Solve each equation. Graph the solution on the number line.
Check your work. The first is done for you.

1. $8 = 2m$ $m = \underline{\ 4\ }$

$$\frac{8}{2} = \frac{2m}{2}$$

$4 = m$ $8 = 2 \cdot 4\ \checkmark$

2. $\frac{a}{4} = 2$ $a = \underline{\ \ \ }$

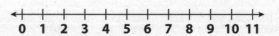

_____

_____

3. $12 = 3s$ $s = \underline{\ \ \ }$

_____

_____

4. $\frac{u}{2} = 5$ $u = \underline{\ \ \ }$

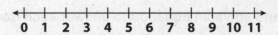

_____

_____

Use the situation below to complete Exercises 5–8.
The first one is done for you.

Jim knows the length of his garden is 12 feet. He knows the area of the garden is 60 ft². What is the width of Jim's garden?

5. Fill in the known values in the picture at the right.

6. Write an equation you can use to solve the problem.

_____

7. Solve the equation. $w = \underline{\ \ \ }$

8. Write the solution to the problem.

_____

w ft $\boxed{A = 60 \text{ ft}^2}$

$\underline{12}$ ft

**LESSON
12-3**

Multiplication and Division Equations
Reteach

Number lines can be used to solve multiplication and division equations.

Solve: $3n = 15$

How many moves of 3 does it take to get to 15?

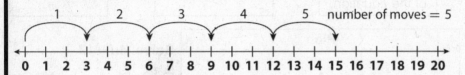

$n = 5$ Check: $3 \bullet 5 = 15$✓

Solve: $\dfrac{n}{3} = 4$

If you make 3 moves of 4, where are you on the number line?

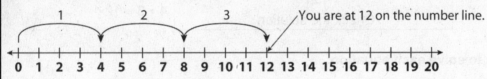

You are at 12 on the number line.

$n = 12$ Check: $12 \div 3 = 4$✓

Show the moves you can use to solve each equation. Then give the solution to the equation and check your work.

1. $3n = 9$

<++++++++++++++++++++>
0 1 2 3 4 5 6 7 8 9 10 11

Solution: $n =$ ____

Show your check:

2. $\dfrac{n}{2} = 4$

<++++++++++++++++++++>
0 1 2 3 4 5 6 7 8 9 10 11

Solution: $n =$ ____

Show your check:

LESSON 12-3

Solving Equations

Reading Strategies: Use a Flowchart

A flowchart gives you a plan. You can use a flowchart to solve equations.

| **1** Decide how to get the variable by itself. | ⇨ | **2** Do the same on both sides of the equation. | ⇨ | **3** Solve the equation. | ⇨ | **4** Check the solution. |

Solve: $\dfrac{x}{6} = 4$

Think: Multiplying by 6 undoes dividing by 6.

$\dfrac{x}{6} \bullet 6 = 4 \bullet 6$

$x = 24$

$\dfrac{24}{6} = 4\checkmark$

Plan

1 Decide on what operation to use.

2 Do the same on both sides.

3 Solve the equation.

4 Check the solution.

Solve: $4n = 12$

Think: Dividing by 4 undoes multiplying by 4.

$\dfrac{4n}{4} = \dfrac{12}{4}$

$n = 3$

$4 \bullet 3 = 12\checkmark$

Use the flowchart to solve each equation.

1.

Plan	Solve: $3r = 24$
1 Decide on what operation to use.	
2 Do the same on both sides.	
3 Solve the equation.	
4 Check the solution.	

2.

Plan	Solve: $\dfrac{b}{8} = 16$
1 Decide on what operation to use.	
2 Do the same on both sides.	
3 Solve the equation.	
4 Check the solution.	

LESSON 12-3

Multiplication and Division Equations

Success for English Learners

Problem 1

Some armadillo mothers had these babies.

Each mother had 4 babies. How many mothers were there?

┌─────────────────┐   ┌─────────────┐
│ 4 babies for   │   │ 32 babies   │
│ each mother   │   │   │
└─────────────────┘   └─────────────┘

$4m = 32$

┌──────────────────┐
│ To undo   │
│ multiplication, │
│ use division.   │
└──────────────────┘

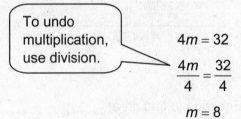

$4m = 32$

$\dfrac{4m}{4} = \dfrac{32}{4}$

$m = 8$

There are 8 mothers.

Problem 2

┌────────────────────────────┐
│ Think: This is a division │
│ equation. I multiply to undo │
│ the multiplication.   │
└────────────────────────────┘

$\dfrac{x}{6} = 12$

$\dfrac{x \bullet 6}{6} = 12 \bullet 6$ Multiply each side by 6.

$x = 72$

$72 \div 6 = 12$ ✓   The answer checks.

1. Explain how to check the solution to Problem 1.

_____

_____

2. Solve $\dfrac{n}{3} = 2$. Show your work.

   Check your work.

3. Solve $5t = 20$. Show your work.
   Check your work.

MODULE 12 **Equations and Relationships**
Challenge

Write and solve an equation to find the unknown measurement. Then use your answer to find the perimeter of each field or court.

> **Remember**
> Area = length • width or $A = l • w$
> Perimeter is the distance around
> or $P = 2l + 2w$

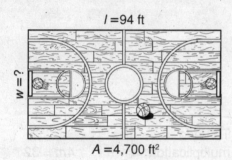

$l = 94$ ft
$w = ?$
$A = 4,700$ ft²

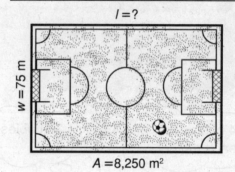

$l = ?$
$w = 75$ m
$A = 8,250$ m²

1. Equation to find area: _____

   Unknown measurement: _____

   Equation to find perimeter:

   $P =$ _____

   Perimeter of court: _____

2. Equation to find area: _____

   Unknown measurement: _____

   Equation to find perimeter:

   $P =$ _____

   Perimeter of field: _____

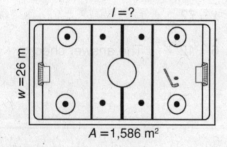

$l = ?$
$w = 26$ m
$A = 1,586$ m²

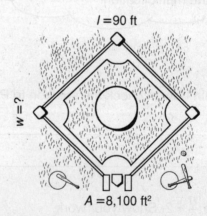

$l = 90$ ft
$w = ?$
$A = 8,100$ ft²

3. Equation to find area: _____

   Unknown measurement: _____

   $P =$ _____

   Perimeter of rink: _____

4. Equation to find area: _____

   Unknown measurement: _____

   $P =$ _____

   Perimeter of diamond: _____

Name _____ Date _____ Class_____

Writing Inequalities

Practice and Problem Solving: A/B

Complete the graph for each inequality.

1. $a > 3$

2. $r \le -2$

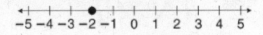

Graph the solutions of each inequality. Check the solutions.

3. $w \ge 0$

Check: _____

4. $b \le -4$

Check: _____

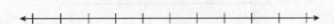

5. $a < 1.5$

Check: _____

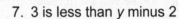

Write an inequality that represents each phrase. Draw a graph to represent the inequality.

6. the sum of 1 and x is less than 5

_____

7. 3 is less than y minus 2

_____

Write and graph an inequality to represent each situation.

8. The temperature today will be at least 10°F. _____

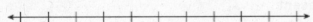

9. Ben wants to spend no more than $3. _____

Write an inequality that matches the number line model.

10. _____

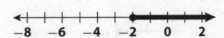

11. _____

LESSON 13-1

Writing Inequalities

Practice and Problem Solving: C

Circle the values that are solutions for each inequality.

1. $a > -2$

    -3.5 -1 0 $4\frac{1}{4}$

2. $r \leq 2$

    -3.5 -1 0 $4\frac{1}{4}$

Graph the solutions of each inequality. Check the solutions.

3. $4 \geq y$

    Check: _____

4. $b \leq 0.5$

    Check: _____

5. $a < 1 - 3$

    Check: _____

Write and graph an inequality to represent each situation. Then determine if 36 is a possible solution. Write *yes* or *no*.

6. The temperature today will be at least 35°F. _____

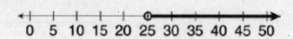

7. Monica wants to spend no more than $35. _____

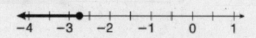

Write an inequality that matches the number line model. Then write a situation that the inequality could represent.

8. _____

       0 5 10 15 20 25 30 35 40 45 50

_____

_____

9. _____

      -4 -3 -2 -1 0 1

_____

_____

LESSON 13-1

Writing Inequalities
Practice and Problem Solving: D

Complete the graph for each inequality. The first one is done for you.

1. $a > 2$

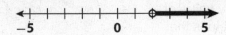

2. $r \leq -1$

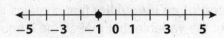

Graph the solutions of each inequality. Check the solutions. The first one is done for you.

3. $m \geq -2$

Check: ___**0 ≥ –2; this is true**___

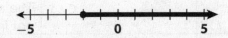

4. $d \leq 3$

Check: _____

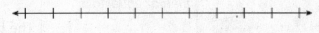

5. $s < -3$

Check: _____

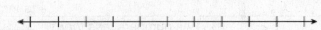

Write an inequality that represents each phrase. Draw a graph to represent the inequality. The first one is done for you.

6. x is less than 4

7. -1 is greater than y

_____**x < 4**_____

_____

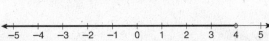

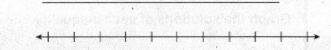

Write and graph an inequality to represent each situation. The first one is done for you.

8. Today's temperature is greater than 0°F. ___**t > 0**___

9. Lyle paid more than $2 for lunch. _____

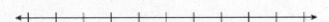

Name _____ Date _____ Class _____

Writing Inequalities
Reteach

An equation is a statement that says two quantities are equal. An **inequality** is a statement that says two quantities are **not** equal.

A **solution of an inequality** that contains a variable is any value or values of the variable that makes the inequality true. All values that make the inequality true can be shown on a graph.

Inequality	Meaning	Solution of Inequality
$x > 3$	All numbers *greater than* 3	 -5 -4 -3 -2 -1 0 1 2 3 4 5 The *open circle* at 3 shows that the value 3 is **not** included in the solution.
$x \geq 3$	All numbers *greater than or equal to* 3	 -5 -4 -3 -2 -1 0 1 2 3 4 5 The *closed circle* at 3 shows that the value 3 **is** included in the solution.
$x < 3$	All numbers *less than* 3	 -5 -4 -3 -2 -1 0 1 2 3 4 5
$x \leq 3$	All numbers *less than or equal to* 3	 -5 -4 -3 -2 -1 0 1 2 3 4 5

Graph the solutions of each inequality.

1. $x > -4$

• Draw an open circle at –4.

• Read $x > -4$ as "x is greater than –4."

• Draw an arrow to the right of –4.

-5 -4 -3 -2 -1 0 1 2 3 4 5

2. $x \leq 1$

• Draw a closed circle at 1.

• Read $x \leq 1$ as "x is less than or equal to 1."

• Draw an arrow to the left of 1.

-5 -4 -3 -2 -1 0 1 2 3 4 5

3. $a > -1$

-5 -4 -3 -2 -1 0 1 2 3 4 5

4. $y \leq 3$

-5 -4 -3 -2 -1 0 1 2 3 4 5

Write an inequality that represents each phrase.

5. the sum of 2 and 3 is less than y

6. the sum of y and 2 is greater than or equal to 6

_____

_____

LESSON 13-1

Writing Inequalities
Reading Strategies: Understand Symbols

An **inequality** is a comparison of two unequal values. This chart will help you understand both words and symbols for inequalities.

The team has scored fewer than 5 runs in each game. "Fewer than 5" means **"less than 5."** Symbol for "less than 5": < 5	No more than 8 people can ride in the elevator. "No more than 8" Means **"8 or less than 8."** Symbol for "less than or equal to 8": ≤ 8
Inequalities	
More than 25 students try out for the team each year. "More than 25" means **"a number greater than 25."** Symbol for "greater than 25": > 25	There are at least 75 fans at each home game. "At least 75" means "75 or more" or **"a number greater than or equal to 75."** Symbol for "greater than or equal to 75": ≥ 75

Use the chart to answer each question.

1. What is an inequality?

_____

2. Explain the difference between the symbols $<$ and $\leq$.

_____

_____

3. Explain the difference between the symbols $>$ and $\geq$.

_____

_____

4. Write an inequality to describe the number of students in each homeroom: There is a limit of 30 students for each homeroom.

_____

5. Is 28 a solution to the inequality you wrote in Exercise 4? How do you know?

_____

LESSON
13-1
Writing Inequalities
Success for English Learners

Problem 1

$w \le 4$

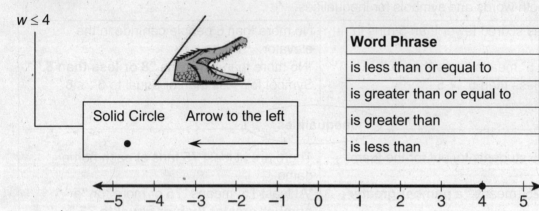

Word Phrase	Symbol
is less than or equal to	$\le$
is greater than or equal to	ε
is greater than	$>$
is less than	$<$

Solid Circle   Arrow to the left

← −5 −4 −3 −2 −1 0 1 2 3 4 5 →

Problem 2

$w > -2$

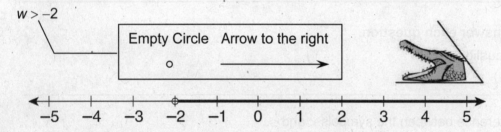

Empty Circle Arrow to the right

← −5 −4 −3 −2 −1 0 1 2 3 4 5 →

1. In Problem 1, is 4 part of the solution set? How do you know?

_____

2. In Problem 2, is −2 part of the solution set? How do you know?

_____

3. When graphing an inequality with a $\ge$ sign, should you use an empty or a solid circle? Why?

_____

4. Graph the solutions of $x \le -2$.

← −5 −4 −3 −2 −1 0 1 2 3 4 5 →

Name _____ Date _____ Class _____

Model and Solve Addition and Subtraction Inequalities

Practice and Problem Solving: A/B

Solve each inequality. Graph and check the solution.

1. $9 > n - 2$ _____

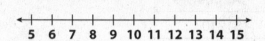

2. $x + 8 < 10$ _____

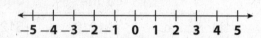

3. $m - 18 \leq 36$ _____

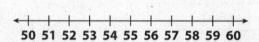

4. $112 \geq b + 128$ _____

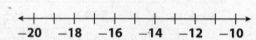

5. $83 \leq p - 183$ _____

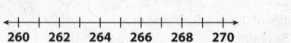

6. $c + 93 \geq 17$ _____

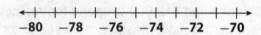

Write an inequality to solve each problem.

7. DeShawn has $53. He needs at least $76 to buy the jacket he wants. How much more money does he need for the jacket?

_____

8. Kristen needs at least 500 points to earn the next trophy on her video game. She has 418 points. How many points must she earn to win the trophy?

_____

9. Abha is hosting a party at a place that can hold up to 125 people. Seventy-eight people have said they are coming. How many more people can Abha invite?

_____

Solve.

10. Write a real-world problem that can be represented by the inequality $r + 32 \geq 56$. Solve the inequality.

_____

_____

Model and Solve Addition and Subtraction Inequalities

LESSON 13-2

Practice and Problem Solving: C

Write an inequality to solve each problem.

The table shows Meagan's family budget for three months of the year.

	June	July	August
Mortgage	$1210	$1210	$1210
Utilities	$403	$455	$461
Food	$680	$572	$905
Savings	$500	$500	$500
Entertainment	$214	$290	$614
Total	$3,007	$3,027	$3,690

1. Meagan had $12,000 to spend for the months of June – September. What is the most Meagan could spend for September?

_____

2. In June and July combined, Meagan spent less on food than she plans to in August and September combined. What is the least that Megan could plan to spend on food in September so that the total of August and September is greater than that of July and August?

_____

3. Meagan does not want to spend more on entertainment in June through September than she does on utilities. If she spends $412 on utilities in September, what is the most she can spend on entertainment?

_____

4. Meagan tries to spend less on food, savings, and entertainment than she does on her mortgage and utilities. How much less could she have spent on entertainment in August to meet that goal?

_____

5. Use the table above to write a problem that can be solved using an inequality. Then find the solution to your problem.

_____

_____

_____

Name _____ Date _____ Class_____

LESSON 13-2

Model and Solve Addition and Subtraction Inequalities
Practice and Problem Solving: D

Solve each inequality. Graph and check the solution. The first one is done for you.

1. $r - 1 > 2$ _____ $r > 3$ _____

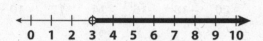

2. $m + 3 \leq 6$ _____

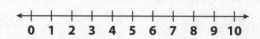

3. $x - 4 < -1$ _____

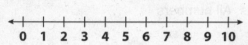

4. $k + 2 \geq 5$ _____

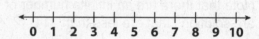

5. $a + 7 > 2$ _____

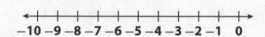

6. $h - 9 \leq 3$ _____

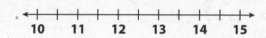

7. $v - 8 < -16$ _____

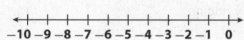

8. $14 + y > -7$ _____

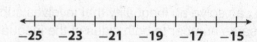

Write an inequality to solve each problem. The first one is done for you.

9. A small car averages up to 29 more miles per gallon of gas than an SUV. If a small car averages 44 miles per gallon, what is the average miles per gallon for an SUV?

   Write and solve an inequality. _____ **$44 - 29 < s$** _____ **$15 < s$** _____

   Write the solution.

   An SUV gets at least 15 miles per gallon.

10. Carlos is taking a car trip that is more than 240 miles. He has already driven 135 miles. How much farther does he have to go?

    Write and solve an inequality. _____

    Write the solution in words.

    _____

LESSON
13-2

Model and Solve Addition and Subtraction Inequalities
Reteach

You can solve an inequality that involves addition by subtracting the
same number from both sides of the inequality sign.

Example:
Solve and graph the inequality.

$$y + 19 < 5$$
$$\underline{-19} < \underline{-19}$$
$$y < -14$$

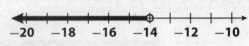

Subtracting 19 from both sides gives us our solution: $y < -14$.

Note that there are an infinite number of solutions. All numbers
are solutions that are less than −14.

Solve each inequality. Graph and check the solution.

1. $x + 15 > 3$ _____

2. $23 \le 58 + y$ _____

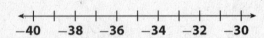

You can solve an inequality that involves subtraction by adding
the same number to both sides of the inequality sign.

Example:
Solve and graph the inequality.

$$x - 164 \le -312$$
$$\underline{+164} < \underline{+164}$$
$$x \le -148$$

Adding 164 to both sides gives the solution: $x \le -148$.

Note that there are an infinite number of solutions. The number −148 is one solution to
this inequality. All numbers less than −148 are also solutions.

Solve each inequality. Graph and check the solution.

3. $x - 21 < 52$ _____

4. $y - 65 \ge 33$ _____

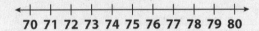
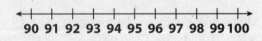

Name _____ Date _____ Class_____

Model and Solve Addition and Subtraction Inequalities

Reading Strategies: Build Vocabulary

Pay close attention to the words used in word problems. There are several different ways to indicate the use of each of the inequality symbols.

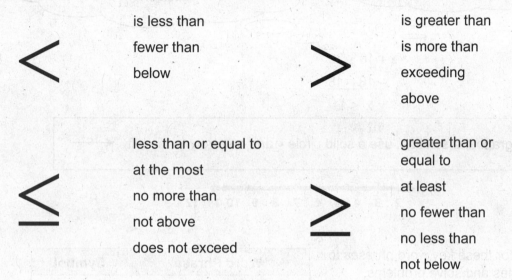

is less than	is greater than
fewer than	is more than
below	exceeding
	above

less than or equal to	greater than or equal to
at the most	at least
no more than	no fewer than
not above	no less than
does not exceed	not below

Here is an example. Look at the language carefully.

Shawn's hot tub holds 325 gallons of water. He has 123 gallons of water in the hot tub. *At the most*, how much more water can Shawn add before the hot tub is filled?

123 gallons plus *w* gallons is *at the most* 325 gallons

$$123 + w \leq 350$$
$$\underline{- 123} \quad \underline{- 123}$$
$$w \leq 227$$

Shawn can add at the most 227 gallons to his hot tub.

Write an inequality to solve each problem. Tell what symbol you will use first.

1. Janelle has a lamp that is 48 inches tall. She is purchasing a table to place the lamp on. The height of the table and lamp combined cannot exceed 72 inches. What height at most can the table Janelle purchases be?

   _____

2. Dani needs $14.25 to pay for his lunch. He has $5 in his pocket, and looks in his wallet to get the rest of the money. How much money must Dani have in his wallet in order to have enough for his lunch bill?

   _____

LESSON 13-2

Model and Solve Addition and Subtraction Inequalities
Strategies for English Learners

Problem 1

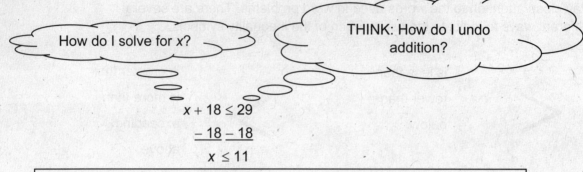

How do I solve for *x*?

THINK: How do I undo addition?

$$x + 18 \leq 29$$
$$-18 \quad -18$$
$$x \leq 11$$

To graph the solution, use a solid circle ● and an arrow to the left. ←

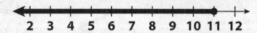

2 3 4 5 6 7 8 9 10 11 12

Problem 2

Use symbols for these key word phrases to write inequalities and solve problems.

Carlos is taking a car trip that is more than 240 miles. He has already driven 135 miles. How much farther does he have to go?

Word Phrase	Symbol
is less than or equal to	≤
is greater than or equal to	≥
is greater than	>
is less than	<

$$135 \text{ miles} + m \text{ miles} > 240 \text{ miles}$$

$$135 + m > 240$$
$$-135 \quad -135$$
$$m > 105$$

Carlos has at least 105 miles to go.

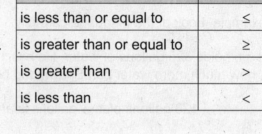

THINK: "is more than" means "is greater than."

Match.

1. 6 is less than $x + 3$ ____

2. 6 is greater than $x + 3$ ____

3. 6 is greater than or equal to $x + 3$ ____

a. $6 \geq x + 3$

b. $6 < x + 3$

c. $6 > x + 3$

**LESSON
13-3**

Multiplication and Division Inequalities with Positive Numbers
Practice and Problem Solving: A/B

Solve each inequality. Graph and check the solution.

1. $9x > 270$ _____

```
27  29  31  33  35  37
```

2. $\dfrac{y}{5} \le 8$ _____

```
33  35  37  39  41  43
```

3. $\dfrac{b}{4} < 4$ _____

```
10  12  14  16  18  20
```

4. $5c \ge 125$ _____

```
22  24  26  28  30  32
```

Solve each inequality.

5. $\dfrac{a}{20} > 12$ _____

6. $\dfrac{r}{13} \le 2$ _____

7. $6b < 720$ _____

8. $\dfrac{s}{4.2} \ge 15$ _____

Write and solve an inequality for each problem.

9. It cost $660 to put on the school play. How many tickets must be sold at $6 apiece in order to make a profit?

_____

10. Jorge's soccer team is having its annual fund raiser. The team hopes to earn at least three times as much as it did last year. Last year the team earned $87. What is the team's goal for this year?

_____

11. Alicia earns $9.00 per hour working at a part-time job. She wants to earn more than $180 this week. How many hours does Alicia have to work?

_____

12. Marc wants to buy a set of 6 antique chairs for his dining room. He has decided to spend no more than $360. How much can he spend per chair?

_____

LESSON 13-3

Multiplication and Division Inequalities with Positive Numbers

Practice and Problem Solving: C

Solve each inequality.

1. $\dfrac{a}{2.5} > 120$ _____

2. $13r \le 19.5$ _____

3. $6b < 73.2$ _____

4. $\dfrac{s}{42} \ge 15$ _____

Write and solve an inequality for each problem.

5. It cost $660 to put on the school play. Tickets sell for $6 each. The drama club has already sold 25 tickets. How many more tickets must be sold at $6 apiece in order to make a profit? Explain.

_____

_____

_____

6. Jorge's soccer team is having its annual fundraiser. The team will sell T-shirts at $10 each. The team hopes to earn at least three times as much as it did last year. Last year the team earned $80 selling hats for $5 each. To meet its goal for this year, how many more T-shirts will the team have to sell than hats it sold last year? Justify your answer.

_____

_____

_____

7. Akiko earns $12.00 per hour babysitting. She also receives a weekly allowance of $10 from her parents. She wants to make more than $190 this week. How many hours does Akiko have to babysit?

_____

_____

_____

8. Marc wants to buy a set of 6 leather chairs for his dining room. He has decided to spend no more than $360. He receives coupons good for $20 off each chair. How much can he spend on each chair? Explain.

_____

_____

_____

Name _____ Date _____ Class_____

LESSON
13-3

Multiplication and Division Inequalities with Positive Numbers
Practice and Problem Solving: D

Use the situation below to complete Exercises 1–3.

Alicia is buying melons. She buys 5 melons and spends more than $10.
How much did she spend on each melon?

1. Let *x* represent the cost of each melon. Write an inequality.

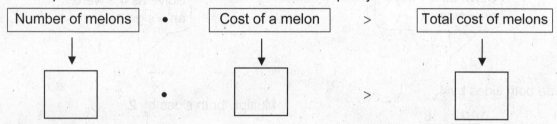

2. The model shows the inequality from
   Exercise 1.

   There are _____ long + tiles, so draw circles to

   separate the one tiles into _____ groups.

   How many units are in each group? _____

3. What values make the inequality you wrote in Exercise 1 true? _____
   Graph the solution of the inequality.

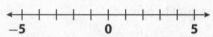

Solve each inequality. Graph and check the solution.

4. $9x > 27$ _____

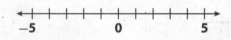

5. $5y \leq 20$ _____

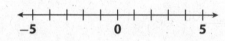

6. $4b < 12$ _____

7. $7c \geq 28$ _____

Solve each inequality. The first one is done for you.

8. $\frac{a}{2} > 12$ _____ $a > 24$ _____

9. $3r \leq 5$ _____

10. $6b < 24$ _____

11. $\frac{s}{2} \geq 14$ _____

Multiplication and Division Inequalities with Positive Numbers
Reteach

When you multiply or divide both sides of an inequality by the same *positive* number, you can solve the inequality just like an equation.

The direction of the inequality symbol remains the same.

Solve as if $<$ were an $=$ sign.	Solve as if $\geq$ were an $=$ sign.

$$4p < 16$$

Divide both sides by 4.

$$\frac{4p}{4} < \frac{16}{4}$$

$$p < 4$$

The inequality symbol remains the same.

$$\frac{x}{2} \geq 19$$

Multiply both sides by 2.

$$2\left(\frac{x}{2}\right) \geq 2(19)$$

$$x \geq 38$$

The inequality symbol remains the same.

Solve.

1. $\dfrac{a}{7} < 5$

   Multiply by ____.

   The inequality symbol

   _____

   $7 \cdot \dfrac{a}{7}$ _____ $7 \cdot 5$

   a _____ 35

2. $3s \geq 24$

   Divide by ____.

   The inequality symbol

   _____

   $\dfrac{3s}{3}$ _____ $\dfrac{24}{3}$

   s _____ 8

Solve. Check each answer.

3. $\dfrac{r}{10} \geq 2$ _____

4. $5b < 45$ _____

5. $4n > 48$ _____

6. $\dfrac{c}{7} < 3$ _____

7. $2t \leq 52$ _____

8. $\dfrac{y}{12} \geq 10$ _____

LESSON 13-3

Multiplication and Division Inequalities with Positive Numbers
Reading Strategies: Analyze Information

Look at the steps for solving multiplication and division inequalities.

Steps for Solving an Inequality	Division Inequality	Multiplication Inequality
Step 1: Isolate the variable.	$\dfrac{x}{8} < 5$	$4y > 12$
Step 2: Multiply both sides of a division equation by the same number. Divide both sides of a multiplication equation by the same number.	$\dfrac{x}{8} \cdot 8 < 5 \cdot 8$	$\dfrac{4y}{4} > \dfrac{12}{4}$
Step 3: Compute to solve.	$x < 40$	$y > 3$

Use the chart to answer the following questions.

1. What do you do to get the variable by itself in a division inequality?

   _____

2. What was $\dfrac{x}{8}$ multiplied by in the example?

   _____

3. What is the solution of the division inequality?

   _____

4. What are three numbers that make the division inequality true?

   _____

5. What do you do to get the variable by itself in a multiplication inequality?

   _____

6. What was $4y$ divided by in the multiplication inequality?

   _____

7. What is the solution to the multiplication inequality?

   _____

8. What are three numbers that are part of the solution?

   _____

LESSON 13-3 Multiplication and Division Inequalities with Positive Numbers
Success for English Learners

Use the information below to help you remember what your solutions mean.

$x < 5$	$x \le 2$	$x > 5$	$x \ge 19$
The solution set is all the numbers less than 5.	The solution set is all the numbers less than or equal to 2.	The solution set is all the numbers greater than 5.	The solution set is all the numbers greater than or equal to 19.

Problem 1

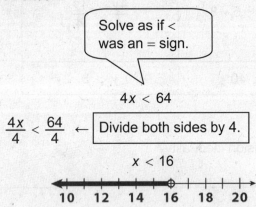

Solve as if $<$ was an $=$ sign.

$4x < 64$

$\dfrac{4x}{4} < \dfrac{64}{4}$ ← Divide both sides by 4.

$x < 16$

The SOLUTION SET is all numbers that are less than 16 such as 10, 8, 0, etc.

Problem 2

Five books cost $45 or less. How much does each book cost?

Let the variable b represent what you are trying to find.

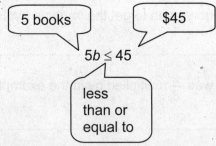

5 books $45

$5b \le 45$

less than or equal to

Divide both sides by 5 to get your solution.
$b \le 9$
A book costs $9 or less.

1. When you graph the solution set of an inequality using an open circle, what does it mean?

   _____

2. How do you check answers to inequality problems?

   _____

   _____

3. Write and solve your own inequality problem.

   _____

   _____

LESSON 13-4

Multiplication and Division Inequalities with Rational Numbers
Practice and Problem Solving: A/B

Solve each inequality. Graph and check the solution.

1. $-3x \geq -18$ _____

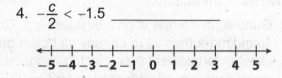

2. $-\dfrac{y}{2} \leq 4$ _____

3. $-11b > 55$ _____

4. $-\dfrac{c}{2} < -1.5$ _____

Solve each inequality.

5. $-\dfrac{x}{5} > \dfrac{1}{20}$ _____

6. $0.9 \leq -r$ _____

7. $-2b > 3$ _____

8. $-\dfrac{a}{0.5} \geq -70$ _____

Solve each problem.

9. Melissa's family is on vacation. They spend $125 per day on food
   and entertainment. They have budgeted only up to $750 for food
   and entertainment. How many days of vacation can they afford?

   _____

10. A marine biologist is doing research on a shellfish that lives 80 feet
    below sea level. The marine biologist dives into the sea at a rate that
    is no less than –5 feet per second. How long will it take the marine
    biologist to reach the shellfish?

    _____

11. Kevin is playing a game at the state fair. For each ball he can toss
    into a jar, he gets –2 points. To win a stuffed animal, he must
    earn a score of –24 or less. How many times does he have
    to toss a ball into a jar?

    _____

LESSON
13-4
Multiplication and Division Inequalities with Rational Numbers
Practice and Problem Solving: C

Solve each inequality.

1. $-\dfrac{x}{4}\left(5^2 - 1\right) > -36$ _____

2. $-\dfrac{1}{9}\left(18 + 3^2\right)y \le -2$ _____

3. $8 \ge -\left(4^2 + 16\right)a$ _____

4. $-7 < \dfrac{1}{8}\left(5^2 - 81\right)b$ _____

Solve each inequality.

5. Guadalupe's family is on a business trip. Guadalupe doesn't want to spend more than $125 per day on hotels and $85 per day for food and client entertainment. Her total trip budget is less than $1,900. How many days can she afford to go on this trip?

_____

6. A diver is diving to reefs that are 480 feet below sea level. He starts at a diving station 30 feet below sea level. From there, he dives into the sea at a rate that is no less than –6 feet per second. How long will it take the diver to reach the reef?

_____

7. Cara is playing a game. For each dart she can toss onto a board, she gets –20 points. To win a stuffed animal, she must earn a score of –240 or less. She gets 5 minutes to play the game. To win a stuffed animal, how many seconds does she have to toss a dart onto the board?

_____

8. Saira's bank deducts $1.75 each time she withdraws money from an out-of-state bank machine. The bank also charges a $10 maintenance fee for each week that Saira's bank balance is less than $500. Saira's current bank balance is $580.25. She is visiting her aunt in another state and wants to withdraw $25 per week for expenses. For how many weeks can she do this without being charged the maintenance fee?

_____

Name _____ Date _____ Class_____

LESSON 13-4

Multiplication and Division Inequalities with Rational Numbers
Practice and Problem Solving: D

Complete the table. The first one is done for you.

Inequality	Do this to each side:	New inequality	New inequality is true or false?	If false, what can you do to make the inequality true?
1. $-\frac{1}{2} < 3$	Multiply by –2	1 < –6	false	reverse the inequality symbol
2. $4 \le 12$	Divide by 4	$1 \le 3$		
3. $-8 > -16$	Divide by –8	1 > 2		
4. $-\frac{1}{3} > -21$	Multiply by –3	1 > 63		

Solve each inequality. Graph and check the solution. The first one is done for you.

5. $-4x \ge -16$ **x ≤ 4**

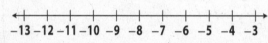

6. $-\frac{y}{2} < 6$ _____

7. $-5a \le -20$ _____

8. $-\frac{b}{2} > -1$ _____

Solve each inequality. The first one is done for you.

9. $-\frac{a}{2} \ge 18$ **a ≤ –36**

10. $-4b \le 24$ _____

11. $-7c < -14$ _____

12. $-\frac{d}{3} > -9$ _____

LESSON
13-4

Multiplication and Division Inequalities with Rational Numbers
Reteach

When you multiply or divide both sides of an inequality by the same *positive* number, the direction of the inequality symbol remains the same.

$3p < -18$

Divide both sides by *positive* 3.

$\dfrac{3p}{3} < \dfrac{-18}{3}$

$p < -6$

$\dfrac{x}{5} \geq -4$

Multiply both sides by *positive* 5.

$5 \cdot \dfrac{x}{5} \geq 5 \cdot -4$

$x \geq -20$

When you multiply or divide both sides of an inequality by the same *negative* number, the direction of the inequality symbol is reversed.

$-6y > -42$

Divide both sides by *negative* 6.

$\dfrac{-6y}{-6} < \dfrac{-42}{-6}$

$y < 7$

$\dfrac{m}{-2} \leq 15$

Multiply both sides by *negative* 2.

$-2 \cdot \dfrac{m}{-2} \geq -2 \cdot 15$

$m \geq -30$

Solve.

1. $\dfrac{a}{8} < -3$

   Multiply by ____. The direction
   of the inequality symbol

   _____.

   $8 \cdot \dfrac{a}{8}$ _____ $8 \cdot -3$

   a _____ -24

2. $-4s \geq -36$

   Divide by ____. The direction of the
   inequality symbol

   _____.

   $\dfrac{-4s}{-4}$ _____ $\dfrac{-36}{-4}$

   s _____ 9

Solve. Check each answer.

3. $\dfrac{r}{-7} \geq 2$

_____

4. $9b < -54$

_____

5. $-3n > -36$

_____

6. $\dfrac{c}{6} < -8$

_____

LESSON 13-4

Multiplication and Division Inequalities with Rational Numbers

Reading Strategies: Use a Graphic Organizer

You can use a graphic organizer to solve an inequality.

$-14x > -28$

Step 1: Solve the inequality. First divide both sides by -14.

$$\frac{-14x}{-14} > \frac{-28}{-14}$$

Step 2: ASK: Did you multiply or divide by a negative number? If yes, reverse the inequality symbol.

$$\frac{-14x}{-14} < \frac{-28}{-14}$$

Step 3: Simplify.

$$x < \frac{-28}{-14}$$
$$x < 2$$

Step 4: Graph.

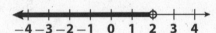

Use the chart to answer the following questions.

1. In the first step, why do you divide by -14?

   _____

2. Why do you divide both sides of the inequality by -14?

   _____

3. What is the second step?

   _____

4. If the answer to the question in Step 2 was "no," what would happen to the inequality symbol?

   _____

LESSON 13-4

Multiplication and Division Inequalities with Rational Numbers
Success for English Learners

Use the information below to help you remember when to change
the direction of the inequality sign.

Multiply or Divide by a **positive** number.	Multiply or Divide by a **negative** number.
↕	↕
Do NOT change the inequality symbol!	**Change the inequality symbol!**

Problem 1

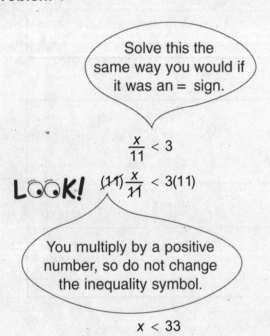

Solve this the same way you would if it was an = sign.

$$\frac{x}{11} < 3$$

LOOK! $(11)\frac{x}{11} < 3(11)$

You multiply by a positive number, so do not change the inequality symbol.

$$x < 33$$

Problem 2

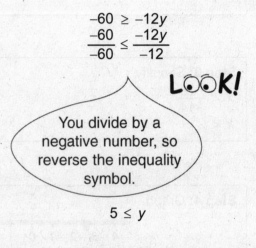

$$-60 \geq -12y$$
$$\frac{-60}{-60} \leq \frac{-12y}{-12}$$

LOOK!

You divide by a negative number, so reverse the inequality symbol.

$$5 \leq y$$

1. The statement " $-x$ is less than -3 " is the same as:

_____

2. When is the only time you reverse an inequality symbol?

_____

MODULE 13

Inequalities and Relationships
Challenge

1. Explain the difference between the solution of the inequality $\frac{x}{3} \geq 2$

   and the solution of the inequality $\frac{x}{-3} \geq 2$. Then solve both

   inequalities.

   _____

   _____

   _____

2. Construct an expression with at least 5 terms so that

   (a) there are at least 3 variable terms with the same variable, and

   (b) when the expression is evaluated for [variable] = 3, the expression
       is equal to 0.

   Show your work.

   _____

   _____

   _____

   _____

3. Can the inequality $-5x > 0$ be solved? Explain why or why not.

   _____

   _____

4. A *compound inequality* is a pair of linked inequalities. Any solution to a
   compound inequality must be in the solution set of <u>both</u> statements.
   Predict whether these pairs of inequalities have any common
   solutions. Then graph both inequalities and check your predictions.

   $x \geq 3$ and $x < -1$ $x < 3$ and $x \geq -2$

   _____   _____

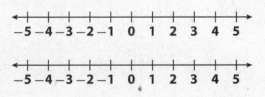
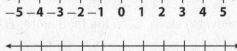
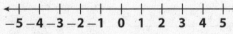

   _____

   _____

Graphing on the Coordinate Plane

Practice and Problem Solving: A/B

Give the coordinates of the points on the coordinate plane.

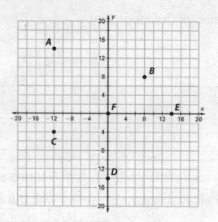

1. *A* (____ , ____)

2. *B* (____ , ____)

3. *C* (____ , ____)

4. *D* (____ , ____)

5. *E* (____ , ____)

6. *F* (____ , ____)

Plot the points on the coordinate plane.

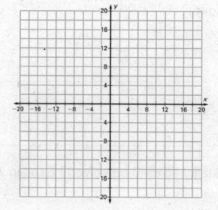

7. *G* (2, 4)

8. *H* (–6, 8)

9. *J* (10, –12)

10. *K* (–14, –16)

11. *M* (0, 18)

12. *P* (–20, 0)

Describe how to go from one store to the next on the map. Use words like *left*, *right*, *up*, *down*, *north*, *south*, *east*, and *west*. Each square on the coordinate plane is a city block.

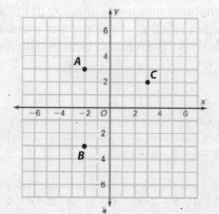

13. The computer store, *A*, to the food store, *B*.

   _____

14. The computer store, *A*, to the hardware store, *C*.

   _____

15. The hardware store, *C*, to the food store, *B*.

   _____

LESSON 14-1

Graphing on the Coordinate Plane

Practice and Problem Solving: C

Label the axes to locate the points on the coordinate planes.

1. *A*(–6, 15), *B*(3, –9), *C*(–9, –9)

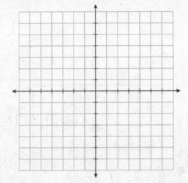

2. *D*(0, 6), *E*(–12, 6), *F*(18, 0)

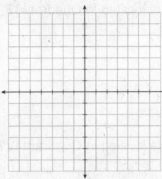

Start with the given point. Give the quadrant in which you end up after following the directions. Then, give the coordinates of the point where you end up.

3. *X*(5, –8) Go down 5, left 7, and down 6 more.

   Quadrant: _____ ; Point: *X*(_____, _____)

4. *Y*(–2, 6) Go up 3, right 5, and up 4 more.

   Quadrant: _____; Point: *Y*(_____, _____)

5. *Z*(0, –5) Go left 5, up 4, right 7, and down 3.

   Quadrant: _____; Point: *Z*(_____, _____)

Give the coordinates of a point that would form a right triangle with the points given. Use the grids for reference. Tell what you know about one of the coordinates of your new point.

6. *P*(2, 4), *Q*(2, 8), *R*(_____, _____)

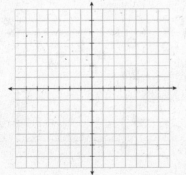

7. *S*(–3, –5), *T*(4, –5), *U*(_____, _____)

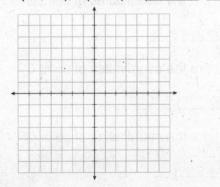

LESSON 14-1

Graphing on the Coordinate Plane

Practice and Problem Solving: D

Use the coordinate plane for Exercise 1–3. Give the letter of the correct answer. The first one is done for you.

1. Which point is located in Quadrant I?

   A   point Q

   B   point P

   C   point X

   __C__

2. Which point is located in Quadrant IV?

   A   point X

   B   point Y

   C   point P

   ____

3. Which point is located in Quadrant II?

   A   point Q

   B   point Y

   C   point X

   ____

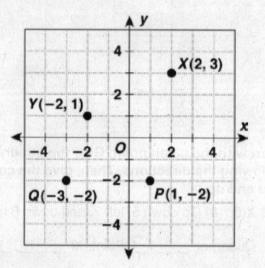

Use the coordinate plane for Exercises 4–7. Give the letter of the correct answer. The first one is done for you.

4. What are the coordinates of point A?

   Go over 3 to the right and down 1, so the x-coordinate is 3 and the y-coordinate is −1, or A(3, −1).

5. What are the coordinates of point B?

   B (_____, _____)

6. What are the coordinates of point C?

   C (_____, _____)

7. What are the coordinates of point D?

   D (_____, _____)

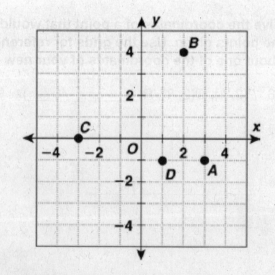

Name _____ Date _____ Class_____

LESSON
14-1
Graphing on the Coordinate Plane
Reteach

Each quadrant of the coordinate plane has a unique combination of positive and negative signs for the *x*-coordinates and *y*-coordinates as shown here.

Quadrant	x-coordinate	y-coordinate
I	+	+
II	–	+
III	–	–
IV	+	–

Use these rules when naming points on the coordinate plane.

Example 1

Draw the point *A*(1, –3) on the coordinate grid.

Solution

According to the table, this point will be in Quadrant IV.

So, go to the *right* (+) one unit, and go *down* (–) three units.

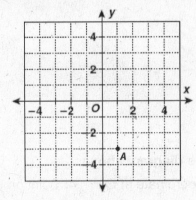

Example 2

What are the coordinates of point *B*?

Solution

According to the table, this point will have a negative *x*-coordinate and a positive *y*-coordinate.

Point *B* is 3 three units to the *left* (–) and four units *up* (+). So the coordinates of point *B* are (–3, 4).

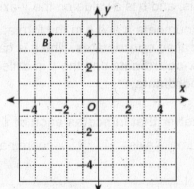

Add the correct sign for each point's coordinates.

1. (___ 3, ___ 4) in

   Quadrant II

2. (___ 2, ___ 5) in

   Quadrant IV

3. (___ 9, ___ 1) in

   Quadrant I

4. In which quadrant is the point (0, 7) located? Explain your answer.

_____

Graphing on the Coordinate Plane

LESSON 14-1

Reading Strategies: Build Vocabulary

This lesson introduces words used to graph numbers. Mathematics uses these words to build new concepts. It is important to remember and to use them. Look at this example. Read each definition, and find it on the picture.

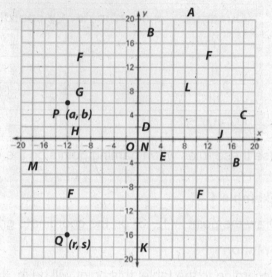

A. The **coordinate plane** includes all of the parts marked on the picture.

B. The **axes** are the darker number lines.

C. The **x-axis** goes left to right, whereas the **y-axis** goes up and down.

D. The axes intersect at the **origin**, which is marked with an "O".

E. The **scale** on the number line is always important in using a coordinate plane. Here, every square on the grid is 2 units.

F. The axes divide the coordinate plane into four **quadrants**. **Quadrant I** is upper right, **Quadrant II** is upper left, **Quadrant III** is lower left, and **Quadrant IV**, which is read "quadrant four," is lower right.

G. Pairs of numbers, called **ordered pairs**, are represented on the coordinate plane as points and in the format *P(a, b)*, where *P* is the point's label, *a* is a value on the x-axis, and *b* is a value on the y-axis.

H. The numbers *a* and *b* in the format *(a, b)* are called **coordinates**. The *a* is called the **x-coordinate** and the *b* is called the **y-coordinate**.

Write a letter that indicates each of the following in the diagram above.

1. point on *x*-axis

2. *x*-coordinate of Q

3. *y*-coordinate of Q

4. point on *y*-axis

_____   _____   _____   _____

5. point on Quadrant I

6. ordered pair for Q

7. Point on Quadrant III

8. origin

_____   _____   _____

LESSON 14-1

Graphing on the Coordinate Plane

Success for English Learners

Problem

This number shows how many units to move right or left.

This number shows how many units to move up or down.

(x, y)

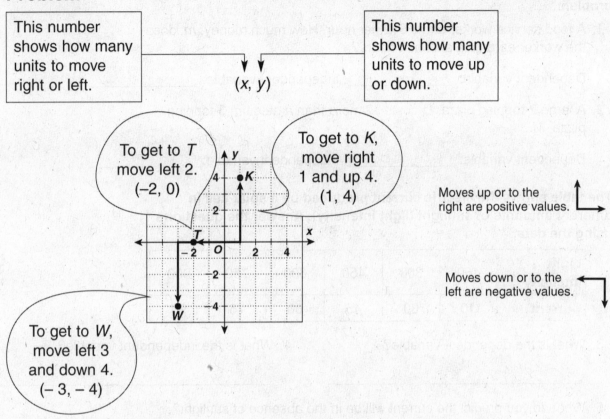

Moves up or to the right are positive values.

Moves down or to the left are negative values.

1. If an ordered pair has an *x*-value of 0, which direction do you move from the origin?

_____

2. A negative *y*-coordinate means that a point may lie in which two quadrants?

_____

3. Does it matter which number comes first in an ordered pair? Explain.

_____

_____

_____

Name _____ Date _____ Class_____

Independent and Dependent Variables in Tables and Charts
Practice and Problem Solving: A/B

Name the *dependent variable* and the *independent variable* in each problem.

1. A food service worker earns $12 per hour. How much money, m, does the worker earn on a shift of h hours?

   Dependent variable: _____; independent variable: _____

2. A large 2-topping pizza, L, costs $2 more than a medium 3-topping pizza, M.

   Dependent variable: _____; independent variable: _____

The table shows the electric current produced by a solar cell in different amounts of sunlight (light intensity). Answer the questions using the data.

Light intensity	150	300	450	600	750	900
Current	10	30	45	60	75	90

3. What is the dependent variable?

   _____

4. What is the independent variable?

   _____

5. What do you predict the current will be in the absence of sunlight? Explain.

   _____

6. What do you predict the current will be if the light intensity is 1,000? Explain.

   _____

A race car driver's time in seconds to complete 12 laps is plotted on the graph.

7. Which axis shows the dependent variable?

   _____

8. Why does the graph begin at $x = 1$?

   _____

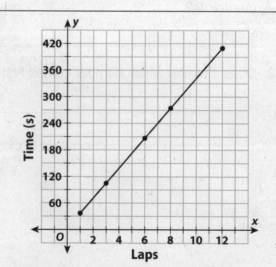

Independent and Dependent Variables in Tables and Charts

LESSON 14-2

Practice and Problem Solving: C

Use the situation below to complete Exercises 1–4.

The commuter bus system collected the data in the table below. All of the data was collected under the same conditions: dry roads, no accidents or traffic jams, same distance each trip, and no mechanical problems with the bus on each trip.

Number of passengers per trip, n	30	35	40	45	50
Average speed, km per hour, s	60	58	55	55	52
Liters of biodiesel fuel used, f	45	48	50	52	54

1. Assume that more passengers cause the bus to travel slower. Of these two factors, which would be the dependent and independent variables?

   Dependent variable: _____; independent variable: _____

2. Assume that an average faster speed causes the bus to consume more fuel. Describe the relationship between bus speed and fuel consumption.

   _____

3. What can you say about the relationship between the number of passengers and the fuel consumption?

   _____

4. What effect does the number of passengers have on bus speed *and* fuel consumption?

   _____

In the graph, the independent variable is the *x*-axis and the dependent variable is the *y*-axis. Use the graph to answer 5–6.

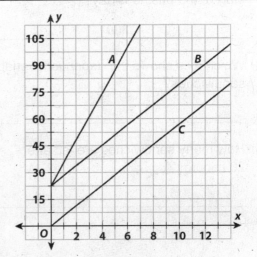

5. Describe and compare how the dependent variables shown by lines *A* and *B* change as the independent variables change.

   _____

6. Describe and compare how the dependent variables shown by lines *B* and *C* change as the independent variables change.

   _____

LESSON 14-2

Independent and Dependent Variables in Tables and Charts

Practice and Problem Solving: D

Answer the questions for each real-world situation. The first one is done for you.

1. The table gives the amount of water in a water tank as it is being filled.

Gallons	50	100	150	200	250
Time (min)	10	20	30	40	50

a. Why is gallons the *dependent* variable?

It depends on how long the water has been filling the tank.

b. Divide gallons by time in each pair of cells. What do you get?

50 ÷ 10 = 100 ÷ 20 = 150 ÷ 30 = 200 ÷ 40 = 250 ÷ 50 = 5; 5

c. If the time is 60 minutes, how would you get the gallons? What would you get?

Multiply 60 times 5, which gives 300 gallons.

2. The table shows how to change miles to kilometers. Divide kilometers by miles for each of the four mileage numbers. How many kilometers do you get?

(km)	3.22	4.83	6.44	8.05
(mi)	2	3	4	5

_____

Answer each question using the graph. The first one is done for you.

3. How many sandwiches are available at the start of the business day?

300

4. Which axis shows the *dependent* variable, sandwiches?

_____

5. How many sandwiches are left after 20 minutes?

_____

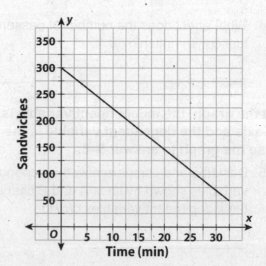

**LESSON
14-2**

Independent and Dependent Variables in Tables and Charts
Reteach

In a table, the *independent variable* is often represented by x. The *dependent variable* is often represented by y. Look at this example.

x	0	1	2	3	4	5	6	7
y	4	5	6	7	8	9	10	?

What y value goes for the question mark?

Step 1   Notice that 4 is added to each value of x to give the y value.

Step 2   So, add 4 to 7. What does this give? $4 + 7 = 11$

On a chart or graph,

- the x-axis is usually used for the *independent variable*, and

- the y-axis is usually used for the *dependent variable*.

Look at the example. ⟶

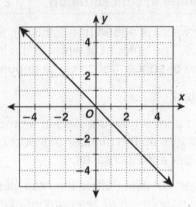

How does y depend on x?

Step 1   Each value of y is the opposite of the value of x.

Step 2   What equation shows this fact?
$y = -x$

Give the relationship between x and y.

1.

x	1	2	3	4	5
y	3	4	5	6	7

_____

2.

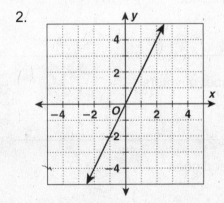

a. What is y when $x = 2$?

_____

b. What value of x gives $y = -2$?

_____

c. Write the equation for the graph.

_____

Independent and Dependent Variables in Tables and Charts

Reading Strategies: Cause and Effect

It can sometimes be useful to think of the **independent variable** as the *cause* of an event. This cause has an *effect* on the **dependent variable**. This type of thinking can be helpful in doing some real-world problems.

Example 1

A middle-school science student did an experiment in which different amounts of water were added on a one-time basis to a solution to see what effect it would have on the solution's concentration. Here are the results.

Water (milliliters)	5	10	15	20
Change in concentration	2	5	10	15

As more water is added (the "cause"), the change in concentration increases. The amount of water is the independent variable. The increase in change of concentration is the dependent variable.

Example 2

The chart shows how the yield of a crop per acre changes as the number of insect pests counted per acre increases.

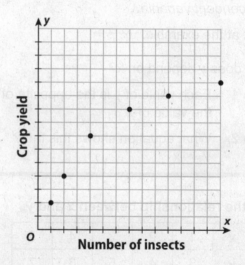

- If the vertical axis (left) is the crop yield, what is happening as the number of insects (horizontal axis) increases?

- The crop yield continues to increase but not as fast as at the beginning.

- The number of insects is the independent variable (the cause), and the crop yield is the dependent variables (the effect).

Identify the cause and the effect in each problem.

1. After a storm, the number of bottles of drinking water available per family decreases as the number of families requesting assistance increases.

_____

2. The number of hours it takes to vote increases as the number of voters per hour increases.

_____

3. The car's mileage, or miles per gallon, increases as its speed goes from 20 miles per hour to 40 miles per hour.

_____

Independent and Dependent Variables in Tables and Charts

LESSON 14-2

Success for English Learners

Problem 1

Let ℓ = length.

Let w = width.

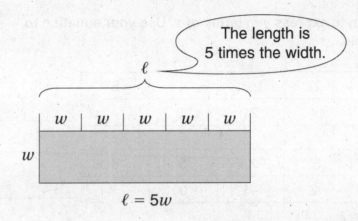

$\ell = 5w$

Problem 2

In Problem 1, the length, *l,* "depends" on the width, *w.*

Independent variable ⟶ width, *w*

Dependent variable ⟶ length, *l*

The variables are related by the formula, *l = 5 w.*

1. Suppose the width of the rectangle in Problem 1 is 10 inches. What is the length of the rectangle?

   _____

2. The table shows the money the school band members collected for washing cars on four different days.

Cars washed	12	15	20	30
Money collected	$120	$150	$200	?

   What is the **dependent variable**?   _____

   What is the **independent variable**?   _____

   How much money is collected for washing 30 cars?

   _____

Name _____ Date _____ Class_____

LESSON 14-3

Writing Equations from Tables

Practice and Problem Solving: A/B

Write an equation to express *y* in terms of *x*. Use your equation to complete the table.

1.

x	1	2	3	4	5
y	7	14	21	28	

_____

2.

x	2	3	4	5	6
y	−3	−2	−1	0	

_____

3.

x	20	16	12	8	4
y	10	8	6	4	

_____

4.

x	7	8	9	10	11
y	11	12	13	14	

_____

Solve.

5. Henry records how many days he rides his bike and how far he rides each week. He rides the same distance each time. He rode 18 miles in 3 days, 24 miles in 4 days, and 42 miles in 7 days. Write and solve an equation to find how far he rides his bike in 10 days.

Number of days, d	3	4	7	10
Number of miles, m	18			

Equation relating *d* and *m* is _____.

The number of miles Henry rides his bike in 10 days is _____.

6. When Cabrini is 6, Nikos is 2. When Cabrini is 10, Nikos will be 6. When Cabrini is 16, Nikos will be 12.When Cabrini is 21, Nikos will be 17. Write and solve an equation to find Nikos' age when Cabrini is 40.

Cabrini's age, x	6	10	16	21	40
Nikos' age, y	2				

Equation relating *x* and *y* is _____.

When Cabrini is 40 years old, Nikos will be _____.

Writing Equations from Tables

LESSON 14-3

Practice and Problem Solving: C

Write an equation to express *y* in terms of *x*. Use your equation to complete the table.

1.

x	1	2	3	4	5
y	1	4	9	16	

_____

2.

x	32	28	24		16
y	−8		−6	−5	−4

_____

3.

x		8	6	4	2
y	4	3.2		1.6	0.8

_____

4.

x	1		3	4	5
y	7	12	17	22	

_____

Solve.

5. $F = \dfrac{9}{5}C + 32$ is an equation that models the relationship in the table.

Equivalent Temperatures					
Celsius, (°C)	−15	−10	−5	0	5
Fahrenheit, (°F)	5	14	23	32	41

What does each variable represent?_____

What is the temperature in °F when it is 20°C? _____.

Is the ordered pair (30, 86) a solution for the equation? Justify your answer.

_____

6. Use the table of values and the equation in Exercise 5 to write an equation for which *F* is the independent variable and *C* is the dependent variable.

An equation relating *F* and *C* is _____.

What is the temperature in °C when it is 59°F? Justify your answer.

_____

LESSON 14-3

Writing Equations from Tables
Practice and Problem Solving: D

Write an equation to express *y* in terms of *x*. The first one is done for you.

1.

x	0	1	2	3
y	2	3	4	5

$y = x + 2$

2.

x	5	10	15	20
y	1	2	3	4

_____

3.

x	3	4	5	6
y	9	12	15	18

_____

4.

x	7	8	9	10
y	5	6	7	8

_____

Solve. The first one is done for you.

5. When George works 8 hours he earns $80. When George works 10 hours he earns $100. When George works 12 hours he earns $120. Complete the table. Circle the letter of the equation that relates the dollars George earns, *y*, to the number of hours he works, *x*.

Number of hours, x	8	10	12
Dollars earned, y	80	100	120

A $y = x \div 10$ Ⓒ $y = 10x$

B $y = x + 72$

6. When Javier is 2, Arianna is 5. When Javier is 3, Arianna is 6. When Javier is 8, Arianna will be 11. When Javier is 20, Arianna is 23. Complete the table. Circle the letter of the equation that relates the age of Arianna, *y*, to the age of Javier, *x*.

Javier's age, x	2	3	8	20
Arianna's age, y	5			

A $y = x \div 2$ C $y = 2x$

B $y = x + 3$

When Javier is 30 years old, Arianna will be _____.

LESSON 14-3
Writing Equations from Tables
Reteach

The relationship between two variables in which one quantity depends
on the other can be modeled by an equation. The equation expresses
the dependent variable y in terms of the independent variable x.

x	0	1	2	3	4	5	6	7
y	4	5	6	7	8	9	10	?

To write an equation from a table of values, first
compare the x- and y-values to find a pattern.
In each, the y-value is 4 more than the x-value.

Then use the pattern to write an equation expressing y in terms of x.
$y = x + 4$

You can use the equation to find the missing value in the table.
To find y when $x = 7$, substitute 7 in for x in the equation.

$y = x + 4$
$y = 7 + 4$
$y = 11$
So, y is **11** when x is 7.

**Write an equation to express y in terms of x. Use your equation to
find the missing value of y.**

1.

x	1	2	3	4	5	6
y	3	6	9	12	15	?

_____

2.

x	18	17	16	15	14	13
y	15	14	13	?	11	10

_____

To solve a real-world problem, use a table of values and an equation.

When Todd is 8, Jane is 1. When Todd is 10, Jane will be 3. When
Todd is 16, Jane will be 9. What is Jane's age when Todd is 45?

Todd, x	8	10	16	45
Jane, y	1	3	9	?

Jane is 7 years younger than Todd.
So $y = x - 7$. When $x = 45$, $y = 45 - 7$. So, $y = 38$.

Solve.

3. When a rectangle is 3 inches wide its length is 6 inches. When it is
4 inches wide its length will be 8 inches. When it is is 9 inches wide its
length will be 18 inches. Write and solve an equation to complete the table.

Width, x	3	4	9	20
Length, y	6			

_____

When the rectangle is 20 inches wide, its length is _____.

LESSON 14-3 Writing Equations from Tables

Reading Strategies: Analyze Information

A table is useful for changing cups to ounces.

Cups	Ounces
1	8
2	16
3	24
4	32
5	40

Use the table above to complete Exercises 1–3.

1. How many ounces are in 1 cup?

   _____

2. How many ounces are in 3 cups?

   _____

3. If "6 cups" were added to the table, how many ounces would be listed?

   _____

An equation shows the relationship between cups and ounces.

ounces = 8 • cups

$y = 8x$

Independent Variable ⟶

Dependent Variable ⟶

x	1	2	3	4	5
y	8	16	24	32	40

The number of ounces depends on the number of cups. The value of y depends on the value of x.

Use the table above to complete Exercises 4–6.

4. Which variable stands for ounces? for cups?

   _____

5. What is the value of y when $x = 2$?

   _____

6. Use the equation to find the number of ounces when the number of cups is 15.

   _____

LESSON 14-3

Writing Equations from Tables

Success for English Learners

Problem 1

The number of inches is 12 times the number of feet.

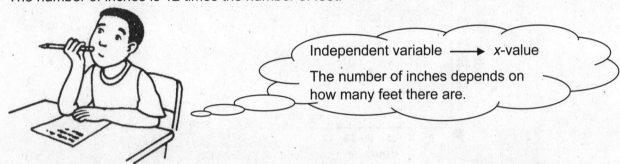

Independent variable ⟶ x-value

The number of inches depends on how many feet there are.

The <u>independent</u> variable is the <u>x-value</u> of the equation.

The <u>dependent</u> variable is the <u>y-value</u> of the equation.

<u>Write an equation</u> to show the relationship between x and y.

number of feet ⟶ x

number of inches ⟶ y

$y = 12x$

Problem 2

Mike has 8 feet of rope. How many inches of rope does he have?

<u>Solve an equation</u> to find a value.

<u>Substitute</u> the value for x into the equation, then <u>solve for y</u>.

y = 12x		
x = 8	Substitute 8 for x.	y = 12(8) = 96

Mike has 96 inches of rope.

1. What does an equation with x and y show?

   _____

   _____

2. What does it mean to substitute a value into the equation?

   _____

3. Suppose Mike has 5 feet of rope. How many inches of rope does he have?

   _____

LESSON 14-4

Representing Algebraic Relationships in Tables and Graphs

Practice and Problem Solving: A/B

An antiques dealer has 24 clock radios to sell at a 12-hour-long antique-radio sale. Use the graph to complete the table.

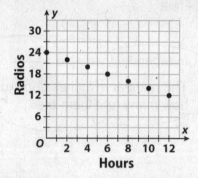

1. Complete the table with the data from the graph.

Radios remaining	24	?	?	?	?	?	?
Hours completed	0	2	4	6	8	10	12

2. What are the dependent (*y*) and independent (*x*) variables?

   dependent: _____; independent: _____

3. Write ordered pairs for the points on the graph and in the table.

   _____

4. How many radios are sold every two hours? _____

5. What happens to the *total* number of radios every two hours?

   _____

6. If *h* is hours and *n* is the number of radios remaining, complete the equation:

   n = _____ × *h* + _____

7. Why is the sign of the number that is multiplied by hours, *h*, negative?

   _____

LESSON 14-4 **Representing Algebraic Relationships in Tables and Graphs**
Practice and Problem Solving: C

Use the graph to answer the questions.

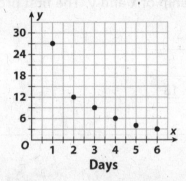

1. A paleontologist is counting fossilized remains of extinct plants at a geological site. Complete the table with data from the graph.

Plant fossils counted, f	____	____	____	____	____	____
Elapsed days of dig, d	1	2	3	4	5	6

2. There are three rates at which the fossils are being counted: Rate *A* for Days 1 and 2, Rate *B* for Days 2 – 4, and Rate *C*: for Days 5 – 6. What is happening to the number of fossils counted as each day passes?

_____

3. Which rate describes the period of time over which the number of fossils counted decreases at the *greatest* rate? Explain your answer.

_____

4. Give the numerical value of each of the rates, *A*, *B*, and *C*. Your answer should be negative and expressed in units of "fossils counted per day" or "fossils/day."

Rate *A*: _____; Rate *B*: _____; Rate *C*: _____

LESSON 14-4

Representing Algebraic Relationships in Tables and Graphs

Practice and Problem Solving: D

Complete the tables. Then, write the ordered pairs. Finally, fill in the blanks to give the algebraic relationship of *x* and *y*. The first problem has been done for you.

1.

x	0	1	2	3
y	4	7	<u>10</u>	<u>13</u>

(0, 4), (1, 7), (2, 10), (3, 13)

$y = \underline{3}x + \underline{4}$

2.

x	0	1	2	4
y	0	−4	___	−16

$y = \underline{\hspace{1cm}}x + \underline{\hspace{1cm}}$

3.

x	0	2	___	6
y	5	11	17	___

$y = \underline{\hspace{1cm}}x + \underline{\hspace{1cm}}$

Write the ordered pairs of three points on the graph. Then, write the algebraic relationship of *x* and *y*. The first one is done for you.

4.
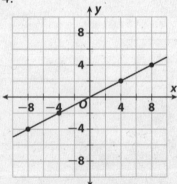

(−8, −4), (4, 2), (8, 4)

$y = \underline{0.5}x + \underline{0}$

5.
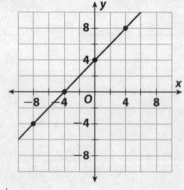

$y = \underline{\hspace{1cm}}x + \underline{\hspace{1cm}}$

6.
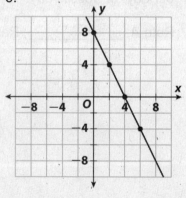

$y = \underline{\hspace{1cm}}x + \underline{\hspace{1cm}}$

LESSON 14-4 Representing Algebraic Relationships in Tables and Graphs
Reteach

The *x* and *y* values in an algebraic relationship should be related in the same way when new values of *x* or *y* are used. This pattern should be seen in a table of values and from a graph of the *x* and *y* values.

Example 1
What is the relationship of the *x* and *y* values in the table?

x	2	4	6	8	10
y	6	12	18	24	30

Solution
First, check to see if there is a simple addition, multiplication, division, or subtraction relationship between the *x* and *y* values.

Here, the *y* values are 3 times the *x* values.

This means that the algebraic relationship is $y = 3x$.

Example 2
What is the relationship between *x* and *y* represented by the graph.

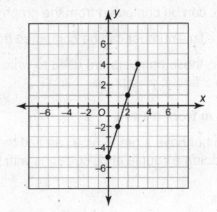

Solution
First, notice that the line through the points crosses the *y*-axis at $y = -5$. This means that part of the relationship between *x* and *y* is given by $y = \underline{\quad} + -5$.

Next, notice that the line through the points goes over to the right by one unit as it "rises" by 3 units. This means that any *x* value is multiplied by 3 over 1 or 3 units as the line goes from one point to another. This is written as $y = 3x$.

Combine these two observations: $y = 3x$ and $y = -5$ give $y = 3x - 5$. Both parts are needed to completely describe the relationship shown.

---

1. Find the relationship of *x* and *y* in the table.

x	0	1	3	6	7
y	1.5	2	3	4.5	5

$y = \underline{\quad\quad} x + \underline{\quad\quad}$

2. Find the relationship of *x* and *y* from a graph of a line that crosses the *y*-axis at $y = 6$ and that goes to the left 2 units and rises 3 units.

$y = \underline{\quad\quad} x + \underline{\quad\quad}$

LESSON 14-4 Representing Algebraic Relationships in Tables and Graphs

Reading Strategies: Reading a Table

In order to write a rule that gives an algebraic relationship, two numbers
have to be identified from a table or a graph.

→ The value of y, often designated by b, on the y-axis at which the
line intercepts that axis

In a table, this is the y value that has an x value of zero (0).

→ A number that is multiplied by x, often designated by m, which
can be computed from the graph of the line

This number can be computed from the x and y values in a table.

Together, these numbers are used to write the algebraic relationship
between x and y: $y = mx + b$.

Finding *m* from a Table

If you do not have a graph, you can find the number m that is multiplied
by x by doing a couple of calculations with the numbers from a table.

Example

Find the number that is multiplied by x for this data:

x	2	4	6	8	1
y	5	10	15	20	25

First, find the difference in consecutive *x*-values.

x	2	4	6	8	10

$$4 - 2 = 2 \quad 6 - 4 = 2 \quad 8 - 6 = 2 \quad 10 - 8 = 2$$

Then, find the difference in consecutive *y*-values.

y	5	10	15	20	25

$$10 - 5 = 5 \quad 15 - 10 = 5 \quad 20 - 15 = 5 \quad 25 - 20 = 5$$

Divide the *difference* of the of the y values by the *difference* of the x values:

5 divided by 2 or $\dfrac{5}{2}$. This number is multiplied by x: $\dfrac{5}{2}x$.

Find the number multiplied by *x* for each table.

1.

x	1	6	11	16	21
y	1	8	15	22	29

2.

x	4	8	12	16	20
y	1	2	3	4	5

_____   _____

LESSON 14-4

Representing Algebraic Relationships in Tables and Graphs

Success for English Learners

Problem 1

Find the algebraic rule from a table.

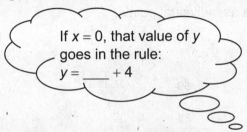

If $x = 0$, that value of y goes in the rule:

$y =$ ____ $+ 4$

What happens to x before it is added to 4 to give 6? Multiplied by 2: 2×1

$y = 2x$

x	0	1	2	3
y	4	6	8	10

Combine the two steps: ⟶ $y = 2x + 4$

Problem 2

Where does the line cross the y-axis?

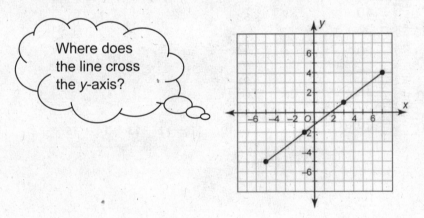

How far over and how far up?

The line crosses the y-axis at -1.

$y =$ _____ $- 1$

The line goes over 4 and up 3.

$y = \dfrac{3}{4}x - 1$

Give the algebraic rule.

1. $(0, 2)$, $(1, 3)$, $(2, 4)$

2. $(0, -1)$, $(2, 3)$, $(4, 7)$

_____   _____

MODULE 14

Relationships in Two Variables
Challenge

Exploring Temperature Data

This activity illustrates the difference between experimental and theoretical data.

1. Complete the tables. Graph the Table 1 data as individual points.
   Show the data in Table 2 as a straight line.

Table 1

data read from
the thermometer

°C	°F
10	
11	
12	
13	
14	
15	

Table 2

data computed
from the equation

$F = C \times \dfrac{9}{5} + 32$

°C	°F
10	
11	
12	
13	
14	
15	

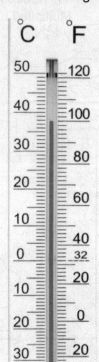

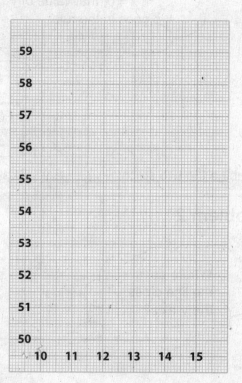

2. Describe the difference between the two data sets and explain why they differ.

_____

_____

_____

LESSON 15-1

Determining When Three Lengths Form a Triangle

Practice and Problem Solving: A/B

Which sides form a triangle? Write "yes" or "no" below each group of measurements.

1. 2 m, 2 m, 4 m

2. 9 in., 4 in., 6 in.

3. 5 mm, 1 mm, 10 mm

_____

_____

_____

Prove your answers to Exercises 1–3.

4. 2 m, 2 m, 4 m

_____

5. 9 in., 4 in., 6 in.

_____

6. 5 mm, 10 mm, 1 mm

_____

Use >, <, and + signs to write inequalities for the relationships among the sides of the triangles. Show your work below the numbers.

7. $\frac{1}{2}$ _____ $\frac{1}{3}$ _____ $\frac{1}{5}$

_____

8. 0.1 _____ 0.15 _____ 0.2

_____

9. The model builder has 4 pieces of balsa wood that are 4 cm, 5 cm, 6 cm, and 7 cm in length. How many different combinations of 3 pieces can be used to make triangles without breaking or cutting the pieces? List the combinations as inequalities.

_____

_____

_____

Complete the triangle inequality.

10. The sum of the length of any two sides of a triangle is _____

than the length of the _____ side.

LESSON 15-1

Determining When Three Lengths Form a Triangle

Practice and Problem Solving: C

List the pairs of unequal whole numbers that could be the sides of the triangles.

1. The longest side is 12. One of the shorter sides is 3 less than the other.

    _____

2. The shortest side is 8. The longest side is 12.

    _____

3. Two of the sides are 11 and 15. The third side is no more than 9.

    _____

In a right triangle, the square of the longest side, the *hypotenuse*, is equal to the sum of the squares of the other two sides, the *legs*. Which triangles are right triangles? Prove your answer.

4. One leg of a triangle is 4 and the other is 2. The hypotenuse is 5.

    _____

5. The longest side of a triangle is twice the length of one of the legs. The other leg is equal to the square root of 3, or $\sqrt{3}$, times the other leg.

    _____

6. A 60-foot long crane is parked in the right lane of a city street. The street is 30 feet wide. How high will the crane have to be raised in order to swing around from one end of its trailer to the other end without striking the building on the opposite side of the street?

    _____

    _____

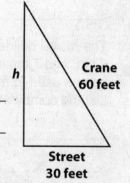

Give the smallest whole number value for the longest sides of triangles with sides *A*, *B*, and *C* so that the other two sides are also whole numbers.

7. $A = \frac{1}{4}B$; $C = 3A$

    _____

    _____

8. $B = 2A$; $6B = 5C$

    _____

    _____

**LESSON
15-1**

Determining When Three Lengths Form a Triangle

Practice and Problem Solving: D

Give the smallest whole number that could equal the length of the side in the picture. The first one is done for you.

1.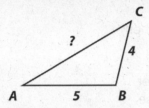

   $5 + 4 >$ ___**6**___

2.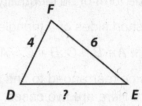

   $4 + 6 >$ _____

3.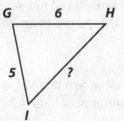

   $6 + 5 >$ _____

4.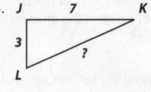

   $3 + 7 >$ _____

Find the smallest whole number for the third side of the triangle. Let A and B be the shorter sides and let C be the longest side. The first one is done for you.

5. $A = 4$, $C = 8$

   $4 + B > 8$

   $B =$ ___**5**___

6. $B = 3$, $C = 9$

   $A + 3 > 9$

   $A =$ _____

7. $A = 5$, $B = 8$

   $5 + 8 > C$

   $C =$ _____

8. A rancher has a 3-sided plot of land that will be used for grazing sheep. One side is 300-yards long and another side is 600 yards long. To the nearest hundred yards, what is the length of the third side of the 3-sided plot of land? Let $300 +$ ____ > 600.

   _____

Name _____ Date _____ Class_____

LESSON 15-1

Determining When Three Lengths Form a Triangle
Reteach

The relationship of the sum of two sides of a triangle to the third side is the rule for finding out if three sides form a triangle. This relationship is often written in the form of an inequality.

If A and B are the short sides of a triangle and C is the longer side, then

$$A + B > C;\ B + C > A;\ C + A > B$$

This inequality can be rearranged to find a missing leg when the other two legs are known. Here are two cases. The third case is in Exercise 1 below.

Case 1
The sides A and C are known but not B. Subtract A from both sides of the inequality and you get $B > C - A$.

Case 2
The sides B and C are known but not A. Subtract B from both sides of the inequality and you get $A > C - B$.

Example 1
If $A = 6$ and $C = 9$, what are two whole-number values of B that could be the lengths of side B? Use $B > C - A$. Substitute: $B > 9 - 6$ or $B > 3$. So, B could be 4 or 5.

Example 2
If $B = 2.5$ and $C = 7.3$, what are two values of A that could be the lengths of side A? Use $A > C - B$. Substitute: $A > 7.3 - 2.5$ or $A > 4.8$. So, A could be 4.9 or 5.0.

A picture of the triangle can also be used to find or measure a missing side if the picture is drawn to scale. In this picture, side $\overline{AB}$ is about 46 units, side $\overline{BC}$ is about 40 units, and side $\overline{AC}$ is about 29 units.

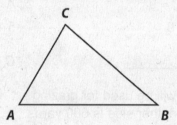

Find the lengths.

1. If $A = 5$ and $B = 10$, find the smallest whole number value of C.

_____

2. If $B = \frac{2}{3}$ and $C = 1\frac{3}{4}$, find the smallest whole number value of A.

_____

LESSON 15-1

Determining When Three Lengths Form a Triangle

Reading Strategies: Using Context Clues

In problems that ask you to determine if three lengths form a triangle, the given information and the words used in the problem setting can provide clues about which math operations to use.

Example

A triangle-shaped piece of flooring tile is 9 inches long along one side and 5 inches long along another side. The third side of the tile has to fit in a space that is no more than 8 inches long. What are the possible lengths of the flooring tile in whole inches?

Solution

Step 1   The relationship among the sides is $A + B > C$. This inequality applies to any combination of the sides:

$$\longrightarrow \quad A + B > C$$
$$\longrightarrow \quad B + C > A$$
$$\longrightarrow \quad C + A > B$$

Step 2   In this problem, the sum of the two known sides, 5 inches and 9 inches, add up to 14 inches, which is greater than the 8-inch long space: $5 + 9 > 8$

However, the problem says that the space is "no more than" 8 inches long, which means that a smaller length would work, too. Finally, the problem asks for possible lengths of flooring "in whole inches."

Step 3   So, two conditions have to be met:

- $5 + 9 > 8$; $5 + 8 > 9$; $8 + 5 > 9$

- The space is *"no more than 8 whole inches."*

What numbers, other than 8, would work? 7? 6? 5? 4?

Do Exercise 1 to find the solution(s) to the Example.

1. Find the third side of the floor tile, other than 8 inches, that is possible for the space that is "no more than 8 inches" in length.

_____

2. The long side of a triangle is 3.45 meters and one of its other sides is 2.5 meters. Explain why the third side cannot be 0.95 meters.

_____

Name ______________________ Date ______________ Class ______________

LESSON 15-1

Determining When Three Lengths Form a Triangle

Success for English Learners

Problem 1

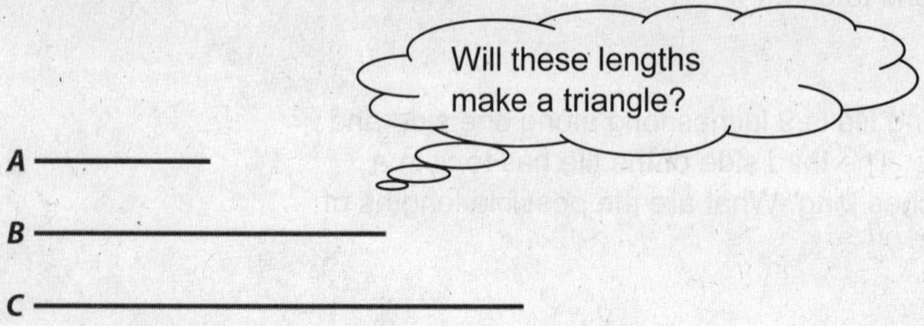

Will these lengths make a triangle?
A
B
C

***A* = 5 units; *B* = 10 units; *C* = 14 units**

You can copy the lengths, cut them out, and find out.

Problem 2

Use the lengths in Problem 1.
Check how the sides relate.

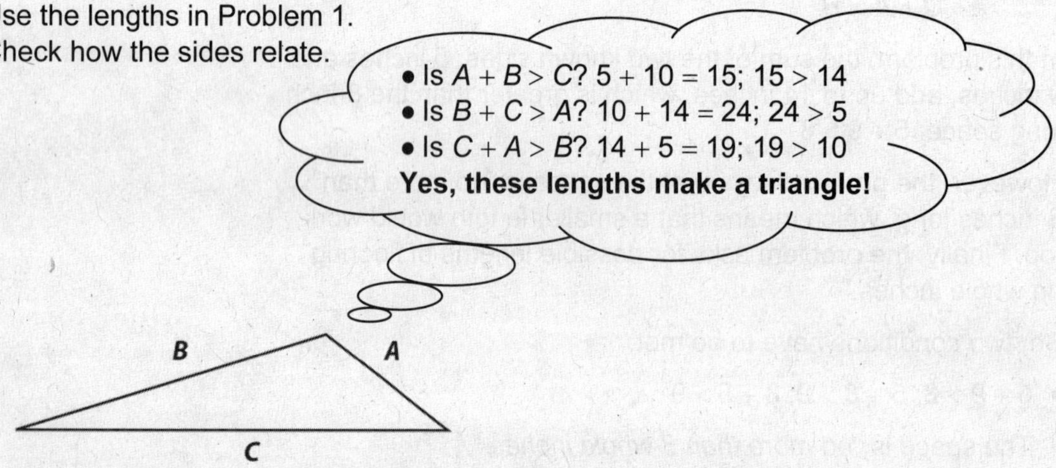

• Is $A + B > C$? $5 + 10 = 15$; $15 > 14$
• Is $B + C > A$? $10 + 14 = 24$; $24 > 5$
• Is $C + A > B$? $14 + 5 = 19$; $19 > 10$
Yes, these lengths make a triangle!
B
A
C

Solve.

1. Make a triangle with the sides 4 yards and 7 yards by picking a third side.

____

2. Do the sides 10 feet, 15 feet, and 25 feet make a triangle? Why or why not?

____

Name _____ Date _____ Class_____

LESSON 15-2

Sum of Angle Measures in a Triangle

Practice and Problem Solving: A/B

Find the missing angle.

1.

_____

2.

_____

3.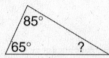

_____

4.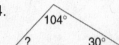

_____

Find the missing angle in a triangle with the given sides.

5. $\angle A = 53°$, $\angle B = 100°$

   $\angle C =$ _____

6. $\angle E = 44°$, $\angle F = 99°$

   $\angle G =$ _____

7. $\angle H = 61°$, $\angle I = 62°$

   $\angle J =$ _____

8. $\angle X = 89°$, $\angle Y = 90°$

   $\angle Z =$ _____

Write an equation that relates the angles in a triangle.

9. The measure of angle *A* is 45 degrees. The measure of angle *B* is *b* degrees. The measure of angle *C* is 3*b* degrees.

_____

10. The measures of angles *X* and *Y* are the same, *x* degrees. The measure of angle *Z* is twice the measure of angle *Y*.

_____

11. What kind of triangle is shown? Why?

_____

12. An isosceles triangle has two equal angles. Give the measure of the third angle that will make triangle *MNO* an isosceles triangle.
$\angle M = 40°$, $\angle N = 70°$

_____

_____

Sum of Angle Measures in a Triangle

LESSON 15-2

Practice and Problem Solving: C

Angles can be measured with calculators and computers in degrees and decimal fractions of a degree, such as 62.5°. Historically, an angle was divided into 60 *minutes* and a minute was divided into 60 *seconds*. The symbol for minutes is the ′. The symbol for seconds is the ″. So, 20 degrees, 15 minutes, and 30 seconds is shown as 20°15′30″.

Find the missing angle measure in each triangle.

1. Angle *A*: 45°15′

   Angle *B*: 77°25′33″

   Angle *C*: _____

2. Angle *D*: 10°25′40″

   Angle *E*: 105°55″

   Angle *F*: _____

Write each angle measure in degrees, minutes, and seconds.

3. Angle *X*: 25.6°

   _____

4. Angle *Y*: 100.25°

   _____

Use the sum of the measures of the angles in a triangle to find the sum of the angles inside each figure.

5.

   Sum of inside angles:

   _____

6.

   Sum of inside angles:

   _____

7.

   Sum of inside angles:

   _____

Find the missing angles in this pair of triangles.

8. In triangle *ABC* and *EFG*, angle *A* is half of angle *E* and also one third of angle *G*. Angle *B* equals the sum of angles *C* and angle *E*. Angle *C* equals angle *G*. Angle *F* equals the sum of angles *A* and *C* and also equals two times angle *E*.

   Angle *A*: _____; angle *B*: _____; angle *C*: _____

   Angle *E*: _____; angle *F*: _____; angle *G*: _____

LESSON 15-2

Sum of Angle Measures in a Triangle

Practice and Problem Solving: D

Find the missing angle measure in the triangle. The first one is done for you.

1.

$85° + 40° + ? = 180°$

___**125**___ $+ ? = 180°$

$? = 180 - $ ___**125°**___

$? = $ ___**55°**___

2.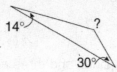

$14° + 30° + ? = 180°$

_____ $+ ? = 180°$

$? = 180° - $ _____

$? = $ _____

3.

_____ $+ $ _____ $+ ? = 180°$

_____ $+ ? = 180°$

$? = $ _____

Find the missing angle. The first one is done for you.

4. $\angle A = 25°$, $\angle B = 63°$, $\angle C = ?$

  $25 + 63 + ? = 180$; $? = 180 - 88 = 92°$

5. $\angle D = 100°$, $\angle E = 10°$, $\angle F = ?$

6. $\angle M = 90°$, $\angle N = 36°$, $\angle O = ?$

7. $\angle P = 125°$, $\angle Q = 3°$, $\angle R = ?$

Write the equation for finding the missing angle, C. The first one is done for you.

8. Angle A is *a* degrees and angle B is *b* degrees.

  $180 = \angle A + \angle B + \angle C$; $180 = a + b + \angle C$; $\angle C = 180 - (a + b) = $ _180 − a − b._

9. Angle A is *x* degrees and angle B is *4x* degrees.

  _____

10. Angle A is 90 degrees and angle B is *x* degrees.

  _____

11. The angle between the lines of sight from a lighthouse to a tugboat and to a cargo ship is 27°. The angle between the lines of sight at the cargo ship is twice the angle between the lines of sight at the tugboat. What are the angles at the tugboat and at the cargo ship?

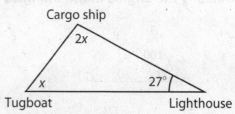

  _____

LESSON 15-2

Sum of Angle Measures in a Triangle
Reteach

Different kinds of triangles have different relationships among their angles. However, in all cases, the angle measures add up to 180° degrees.

Equilateral triangles

Equilateral triangles have three equal sides and three equal angles. By the rule for the sum of the angles in a triangle, each angle in an equilateral triangle has a measure of 60°.

Isosceles triangles

Isosceles triangles have two sides that are equal and two angles that are equal. If the largest angle in an isosceles triangle is a right angle, or 90°, the other two angles have measures of 45° each.

Scalene triangles

Scalene triangles have three *unequal* sides and three *unequal* angles. For example, a triangle with angles measuring 20°, 60°, and 100° is a scalene triangle.

Sometimes, the angles in a triangle are classified as *acute*, *obtuse*, or *right* angles, depending on their angle measures.

Acute angles have a measure less than 90° degrees. A 27° angle is an acute angle.	**Obtuse angles** have measures that are greater than 90°. A 95° angle is an obtuse angle.

Classify the triangles with the angle measures shown.

1.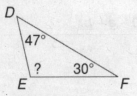

2.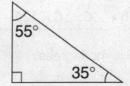

3.

_____   _____   _____

Classify the angles in the triangles as *acute*, *obtuse*, or *right* angles.

4.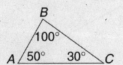

5.

_____   _____

Sum of Angle Measures in a Triangle
Reading Strategies: Analyze Information

To find a missing angle in a triangle problem, you also need to analyze information. You look for what is known and what is unknown. By organizing your analysis into steps, you can make sure that you use all of the information that is available in the problem.

Example

Find the missing angle.

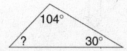

Step 1   Find the missing angle.

Look at the picture. What do you know?

⟶   One angle measures 104°.

⟶   Another angle measures 30°.

Step 2   What rule do you know for this problem?

⟶   The sum of the measures of the three angles is 180°.

Step 3   Put the information together.

104° + 30° + ? = 180°

Step 4   Do the math. What is 104 plus 30? <u>134</u>

What has to be added to 134 to get 180?

180 − 134 = 46

The missing angle is 46°.

The number of steps you use may vary, and will depend on the problem.

Solve. Show your work.

1. Triangle *ABC* is an isosceles triangle. One of the equal angles has a measure of 30°. What is the measure of the third angle?

_____

2. Right triangle *DEF* has a second angle with a measure of 14°. What is the measure of the third angle?

_____

3. Triangle *GHI* is an equilateral triangle. What do you know about the angles?

_____

**LESSON
15-2**

Sum of Angle Measures in a Triangle
Success for English Learners

Problem

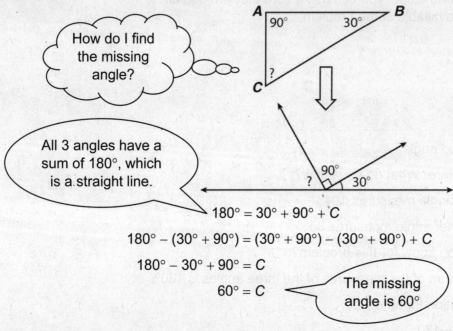

How do I find the missing angle?

All 3 angles have a sum of 180°, which is a straight line.

$$180° = 30° + 90° + C$$
$$180° - (30° + 90°) = (30° + 90°) - (30° + 90°) + C$$
$$180° - 30° + 90° = C$$
$$60° = C$$

The missing angle is 60°

1. Why did you subtract the known angle measures from 180°?

   _____

   _____

2. Is it possible for one of the angles to be 100° and another to be 90°? Explain.

   _____

3. If one angle in a triangle measures 90°, what do you know about the sum of the other two angle measures?

   _____

Name _____ Date _____ Class_____

Relationships Between Sides and Angles in a Triangle
Practice and Problem Solving: A/B

Use the triangles shown below to complete Exercises 1–6.

1.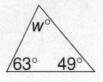

∠w = _____

2.

∠y = _____

3.

∠r = _____

4. The longest side in the triangle in Exercise 1 is opposite the _____ angle.

5. How do the lengths of the sides compare in the triangle in Exercise 2?

_____

6. The shortest side in the triangle in Exercise 3 is opposite the _____ angle(s).

Solve. Show your work.

7. The shortest side of triangle *ABC* is half of the second side and a third
   of the longest side. How does the perimeter of the triangle compare to
   the longest side?

   _____

   _____

8. In triangle *DEF*, side *DE* is 3 inches, side *EF* is 4 inches, and side *DF*
   is 5 inches. The largest angle is opposite which side? Explain your
   choice.

   _____

9. Angle *X* is the largest angle in triangle *XYZ*. Angle *Y* is the smallest
   angle. How does the sum of the measures of angles *Y* and *Z* compare
   to the measure of angle *X*? Explain.

   _____

Describe each statement as *always*, *never*, or *sometimes* true.

10. An obtuse triangle is a scalene triangle. _____

11. A scalene triangle is an isosceles triangle. _____

12. A right triangle is an isosceles triangle. _____

LESSON 15-3

Relationships Between Sides and Angles in a Triangle

Practice and Problem Solving: C

Use the picture to complete Exercises 1–2.

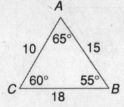

1. How would you change the measure of angle *B* so that the length of *BC* would equal the length of *AC*?

   _____

2. If the measure of angle *B* is *decreased* to 30° by stretching side *BC* to the right while leaving the vertices of angles *A* and *C* where they are, what happens to the other angle and side measures in triangle *ABC*?

   _____

   _____

Draw lines connecting the vertices of the trapezoid to form two triangles, △ABC and △DCA and also △ADB and △BDC. Then use the diagram to complete Exercises 3–5.

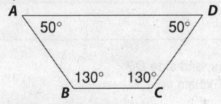

3. Name any of the angle measures and sides of the triangles formed that are the same.

   _____

   _____

4. The angles opposite the common side of the two triangles are unequal. Why don't they have equal angle measures? Explain.

   _____

   _____

5. What is the sum of the other two angle measures in the triangles that have 50° and 130° angles?

   _____

   _____

Name _____ Date _____ Class_____

Relationships Between Sides and Angles in a Triangle
Practice and Problem Solving: D

Use the picture to answer each question. The first one is done for you.

1.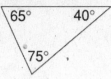

What angle is opposite the longest side?

_____**75°**_____

2.

What angle is opposite the shortest side?

_____

3.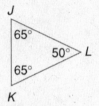

Give the letter name of the side that is opposite the shortest side.

_____

4.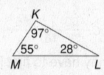

Which side is opposite the middle-size angle? Give its letter name.

_____

Write the words that apply to each triangle: equilateral, isosceles, right, and scalene. You can use more than one word. The first one is done for you.

5.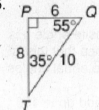

_____**right; scalene**_____

6.

_____

7.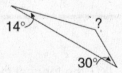

Given: ? = 136°

_____

8.

Given: ? = 45°

_____

LESSON
15-3

Relationships Between Sides and Angles in a Triangle
Reteach

The rule in this lesson that describes how angles and sides are related applies to all of the types of triangles presented so far.

→ *In a triangle, the side opposite the larger of two angles is longer than the side that is opposite the smaller angle.*

For example, in triangle *ABC*, the largest angle is angle *A* which has a measure of 65°. The side opposite angle *A*, side *CB*, is also the longest side of the three sides of the triangle.

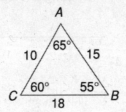

In special triangles, you may have to first identify the general way that angles and sides are related before you can label an angle or side. The examples show two of these cases.

Example 1
What is the longest side in triangle *DEF*?

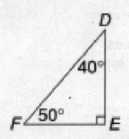

The square between the sides *DE* and *EF* indicates a right angle, which has a measure of 90°.
If a triangle has a 90° angle, neither of other two angles will be greater than 90°.
Therefore, the side opposite the 90° angle will be the longest side, which is side *DF* in this example.

Example 2
Which side of the triangle is the shortest?

It appears that the side opposite angle *u* is the shortest. To be sure, notice that this is an *isosceles* triangle with two equal angles and equal sides.
Since the two equal angles add up to 150°, angle *u* has to be 180° minus 150°, or 30°.
Since angle *u* is 30°, the side opposite it is the shortest side.

Answer the questions.

1. In triangle *XYZ*, angle *X* is 95 degrees. How do you know that the side opposite angle *X* is the longest without computing the other angles and sides?

2. In isosceles triangle *JKL*, the longest side is opposite angle *L*. What does this mean about the other two angles and sides?

_____ _____

LESSON 15-3

Relationships Between Sides and Angles in a Triangle
Reading Strategies: Use Graphic Aids

Sometimes, drawing a diagram can help you understand the information
in a problem. This is especially true for directional words that do not always
have precise meanings, like "north" and "southwest."

Example

A school plans to build a courtyard "honor" walk 50 feet long and due north
from the school flag pole. From there, the sidewalk will go 100 feet
southeast to a dedication marker. The sidewalk will then be extended
northwest back to the flag pole. Is the last part of the sidewalk the longest
side of the triangle formed by the three sections? Explain your answer.

Solution

Step 1   This problem is best visualized with a diagram or a
picture. For example, this diagram shows the three
sidewalks as the sides of a triangle *ABC*.

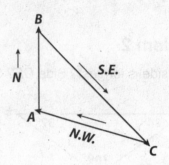

Step 2   First, draw the "due north" sidewalk from point *A* to point *B* that is 50 feet long.
Pick a map or drawing length for it, which will be doubled for the next part of
the sidewalk.

Step 3   Next, draw the "southeast" sidewalk between points *B* and *C* with a length of 100
feet, *twice* that between points *A* and *B*. This part will point in a direction of roughly
45°, down and to the right. The choice of 45° is not the only direction for
"southeast," but it divides the map "half way" between "east" and "south."

Step 4   Finally, draw the last part of the sidewalk "northwest" from point *C* back to point *A*.
Here, "northwest" *is* an exact direction since it connects points *C* and *A*.

Step 5   It is not possible to calculate an exact length for the third part of the sidewalk with
what you have learned up to this point. However, a reasonable estimate would be
that the third part of the sidewalk is *not* as long as the part between points *B* and *C*.

1. Make a drawing of the problem in the example. Measure the sides of
   triangle *ABC* to see if their measures confirm the conclusion from Step 5.

_____

2. Can the direction of "northwest" be changed so that the sidewalk
   between points *A* and *C* will be longer than the sidewalk from point *B*
   to point *C*? Explain.

_____

LESSON 15-3

Relationships Between Sides and Angles in a Triangle

Success for English Learners

Problem 1

Which is the largest angle? Angle *A*, angle *B*, or angle *C*?

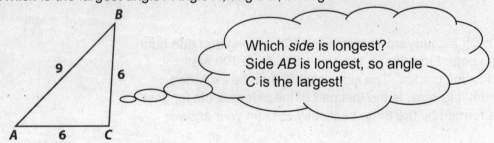

Which *side* is longest?
Side *AB* is longest, so angle
C is the largest!

Problem 2

Which side is longest? Side *DE*? Side *EF*? Side *DF*?

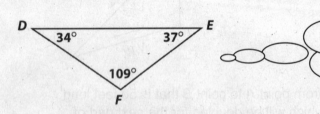

Which *angle* is largest?
Angle *F* is largest, so side
DE is the longest!

Complete the missing part.

1. Which is the longest side?

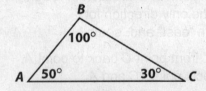

the side opposite angle _____

side _____

2. Which is the largest angle?

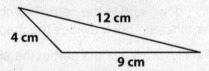

the angle opposite the _____

centimeter side

MODULE 15
Angles, Triangles, and Equations
Challenge

Figure *ABCD* is a square. Answer the questions about the diagram. Explain your answers.

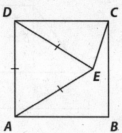

1. What kind of triangle is *ADE*?

   _____

2. Draw a straight line between points *B* and *E*. What kind of triangle is formed by points *B*, *C*, and *E*?

   _____

   _____

3. What is the sum of the measures of angles *ADE* and *CDE*?

   _____

4. What is the measure of angle *ADE*?

   _____

5. What is the measure of angle *CDE*?

   _____

6. What is the sum of the measures of angles *CDE* and *BCE*?

   _____

7. Is it possible to find the measure of angle *BCE*? Why or why not? If so, give the measure of angle *BCE*.

   _____

   _____

8. Find the measure of angle *CEB*.

   _____

LESSON 16-1

Area of Quadrilaterals

Practice and Problem Solving: A/B

Find the area of each parallelogram.

1.
18 ft
16 ft

_____

2.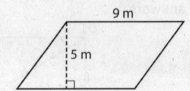
9 m
5 m

_____

Find the area of each trapezoid.

3.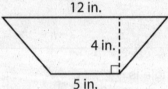
12 in.
4 in.
5 in.

_____

4.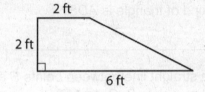
2 ft
2 ft
6 ft

_____

Find the area of each rhombus.

5.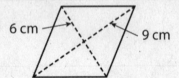
6 cm
9 cm

_____

6.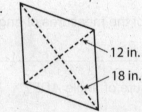
12 in.
18 in.

_____

Solve.

7. A desktop in the shape of a parallelogram has a base of 30 inches and a height of 40 inches. What is the area of the desktop?

_____

8. A rhombus has one diagonal that is 14 centimeters long and one diagonal that is 12 centimeters long. What is the area of the rhombus?

_____

9. The bases of a trapezoid are 24 feet and 16 feet. The height of the trapezoid is 12 feet. What is the area of the trapezoid?

_____

Name _____ Date _____ Class_____

LESSON 16-1

Area of Quadrilaterals

Practice and Problem Solving: C

Find the area of each figure.

1.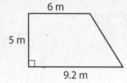

   6 m
   5 m
   9.2 m

   _____

2.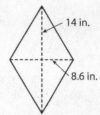

   14 in.
   8.6 in.

   _____

3.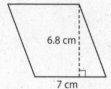

   6.8 cm
   7 cm

   _____

4.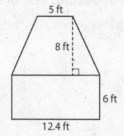

   5 ft
   8 ft
   6 ft
   12.4 ft

   _____

Solve.

5. A section of a stained-glass window is shaped like a parallelogram. Its base is 6.5 inches, and its height is 4 inches. How much glass is needed to cover the section completely?

   _____

6. The base of a statue is in the shape of a trapezoid. The bases of the statue are 7.5 feet and 4.75 feet. Its height is 6 feet. What is the area of the base of the statue?

   _____

7. The front view of a piece of art is in the shape of a rhombus. The front view of the art has diagonals that are 1.4 yards long and 0.8 yards long. What is the area of the front view of the piece of art?

   _____

8. A decorative pillow is in the shape of a parallelogram. Its base is 28 centimeters, and its height is 24.5 centimeters. What is the area of the front surface of the pillow?

   _____

LESSON 16-1

Area of Quadrilaterals
Practice and Problem Solving: D

Find the area of each parallelogram. The first one is done for you.

1.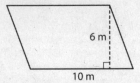

6 m
10 m

$A = 10 \cdot 6 = 60 \text{ m}^2$

2.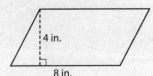

4 in.
8 in.

_____

Find the area of each trapezoid. The first one is done for you.

3.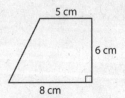

5 cm
6 cm
8 cm

$A = \dfrac{1}{2} \cdot 6 \cdot (8 + 5) = 39 \text{ cm}^2$

4.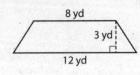

8 yd
3 yd
12 yd

_____

Find the area of each rhombus. The first one is done for you.

5.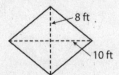

8 ft
10 ft

$A = \dfrac{1}{2} \cdot 8 \cdot 10 = 40 \text{ ft}^2$

6.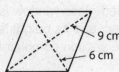

9 cm
6 cm

_____

Solve.

7. A countertop in the shape of a parallelogram has a base of 90 centimeters and a height of 50 centimeters. What is the area of the countertop?

_____

8. A rhombus has one diagonal that is 10 inches long and one diagonal that is 15 inches long. What is the area of the rhombus?

_____

9. The bases of a trapezoid are 4 yards and 6 yards. The height of the trapezoid is 5 yards. What is the area of the trapezoid?

_____

LESSON 16-1
Area of Quadrilaterals
Reteach

You can use formulas to find the areas of quadrilaterals.

The area A of a **parallelogram** is the product of its base b and its height h.

$$A = bh$$

$$\begin{aligned} A &= bh \\ &= 3 \cdot 7 \\ &= 21 \text{ cm}^2 \end{aligned}$$

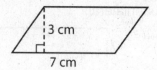

The area of a **trapezoid** is half its height multiplied by the sum of the lengths of its two bases.

$$A = \frac{1}{2}h(b_1 + b_2)$$

$$\begin{aligned} A &= \frac{1}{2}h(b_1 + b_2) \\ &= \frac{1}{2} \cdot 6(5 + 9) \\ &= \frac{1}{2} \cdot 6(14) \\ &= 3 \cdot 14 \\ &= 42 \text{ m}^2 \end{aligned}$$

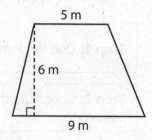

The area of a **rhombus** is half of the product of its two diagonals.

$$A = \frac{1}{2}d_1 d_2$$

$$\begin{aligned} A &= \frac{1}{2}d_1 d_2 \\ &= \frac{1}{2}(5)(8) \\ &= 20 \text{ in}^2 \end{aligned}$$

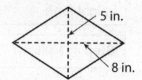

Find the area of each figure.

1.
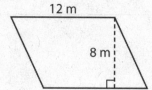

_____

2.
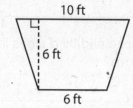

_____

3.
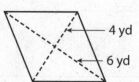

_____

4.
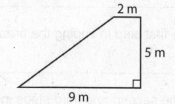

_____

LESSON
16-1

Area of Quadrilaterals

Reading Strategies: Follow a Procedure

Parallelograms and trapezoids are two different types of quadrilaterals.
You can follow a procedure to help you find the area of each type
of quadrilateral.

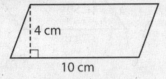

4 cm

10 cm

6 in.

4 in.

8 in.

Step 1: Use the formula $A = bh$.

↓

Step 2: Substitute the length of the
base for b.

↓

Step 3: Substitute the length of the
height for h.

↓

Step 4: Multiply.

Step 1: Use the formula $A = \frac{1}{2}h(b_1 + b_2)$.

↓

Step 2: Substitute the length of the height
for h.

↓

Step 3: Substitute the length of the bases
for b_1 and b_2 and add.

↓

Step 4: Multiply.

Solve.

1. What is the first step in finding the area of the parallelogram above?

   _____

2. What are the second and third steps in finding the area of the
   parallelogram above?

   _____

3. What is the area of the parallelogram above?

   _____

4. What is the first step in finding the area of the trapezoid?

   _____

5. What are the second and third steps in finding the area of the
   trapezoid above?

   _____

6. What is the area of the trapezoid above?

   _____

LESSON
16-1

Area of Quadrilaterals

Success for English Learners

Problem 1

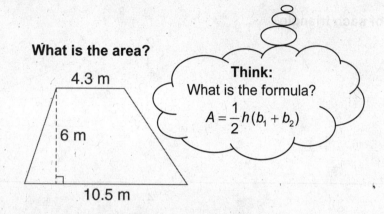

What is the area?

4.3 m

6 m

10.5 m

Think:
What is the formula?

$A = \frac{1}{2}h(b_1 + b_2)$

Remember	
A = Area	h = height
b_1 = base on top	b_2 = base on bottom

What is the height? $h = 6$ m

What is the base on top? $b_1 = 4.3$ m

What is the base on the bottom? $b_2 = 10.5$ m

$A = \frac{1}{2}h(b_1 + b_2)$ Use formula.

$A = \frac{1}{2}(6)(4.3 + 10.5)$ Substitute.

$A = (3)(4.3 + 10.5)$ Multiply.

$A = (3)(14.8)$ Add.

$A = 3 \bullet 14.8 = 44.4$ Multiply.

$A = 44.4 \, m^2$

So, the area is 44.4 m².

1. Does it matter which length you use for b_1 and which you use for b_2?
   Explain.

   _____

2. Describe another way to find the area of a trapezoid.

   _____

3. Find the area of the trapezoid shown.

   _____

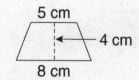

5 cm

4 cm

8 cm

**LESSON
16-2**

Area of Triangles

Practice and Problem Solving: A/B

Find the area of each triangle.

1.

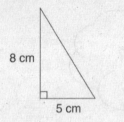

8 cm

5 cm

_____

2.

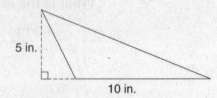

5 in.

10 in.

_____

3.

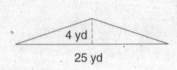

4 yd

25 yd

_____

4.

4 ft

3.5 ft

_____

Solve.

5. The front part of a tent is 8 feet long and 5 feet tall.
   What is the area of the front part of the tent?

   _____

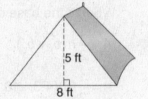

5 ft

8 ft

6. Kathy is playing a board game. The game pieces are
   each in the shape of a triangle. Each triangle has a
   base of 1.5 inches and a height of 2 inches. What is
   the area of a game piece?

   _____

7. A triangular-shaped window has a base of 3 feet and a height
   of 4 feet. What is the area of the window?

   _____

8. Landon has a triangular piece of paper. The base of the paper
   is $6\frac{1}{2}$ inches. The height of the paper is 8 inches. What is the
   area of the piece of paper?

   _____

Name _____ Date _____ Class_____

LESSON 16-2

Area of Triangles
Practice and Problem Solving: C

Find the area of each triangle.

1.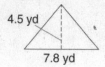

4.5 yd

7.8 yd

_____

2.

$4\frac{1}{2}$ ft

$3\frac{3}{4}$ ft

_____

3.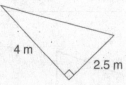

4 m

2.5 m

_____

4.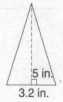

5 in.

3.2 in.

_____

Solve.

5. If you wanted to find the total area of the triangles in Exercises 1, 2, and 4, what could you do?

_____

_____

6. A scale model of a street sign is in the shape of a triangle. The base is 4.25 centimeters and the height is 8.8 centimeters. What is the area of the street sign?

_____

7. Rachel's earrings are in the shape of a triangle. The height of the earrings is $1\frac{1}{2}$ inches and the base is $\frac{3}{5}$ inch. What is the area of both of Rachel's earrings?

_____

8. The face of a watch is in the shape of a triangle with a base of 6 centimeters and a height of 7.75 centimeters. What is the area of the face of the watch?

_____

9. A flag in the shape of a triangle has an area of 25.2 square inches. The base of the flag is 6 inches. What is the height of the flag?

_____

Name _____ Date _____ Class_____

Area of Triangles

Practice and Problem Solving: D

Find the area of each triangle. The first one is done for you.

1.

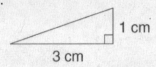

1 cm
3 cm

$A = \frac{1}{2} \cdot 3 \cdot 1 = 1.5 \text{ cm}^2$

2.

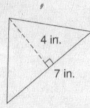

4 in.
7 in.

3.

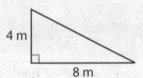

4 m
8 m

4.

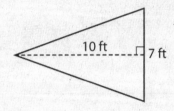

10 ft   7 ft

5.

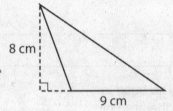

8 cm
9 cm

6.

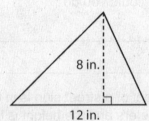

8 in.
12 in.

Solve each problem. The first one is done for you.

7. A triangular-shaped rug has a base of 8 feet and a height of 7 feet. What is the area of the rug?

$A = \frac{1}{2} \cdot 8 \cdot 7 = 28 \text{ ft}^2$

8. The sail on a sailboat is in the shape of a triangle that has a base of 12 feet and a height of 14 feet. What is the area of the sail?

9. The front view of a square pyramid is in the shape of a triangle that has a base of 30 yards and a height of 40 yards. What is the area of the front view of the square pyramid?

LESSON 16-2

Area of Triangles

Reteach

To find the area of a triangle, first turn your triangle into a rectangle.

Next, find the area of the rectangle. $6 \cdot 3 = 18$ square units

The triangle is half the area of the formed rectangle or $A = \dfrac{1}{2}bh$, so

divide the product by 2.

$18 \div 2 = 9$ So, the area of the triangle is 9 square units.

Find the area of each triangle.

1.

4 cm
6 cm

_____

2.

3 ft
4 ft

_____

3.

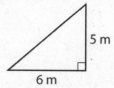
5 m
6 m

_____

4.

3 mm
6 mm

_____

5.

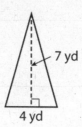
7 yd
4 yd

_____

6.

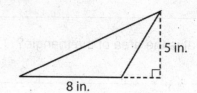
5 in.
8 in.

_____

LESSON 16-2

Area of Triangles

Reading Strategies: Follow a Procedure

You can follow a procedure to help you find the area of a triangle.

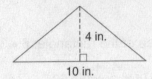

4 in.

10 in.

Step 1: Use the formula $A = \frac{1}{2}bh$.

↓

Step 2: Substitute the length of the base for b.

↓

Step 3: Substitute the length of the height for h.

↓

Step 4: Multiply.

Answer each question.

1. What is the first step in finding the area of the triangle?

_____

2. What are the second and third steps in finding the area of the triangle?

_____

3. What is the area of the triangle?

_____

4. What is the area of a triangle with base 18 meters and height 6 meters?

_____

5. What is the area of a triangle with base 3.6 feet and height 2.5 feet?

_____

6. How would you vary this procedure if you were given the area and base of a triangle and asked to find its height?

_____

LESSON 16-2

Area of Triangles

Success for English Learners

Problem 1

What is the area?

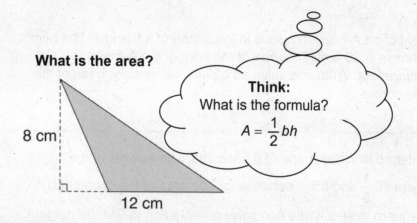

8 cm

12 cm

Think:
What is the formula?
$A = \frac{1}{2}bh$

Remember:
A = Area b = base h = height
Examples of square units: ft², yd², cm²

The base is 12 cm.

The height is 8 cm.

$A = \frac{1}{2}bh$ Use formula.

$A = \frac{1}{2}(12 \bullet 8)$ Use measurements.

$A = \frac{1}{2}(96)$ Multiply. 12 • 8 = 96

$A = \frac{1}{2}(96) = 48$ Divide. 96 ÷ 2 = 48

$A = 48$ cm²

So, the area is 48 cm².

1. Does it matter which side of the triangle you use as the base and which you use as the height? Explain.

_____

2. Why is the expression $(\frac{1}{2} \bullet 12) \bullet 8$ the same as $\frac{1}{2} \bullet (12 \bullet 8)$?

_____

3. Find the area of the triangle shown.

_____

8 ft

4 ft

LESSON 16-3

Solving Area Equations
Practice and Problem Solving: A/B

Solve.

1. The front of an A-frame house is in the shape of a triangle. The height of the house is 20 feet. The area of the front of the A-frame is 600 square feet. Write and solve an equation to find the base of the A-frame house.

   _____

2. A countertop is in the shape of a trapezoid. The lengths of the bases are $70\frac{1}{2}$ and $65\frac{1}{2}$ inches long. The area of the countertop is 1,224 square inches. Write and solve an equation to find the height of the countertop.

   _____

3. The top of a coffee table is in the shape of a rectangle. The length of the top of the coffee table is 3.5 feet and the area is 10.5 square feet. What is the width of the top of the coffee table?

   _____

4. Jacob made a banner for a sporting event in the shape of a parallelogram. The area of the banner is $127\frac{1}{2}$ square centimeters. The height of the banner is $4\frac{1}{4}$ centimeters. What is the base of the banner?

   _____

5. McKenzie has enough paint to paint 108 square feet. She wants to paint her garage door, which has a height of 12 feet. The garage door is in the shape of a rectangle. If McKenzie has just enough paint to cover the garage door, what is the width of the door?

   _____

LESSON
16-3

Solving Area Equations
Practice and Problem Solving: C

Solve.

1. The front of a podium is in the shape of a trapezoid with base lengths 4 and 8.5 feet. The height is 2 feet. A gallon of paint covers about 350 square feet. How many front frames of a podium can Lillian paint with 2 gallons of paint?

   _____

2. Kenneth's back yard is in the shape of a rectangle with a length of 12 yards and a width of 10 yards. A bag of grass seed costs $25.99 and covers 400 square feet. How much will Kenneth spend on grass seed to cover his back yard?

   _____

3. The area of a triangular piece of stained glass is 50 square centimeters. If the height of the triangle is four times the base, how long are the height and base of the piece of stained glass?

   _____

4. A park is in the shape of a parallelogram. The park has an area of $776\frac{1}{4}$ square yards. The base of the park is $34\frac{1}{2}$ yards. Marta wants to jog 10 sprints. Each sprint is the same distance as the height of the park. How far will Marta sprint?

   _____

5. A quilt contains cuts of congruent right triangular pieces with a base of $8\frac{1}{2}$ centimeters and a height of $8\frac{1}{2}$ centimeters. How many triangular pieces are needed to make a rectangular quilt with an area of 4,335 square centimeters?

   _____

LESSON
16-3

Solving Area Equations

Practice and Problem Solving: D

Solve each problem. The first one is done for you.

1. Jennifer has a picture frame in the shape of a rectangle. The area of the picture frame is 35 square inches. The length of the picture frame is 7 inches. What is the width of the frame?

$$A = lw$$
$$35 = 7w$$

5 in._____ $5 = w$

2. Christopher's back yard is in the shape of a trapezoid. The bases of his back yard are 30 and 40 feet long. The area of his back yard is 525 square feet. Write and solve an equation to find the height of Christopher's back yard.

_____

3. Cindy made a triangular shaped sculpture with an area of 63 square inches. The height of the sculpture is 9 inches. What is the base length of the sculpture?

_____

4. A floor mat is in the shape of a parallelogram. The mat has an area of 480 square inches. If the base of the mat is 24 inches, what is the height of the mat?

_____

5. A trading token is in the shape of a trapezoid and has an area of 25 square centimeters. If the bases are 3 and 7 centimeters, what is the height of the token?

_____

6. The back frame of a dog house is in the shape of a triangle with an area of 6 square feet. The height of the frame is 4 feet. What is the width of the frame?

_____

Solving Area Equations

LESSON 16-3

Reteach

You can use area formulas to find missing dimensions in figures.

The formula for area of a parallelogram is $A = bh$.

The formula for area of a trapezoid is $A = \frac{1}{2}h(b_1 + b_2)$.

The formula for area of a rhombus is $A = \frac{1}{2}d_1d_2$.

The formula for area of a triangle is $A = \frac{1}{2}bh$.

Suppose you know the area of a triangle is 28 square feet. You also know the length of the base of the triangle is 7 feet. What is the height of the triangle?

Use the formula for area of a triangle. $A = \frac{1}{2}bh$

Substitute known values. $28 = \frac{1}{2}(7)h$

Multiply both sides by 2. $56 = 7h$
Divide both sides by 7. $8 = h$

The height of the triangle is 8 feet.

Solve.

1. The area of a parallelogram is 150 square meters. The height of the parallelogram is 15 meters. What is the length of the parallelogram?

   _____

2. The length of one diagonal of a rhombus is 8 cm. The area of the rhombus is 72 square centimeters. What is the length of the other diagonal of the rhombus?

   _____

3. The area of a triangle is 32 square inches. The height of the triangle is 8 inches. What is the length of the base of the triangle?

   _____

4. The area of a rectangle is 34 square yards. The length of the rectangle is 17 yards. What is the width of the rectangle?

   _____

5. The area of a trapezoid is 39 square millimeters. The height of the trapezoid is 6 millimeters. One of the base lengths of the trapezoid is 5 millimeters. What is the length of the other base of the trapezoid?

   _____

Name _____ Date _____ Class_____

Solving Area Equations
Reading Strategies: Draw a Diagram

You can find missing measurements of figures when you know the formula for the figure and when you are given other information about the figure.

First, you need to know the different area formulas for common figures.

Figure	Area Formula
Parallelogram	$A = bh$
Trapezoid	$A = \frac{1}{2}h(b_1 + b_2)$
Rhombus	$A = \frac{1}{2}d_1 d_2$
Triangle	$A = \frac{1}{2}bh$

First, you should draw a diagram. Be sure to label the diagram with all the information you are given.

For example, a triangular-shaped poster has an area of 16 square meters and a base length of 8 meters. What is the height of the poster?

Draw a diagram. Label the diagram with the given information.

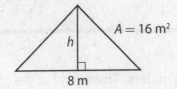

$A = 16\text{ m}^2$

h

8 m

Now, use the given information with the formula for area of a triangle.

$A = \frac{1}{2}bh$ Write the formula for area of a triangle.

$16 = \frac{1}{2}(8)(h)$ The area is 16 and the base is 8.

$16 = 4h$ Multiply $\frac{1}{2}$ and 8.

$4 = h$ Divide both sides by 4.

The height of the poster is 4 meters.

Solve.

1. A parallelogram has an area of 60 square inches. If the base of the parallelogram is 12 inches, what is the height of the parallelogram?

_____

2. A trapezoid and has an area of 45 square centimeters. If the bases are 10 and 5 centimeters, what is the height of the trapezoid?

_____

LESSON 16-3
Solving Area Equations
Success for English Learners

Problem 1

If you are given the length of the base and the area, you can find the height of a parallelogram.

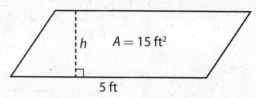

$A = bh$ Write the formula for area.

$15 = 5h$ The area is 15 and the length of the base is 5.

$3 = h$ Divide both sides by 5.

Problem 2

If you are given the height and the area, you can find the length of the base of a triangle.

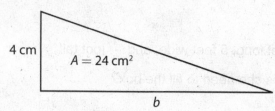

$A = \dfrac{1}{2}bh$ Write the formula for area.

$24 = \dfrac{1}{2}(b)(4)$ The area is 24 and the height is 4.

$24 = 2b$ Multiply $\dfrac{1}{2}$ and 4.

$12 = b$ Divide both sides by 2.

1. When given the area and known dimensions, what is the first step in finding an unknown measure in a figure?

_____

2. What is the next step?

_____

Name _____ Date _____ Class _____

LESSON 16-4
Solving Volume Equations
Practice and Problem Solving: A/B

Find the volume of each figure.

1.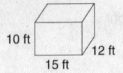
10 ft 12 ft 15 ft

_____

2.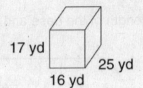
17 yd 25 yd 16 yd

_____

3.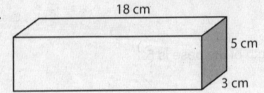
18 cm 5 cm 3 cm

_____

4.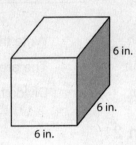
6 in. 6 in. 6 in.

_____

Solve.

5. Fawn built a sandbox that is 6 feet long, 5 feet wide, and $\frac{1}{2}$ foot tall. How many cubic feet of sand does she need to fill the box?

_____

6. A pack of gum is in the shape of a rectangular prism with a length of 8 centimeters and width of 2 centimeters. The volume of the pack of gum is 48 cubic centimeters. What is the height of the pack of gum?

_____

7. A block of cheese is in the shape of a rectangular prism with a width of 2.5 inches and a height of 5 inches. The volume of the block of cheese is 75 cubic inches. What is the length of the block of cheese?

_____

8. A tissue box is in the shape of a rectangular prism with an area of 528 cubic inches. The length of the box of tissues is 12 inches and the height is $5\frac{1}{2}$ inches. What is the width of the box of tissues?

_____

Name _____ Date _____ Class _____

LESSON
16-4

Solving Volume Equations

Practice and Problem Solving: C

Find the volume of each figure.

1.   4 m
      ╱_____╱ 0.02 m
      6 m

2.

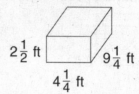

$2\frac{1}{2}$ ft $9\frac{1}{4}$ ft

$4\frac{1}{4}$ ft

_____   _____

3.   16.2 cm

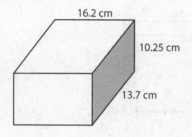

10.25 cm

13.7 cm

4.

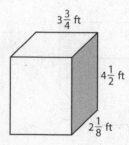

$3\frac{3}{4}$ ft

$4\frac{1}{2}$ ft

$2\frac{1}{8}$ ft

_____   _____

Solve.

5. If you changed the measures in Exercises 1 and 3 to fractions and

   mixed numbers, would you get the same volumes? _____

6. A rectangular prism's base is 8 feet long. It is $2\frac{1}{2}$ times taller than it is

   long and $\frac{1}{2}$ as wide as it is tall. What is the volume of that prism?

   _____

7. A box of mashed potato flakes has a volume of 220 in³. The box is
   8 inches long and 11 inches tall. What is the width of the box of
   mashed potato flakes?

   _____

8. A building shaped like a rectangular prism is 42 yards long, 30 yards
   wide, and 120 yards tall. On average, it cost $0.02 per cubic yard to
   provide heat and electricity for one month. What is the heat and electric
   bill for one month?

   _____

9. A 12 inches by 12 inches by 12 inches container of water was placed in the
   freezer. Water expands 4% when it is frozen. What is the volume of the
   container when it is frozen? Give your answer in cubic inches and cubic feet.

   _____

LESSON 16-4

Solving Volume Equations
Practice and Problem Solving: D

Find the volume of each figure. The first one is done for you.

1.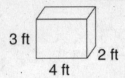
   3 ft, 2 ft, 4 ft

   $V = 3(4)(2) = 24; 24 \text{ ft}^3$

2.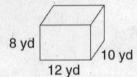
   8 yd, 10 yd, 12 yd

   _____

3.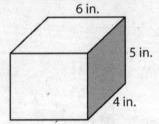
   6 in., 5 in., 4 in.

   _____

4.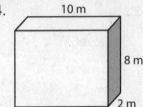
   10 m, 8 m, 2 m

   _____

Solve each problem. The first one is done for you.

5. Tim made a toy chest for his little sister's square building blocks. If 6 layers of blocks can fit in the box, and each layer has 15 blocks, how many building blocks can the toy chest hold in all?

   $V = 15(6) = 90; 90 \text{ blocks}$

6. Kathy bought a jewelry box in the shape of a rectangular prism. The volume of the jewelry box is 192 cubic inches. The length and width of the jewelry box are 8 and 6 inches respectively. What is the height of the jewelry box?

   _____

7. A filing cabinet has a height of 4 feet and a length of 2 feet. The volume of the filing cabinet is 24 cubic feet. What is the width of the filing cabinet?

   _____

8. A box of business cards is in the shape of a rectangular prism. The volume of the box of cards is 360 cubic centimeters. The length of the box is 12 centimeters and the height of the box is 5 centimeters. What is the width of the box of business cards?

   _____

Name _____ Date _____ Class_____

LESSON 16-4

Solving Volume Equations
Reteach

Volume is the number of cubic units needed to fill a space. To find the volume of a rectangular prism, first find the area of the base.

length = 3 units

width = 2 units

$A = lw = 3 \cdot 2 = 6$ square units

The area of the base tells you how many cubic units are in the first layer of the prism.

The height is 4, so multiply 6 by 4.

$6 \cdot 4 = 24$

So, the volume of the rectangular prism is 24 cubic units.

Find each volume.

1.

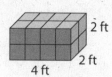

2 ft
2 ft
4 ft

_____

2.

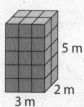

5 m
2 m
3 m

_____

3.

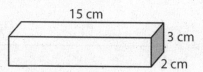

15 cm
3 cm
2 cm

_____

4.

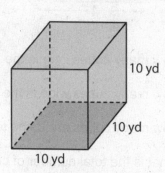

10 yd
10 yd
10 yd

_____

5.

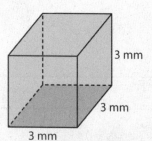

3 mm
3 mm
3 mm

_____

6.

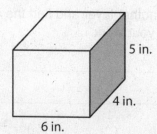

5 in.
4 in.
6 in.

_____

Original content Copyright © by Houghton Mifflin Harcourt. Additions and changes to the original content are the responsibility of the instructor.

337

LESSON 16-4

Solving Volume Equations

Reading Strategies: Analyze Information

You can think of the **volume** of a prism as the number of unit cubes it contains.

Look at the first layer of cubic units in this rectangular prism.

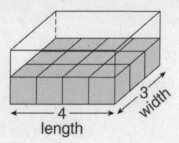

1. How many cubes long is the first layer?   _____

2. How many cubes wide is the first layer?   _____

3. How many cubes are in the first layer?   _____

Now look at the next layer of cubes.

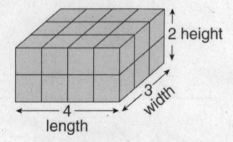

4. How many cubes long is the top layer?   _____

5. How many cubes wide is the top layer?   _____

6. How many cubes are in the top layer?   _____

7. What is the total number of cubes in both layers?   _____

8. What is the total volume of the rectangular prism?   _____

9. Add another layer and find the volume for the new figure.
   Show your work.

   _____

   _____

Solving Volume Equations

Success for English Learners

Problem 1

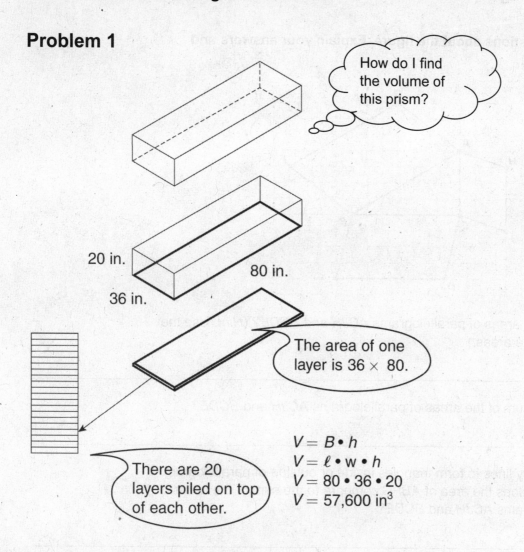

How do I find the volume of this prism?

20 in.

80 in.

36 in.

The area of one layer is 36×80.

There are 20 layers piled on top of each other.

$V = B \cdot h$
$V = \ell \cdot w \cdot h$
$V = 80 \cdot 36 \cdot 20$
$V = 57{,}600 \text{ in}^3$

1. Describe how to find the volume of a rectangular prism.

_____

2. How are units for volume different than units for area?

_____

Volume and Surface Area
Challenge

Answer the questions about the figure. Explain your answers and show your work.

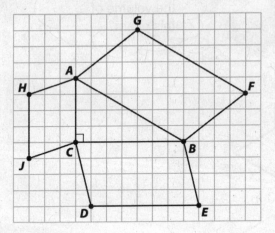

1. What are the areas of parallelograms *ACJH* and *BCDE*? (*Hint:* Use the grid to find the areas.)

   _____

2. What is the sum of the areas of parallelograms *ACJH* and *BCDE*?

   _____

3. Draw auxiliary lines to form triangles inside or outside of parallelogram *ABFG*. How does the area of *ABFG* compare *to* the sum of the areas of parallelograms *ACJH* and *BCDE*?

   _____

4. Use the Pythagorean Theorem, $a^2 + b^2 = c^2$, to find the length of side *AB* of right triangle *ABC*.

   _____

5. How does the length of *AB* affect the area of *ABFG* as it relates to the sum of the areas of parallelograms *ABFG*, *ACJH*, and *BCDE*?

   _____

Name _____ Date _____ Class _____

Measures of Center
Practice and Problem Solving: A/B

Use the situation below to complete Exercises 1–4.

The heights (in inches) of the starting players on a high school basketball team are as follows: 72, 75, 78, 72, 73.

1. How many starting players are there? _____

2. What is the mean height? _____

3. What is the median height? _____

4. Does one measure describe the data better than the other? Explain.

_____

In Exercises 5–7, find the mean and median of each data set.

5. Daily high temperatures (°F): 45, 50, 47, 52, 53, 45, 51

   Mean: _____   Median: _____

6. Brian's math test scores: 86, 90, 93, 85, 79, 92

   Mean: _____   Median: _____

7. Players' heart rates (beats per minute): 70, 68, 70, 72, 68, 66, 65, 73

   Mean: _____   Median: _____

8. Hikers spent the following amounts of time (in minutes) to complete a nature hike: 48, 46, 52, 57, 58, 52, 61, 56.

   a. Find the mean and median times.

   Mean: _____   Median: _____

   b. Does one measure describe the data better than the other? Explain.

   _____

   c. Suppose another hiker takes 92 minutes to complete the hike. Find the mean and median times including this new time.

   Mean: _____   Median: _____

   d. Does one measure describe the data better than the other now? Explain.

   _____

   _____

LESSON
17-1

Measures of Center
Practice and Problem Solving: C

Find the mean and median of each data set.

1. Monthly rainfall (in inches): 7.6, 6.7, 8.1, 6.2, 6.0, 6.2

   Mean: _____   Median: _____

2. Dylan's weekly earnings (in dollars): 200, 167, 185, 212, 195, 193, 188, 140

   Mean: _____   Median: _____

3. Fundraising calendars sold per person: 22, 13, 47, 11, 8, 16, 15, 14, 13, 17

   Mean: _____   Median: _____

The line plot below shows the number of kilometers Clara ran each day for 14 days. Use the line plot for Exercises 4 and 5.

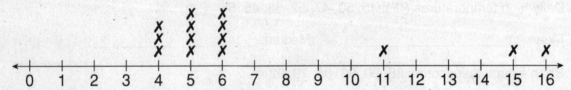

4. Find the mean and median for the data.

   _____

5. Does one measure describe the data better than the other? Explain.

   _____

   _____

In Exercises 6 and 7, use the given measure to find the missing value in each data set.

6. The mean of the ages of 5 brothers is 13 years.

   12, 16, ☐, 14, 8

7. The median number of students in each music class is 19 people.

   16, ☐, 24, 17, 20, 21

8. Write a data set where both the mean and the median describe the data equally well. Explain your reasoning.

   _____

   _____

Name _____ Date _____ Class_____

Measures of Center

LESSON 17-1

Practice and Problem Solving: D

Use the situation below to complete Exercises 1 and 2. The first step in Exercise 1 is done for you.

The heights (in meters) of the trees in a park are as follows:
7, 11, 9, 7, 6, 8.

1. Follow the steps to find the mean.

   a. Find the sum of the data values.

      48
   _____

   b. Divide to find the mean.

      $$\text{Mean} = \frac{\text{sum of data values}}{\text{number of data values}} = \frac{\square}{\square} = \square$$

      The mean height is _____.

2. Follow the steps to find the median.

   a. Write the data values in order from least to greatest.

      _____, _____, _____, _____, _____, _____

   b. Find the middle value.

      The data set has two middle values: _____ and _____.

      $$\text{Median} = \frac{\square + \square}{\square} = \frac{\square}{\square} = \square$$

      The median height is _____.

The points scored by a football team in each game are shown in the table. Use this data to complete Exercises 3–5. The first one is done for you.

Game	Points Scored
1	7
2	20
3	24
4	17
5	28
6	24

3. How many data values are there?

   6
   _____

4. What is the mean and median?

   Mean: _____

   Median: _____

5. Does one measure describe the data better than the other? Explain.

   _____

   _____

Measures of Center

LESSON 17-1

Reteach

When calculating the mean, you can use *compatible numbers* to find the sum of the data values. Compatible numbers make calculations easier. For example, adding multiples of 5 or 10 is easier than adding all of the individual data values.

A group of students are asked how many hours they spend watching television during one week. Their responses are: 15, 7, 12, 8, 4, 13, 11. What is the mean?

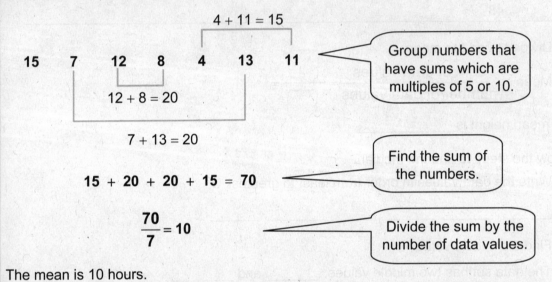

The mean is 10 hours.

Use compatible numbers to find the mean.

1. The costs (in dollars) of items on a lunch menu are 9, 14, 11, 6, 16, 10.

   Mean: _____

2. The numbers of students in Mr. Silva's math classes are 19, 18, 22, 24, 20, 18, 26.

   Mean: _____

3. In the television viewing data above, is there more than one way to pair the data values to form compatible numbers? Explain.

   _____

   _____

LESSON
17-1

Measures of Center

Reading Strategies: Use Graphic Aids

Tim's bowling scores from 5 different games are 89, 98, 110, 98, 105. The scores are shown on the number line below. The number line is a graphic aid that lets you see whether the scores are close together or spread apart.

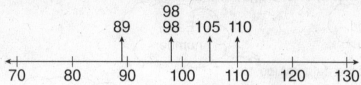

Use the bowling scores above to complete Exercises 1–3.

1. Are the bowling scores close together or spread out? _____

2. Find the mean and the median bowling scores.

   Mean: _____   Median: _____

3. Does one measure describe the data better than the other? Explain.

   _____

   _____

The number line below shows Pranav's bowling scores from 5 different games. The scores, shown on the number line, are: 94, 90, 111, 86, 129. Use the number line to complete Exercises 4–6.

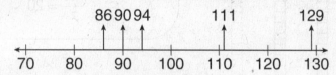

4. Are the bowling scores close together or spread out? _____

5. Find the mean and the median bowling scores.

   Mean: _____   Median: _____

6. Does one measure describe the data better than the other? Explain.

   _____

   _____

7. Explain why you think the mean and median are called "measures of center."

   _____

   _____

Measures of Center
Success for English Learners

LESSON 17-1

Problem 1

Steps to find the mean, or average, of a data set.

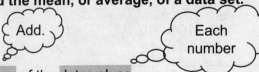

Add.

Each number

1. Find the sum of the data values.

Count each number.

2. Divide the sum by the number of data values.

Problem 2

Use a visual model to examine the data.

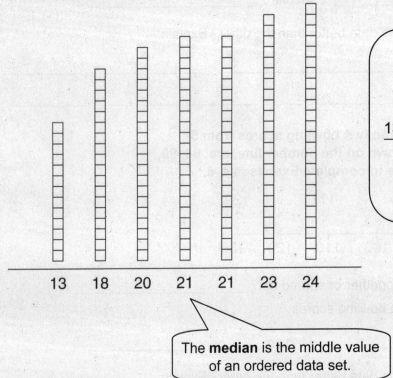

13 18 20 21 21 23 24

The **median** is the middle value of an ordered data set.

The **mean** is the average.

$$\frac{\text{sum of data values}}{\text{number of data values}} =$$

$$\frac{13+18+20+21+21+23+24}{7} =$$

$$\frac{140}{7} = 20$$

1. What is an "ordered data set"?

_____

2. How do you find the median if there are an even number of data values?

_____

Name _____ Date _____ Class_____

LESSON 17-2 Box Plots
Practice and Problem Solving: A/B

High Temperatures						
69	73	72	66	64	64	61
70	78	78	74	69	61	62

The high temperatures for 2 weeks are shown at the right. Use the data set for Exercises 1–7.

1. Order the data from least to greatest.

_____

2. Find the median. _____

3. Find the lower quartile. _____

4. Find the upper quartile. _____

5. Make a box plot for the data.

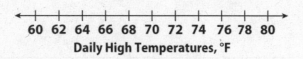

Daily High Temperatures, °F

6. Find the IQR. _____   7. Find the range. _____

Use the situation and data given below to complete Exercises 8–10.

Two classes collected canned food for the local food bank. Below are the number of cans collected each week.

    Class A: 18 20 15 33 30 23 38 34 40 28 18 33

    Class B: 18 27 29 20 26 26 29 30 24 28 29 28

8. Arrange the data for each class in order from least to greatest.

    Class A: _____

    Class B: _____

9. Find the median, the range, and the IQR of each data set.

    Class A: median:_____ range:_____ IQR:_____

    Class B: median:_____ range:_____ IQR:_____

10. Compare and contrast the box plots for the two data sets.

_____

_____

Box Plots

LESSON 17-2

Practice and Problem Solving: C

Use the data set at the right for Exercises 1–3.

A math test had 50 questions. The data set shows how many questions were answered correctly in one class.

Questions Correctly Answered
48 50 48 40 42 42 47 48 48 41
40 48 43 49 50 43 47 43 42 44

1. What is the first step you need to do to make a box plot? Complete that step now.

   _____

   _____

2. Find the median, the range, and the IQR of the data set.

   median:_____   range:_____   IQR:_____

3. Make a box plot for the data.

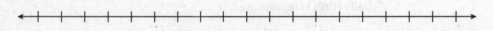

Questions Correctly Answered

Use the situation below to complete Exercises 4–7.

Below are the prices of various rooms at two different resort city hotels.

   Hotel A: 360 100 180 220 240 200

   Hotel B: 300 250 180   80 120 340 220

4. Make box plots for each set of data.

   Hotel A

   Hotel B

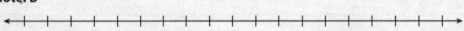

Comparative Room Rates

5. Which hotel has the greater median room price? _____

6. Which hotel has the greater interquartile range of room prices? _____

7. Which hotel appears to have more predictable room prices? Explain.

   _____

   _____

Box Plots
Practice and Problem Solving: D

The data set at the right shows the money Joe earned in 8 weeks. Use the data set to complete Exercises 1–7. The first one is done for you.

Weekly Earnings ($)
20 12 10 6 12 15 8 15

1. Order the data from least to greatest.

   6, 8, 10, 12, 12, 15, 15, 20

2. Find the median. _____

3. Find the lower quartile. _____

4. Find the upper quartile. _____

5. Complete the box plot for the data.

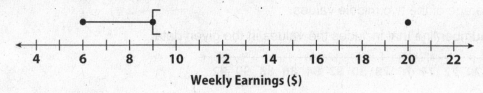

Weekly Earnings ($)

6. Find the IQR. _____

7. Find the range. _____

Use the situation and data given below to complete Exercises 8–11.

Below are the number of books read each week for Juan and Mia.

   Juan: 2, 6, 4, 1, 2, 6, 8, 4, 3

   Mia: 6, 6, 2, 5, 2, 2, 4, 5, 6

8. Arrange the data for each person in order from least to greatest.

   Juan: _____

   Mia: _____

9. Who had the higher median number of books read? _____

10. Who had the greater range in number of books read? _____

11. Who had the higher IQR in number of books read? _____

Box Plots
LESSON 17-2
Reteach

A **box plot** gives you a visual display of how data are distributed.

Here are the scores Ed received on 9 quizzes: 76, 80, 89, 90, 70, 86, 87, 76, 80.

Step 1: List the scores in order from least to greatest.

Step 2: Identify the least and greatest values.

Step 3: Identify the median.
If there is an odd number of values, the median is the middle value.

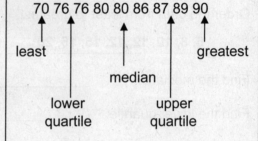

Step 4: Identify the lower quartile and upper quartile. If there is an even number of values above or below the median, the lower or upper quartile is the average of the two middle values.

Step 5: Draw a number line that includes the values in the given data.

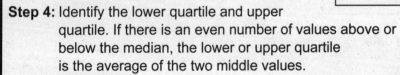

Step 6: Place dots above the number lines at each value you identified in Steps 2–4. Draw a box starting at the lower quartile and ending at the upper quartile. Mark the median, too.

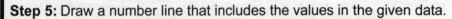

Use the data at the right for Exercises 1–5. Complete each statement.

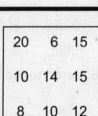

1. List the data in order: _____

2. Least value: _____ Greatest value: _____

3. Median:_____

4. Lower quartile:_____ Upper quartile:_____

5. Draw a box plot for the data.

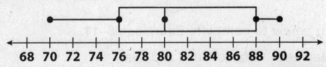

**LESSON
17-2**

Box Plots

Reading Strategies: Use Graphic Aids

A **box plot** shows a set of data divided into four equal parts called **quartiles**.

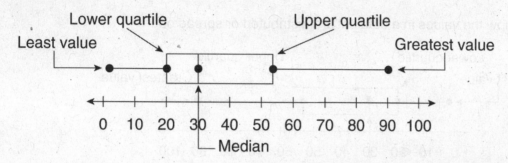

- The median score divides the set of data in half. The median score for this plot is 30.

- The box shows the middle half of the data, located on either side of the median. The box extends from 20 to 53.

- The two "whiskers" identify the remaining half of the data. One whisker extends from the box to the greatest value: from 53 to 90. The other whisker extends from the box to the least value: from 2 to 20.

Answer each question.

1. What does the box stand for in a box plot?

   _____

2. How are the whiskers determined?

   _____

   _____

3. Why is it important to find the median score?

   _____

Describe where these scores are located in the box plot above.

4. 18 is between the _____ and the _____.

5. 75 is between the _____ and the _____.

6. 45 is between the _____ and the _____.

Name _____ Date _____ Class_____

LESSON 17-2 Box Plots

Success for English Learners

A **box plot** shows a set of data divided into four equal parts.

Problem 1

A box plot shows how the values in a data set are distributed or spread out.

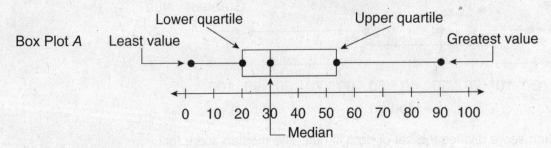

Problem 2

To make a box plot, start by putting the data in order from least to greatest.

Identify the least and greatest values. In box plot *A*, the least value is 2 and the greatest value is 90.

Identify the middle value. This is the **median**. The median for box plot *A* is 30.

Identify the lower quartile. The **lower quartile** is the middle value between the least value and the median. In box plot *A*, the lower quartile 20.

Identify the upper quartile. The **upper quartile** is the middle value between the median and the greatest value. In box plot *A*, the upper quartile 53.

Plot each identified value on a number line and draw a box from the lower quartile to the upper quartile with a line drawn at the median. Draw a line segment from the least value to the lower quartile and from the upper quartile to the greatest value.

Use box plot *B* and box plot *C* to complete the table.

Box Plot *B*

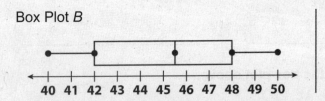

Box Plot *C*

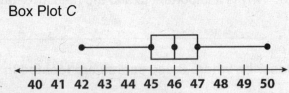

		Median	Least Value	Greatest Value	Lower Quartile	Upper Quartile
1.	Box Plot *B*					
2.	Box Plot *C*					

3. Which box plot has the middle half of the data closer together? _____

Dot Plots and Data Distribution
Practice and Problem Solving: A/B

Tell whether each question is a statistical question. If it is a statistical question, identify the units for the answer.

1. How far do you travel to get to school? _____

2. How tall is the door to this classroom? _____

Use the data set at the right and the description below to complete Exercises 3–6.

The class took a survey about how many people live in each student's home. The results are shown at the right.

People in Our Homes
4, 2, 5, 4, 2, 6, 4, 3, 4, 3, 5, 6, 2, 7, 3, 2, 5, 3, 4,11, 4, 5, 3

3. Make a dot plot of the data.

<----+---+---+---+---+---+---+---+---+---+---+---+---->
0   1   2   3   4   5   6   7   8   9 10 11
People in Our Homes

4. Find the mean, median, and range of the data.

mean:_____; median:_____; range:_____

5. Describe the spread, center, and shape of the data distribution.

_____

_____

6. Which number is an outlier in the data set? Explain what effect the outlier has on the measures of center and spread.

_____

_____

7. Survey 12 students to find how many people live in their homes. Record the data below. Make a box plot at the right.

_____

_____   <----+---+---+---+---+---+---+---+---+---->

Name _____ Date _____ Class_____

Dot Plots and Data Distribution
Practice and Problem Solving: C

Use the data set at the right and the description below to complete Exercises 1–4.

The class counted the cars in the parking lot each hour from 9 A.M. to 3 P.M. for 3 days. The results are shown in the data set.

Cars in the Parking Lot
30, 22, 33, 22, 26, 24, 33, 8, 30, 33, 40, 28, 38, 30, 38, 33, 33, 28, 22, 28, 30

1. Make a dot plot of the data.

```
←┼──┼──┼──┼──┼──┼──┼──┼──┼──┼──┼──┼──┼──┼──┼──┼──┼──┼→
  8  10 12 14 16 18 20 22 24 26 28 30 32 34 36 38 40
```
Cars in the Parking Lot

2. Find the mean, median, and range of the data.

   mean:_____; median:_____; range:_____

3. Describe the spread, center, and shape of the data distribution.

   _____

   _____

4. Which number is an outlier in the data set? Explain what effect the outlier has on the measures of center and spread.

   _____

   _____

Answer the questions below.

5. Write a survey question that you can ask at least 15 people.

   _____

6. Complete your survey. List the results.

   _____

   _____

7. In the blank space at the right, make a dot plot to show the results of your survey.

8. Find each of the following.

   mean:____ ; median:____ ; range:____

LESSON 17-3 Dot Plots and Data Distribution

Practice and Problem Solving: D

Use the data set at the right and the description below for Exercises 1–3. The first one is done for you.

The class took a survey about how many dogs and cats each student has. The results are shown in the data set.

Dogs and Cats in Our Homes
1, 0, 3, 5, 1, 3, 2, 4, 2, 1, 2, 0, 5, 3, 1, 2, 0, 0, 2, 3

1. Make a dot plot of the data.

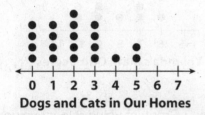

Dogs and Cats in Our Homes

2. Find the mean, median, and range of the data.

   mean:_____; median:_____; range:_____

3. Choose the best description of shape of the data distribution.

   A. symmetric   B. not symmetric

Answer the questions below.

4. The data set at the right shows the hours that a group of students spent volunteering each weekend. Make a dot plot of the data. Then use your dot plot to complete Exercises 5–7.

Hours Spent Volunteering on Weekends
5, 3, 2, 6, 5, 4, 2, 14, 1, 2

Hours Spent Volunteering on Weekends

5. Find the mean, median, and range of the data.

   mean:_____; median:_____; range:_____

6. Choose the best description of shape of the data distribution.

   A. symmetric   B. not symmetric

7. 14 is far away from the other data. What is 14 called? _____

LESSON 17-3
Dot Plots and Data Distribution
Reteach

A **dot plot** gives you a visual display of how data are distributed.

Example: Here are the scores Yolanda received on math quizzes: 6, 10, 9, 9, 10, 8, 7, 7, and 10. <u>Make a dot plot for Yolanda's quiz scores.</u>

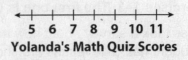
Yolanda's Math Quiz Scores

Step 1: Draw a number line.

Step 2: Write the title below the number line.

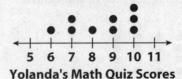
Yolanda's Math Quiz Scores

Step 3: For each number in the data set, put a dot above that number on the number line.

<u>Describe the dot plot by identifying the **range,** the **mean,** and the **median.**</u>

Step 4: Identify the range. $10 - 6 = 4$

Step 5: Find the mean. $76 \div 9 = 8.4$

Step 6: Find the median. 9

Range: Greatest value – least value

Mean: $\dfrac{\text{Sum of data valuse}}{\text{Number of data values}}$

Median: Middle value

Use the data set at the right to complete Exercises 1–4.

1. Draw a dot plot for the data.

Game Scores			
12	6	15	10
14	15	8	10
12	21	15	8

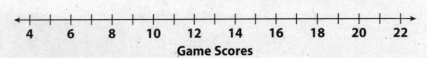
Game Scores

2. Find the range. _____

3. Find the mean. _____

4. Find the median. _____

Name _____ Date _____ Class_____

LESSON 17-3

Dot Plots and Data Distribution
Reading Strategies: Build Vocabulary

When people study data, they are often asked questions that have a mathematical answer. Some such questions are **statistical**, meaning they have answers that can vary. Some are **not statistical**, meaning they have a single correct answer. For example:

<u>Statistical question:</u> How many books does a typical student read in a week?

<u>Not a statistical question:</u> How many books did Dave read last week?

Statistical questions are answered by collecting and analyzing data.

The data below was collected as an answer to the statistical question above. The data is shown in the dot plot at the right.

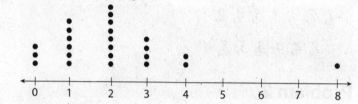

A **dot plot** is a visual way of displaying data.

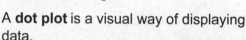

4	2	1	0	3	2	4	1
1	2	3	8	2	1	0	2
2	3	3	1	1	2	2	0

You can describe the spread, the center, and the shape of a dot plot.

Spread: Range or difference between least and greatest values

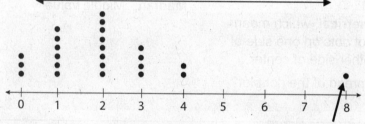

The **shape** of this dot plot is **not symmetrical**, which means there are more dots on one side of the center of the range than on the other side of center.

An **outlier** is a data value much greater or less than other data values.

Measures of **center**:

Mean: $\dfrac{\text{Sum of data values}}{\text{Number of data values}}$

Median: Middle value

Mean, median, and range might be affected by an **outlier**.

Use the dot plot above to answer each question.

1. How would you describe the spread of the dot plot?

   _____

2. What is the mean? What is the median?

   _____

3. What do you think it means if a dot plot is symmetrical?

   _____

LESSON 17-3

Dot Plots and Data Distribution

Success for English Learners

A **dot plot** provides a visual way to display data.

Problem 1

The data below is shown in the dot plot at the right.

Summer Hours I Spent Horseback Riding

1, 7, 4, 3, 5, 4, 2,

7, 4, 4, 3, 5, 5, 4

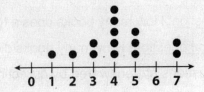

Summer Hours I Spent Horseback Riding

Problem 2

You can describe the spread, the center, and the shape of a dot plot.

Spread: Range or difference between least and greatest values

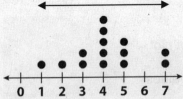

Measures of **center**:

Mean: $\dfrac{\text{Sum of data values}}{\text{Number of data values}}$

Median: Middle value

The **shape** of this dot plot is **symmetrical**, which means there are about the same number of dots on one side of the center of the range as on the other side of center.

1. How would you describe the spread of the dot plot?

   _____

2. Find the mean of the data. _____

3. Find the median of the data. _____

4. What does it mean if the shape of a dot plot is **not** symmetrical?

   _____

Stem-and-Leaf Plots and Histograms

LESSON 17-4

Practice and Problem Solving: A/B

Use the data at the right and the description below to complete Exercises 1–6.

The data set lists the heights of the Houston Rockets players during the 2011–2012 basketball season.

Players' Heights						
81	80	79	72	72	78	82
80	80	76	87	65	79	82
80	79	81	71	77		

1. Complete the stem-and-leaf plot for the data.

Players' Heights

Stem	Leaves
6	
7	
8	

2. Complete the frequency table. Use an interval of 5.

Players' Heights	
Heights (in.)	Frequency
65–69	

3. Complete the histogram.

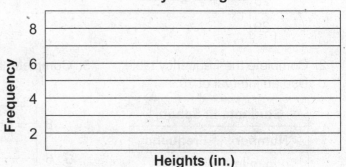

Solve.

4. Find the range, the median, and the mean of the players' heights.

   a. range   b. median   c. mode

   _____   _____   _____

5. Based on this data, what do you think is the average height of players in the National Basketball Association? Explain how you decided on your answer including which display of data you used.

   _____

   _____

   _____

Stem-and-Leaf Plots and Histograms

LESSON 17-4

Practice and Problem Solving: C

Use the data set at the right and the description below to complete Exercises 1–6.

The data set shows a list of the number of students at school each day during the month of January.

Students in School				
281	260	279	253	275
278	255	280	220	266
287	252	279	282	293
277	288	254	256	285

1. Complete the stem-and-leaf plot for the data.

Students in School

Stem	Leaves
22	
23	
24	
25	
26	
27	
28	
29	

2. Complete the frequency table. Use an interval of 20.

Students in School	
Number	**Frequency**
220–239	

3. Complete the histogram.

Students in School

Frequency: 8, 6, 4, 2

4. Find the range, the median, and the mean of the data.

Range: _____ ; Median: _____ ; Mean: _____

5. Identify the outlier and give a possible explanation for its occurrence.

_____

6. Identify what effect, if any, the outlier has on the measures of center.

_____

Stem-and-Leaf Plots and Histograms

Practice and Problem Solving: D

At the right is a list of the heights of trees that are for sale at a nursery. Use the data for Exercises 1–8. The first one is done for you.

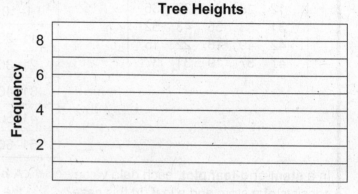

Tree Heights							
70	75	65	70	74	64	77	61
77	73	75	79	68	86	79	75

1. Complete the frequency table. Use an interval of 5.

2. Complete the histogram for the data.

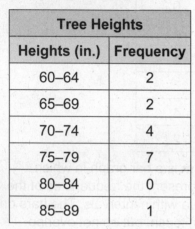

Tree Heights	
Heights (in.)	**Frequency**
60–64	2
65–69	2
70–74	4
75–79	7
80–84	0
85–89	1

3. Complete the stem-and-leaf plot for the data.

Tree Heights

Stem	Leaves
6	
7	
8	

Answer the questions below. The first one is done for you.

4. What is the range of the tree heights? _____**25**_____

5. What is the median of the tree heights? _____

6. What is the mean of the tree heights? _____

7. The nursery wants a sign that tells what trees are available for sale by height. What measure of center would you use for the sign? _____

8. In the space below, make a sign for the trees for sale at the nursery.

LESSON 17-4

Stem-and-Leaf Plots and Histograms
Reteach

Both stem-and-leaf plots and histograms can be used to display the same data. When intervals of 10 are used, you can compare the visual results.

Pounds of Newspapers Collected for Recycling

12	28	24	32	35
31	38	55	43	52
42	49	18	22	15
47	37	19	31	37

Pounds of Newspapers

Interval	Frequency
1–10	0
11–20	4
21–30	3
31–40	7
41–50	4
51–60	2

In a **stem-and-leaf plot,** each data value consists of a stem and a leaf. In this case, the tens digit is the **stem** and the ones digit is the **leaf**.

A **histogram** is a bar graph in which the bars represent the frequencies of the numeric data within intervals. The bars on a histogram touch, but do not overlap.

Pounds of Newspapers Collected

Stem	Leaves
1	2 5 8 9
2	2 4 8
3	1 1 2 5 7 7 8
4	2 3 7 9
5	2 5

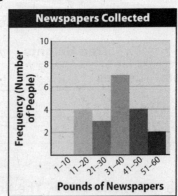

Use the stem-and-leaf plot and histogram to complete Exercises 1–4.

1. How are the stem-and-leaf plot and histogram alike?

_____

_____

2. How do the stem-and-leaf plot and histogram differ?

_____

_____

3. Which display can you use to find the median? _____

4. What is the median of the data? _____

LESSON
17-4

Stem-and-Leaf Plots and Histograms
Reading Strategies: Compare and Contrast Displays

Statistical data can be displayed in different ways. Each of the following displays shows the high temperature on the 15th of each month in one city.

Ordered List	Line Plot
High Temperatures 2 15 18 22 30 30 30 32 45 65 65 90	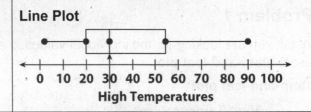

Frequency Table

High Temperatures	
Temperatures	**Frequency**
0–19	3
20–39	5
40–59	1
60–79	2
80–99	1

Stem-and–Leaf Plot

High Temperatures	
Stem	**Leaves**
0	2
1	5 8
2	2
3	0 0 0 2
4	5
5	
6	5 5
7	
8	
9	0

Dot Plot

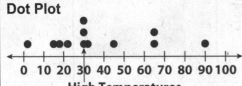

Histogram

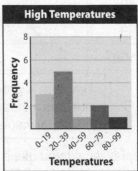

1. Compare and contrast the ability to identify the measures of center with each type of display.

_____

_____

LESSON 17-4

Stem-and-Leaf Plots and Histograms
Success for English Learners

Both the **stem-and-leaf plot** and the **histogram** provide a visual way to
display data that involves greater numbers.

Problem 1

When you are looking for the individual values in a data set, you can
use a **stem-and-leaf plot**.

stem-and-leaf plot

High Temperatures	
Stem	**Leaves**
6	0 5 8
7	2 5 6 7 9
8	1
9	0 6
10	2

Reading the numbers:

9 | 0 6

↑ first digit   ↖↖ second digits

So, 9 | 0 6 represents 90 and 96.

Problem 2

When you are not looking for the individual values in a data set, you can
use a **frequency table** or a **histogram**.

frequency table

High Temperatures	
Temperatures	**Frequency**
60–69	3
70–79	5
80–89	1
90–99	2
100–109	1

histogram

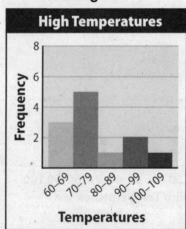

The data is grouped by
intervals instead of
individual values.

1. Which display would you use if being able to identify the median
   and the mean is important? Explain.

   _____

2. What does the shape of the histogram tell you about the high
   temperatures?

   _____

LESSON 17-5

Categorical Data

Practice and Problem Solving: A/B

Use the situation to complete Exercises 1–2.

Students in Mr. Downey's class chose their favorite bird. Seven chose the eagle, 6 chose the bluejay, 4 chose the robin, 7 chose the cardinal, and 2 chose the swan.

1. Complete the dot plot of favorite birds.

2. Identify the mode(s) of the data. _____

Favorite Birds

_____

bluejay cardinal eagle robin swan

Use the situation to complete Exercises 3–5.

A sports store asked 50 customers to name their favorite type of summer Olympic sport. Five named cycling, 10 named swimming, 10 named athletics, 20 named gymnastics, and the rest named fencing.

3. Make a relative frequency table of the data that shows both the fractions and percents.

Favorite Type of Summer Olympic Sport					
Sport	athletics	cycling	fencing	gymnastics	swimming
Relative Frequency					

4. Complete the percent bar graph of the relative frequencies of the favorite type of summer Olympic sport.

5. Identify the mode(s) of the data.

_____

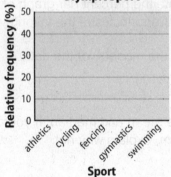

Favorite Type of Summer Olympic Sport

Solve.

6. Take survey of 20 people. Ask them to choose their favorite color from the colors listed below. Record the results for each color.

red____, white____, yellow____

blue____, green____, orange____

7. Make a dot plot from your data.

8. Identify the mode(s) of the data.

_____

Favorite Colors

_____

red   white   yellow   blue   green   orange

LESSON
17-5

Categorical Data

Practice and Problem Solving: C

Take a survey of 20 people. Ask them to choose their favorite fruit from the ones listed below.

1. Record the results below.

   apple____, banana____, mango____,

   grape____, orange____

2. Make a dot plot from your data.

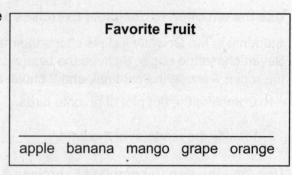

Favorite Fruit

_____

apple   banana   mango   grape   orange

Use the situation below to complete Exercises 3–6.

Two hundred students were asked to choose their favorite even number. Fifty students chose 8, 40 students chose 4, 30 students chose 6, 30 students chose 2, and the rest chose 0.

3. Make a relative frequency table of the data that shows both the fractions and percents.

Favorite Even Number					
Number	0	2	4	6	8
Relative Frequency					

4. Complete the percent bar graph of the relative frequencies of the favorite even number.

5. Identify the mode(s) of the data.

   _____

6. Find the mean and median. If you cannot find them, explain why not.

   _____

   _____

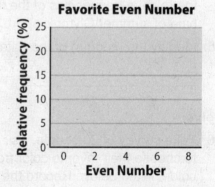

Answer the questions below.

7. A charitable group sold 400 toys to raise money. The graph shows the type of toys that were sold.

   a. How many dolls were sold? _____

   b. How many more games than puzzles were sold?

   _____

LESSON
17-5

Categorical Data
Practice and Problem Solving: D

Use the description to complete Exercises 1 and 2.
The first one has been started for you.

Students in Ms. McAlister's class chose their favorite
flower. Four chose daisies, 1 chose pansies,
4 chose roses, and 5 chose tulips.

1. Complete the dot plot of favorite flowers.

2. Identify the mode(s) of the data. _____

Favorite Flowers
•
•
•
•   •
daisies   pansies   tulips   roses

Use the description to complete Exercises 3–6.
The first one has been started for you.

A sports store asked 100 customers to name their favorite type of water
sport. Forty named swimming, 25 named boating, 5 named skiing,
20 named fishing, and 10 surfing.

3. Make a relative frequency table of the data that shows both the
   fractions and percents.

Favorite Type of Water Sport					
Sport	boating	fishing	skiing	surfing	swimming
Relative Frequency	$\frac{25}{100} = 25\%$	$\frac{20}{100} = 20\%$			

4. Complete the percent bar graph of the relative frequencies of the
   favorite type of water sport.

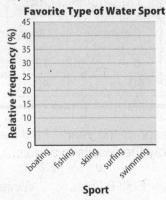

5. Identify the mode(s) of the data. _____

6. Suppose you want to change the graph to make it easier to compare
   the relative frequencies. In what order would you order the sports?

_____

Categorical Data

LESSON 17-5

Reteach

The **relative frequency** of a data item tells what percent each data item is when related to the whole. Categorical data can be recorded with relative frequencies.

At the right are the results of a classroom survey that asked, "What kind of book was the last one you checked out from the school library?"

Cooking books	4	Mystery	12
Biography	8	Adventure	10
Fantasy	6		

Find the relative frequency of each response.

$$\text{relative frequency of a data item} = \frac{\text{frequency of item}}{\text{total number of data items}}$$

Add to find the total number of data items: $4 + 8 + 6 + 12 + 10 = 40$

Divide each result by 40 to find the relative frequency:

Cooking books: $\frac{4}{40} = 0.10$ or 10%   Mystery: $\frac{12}{40} = 0.30$ or 30%

Biography: $\frac{8}{40} = 0.20$ or 20%   Adventure: $\frac{10}{40} = 0.25$ or 25%

Fantasy: $\frac{6}{40} = 0.15$ or 15%

Display the categorical data in a table.

The Kind of Books We Checked Out					
Kind	**Cooking**	**Biography**	**Fantasy**	**Mystery**	**Adventure**
Relative Frequency	$\frac{4}{40} = 10\%$	$\frac{8}{40} = 20\%$	$\frac{6}{40} = 15\%$	$\frac{12}{40} = 30\%$	$\frac{10}{40} = 25\%$

1. A survey asked, "What is your favorite season of the year?" Find the relative frequency of each response. Display the results in a table.

Spring: 12 votes   Summer: 22 votes   Fall: 6 votes   Winter: 10 votes

Relative Frequency				

Name _____ Date _____ Class_____

Categorical Data

LESSON 17-5

Reading Strategies: Analyze Data

You can analyze the data in a problem to plot the data by category in a table.

Example:

A sporting complex is going to expand by adding another activity. The owner surveyed his customers to see what new activity they would like. Eighty surveys were completed by customers. Twenty customers chose a handball court, 15 chose an indoor tennis court, 10 chose a dance studio, and the rest chose a trampoline training room. The owner is going to post a table of the results to show customers what new activity is being planned.

Analyze the survey results by finding the relative frequency of each activity. Display the results in a table.

Analyze the given information to find how many customers chose a trampoline training room.

$$20 + 15 + 10 + ? = 80 \rightarrow 45 + ? = 80 \rightarrow ? = 35$$

Remember: relative frequency of a data item = $\dfrac{\text{frequency of item}}{\text{total number of data items}}$

Divide the number of votes for each activity by 80.

Handball court: $\dfrac{20}{80} = 0.25$ or 25%   Indoor tennis court: $\dfrac{15}{80} = 0.1875$ or 18.75%

Dance studio: $\dfrac{10}{80} = 0.125$ or 12.5%   Trampoline training room: $\dfrac{35}{80} = 0.4375$ or 43.75%

New Activity Survey Results				
Activity	**Handball Court**	**Indoor Tennis Court**	**Dance Studio**	**Trampoline Training Room**
Relative frequency	$\dfrac{20}{80} = 25\%$	$\dfrac{15}{80} = 18.75\%$	$\dfrac{10}{80} = 12.5\%$	$\dfrac{35}{80} = 43.75\%$

Analyze the survey results by finding the relative frequency of each activity. Display the results in a table.

1. A youth group is planning an activity night. Each member was asked what they wanted to do. Twelve chose swimming, 10 chose volleyball, 3 chose skating, and the rest chose bowling. There are 30 members in the group.

Activity Night Survey Results				
Activity				
Relative frequency				

Original content Copyright © by Houghton Mifflin Harcourt. Additions and changes to the original content are the responsibility of the instructor.

369

LESSON 17-5

Categorical Data

Success for English Learners

Categorical data are data that are not numerical. The data can be sorted by types or categories.

Problem 1

You can use a **dot plot** to display categorical data.

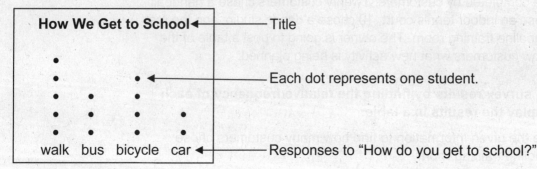

Problem 2

The relative frequency of a data item tells what percent each data item is when related to the whole. Categorical data can be recorded with relative frequencies.

$$\text{relative frequency of a data item} = \frac{\text{frequency of item}}{\text{total number of data items}}$$

You can display the categorical data in a table.

How We Get to School				
Method	**walk**	**bus**	**bicycle**	**car**
Relative frequency	$\frac{5}{14} \approx 35.7\%$	$\frac{3}{14} \approx 21.4\%$	$\frac{4}{14} \approx 28.6\%$	$\frac{2}{14} \approx 14.3\%$

Relative frequency can be given as a fraction or a percent.

You can also display categorical data in a bar graph.

The mode of the data is the category that is chosen most often.

The sum of the relative frequencies is 1 whole or 100%.

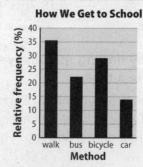

1. What is the mode of the data in the above examples? _____

2. Suppose 3 of 4 categories are 84% of the responses. What percent is the fourth category? How do you know?

Displaying, Analyzing, and Summarizing Data
Challenge

The box plot has 6 data points between the third quartile (Q3) and the largest value (MAX) of the data set. The minimum value (MIN) of the data set is 21. The interquartile range (IQR) is 27.

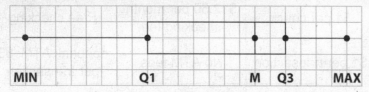

Solve.

1. How many data points are in the distribution? _____

2. Write an inequality for the value, *V1*, of any of the data points between the first quartile (Q1) and the median (M).

   _____

3. Write an inequality for the value, *V2*, of any of the data points between the minimum-value point (MIN) and the first quartile (Q1).

   _____

4. Write an inequality for the value of *V1* in terms of the minimum data point's value.

   _____

5. Use the grid to find the values of Q1, M, Q3, and MAX.

   Q1: _____ M: _____ Q3: _____ MAX: _____

6. Given what you have found, create a data set of the values shown in the box plot. Check to make sure that *all* of the values you come up with are consistent with the features of the box plot.

   _____

   _____

   _____

7. On the back of this sheet or on a separate sheet of paper, draw a stem-and-leaf plot of the data points you created in Exercise 6.

LESSON 18-1

Choosing a Bank

Practice and Problem Solving: A/B

Use the table and the situation given below to complete Exercises 1–4.

	First State Bank	National Bank	Third City Bank
Checks	$1 per check	$12.50 per month checking fee	Free checking
ATM transactions	$1 per transaction	No ATM fees	nonbank ATM: $3 per transaction
Debit Cards	No debit card fees	No debit card fees	$0.75 per debit card transaction

One month you write 5 checks and use the bank's ATM machine 3 times.

You use a nonbank ATM twice and your debit card 8 times. Find the total amount of fees you would pay from each bank.

1. First State Bank _____

2. National Bank _____

3. Third City Bank _____

4. You use your checking account mainly to make debit purchases.
   You write only 3 checks each month. What other factors might
   you consider when choosing which of the three banks to use?

   _____

   _____

Solve.

5. Enter the following information into the check register below.

   Check 123 to Bruns' Bowling Alley for $16.63 on May 5
   Debit card purchase at Z-Store of $20.55. (no fees) on May 8
   ATM withdrawal of $40.00 ($2 ATM fee) on May 14
   Deposit of $93.00 on May 15.

6. Balance the check register.

Check Number	Date	Transaction	Deposit		Withdrawal		Balance	
		Beginning balance					$140	00

Name _____ Date _____ Class _____

 LESSON 18-1

Choosing a Bank

Practice and Problem Solving: C

Use the table and the situation given below for Exercises 1–4.

	First State Bank	**National Bank**	**Third City Bank**
Checks	first 10 checks free $1 per check over 10	$12.50 per month checking fee	Free checking
ATM transactions	$1.50 per transaction	No ATM fees	nonbank ATM: $2.50 per transaction
Debit Cards	No debit card fees	No debit card fees	$0.50 per debit card transaction
Hours	Open Mon.-Fri. 9-7; Sat. 9-12	Open Mon.-Fri. 8-5	Open Mon.-Sat. 10-4

One month you write 15 checks, use a nonbank ATM twice, and use your debit card 8 times. Find the fees you would pay from each bank.

1. First State Bank _____ 2. National Bank _____

3. Third City Bank _____

4. You use your checking account only to make debit purchases and ATM withdrawals. Which bank would you choose? Explain your choice.

_____

_____

Solve.

5. Enter each transaction. Then balance the check register.

        Check 123 to Gloria's Grill for $18.45 on May 5
        Debit card purchase at Stan's Shop for $39.45 (no fees) on May 8
        ATM withdrawal of $20.00 ($1.50 ATM fee) on May 14
        Deposit of $108.50 on May 15.

Check Number	Date	Transaction	Deposit		Withdrawal		Balance	
		Beginning balance					$208	04

Name _____ Date _____ Class_____

Choosing a Bank

Practice and Problem Solving: D

Use the table to complete Exercises 1–4. The first one is done for you.

	First State Bank	National Bank	Third City Bank
Checks	$1 per check	$12.50 per month checking fee	Free checking
ATM transactions	$1 per transaction	No ATM fees	nonbank ATM: $3 per transaction
Debit Cards	No debit card fees	No debit card fees	$0.50 per debit card transaction

1. You write 16 checks each month. You do not use the ATM or a debit card. Which bank should you choose?

   Third City Bank

2. You only use your debit card or the ATM machine. You do not write checks. Which bank should you choose?

   _____

3. You write 2 checks each month. You use your debit card but not the ATM machine. Which bank should you choose?

   _____

4. Suppose you live very close to Third City Bank. Give some reasons why you might NOT choose to bank at the Third City Bank.

   _____

   _____

Use the check register below to complete Exercises 5 and 6. The first step in Exercise 5 is done for you.

5. Enter the following information into the check register.

   Check 123 to Al's Flower Shop for $30 on May 5
   Debit card purchase at Carla's Shop for $20 (no fees) on May 8
   ATM withdrawal of $30.00 ($1 ATM fee) on May 14
   Deposit of $40.00 on May 15.

6. Balance the check register.

Check Number	Date	Transaction	Deposit		Withdrawal		Balance	
		Beginning balance					$200	00
123	5/5	Al's Flower Shop			$30	00	$170	00

Name _____ Date _____ Class_____

LESSON 18-1

Choosing a Bank
Reteach

Having money in a **checking account** can be much safer than having cash on hand. A checking account lets you spend your money more easily than a savings account.

Here are ways to use a checking account and the fees banks charge.

Write **checks**.   Fees vary: can be free, can cost a monthly fee, can cost a per check fee

Use a **debit card**.   Fees vary: can be free, can cost a per debit fee

Use an **ATM card**.   Fees vary: can be free (usually if you use the bank's ATM), can cost a per withdrawal fee (usually much higher than a debit card fee)

Use a **credit card**.   Fees vary: usually costs a fixed percentage of the balance on the credit card

When you withdraw or deposit money, you record the transaction in a **check register**. **Balancing the check register** means adding deposits and subtracting withdrawals to find the balance in the account.

Check #	Date	Transaction	Deposit		Withdrawal		Balance	
		Beginning balance					$140	00
123	9/19	J's Flower Shop			17	40	$122	60
	9/21	ATM withdrawal			40	00	$82	60
	9/21	ATM fee			2	00	$80	60
	9/28	Deposit	35	25			$115	85

> Be sure to subtract any fees for the transaction.

1. Enter each transaction given below in the check register. Then balance the check register.

   Check 140 to CP Mart for $25 on June 1

   ATM withdrawal of $20.00 ($1.50 ATM fee) on June 5

   Deposit of $50 on June 15.

Check	Date	Transaction	Deposit		Withdrawal		Balance	
		Beginning balance					$85	00

Original content Copyright © by Houghton Mifflin Harcourt. Additions and changes to the original content are the responsibility of the instructor.

375

Name _____ Date _____ Class_____

Choosing a Bank
Reading Strategies: Compare and Contrast

Banks offer many services. Some examples are checking accounts, debit cards, and credit cards. When choosing a bank, you can compare and contrast the fees that various banks charge. Sometimes the location of a bank or ATM machines and hours of operation may affect your choice of banks.

Bank	Fees	Location	Hours
Bank A	Checks: $1 per check Debit card: no fees ATM: $2 per use	Within 2 blocks of where you live; ATMs all over town	Mon.-Fri. 8-6 Closed Saturday Closed Sunday
Bank B	Free checks Debit card: $0.25 per use Downtown ATM: free; $1.50 per nonbank ATM	About 2 miles from where you live; bank ATM only at bank location	Mon.-Fri. 9-5 Saturday 9-1 Closed Sunday

Complete.

How you use your account	Compare costs of checks	Compare debit cards	Compare ATM fees	Do location and hours matter?	Which bank is best? Why?
1. You write 2 checks a month, use the debit and ATM card every week, and mail in checks to deposit.	Bank B is better.	Bank A is better.	Bank B is better IF I use their ATM.	No, Bank B is still better.	
2. You write 2 checks a month, use the debit card 10 times a month, and use the ATM once a week. You deposit cash you earn twice a week.					

Compare and contrast the advantages and disadvantages of using a debit card or a credit card. Tell which is better to use in each situation.

3. You want to buy a new coat for $39. You have $60 in your checking account.

_____

_____

4. You need to buy a gift worth $15 for a friend's birthday tomorrow. You have $10 in your checking account.

_____

_____

Name _____ Date _____ Class_____

LESSON 18-1

Choosing a Bank
Success for English Learners

A bank provides many services to its customers. Customers should compare the services offered before opening a checking account.

Problem 1

A checking account can offer these services. Some of them cost money.

Checks	Debit Card	ATM Card	Credit Card
• May be free • May cost a monthly fee • May cost per check written and/or deposit made	• May be free • May have cost per **transaction**, or use	• May be free if you use the bank's ATM • May cost a fee per withdrawal and is usually higher than a debit card fee	• May have a yearly fee • Usually costs a fixed percentage of the balance on the credit card

You can record each withdrawal from or deposit into a checking account in a check register. A **check register** allows you to write details about each transaction, like the date and the amount of a check or the amount of an ATM withdrawal and any fees charged.

To **balance the check register,** find the balance in the account by adding and subtracting.

Check #	Date	Transaction	Deposit		Withdrawal		Balance	
		Beginning balance					$138	00
123	9/19	J's Flower Shop			17	40	$120	60
	9/21	ATM withdrawal			40	00	$80	60
	9/21	ATM fee			2	00	$78	60
	9/28	Deposit	35	25			$113	85

Be sure to subtract any fees for a given transaction.

1. Explain why might you want to use a debit card instead of a credit card.

_____

2. Enter each transaction in the check register below. Then balance the check register.

Check 140 to Betty's Bakery for $12.50 on June 1

ATM withdrawal of $20.00 ($1.75 ATM fee) on June 5

Deposit of $30 on June 15

Check #	Date	Transaction	Deposit		Withdrawal		Balance	
		Beginning balance					$65	00

LESSON 18-2 Protecting Your Credit

Practice and Problem Solving: A/B

Solve.

1. Match each credit history below with a credit score. The credit scores are: 660, 580.

   a. Monthly income: $2,500.
   Credit card payment: $300.
   Usually pays credit card on time.
   One late phone payment.

   _____

   b. Monthly income: $3,500.
   Credit card payment: $100.
   Car loan payment: $400
   Pays credit card on time.

   _____

Use the situation below to complete Exercises 2–4.

Jan has no credit history. Tell whether each of the following would help her establish a credit history. Write *will help* or *will not help*.

2. Taking out a small loan from a credit union and paying it back on time. _____

3. Taking a loan from her aunt and paying it on time. _____

4. Getting a credit card and maxing it out to buy a new television. _____

Answer the questions below.

5. Ms. McElaney and Ms. Hernandez each want to buy a car and obtain a loan of $10,000. Each wants a 4-year loan. Ms. McElaney has fair credit and her payments will be $256 per month. Ms. Hernandez has excellent credit and her payments will be $224 per month.

   a. How much will Ms. McElaney repay the lender over 4 years?

   _____

   b. How much will Ms. Hernandez repay the lender over

   4 years?_____

   c. How much more will a 4-year, $10,000 loan cost Ms. McElaney than it will cost Ms. Hernandez?

   _____

6. What factors may <u>lower</u> your credit score when you have a credit card?

_____

_____

7. Why is it a good idea to check your credit report regularly? What should you do if you think there are errors on the report?

_____

_____

Protecting Your Credit

Practice and Problem Solving: C

Answer the questions below.

1. Ewan has no credit history.

    a. Explain how Ewan could establish a credit history.

    _____

    b. Explain how Ewan could maintain a good credit rating once he has a credit history.

    _____

2. A new car dealer uses the table at the right to estimate car payments based on credit scores.

    a. Find the monthly payment on a 48-month new car loan for $15,000 with a credit score of 700.

    _____

    b. Find the monthly payment on a 48-month new car loan for $15,000 with a credit score of 600.

    _____

Payments on 48-month new car loan	
Credit Score	**Monthly payment per $1,000 financed**
720-850	$22.50
690-719	$23.00
660-689	$24.00
620-659	$25.50
590-619	$28.00

    c. Family A has a credit rating of 628. Family B has a credit rating of 760. Each family takes out a $14,000 new car loan for 48 months. Over the 4-year period, how much more will family A pay than family B pays?

    _____

3. The Slovacek family wants to buy a $200,000 house. With excellent credit, their monthly payments on the loan will be $843 per month for 30 years. With a fair credit rating, monthly payments will be $954 per month.

    a. How much will that $200,000 house cost over the 30-year period if they have excellent credit?

    _____

    b. How much will that $200,000 house cost over the 30-year period if they have fair credit?

    _____

    c. How much more will that $200,000 house cost over the 30-year period if they have fair credit rather than excellent credit?

LESSON 18-2

Protecting Your Credit
Practice and Problem Solving: D

Solve. The first part of Exercise 1 is done for you.

1. Tell whether each person listed below has an excellent credit rating or poor credit rating.

   a. Mr. Andrews:
   Monthly income: $2,500
   Credit card payment: $300
   Pays on credit card late
   Several late phone payments

   b. Ms. Polcari:
   Monthly income: $3,500
   Credit card payment: $100
   Car loan payment: $200
   Pays on credit card on time

   _____poor credit rating_____   _____

Use the situation below to complete Exercises 2–4.

Paul has no credit history. Tell whether each of the following would help him establish a credit history. Write *will help* or *will not help*. The first one is done for you.

2. Taking out a small loan from a bank and making 2 late payments   __will not help__

3. Taking a loan from his uncle and paying it on time   _____

4. Getting a credit card and making all payments on time   _____

Answer the questions below. The first one is done for you.

5. Mr. Alfredo and Ms. Walton each want to buy a car that costs $10,000. Each wants a 4-year loan. Mr. Alfredo has very good credit and his payments will be $230 per month. Ms. Walton has poor credit and her payments will be $280 per month.

   a. How much will Mr. Alfredo repay the lender over 4 years? ____**$11,040**____

   b. How much will Ms. Walton repay the lender over 4 years? _____

   c. How much more will a 4-year, $10,000 loan cost Ms. Walton

      than it will cost Mr. Alfredo? _____

6. What factors can help you create a good credit score when you have a credit card?

   _____

   _____

LESSON 18-2
Protecting Your Credit
Reteach

People in every society sometimes have to use **credit** instead of cash to pay for certain goods and services.

There are some important things that everyone should need to know about credit.

Your **credit history** tells about how you manage money and pay debts.

To **establish a credit history** you need to take out a small loan or buy something using credit instead of cash. Then you must make payments on that loan or credit line.

Once you have established a credit history, the lender will send information to the credit reporting agencies. These agencies create your **credit report**. This report includes information on the following:

where you live	what credit cards or loans you have
where you work	how much you owe on credit
how much money you earn	whether you pay your bills on time

The information in your credit report creates your **credit score**. Credit scores generally are between 300 and 850. The higher your credit score, the better your chance of getting a loan or credit card. The lower your credit score, the more you will pay to get credit.

A **high credit score** means:	A **low credit score** means:
• You probably pay your bills on time.	• You might have too many late payments.
• Your ratio of debt to earnings is acceptable.	• Your ratio of debt to earnings is too high.
• You have a good work record at your job.	• You have been on your job a short time.
• You can get a loan or credit card with a reasonably low interest rate.	• IF you can get a credit card or loan, you will pay a high interest rate.

Mike has no credit history. Tell whether each of the following would help him establish a credit history. Write *will help* or *will not help*.

1. Opening a saving account at a local bank and adding to it every week. _____

2. Taking out a small loan from a local bank and paying it back on time. _____

3. Taking a loan from your best friend and paying it back on time. _____

4. Getting a credit card and paying it off each month. _____

Match the credit history with the credit score. Credit scores: 660, 580

5. Monthly income: $4,000.
   Credit card payment: $200.
   Pays on credit card on time.
   Car loan payment: $200.

6. Monthly income: $3,500.
   Credit card payment: $100.
   Car loan payment: $400.
   Sometimes pays bills late.

_____   _____

Protecting Your Credit

Reading Strategies: Using Information in a Table

Your credit score helps a lender estimate how much your monthly payments will be. Below is an example of such a table.

Payments on a 48-month New Car Loan

Credit Score	Monthly payment per $1,000 financed
720-850	$22.50
690-719	$23.00
660-689	$24.00
620-659	$25.50
590-619	$28.00

You can use information in a table like the one above to calculate monthly payments on loans.

Example: You mother wants to buy a car that costs $13,000. She is putting down $2,000 and wants a 4-year loan. Her credit score is 673. Find out approximately what her monthly payment will be.

Find out how much she will be borrowing.

$13,000 – $2,000 = $11,000

Find her credit score and the monthly payment per $1,000 financed.

673 → $24 per $1,000 financed

Find her monthly payment.

11 × $24 = $264 ⟵ Think: $11,000 ÷ $1,000 = 11

Use the table above to complete Exercises 1–2.

1. Mr. Adams is buying a new car costing $18,500. He is putting down $2,500 and wants a 4-year loan. His credit score is 635. Find his monthly payment.

   _____

2. Mrs. Williams is buying a $21,000 new car. She is putting down $3,000 and wants a 4-year loan. Her credit score is 750. Find her monthly payment.

   _____

Protecting Your Credit

LESSON 18-2

Success for English Learners

People in every society sometimes have to use **credit** instead of cash to pay for certain goods and services.

Problem 1

To get credit, you need to create or **establish** a credit history.

Credit History
determined by

This tells how you manage your money and pay your bills.

- what credit cards or loans you have
- how much you owe on credit
- whether you pay your bills on time

- where you live
- where you work
- how much you earn

Problem 2

Once you have established a credit history you get a **credit score**.

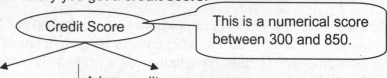

Credit Score

This is a numerical score between 300 and 850.

A high credit score means:	A low credit score means:
• You probably pay your bills on time.	• You might have too many late payments.
• Your ratio of debt (what you owe) to earnings (what you earn) is acceptable.	• Your ratio of debt (what you owe) to earnings (what you earn) is too low.
• You have a good work record at your job.	• You have been on your job a short time.
• You can get a loan or credit card with a reasonably low interest rate.	• IF you can get a credit card or loan, you will pay a high interest rate.

Ms. Jones has no credit history. Tell whether each of the following will help her establish a credit history. Write *will help* or *will not help*.

1. Buying a very expensive car for cash. _____

2. Taking out a small loan from a local bank and paying it back on time. _____

3. Buying a used car and making payments on time. _____

Match each credit history below with a credit score. The credit scores are 700 and 550.

4. Monthly income: $4,000.
   Credit card payment: $200.
   Pays on most bills on time.
   Car loan payment: $600.

5. Monthly income: $3,500.
   Credit card payment: $100.
   Student loan payment: $200
   Pays all bills on time.

_____   _____

Paying for College

Practice and Problem Solving: A/B

Put each of the following into the correct category: grant, savings, loan, work-study, scholarship. You may list more than one category for each description.

1. Money you earn for yourself. _____

2. Money you have to repay. _____

3. Money you do not have to repay. _____

Solve each problem. Show your work.

4. Jeff wants to go to a university where the tuition is $9,000 per year. He has a scholarship that pays for 70% of his tuition. He has saved $3,000 toward the first year's tuition. Does he have enough to pay for the first year's tuition? Explain.

   _____

5. Meghan is attending a college where tuition is $6,600 per year. She received a $2,000 grant and her parents will give her another $1,500. How much will Meghan have to earn on a work-study program to pay for the first year's tuition?

   _____

6. The Winkler family saved $100 month from the time Sarah was born until she started college. Sarah started college on her 18th birthday. The college that Sarah wants to attend charges $7,200 tuition per year. Has the family saved enough to pay for 4 years' tuition? Explain.

   _____

7. Juan is going to a school where tuition is $5,000 per year. He has a scholarship that pays 60% of his tuition. He has a grant for $1,000 per year. How much will Juan need to borrow to pay tuition each year?

   _____

There are expenses besides tuition when you attend college. For Exercises 8–10, tell how you might pay less for that expense.

8. Room and board _____

9. Books and supplies _____

10. Transportation and personal expenses _____

Paying for College

Practice and Problem Solving: C

LESSON 18-3

Solve each problem.

1. Phillip is going to a college where tuition is $7,000 per year. He has a scholarship that pays 75% of tuition. He has a grant that pays $1,500 per year. How much will he need to borrow to pay tuition each year?

   _____

2. Lurinda's college tuition is $9,000 per year. Other expenses are expected to be $5,000 per year. Her scholarship pays $6,500 per year. She has a grant for $2,000 for one year only. She has saved $13,000. How much more does Lurinda need to pay for four years of college?

   _____

3. Gavin is attending a college where tuition is $6,600 per year. He estimates his other expenses are 80% of his tuition. He received a $4,000 grant and his parents gave him another $4,500. How much will Gavin have to earn on a work-study program just to pay for the first year's tuition and other costs?

   _____

Colton is going to college. He made a table of estimated income and expenses. Use the table to complete Exercises 4–8.

Income			Expenses				
Scholarship	**Grant**	**Savings**	**Tuition**	**Books and Fees**	**Room and Board**	**Car and Travel**	**Personal**
$7,000 per year	$4,000 per year	$12,000 total	$9,000 per year	$1,000 per year	$300 per month	$100 per month	$200 per month

4. Find the total expenses Colton estimates for 1 year, assuming he is at college for 9 months a year. Then find the total expenses for 4 years.

   _____

5. Find the total amount of income Colton estimates for 4 years.

   _____

6. How much more money will Colton need for the 4 years of college?

   _____

7. The rest of the needed money Colton hopes to save during four summers. How much will he have to save each summer?

   _____

Name _____ Date _____ Class_____

LESSON 18-3

Paying for College
Practice and Problem Solving: D

Match each of the following with the source of money on the left.
The first one is done for you.

1. Money you earn for yourself. **B**   A. loan

2. Money you have to repay. ____   B. work-study earnings

3. Money you do not have to repay. ____   C. scholarship

Solve each problem. The first one has been done for you.

4. Kristy is going to a college where tuition is $8,000 per year. She has a scholarship that pays 80% of tuition. Her aunt is giving her $1,000 per year. How much will Kristy need to borrow to pay tuition each year?

   $600; 80% of 8,000 = $6,400; $6,400 + $1,000 = $7,400; $8,000 − $7,400 = $600
   _____

5. Jacob wants to go to a college where the tuition is $9,000 per year. His scholarship pays $5,500 toward tuition. He saved $3,000 toward tuition. Does he have enough to pay for the first year's tuition? Explain.
   _____
   _____

6. Sierra is attending a university where tuition is $8,600 per year. She received a $4,000 grant and her parents will give her another $2,500. How much will Sierra have to earn on a work-study program to pay for the first year's tuition?
   _____
   _____

7. Tuan is going to a school where tuition is $5,000 per year. He has a scholarship that pays 60% of his tuition. He has a grant for $1,000 per year. How much will Tuan need to borrow to pay tuition each year?
   _____
   _____

There are expenses besides tuition when you attend college.
For each, tell how you might pay less for that expense.

8. Room and board: the place where you stay, cable television costs, and cost of food
   _____
   _____

9. Books and supplies: books used for class and supplies like paper, calculators, etc.
   _____
   _____

LESSON 18-3

Paying for College
Reteach

There are many expenses associated with attending college. There are also difference **sources of money** to pay for college **expenses**.

Sources of Money	Expenses
Scholarships	Tuition
Grants	Books and Fees
Loans	Room and Board
Work-Study Programs	Transportation and Travel
Gifts	Personal Spending
Savings	

Example: Angie is going to a college where tuition is $8,500 per year. She has a scholarship that pays 65% of tuition. She has a grant that pays $2,000 per year. How much more will she need to pay for tuition each year?

Solution: 65% of $8,500 is 0.65 × $8,500 = $5,525

$5,525 + $2,000 = $7,525

$8,500 − $7,525 = $975

Angie needs $975 more to pay for tuition each year.

Solve.

1. Dylan is going to a college where tuition is $8,000 per year. He has a scholarship that pays 80% of tuition. His uncle is giving him $1,000 per year. How much will Dylan need to borrow to pay tuition each year?

   _____

2. Lynne wants to go to a college where the tuition is $9,500. Her scholarship pays $5,500 toward tuition. She saved $3,000. Does she have enough to pay for the first year's tuition? Explain.

   _____

3. Diego is attending a college where tuition is $10,600 per year. He received a $3,000 grant and his parents will give him another $5,000. How much will Diego have to earn to pay for the first year's tuition?

   _____

4. Tia is going to a school where tuition and books cost $11,000. She has a scholarship that pays 100% of tuition. She has a grant for $1,000. Does she have enough to pay for tuition and books?

   _____

   _____

Name _____ Date _____ Class_____

Paying for College

Reading Strategies: Classifying information

In order to attend college, you have to be able to pay for college. Here
are some sources of money to pay for college.

Sources of money you do not have to pay back	Sources of money you have to pay back	Other sources of money
Scholarships Grants	Loans	Savings Gifts Work-Study Programs

Below are some of the expenses involved in going to college.

Expenses set by the college	Other college expenses
Tuition Books Fees	Room and Board Car and Travel Personal

Classify each of the following as a Source of Money (S) or an Expense (E).

1. Money from your aunt ____

2. Room and food ____

3. Work-study money ____

4. Scholarship ____

5. Books ____

6. Federal grant ____

Solve.

7. Isak is going to a college where tuition is $6,900 per year. He has a
   scholarship for $5,000 and a grant for $1,500 per year. How much
   more does Isak need to pay for one year of tuition?

   _____

8. Rowena's college tuition is $8,000 per year. Books and fees are
   $1,200 per year. Her other expenses are $2,000 per year. Her parents
   have saved $20,000. She has a grant for $5,000 a year. Can she pay
   for 4 years of college? If not, how much more does she need?

   _____

**Sophie made this list: room and board: $1,000; tuition: $8,200; grant:
$5,000; books and fees: $700; savings: $590; loan: $3,000; spending
money: $900. Separate her list into income and expenses.**

9. Income: _____

10. Expenses: _____

11. Does Sophie have enough for one year of college? _____

Original content Copyright © by Houghton Mifflin Harcourt. Additions and changes to the original content are the responsibility of the instructor.

388

Paying for College
LESSON 18-3

Success for English Learners

In order to go to college, you have to be able to pay for tuition, books, and other expenses.

Problem 1

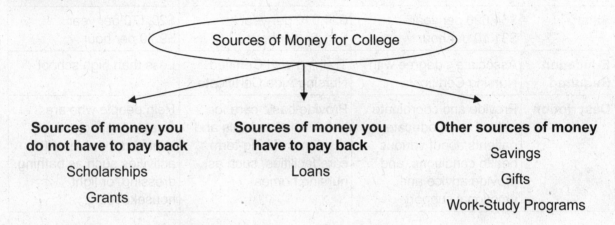

Sources of Money for College

Sources of money you do not have to pay back

Scholarships

Grants

Sources of money you have to pay back

Loans

Other sources of money

Savings

Gifts

Work-Study Programs

Problem 2

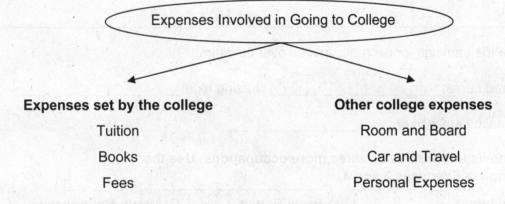

Expenses Involved in Going to College

Expenses set by the college

Tuition

Books

Fees

Other college expenses

Room and Board

Car and Travel

Personal Expenses

Tell whether each is a source of money (S) or an expense (E).

1. Car and Travel ____

2. Room and food ____

3. Work-study money ____

4. Scholarship ____

5. Books ____

6. Federal grant ____

Name _____ Date _____ Class_____

Wages, Salaries, and Careers
LESSON 18-4
Practice and Problem Solving: A/B

The table shows information on three occupations. Use the table to complete Exercises 1 and 2.

Occupation	Registered Nurses	Nursing Aides	Home Health Care Worker
Salary	$64,690 per year $31.10 per hour	$24,010 per year $11.54 per hour	$20,170 per year $9.70 per hour
Education Required	Associate's degree with Nursing Certification	Training with Certified Nursing Aide Certificate	Less than high school
Description	Provide and coordinate patient care, educate patients about various health conditions, and provide advice and emotional support	Provide basic care for patients in hospitals and residents of long-term care facilities, such as nursing homes	Help people who are disabled, ill, cognitively impaired, or older with activities such as bathing, dressing, or light housekeeping

1. Compare and contrast the occupations.

   _____

   _____

2. Estimate the earnings for each occupation over 30 years.

   Registered nurse:_____ Nursing aide:_____

   Home health care worker:_____

The table shows information on three more occupations. Use the table to complete Exercises 3 and 4.

Architect	Auto Body Repair	Grounds Maintenance
$72,550 per year $34.88 per hour	$37,580 per year $18.07 per hour	$23,740 per year $11.41 per hour
Bachelor's degree	High school diploma and training	High school diploma and work experience

3. Which occupation would you be most interested in? Why?

   _____

4. Estimate how much each occupation will make over 30 years.

   Architect:_____ Auto Body Repair:_____

   Grounds Maintenance:_____

LESSON 18-4

Wages, Salaries, and Careers

Practice and Problem Solving: C

The table shows information on three occupations. Use the table to complete Exercises 1 and 2.

Occupation	Accountant/Auditor	Middle-School Teacher	Librarian
Median Salary	$61,690 per year $29.66 per hour	$51,960 per year	$54,500 per year $26.20 per hour
Education Required	Bachelor's degree	Bachelor's degree	Master's degree

1. Compare and contrast the three occupations.

   _____

   _____

   _____

2. Estimate how much each occupation will make over 30 years.

   Accountant/Auditor:_____ Librarian:_____

   Middle-School Teacher:_____

Use the library or the Internet to find information on two occupations that interest you. Complete the table below with the information.

Occupation	3.	4.
Median Salary		
Education Required		
Description of Duties		
Estimated Earnings over 30 Years		
Why did you choose this occupation?		

Name _____ Date _____ Class_____

Wages, Salaries, and Careers

Practice and Problem Solving: D

The table shows information on two occupations. Use the table to complete Exercises 1–3. The first one is done for you.

Occupation	Flight Attendant	EMT/Paramedics
Salary	$37,740 per year	$30,360 per year
Education Required	High school diploma or equivalent	Postsecondary non-degree award
Description	Provide personal services to ensure the safety and comfort of airline passengers	Care for the sick or injured in emergency medical settings

1. Estimate how much a flight attendant will make over 30 years. _____**$1,132,200**_____

2. Estimate how much a paramedic will make over 30 years. _____

3. Compare and contrast the two occupations.

   _____

   _____

   _____

The table below shows information on three more occupations.
Use the table to complete Exercises 4 and 5.

Bank Manager	Tellers	Bank Examiner
$103,910 per year $49.96 per hour	$24,100 per year $11.59 per hour	$74,940 per year $36.03 per hour
Bachelor's degree	High school diploma	Bachelor's degree

4. Would you be interested in any of these three occupations? Why or why not?

   _____

   _____

   _____

5. Estimate how much each occupation will make over 30 years.

   Bank Manager:_____ Teller:_____

   Bank Examiner:_____

Name _____ Date _____ Class_____

 LESSON 18-4

Wages, Salaries, and Careers
Reteach

When considering a job or a career, there are many different things to think about.

What kind of work am I interested in doing?

What kind of background and education are required for this career?

Is there a demand for this career—will it be around in the future?

Can I pursue this career in the area where I want to live?

Does this career offer advancement in this field?

What is the typical salary for this career?

When comparing careers, you can compare salaries to estimate how much you would earn over a 30-year career in each occupation (not including annual adjustments to salaries).

Occupation	Veterinarian	Telecommunications Technician
Median Salary	$82,040 per year $39.44 per hour	$54,710 per year $26.30 per hour

Veterinarian: 30 × $82,040 = 2,461,200

Telecommunications technician: 30 × $54,710 = 1,641,300

Below are three occupations. Read the information in the table. Then complete Exercises 1 and 2.

Occupation	Customer Service Representative	Police Dispatcher	Receptionist
Salary	$30,460 per year $14.64 per hour	$35,370 per year $17.00 per hour	$25,240 per year $12.14 per hour
Education Required	High school diploma or equivalent	High school diploma or equivalent	High school diploma or equivalent

1. Do any of these occupations appeal to you? Why or why not?

_____

_____

2. Estimate the earnings for each occupation over a 30-year career.

Police dispatcher:_____   Receptionist:_____

Customer service representative:_____

Name _____ Date _____ Class_____

Wages, Salaries, and Careers
Reading Strategies: Interpret Information in a Table

When you research a career on the Internet, a lot of information is provided in a table format. Being able to interpret that information is important.

Occupations (Numbers are in 1,000s)	Employment		Change, 2010–20		Median annual wage, 2010
	2010	2020	Number	Percent	
Architecture and Engineering	2,433.4	2,686.2	252.8	10.4	70,610
Community and Social Service Occupations	2,402.7	2,985.0	582.3	24.2	39,280
Healthcare Support	4,190.0	5,633.7	1,443.7	34.5	24,760
Sales and Related	14,915.6	16,784.7	1,869.1	12.5	24,370
Farming, Fishing, and Forestry Occupations	972.1	952.6	−19.4	−2.0	19,630

Source: Employment Projections program, U.S. Department of Labor, U.S. Bureau of Labor Statistics

Note: Numbers are in thousands, so 2,433.4 represents 2,433,400.	These two columns estimate how many workers (in thousands) there will be in each type of occupation.	These columns show the estimated change in number of workers (again in thousands) and the percent of change.	This column gives the median yearly income for 2010.

Use the table above to complete Exercises 1–6.

1. Which occupational group had the greatest number of workers in 2010?

   _____

2. Which two occupational groups had about the same number of workers in 2010?

   _____

3. Of the five occupational groups listed, which one is expected to have the greatest growth in workers between 2010 and 2020?

   _____

4. Of the five occupational groups listed, which one is expected to have a decrease in workers between 2010 and 2020?

   _____

5. Of the five occupational groups listed, which two had approximately the same median wage in 2010?

   _____

6. Why is information in this table useful when deciding upon a career?

   _____

Name _____ Date _____ Class_____

Wages, Salaries, and Careers
Success for English Learners

When considering a job or a career, there are many different things to think about.

Problem 1

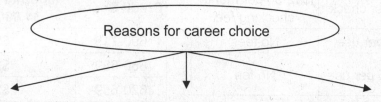

Reasons for career choice

I like this kind of work. I am interested in doing this kind of work.

I have the background and education that are required for this career.

There is a demand for this career. I think this career will be around in the future.

Problem 2

Important factors in choosing a career

Can I pursue this career in the area where I want to live?

Does this career offer advancement in this field?

What is the typical salary for this career?

Choose a career in which you are interested. Use the library or Internet to find more information about that career. Complete the table below.

Reasons for career choice		
This kind of work interests me because:	The education or background I will need is:	I think this career will be around in the future because:
Important factors in choosing a career		
Can I pursue this career in the area in which I want to live?	Does this career offer advancement in this field?	What is the typical salary for this career?

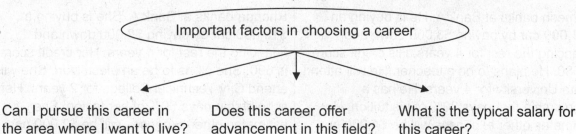

Becoming a Knowledgeable Consumer and Investor

MODULE 18

Challenge

Ramesh and Rhonda are teenagers who are planning their futures. Here is some information you will need to complete each person's story.

	Bank A	Bank B
Checks	$1 per check	$12.50 per month checking fee
ATM	$1 per use	No fees
Debit Cards	$0.25 per use	No fee

Payments on 48-month new car loan

Credit Score	Monthly payment per $1,000 financed
690-719	$23.00
660-689	$24.00
620-659	$25.50

	Teacher	Electrician
Median Pay	$51,960 per year	$48,250 per year
Education	Bachelor's degree	Associate's degree

School	Tuition per year
State University	$6,000
City Technical College	$2,500

Ramesh banks at Bank A. He is buying an $11,000 car by paying $3,000 down and financing the rest for 4 years. His credit score is 680. He plans to be a teacher. He will attend State University for 4 years. He has a scholarship that pays 90% of his tuition. He estimates other expenses will be $4,000 per school year plus the payments on his car.

Rhonda banks at Bank A. She is buying a $15,000 car by paying $2,000 down and financing the rest for 4 years. Her credit score is 690. She plans to be an electrician. She will attend City Technical College for 2 years. Her scholarship pays 60% of her tuition. She estimates other expenses will be $2,000 per year plus the payments on her car.

1. In an average month, Ramesh writes 4 checks, takes money from an ATM 4 times, and uses his debit card 8 times.

   Monthly bank fees are _____.

2. Ramesh's monthly car payments will be

   _____.

3. For Ramesh to go to State University for 4 years, he will have to come up with

   $ _____ plus his car payments.

4. Suppose Ramesh works as a teacher for 30 years. How much will he earn during his 30-year career?

   _____

5. In an average month, Rhonda writes 9 checks, takes money from an ATM 2 times, and uses her debit card 8 times.

   Monthly bank fees are _____.

6. Rhonda's monthly car payments will be

   _____.

7. For Rhonda to go to City Technical for 2 years, she will have to come up with

   $ _____ plus her car payments.

8. Suppose Rhonda works as an electrician for 30 years. How much will she earn during her 30-year career?

   _____

UNIT 1: Numbers

MODULE 1 Integers

LESSON 1-1

Practice and Problem Solving: A/B

1. +85 or 85

2. –3

3. –5

4. +98 or 98

5.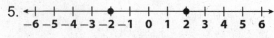

6.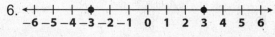

7.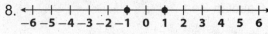

8.

9. –4

10. +2 or 2

11. +535 or 535

12. –8

13. Death Valley: –282; Mount McKinley: +20,320 or 20,320

14. No. There are no whole numbers between 0 and 1, so there are no integers between 0 and 1.

Practice and Problem Solving: C

1. +7 or 7; –3

2. +30 or 30; –12

3. –5; +11 or 11

4. +32 or 32; –32

5. –8.

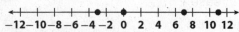

9. +120 or 120; –120

10. –23; +23 or 23

11. 0; –32

12. –212; –100; no

13. An integer and its opposite are the same distance (in the opposite directions) from 0 on the number line. For example, –7 and 7 are opposites and are the same distance from 0 on the number line.

Practice and Problem Solving: D

1. B

2. B

3. +2 or 2

4. –3

5. +20 or 20

6. –25

7. –38

8. –20

Reteach

1. +3 or 3

2. –10

3. +25 or 25

4. –5

5. –1; 1

6. 9; –9

7. 6; –6

8. –5; 5

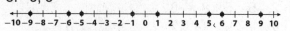

Reading Strategies

1. +25 or 25

2. +1,195 or 1,195

3. +12 or 12

4. –50

5. –87

6. –3,000

Success for English Learners

1. saving money

2. all negative numbers and zero

LESSON 1-2

Practice and Problem Solving: A/B

1. $10 > -2$
2. $0 < 3$
3. $-5 < 0$
4. $-7 < 6$
5. $-6 > -9$
6. $-8 > -10$
7. $-2, 5, 6$
8. $-3, 0, 9$
9. $-1, 1, 6$
10. $1, 0, -1$
11. $2, 1, -12$
12. $-10, -11, -12$
13. $205, 50, -5, -20$
14. $78, 9, -78, -89$
15. $0, -2, -55, -60$
16. $28, 0, -8, -8$
17. $38, 37, -37, -38$
18. $11, 1, -1, -111$
19. Brenda, Tim, Carl, Ali
20. Tuesday, Wednesday, Monday

Practice and Problem Solving: C

1. $7 < 10 > -3 < 0$
2. $-5 < 5 < 8 > -8$
3. $-1 < 2 > -3 < 4$
4. $2 > -1 > -2 < 0$
5. $-9 < 6 > -8 < 7$
6. $2 > -1 < 0 < 1 > -2$
7. $-1, 0, 8, 9$ and $9, 8, 0, -1$
8. $-3, -2, 0, 2, 3$ and $3, 2, 0, -2, -3$
9. $-11, -1, 0, 1, 11$ and $11, 1, 0, -1, -11$
10. $-13, -5, 0, |-7|, 13$ and $13, |-7|, 0, -5, -13$
11. $-8, -7, 0, |7|, |-8|$ and $|-8|, |7|, 0, -7, -8$
12. $-15, -13, 14, |-15|, |16|$ and $|16|, |-15|, 14, -13, -15$
13. Davio, Beth, Abe, Casey, Eric
14 a. $5, -3, 7, -2, 2, -4$
   b. up 7 floors

c. down 2 and up 2
d. higher at the finish
e. the 23rd floor

Practice and Problem Solving: D

1. $>$
2. $<$
3. $<$
4. $-3, 2, 4$
5. $-2, 2, 3$
6. $-1, 0, 3$
7. $-3, -1, 0, 1, 3$
8. C
9. B
10. $-8,327, -1,349; -8,327;$ Bentley Subglacial Trench, $-8,327$
11. Caspian Sea

Reteach

1. $>$
2. $<$
3. $<$
4. $>$
5. $>$
6. $<$
7. $-5, -2, -1$
8. $-5, 0, 5$
9. $-5, -3, 2$
10. $-4, -1, 3$
11. $-5, 0, 3$
12. $-4, -2, 1$

Reading Strategies

1. increase
2. decrease
3. right
4. left
5. -3 is to the left of 3, or 3 is to the right of -3
6. $-3 < 3$, or $3 > -3$

7. −1 is the right of −4, or −4 is to the
left of −1

8. −1 > −4, or −4 < −1

Success for English Learners

1. −3 is to the right of −5 on the number line.

LESSON 1-3

Practice and Problem Solving: A/B

1–4.

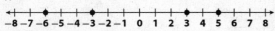

5. 6

6. 3

7. 8

8. 6

9. 3

10. 5

11. The absolute values of 6 and −6 are
the same.

12. opposites

13. −20

14. −6

15. −8

16. 20

17. 6

18. 15

19. Monday; the greatest negative number
shows the greatest amount spent.

20. |3 + 10| = |13| = 13; |3| = 3 and |10| =
10; 3 + 10 = 13; 13 = 13

21. two; possible answer: −4 and 4

Practice and Problem Solving: C

1. 2,300

2. Elan; 2,910

3. Pietro; 2,080

4. Bill, Jorge

5. Bill, Jorge

6. Elan

7. +186

8. 324

9. Their absolute values are the same.

10. Negative deviations would decrease by
100; positive differences would increase
by 100.

Practice and Problem Solving: D

1–4.

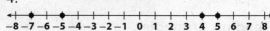

5. 4

6. 5

7. 7

8. 5

9. 4

10. 6

11. same

12. opposites

13. −5

14. −2

15. −3

16. no

17. 5

18. 2

19. 3

20. Monday

21. Thursday

22. absolute value

Reteach

1. c

2. a or d

3. b

4. a

5. c

6. 3

7. 5

8. 7

9. 6

10. 0

11. 2

12. 10

13. $\frac{3}{4}$

14. 0.8

15. Sample answer: The absolute value of a number is the number's distance from 0 on the number line. Since the distance is positive or 0, absolute value is always positive or 0. For example $|-5| = 5$ and $|5| = 5$.

Reading Strategies

1. above, sea level, scored
2. loss, below sea level
3. rising 17 feet; 17 or +17
4. 5 feet below the surface, −5
5. losing 6 points; −6
6. paying a fee of $35; −35
7. penalty of 5 yards; −5
8. adding 32 MB; +32 or 32
9. award of $50; +50 or 50
10. crediting $60; +60 or 60

Success for English Learners

1. −5, 5
2. 6
3. 4
4. 3
5. 0
6. 2
7. 2
8. They both have an absolute value of 2.

MODULE 1 Challenge

1.

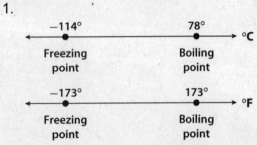

The Celsius degree is larger, or the Fahrenheit degree is smaller.

2. a. −3, −6, −6, −6, −7, −6, −4

 b. −7, −6, −6, −6, −6, −4, −3

 c. 5, 9, 18, 8, 21, 12, 12

 d. 5, 8, 9, 12, 12, 18, 21

 e. none

MODULE 2 Rational Numbers

LESSON 2-1

Practice and Problem Solving: A/B

1. $\frac{3}{10}$

2. $\frac{23}{8}$

3. $-\frac{5}{1}$

4. $\frac{16}{1}$

5. $-\frac{7}{4}$

6. $-\frac{9}{2}$

7. $\frac{3}{1}$

8. $\frac{11}{100}$

9–15.

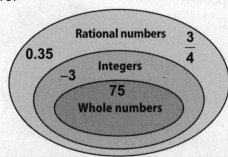

9. integers, rational numbers
10. rational numbers
11. whole numbers, integers, rational numbers
12. rational numbers
13. rational numbers
14. whole numbers, integers, rational numbers
15. rational numbers

Practice and Problem Solving: C

1. $-\frac{4}{1}$

2. Possible answer: $\frac{0}{5}$

3. $\frac{16}{3}$

4. $\dfrac{675}{100} = \dfrac{27}{4}$

5. $\dfrac{17}{8}$

6. $-\dfrac{35}{100} = -\dfrac{7}{20}$

7. $\dfrac{78}{10} = \dfrac{39}{5}$

8. $-\dfrac{48}{5}$

9–15.

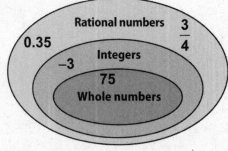

9. rational numbers

10. whole numbers, integers, rational numbers

11. integers, rational numbers

12. rational numbers

13. Sample answers: 9, 11

14. Sample answers: −3, −8

15. Sample answers: −0.54, $-\dfrac{2}{5}$

Practice and Problem Solving: D

1. $\dfrac{31}{6}$

2. $-\dfrac{6}{1}$

3. $\dfrac{97}{100}$

4. $\dfrac{18}{1}$

5. $\dfrac{33}{10}$

6. $-\dfrac{17}{8}$

7. integers, rational numbers

8. rational numbers

9. whole numbers, integers, rational numbers

10–12.

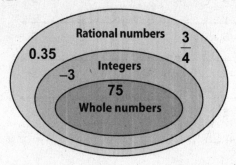

10. rational numbers

11. integers, rational numbers

12. whole numbers, integers, rational numbers

Reteach

1. $-\dfrac{12}{1}$; integers, rational numbers

2. $\dfrac{73}{10}$; rational numbers

3. $\dfrac{41}{100}$; rational numbers

4. $\dfrac{6}{1}$; whole numbers, integers, rational numbers

5. $\dfrac{7}{2}$; rational numbers

Reading Strategies

1. rational number

2. integer; rational number

3. rational number

4. whole number, integer, rational number

Success for English Learners

1. Change the mixed number to an improper fraction, $\dfrac{26}{5}$.

2. Every whole number can be written as a fraction with a denominator of 1.

3. No, some integers are negative. So a number like −2 is an integer, but not a whole number.

LESSON 2-2

Practice and Problem Solving: A/B

1.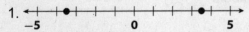
   number line from −5 to 5 with points at −4 and 4

2. number line from −5 to 5 with points at −2 and 2

3. number line from −5 to 5 with points at −2.5 and 2.5

4. number line from −5 to 5 with points at −1 and 1

5. −4.25

6. $5\frac{1}{4}$

7. $-\frac{1}{2}$

8. $2\frac{1}{3}$

9. 3.85

10. 6.1

11. A: −15.6; B −17.1; C: −5.2; D: 6.5; E: 18.5

12. checkpoint C

13. checkpoint E; When you find the absolute value of each elevation, 18.5 is the furthest from 0 (sea level).

Practice and Problem Solving: C

1. $\frac{2}{3}$; $\frac{2}{3}$

2. $-1\frac{1}{7}$; $1\frac{1}{7}$

3. 0.89; 0.89

4. −3.47; 3.47

5. $-\frac{7}{5}$; $\frac{7}{5}$

6. $-5\frac{2}{3}$; $5\frac{2}{3}$

7. 4.03; 4.03

8. 1.11; 1.11

9. when the rational number is negative

10. |−5.47| = 5.47. The distance from −5.47 to 0 is 5.47 and the distance from 0 to 5.47 is 5.47. So, the total distance between the two points is 10.94.

11. Tuesday and Friday

12. greatest to least: 3.4, 2.1, −1.2, −3.4, −7.1; greatest to least absolute value: 7.1, 3.4, 3.4, 2.1, 1.2

Practice and Problem Solving: D

2. number line from −5 to 5 with points at −2 and 2

3. number line from −5 to 5 with points at −3 and 3

4. number line from −5 to 5 with points at −1.5 and 1.5

5. −3

6. 4.5

7. $-\frac{1}{3}$

8. 4.0

9. $2\frac{1}{2}$

10. $\frac{2}{3}$

11. Camille

12. −$7.45

13. $1.50

14. $5.25

Reteach

1. yes; 6.5, 6.5

2. no; $-3\frac{2}{5}$, $3\frac{2}{5}$

3. Answers will vary. Accept any negative rational number.

4. Answers will vary. Accept any positive rational number.

Reading Strategies

1. positive; 2.7

2. negative; $-3\frac{1}{8}$

3. negative; $-\frac{2}{7}$

4. positive; 0.9

5. No. All absolute values are positive.

6. It is the distance from 0 and the number and since distance is positive, it is positive.

Success for English Learners

1.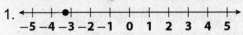
   −3 and −4

2. ![number line from −5 to 5 with point between 3 and 4]
   3 and 4

3. $3\dfrac{2}{7}$

4. $3\dfrac{2}{7}$

5. They are opposites, and they are the same distance from 0 on the number line.

6. Answers will vary. Sample answer: 2.45 and −2.45; absolute value of both numbers: 2.45

LESSON 2-3

Practice and Problem Solving: A/B

1. 0.375
2. 1.4
3. 3
4. 1.67
5. $\dfrac{11}{20}$
6. $10\dfrac{3}{5}$
7. $-7\dfrac{2}{25}$
8. .05, .05, $\dfrac{5}{8}$
9. 1.3, $1\dfrac{1}{3}$, 1.34
10. −2.67, 2.07, 2.67, $2\dfrac{7}{10}$
11. 0.422
12. 20
13. 23
14. 0.6, 39 mph
15. $\dfrac{7}{100}$, 7 cents
16. $\dfrac{373}{500}$; 0.746

Practice and Problem Solving: C

1. less than; 0.625
2. greater than; 2.2
3. equal to; 1
4. less than; 0.57
5. fraction; $\dfrac{17}{20}$
6. mixed number; $3\dfrac{4}{5}$
7. mixed number; $-11\dfrac{4}{25}$
8. 0.867; yes
9. $0.8\overline{3}$; no
10. −5.9, $-5\dfrac{7}{8}$, 5.78
11. $\dfrac{3}{7}$, $\dfrac{4}{9}$, 0.45
12. −0.38, $-\dfrac{3}{8}$, −0.04
13. blue: $\dfrac{14}{25}$, 0.56; red: $\dfrac{11}{25}$, 0.44
14. 0.1, 7.5 widgets

Practice and Problem Solving: D

1. $\dfrac{5}{10}$ or $\dfrac{1}{2}$
2. $\dfrac{2}{25}$ or $\dfrac{1}{4}$
3. $\dfrac{75}{100}$ or $\dfrac{3}{4}$
4. $\dfrac{4}{10}$ or $\dfrac{2}{5}$
5. $\dfrac{8}{10}$ or $\dfrac{4}{5}$
6. $1\dfrac{2}{10}$ or $1\dfrac{1}{5}$
7. 0.36
8. 0.6
9. 1.4
10. B
11. B
12. basketball game

Reteach

1. $\dfrac{61}{100}$

2. $3\dfrac{43}{100}$

3. $\dfrac{9}{1000}$

4. $4\dfrac{7}{10}$

5. $1\dfrac{5}{10}$ or $1\dfrac{1}{2}$

6. $\dfrac{13}{100}$

7. $5\dfrac{2}{1000}$ or $5\dfrac{1}{500}$

8. $\dfrac{21}{1000}$

Reading Strategies

1. $0.1\overline{6}$; ; repeating

2. 0.125; terminating

3. $0.\overline{09}$; repeating

4. $0.\overline{2}$; repeating

5. 0.8; terminating

6. $0.\overline{5}$; repeating

7. 0.5; terminating

8. $0.\overline{7}$; repeating

Success for English Learners

1. A terminating decimal ends, while in a repeating decimal one or more digits repeats.

2. Divide the numerator by the denominator.

MODULE 2 Challenge

1. Divide the weight of the oranges by the number of boxes on each day to find a rational number for the weight of each box.

The weights are:

Monday: $\dfrac{113}{45} = 2.51$ lb

Tuesday: $\dfrac{116}{43} = 2.69$ lb

Wednesday: $\dfrac{144}{50} = 2.88$ lb

Thursday: $\dfrac{129}{40} = 3.225$ lb

Friday: $\dfrac{109}{35} = 3.11$ lb

a. The boxes packed on Thursday and Friday will not ship.

b. The boxes packed on Wednesday will sell for the highest price.

2. The inequality can be corrected in three moves.

$$2 \leq -\dfrac{1}{8} \leq -10 \leq -0.125 \leq -\dfrac{15}{2}$$

Move 1: Swap -10 and 2.

$$-10 \leq -\dfrac{1}{8} \leq 2 \leq -0.125 \leq -\dfrac{15}{2}$$

Move 2: Swap $-\dfrac{15}{2}$ and 2.

$$-10 \leq -\dfrac{1}{8} \leq -\dfrac{15}{2} \leq -0.125 \leq 2$$

Move 3: Swap $-\dfrac{15}{2}$ and $-\dfrac{1}{8}$.

$$-10 \leq -\dfrac{15}{2} \leq -\dfrac{1}{8} \leq -0.125 \leq 2$$

UNIT 2: Number Operations

MODULE 3 Multiplying and Dividing Fractions

LESSON 3-1

Practice and Problem Solving: A/B

1. 2

2. 2

3. 2

4. $\frac{1}{8}$

5. $\frac{1}{6}$

6. $\frac{1}{2}$

7. 20

8. 12

9. $7\frac{7}{8}$

10. 3 h

11. $4\frac{1}{2}$ h

12. $1\frac{1}{5}$ T

13. $\frac{1}{6}$ of a pizza

Practice and Problem Solving: C

1. $2\frac{1}{3}$

2. $3\frac{3}{5}$

3. $7\frac{1}{3}$

4. $\frac{12}{35}$

5. $\frac{1}{6}$

6. $\frac{28}{45}$

7. 14

8. $4\frac{7}{8}$

9. $7\frac{7}{8}$

10. $7\frac{3}{4}$ h

11. $18\frac{3}{4}$ ft

12. flour: 2 c; sugar: $\frac{1}{2}$ c; butter: $1\frac{1}{3}$ T, salt: $\frac{1}{3}$ t, fruit: $2\frac{2}{3}$ c

13. $\frac{7}{24}$ of the pizza

Practice and Problem Solving: D

1. 3

2. 3

3. 4

4. $\frac{1}{6}$

5. $\frac{2}{15}$

6. $\frac{1}{2}$

7. 9

8. 15

9. $4\frac{2}{7}$

10. $\frac{1}{4} \cdot 24 = 6$; 6 oz

11. 20 h

12. 3 h

13. $4\frac{3}{8}$ c

Reteach

1. $\frac{21}{32}$

2. $\frac{2}{9}$

3. $\frac{1}{2}$

4. $3\frac{1}{3}$

5. $2\frac{2}{5}$

6. $5\frac{5}{6}$

7. $\frac{8}{27}$

8. $1\frac{7}{8}$

9. $\frac{2}{7}$

Reading Strategies

1. $\frac{2}{3}$

2. 4

3. $4 \cdot \frac{2}{3} = \frac{8}{3}$

4. $\frac{3}{5}$

5. 3

6. $3 \cdot \frac{3}{5} = \frac{9}{5} = 1\frac{4}{5}$

7. $1\frac{1}{7}$

8. $3\frac{3}{4}$

9. $\frac{2}{3}$

10. $1\frac{5}{7}$

11. $1\frac{2}{3}$

12. $1\frac{9}{13}$

13. Sample answer: You would need to make or draw many fraction strips.

Success for English Learners

1. Write the whole number as a fraction over 1.

2. When multiplying, you multiply numerators, then denominators. When adding, you change the fractions to fractions with a common denominator and then add the numerators.

LESSON 3-2

Practice and Problem Solving: A/B

1. $\frac{2}{3}$

2. $\frac{24}{25}$

3. $\frac{5}{6}$

4. $\frac{9}{20}$

5. $\frac{3}{5}$

6. $\frac{8}{15}$

7. $\frac{5}{14}$

8. $\frac{11}{15}$

9. $\frac{3}{16}$

10. $\frac{14}{15}$

11. $\frac{3}{4}$

12. $\frac{7}{12}$

13. $1\frac{11}{15}$

14. $6\frac{1}{4}$

15. $5\frac{5}{6}$

16. $\frac{7}{8}$ m

17. 30 pencils

18. 275 mi

19. $9\frac{3}{4}$ ft^3

Practice and Problem Solving: C

1. no; $\frac{2}{5}$

2. no; $\frac{13}{64}$

3. yes; $1\frac{1}{5}$

4. $3\frac{1}{3}$

5. $4\frac{2}{3}$

6. $8\frac{1}{6}$

7. no

8. yes

9. no

10. $159\frac{9}{10}$ ft^2

11. a. $5\frac{1}{4}$ c; $1\frac{5}{8}$ c

    b. 3 eggs; 1 egg

    c. 10 T; $3\frac{1}{3}$ T

    d. 2 c; $\frac{2}{3}$ c

Practice and Problem Solving: D

1. 3; $\frac{1}{2}$

2. 5; 1

3. 7; $1\frac{2}{5}$

4. 9; $\frac{4}{7}$

5. 4; $\frac{8}{27}$

6. 7; $\frac{1}{3}$

7. $\frac{9}{10}$

8. $\frac{2}{3}$

9. $\frac{1}{2}$

10. $3\frac{1}{15}$

11. $8\frac{2}{3}$

12. $1\frac{1}{2}$

13. $\frac{5}{6}$ h

14. $37\frac{4}{5}$ pages

Reteach

1. $\frac{4}{3}$; yes; GCF: 4; $\frac{1}{3}$

2. $\frac{5}{2}$; no; $\frac{5}{12}$

3. $\frac{3}{2}$; no; $\frac{3}{16}$

4. $\frac{7}{5}$; no; $\frac{7}{15}$

5. $\frac{4}{3}$, $\frac{5}{3}$; no; $2\frac{2}{9}$

6. $\frac{3}{2}$, $\frac{4}{3}$; yes; GCF: 2,3; 2

7. $\frac{7}{4}$, $\frac{5}{2}$; no; $4\frac{3}{8}$

8. $\frac{7}{6}$; $\frac{8}{3}$; yes; GCF: 2; $3\frac{1}{9}$

9. $1\frac{1}{3}$

10. $\frac{1}{2}$

Reading Strategies

1. $2\frac{1}{2}$

2. $\frac{5}{2}$

3. 5

4. Multiply the denominator by the whole number: $3 \cdot 5 = 15$.

5. Add the numerator: $15 + 2 = 17$.

6. $\frac{17}{5}$

Success for English Learners

1. Because you must also multiply 1 by $\frac{1}{3}$

   Or "flip" the numerator and denominator

2. Write the problem as a multiplication problem by using the reciprocal of $\frac{1}{3}$, which is $\frac{3}{1}$. Multiply to find the product and simplify the fractions, $\frac{5}{8} \cdot \frac{3}{1} = \frac{15}{8} =$ $1\frac{7}{8}$.

3. 1; Sample answer: $\frac{2}{7} \cdot \frac{7}{2} = \frac{14}{14} = 1$

LESSON 3-3

Practice and Problem Solving: A/B

1. $\frac{7}{5}$

2. $\frac{4}{3}$

3. $\frac{5}{3}$

4. 10

5. $\frac{9}{4}$

6. $\frac{14}{13}$

7. $\frac{12}{7}$

8. $\frac{10}{3}$

9. $\frac{8}{5}$

10. $1\frac{2}{3}$

11. $1\frac{5}{16}$

12. $1\frac{1}{5}$

13. $\frac{1}{12}$

14. $\frac{7}{9}$

15. $2\frac{7}{9}$

16. $1\frac{1}{9}$

17. $1\frac{1}{24}$

18. $\frac{3}{4}$

19. 24 sandwiches

20. $10\frac{1}{2}$ lb

21. 36 points

Practice and Problem Solving: C

1. $\frac{7}{3}$; greater

2. $\frac{4}{3}$; greater

3. $\frac{5}{8}$; less

4. $\frac{11}{1}$; greater

5. $\frac{9}{8}$; greater

6. $\frac{4}{13}$; less

7. It is greater than 1.

8. It is less than 1.

9. 1

10. $1\frac{1}{4}$

11. $1\frac{11}{24}$

12. $2\frac{2}{9}$

13. $\frac{5}{6}$

14. $\frac{45}{49}$

15. $\frac{11}{15}$

16. They are greater than 1.

17. They are less than 1.

18. greater

19. 14; $7\frac{1}{2}$ min

Practice and Problem Solving: D

1. $\frac{3}{2}$

2. $\frac{9}{7}$

3. $\frac{5}{8}$

4. $\frac{9}{1}$

5. $\frac{10}{9}$

6. $\frac{10}{3}$

7. $\frac{7}{4}$

8. $\frac{1}{8}$

9. $\frac{7}{6}$

10. $1\frac{1}{2}$

11. $1\frac{1}{20}$

12. $1\frac{1}{9}$

13. $\frac{9}{25}$

14. $\frac{7}{9}$

15. $\frac{21}{25}$

16. $1\frac{1}{6}$

17. $1\frac{3}{8}$

18. $\frac{13}{14}$

19. $\frac{16}{3}$; 64; $21\frac{1}{3}$

20. 9 in.

21. $\frac{1}{5}$ h

Reteach

1. $\frac{1}{4} \cdot \frac{3}{1} = \frac{3}{4}$

2. $\frac{1}{2} \cdot \frac{4}{1} = 2$

3. $\frac{3}{8} \cdot \frac{2}{1} = \frac{6}{8} = \frac{3}{4}$

4. $\frac{1}{3} \cdot \frac{4}{3} = \frac{4}{9}$

5. $\frac{2}{5}$

6. $\frac{1}{4}$

7. $\frac{5}{16}$

8. $\frac{1}{4}$

Reading Strategies

1. 3; $\frac{1}{2}$

2. $\frac{7}{8} \cdot 4$

3. 3

4. $\frac{4}{8}$; $\frac{1}{2}$

5. $3\frac{1}{2}$

6. The answer is the same.

Success for English Learners

1. Sample answer: When you divide mixed numbers, you have to change the division to multiplication and also change the divisor to its reciprocal.

2. Change all mixed numbers to improper fractions.

3. We know that $8 \times 7 = 56$, and the area of the rectangle is greater than 56. Since $8\frac{1}{2} \times 7$ is greater than 56, then the width would need to be approximately 7 feet.

LESSON 3-4

Practice and Problem Solving: A/B

1. $\frac{2}{21}$; $\frac{21}{2} \times \frac{2}{21} = 1$

2. $\frac{7}{45}$; $\frac{45}{7} \times \frac{7}{45} = 1$

3. $\frac{9}{26}$; $\frac{26}{9} \times \frac{9}{26} = 1$

4. $\frac{4}{61}$; $\frac{4}{61} \times \frac{61}{4} = 1$

5. $\frac{3}{29}$; $\frac{3}{29} \times \frac{29}{3} = 1$

6. $\frac{8}{61}$; $\frac{61}{8} \times \frac{8}{61} = 1$

7. $\frac{24}{55}$

8. $1\frac{1}{13}$

9. $1\frac{3}{5}$

10. $1\frac{17}{19}$

11. $1\frac{16}{19}$

12. $\frac{22}{63}$

13. $4\frac{20}{39}$

14. $2\frac{16}{145}$

15. $1\frac{25}{62}$

16. $36\frac{5}{6} \div 5\frac{2}{3} = 6\frac{1}{2}$; No, the slab is not long enough for a 7-ft picnic table since $36\frac{5}{6} \div 5\frac{2}{3} = 6\frac{1}{2}$ ft.

17. $225 \div 13\frac{3}{4} = 16\frac{4}{11}$; The space is wide enough, but since $225 \div 13\frac{3}{4} = 16\frac{4}{11}$ in. and $16\frac{4}{11} > 16$, the space is not long enough to fit the mirror.

18. $16\frac{1}{5} \div 5\frac{2}{5}$; 3 costumes

Practice and Problem Solving: C

1. 21 in.

2. He can make 5 pillowcases, and will have $2\frac{11}{12}$ yd left over.

3. He has hiked $3\frac{11}{12}$ mi.

4. She can make 2 bows.

5. $\frac{2}{3}$ oz

6. He can make 14 more bowls. He can make a total of $15\frac{5}{8} \div \frac{7}{10}$ or 22 bowls in all. $22 - 8 = 14$.

Practice and Problem Solving: D

1. $\frac{(9 \times 2) + 1}{2} = \frac{19}{2}$; $\frac{2}{19}$

2. $\frac{(5 \times 7) + 3}{7} = \frac{38}{7}$; $\frac{7}{38}$

3. $\frac{(1 \times 9) + 8}{9} = \frac{17}{9}$; $\frac{9}{17}$

4. $\dfrac{(14 \times 4)+1}{4} = \dfrac{57}{4}$; $\dfrac{4}{57}$

5. $\dfrac{(8 \times 3)+2}{3} = \dfrac{26}{3}$; $\dfrac{3}{26}$

6. $\dfrac{(6 \times 8)+5}{8} = \dfrac{53}{8}$; $\dfrac{8}{53}$

7. $\dfrac{21}{40}$

8. $1\dfrac{1}{6}$

9. $1\dfrac{11}{12}$

10. $\dfrac{11}{12}$

11. $9\dfrac{3}{5} \div 2\dfrac{2}{5} = \dfrac{48}{5} \div \dfrac{12}{5} = \dfrac{48}{5} \times \dfrac{5}{12} = \dfrac{48}{12} = 4$;
    4 vests

12. $20\dfrac{5}{6} \div 3\dfrac{1}{2} = \dfrac{125}{6} \div \dfrac{7}{2} = \dfrac{125}{6} \times \dfrac{2}{7}$
    $= \dfrac{250}{42} = 5\dfrac{40}{42} = 5\dfrac{20}{21}$; $5\dfrac{20}{21}$ ft long

Reteach

1. $\dfrac{14}{9}$

2. $\dfrac{2}{7}$

3. $\dfrac{3}{32}$

4. $\dfrac{18}{5} \div \dfrac{9}{4}$
   $\dfrac{18}{5} \times \dfrac{4}{9}$
   $\dfrac{72}{45} = \dfrac{8}{5} = 1\dfrac{3}{5}$

5. $\dfrac{3}{2} \div \dfrac{5}{4}$
   $\dfrac{3}{2} \times \dfrac{4}{5}$
   $\dfrac{12}{10} = \dfrac{6}{5} = 1\dfrac{1}{5}$

6. $\dfrac{5}{12} \div \dfrac{15}{8}$
   $\dfrac{5}{12} \times \dfrac{8}{15}$
   $\dfrac{40}{180} = \dfrac{2}{9}$

7. $6\dfrac{1}{4}$

8. $\dfrac{7}{16}$

9. $1\dfrac{2}{3}$

Reading Strategies

1. Draw a single square and label it $\dfrac{1}{2}$.

2. to find the number of $\dfrac{1}{2}$-ft servings in $2\dfrac{1}{2}$ ft.

3. 5

4. 5

Success for English Learners

1. Sample answer: When you divide mixed numbers, you have to change the division to multiplication and also change the divisor to its reciprocal.

2. Change all mixed numbers to improper fractions.

3. We know that $8 \times 7 = 56$, and the area of the rectangle is greater than 56. Since $8\dfrac{1}{2} \times 7$ is greater than 56, then the width would need to be approximately 7 feet.

MODULE 3 Challenge

1. Find the prices of the rugs by multiplying the area of each rug by $8.

Type of Rug	Length (ft)	Width (ft)	Area (ft²)	Price ($)
Classic	$8\frac{1}{2}$	$10\frac{3}{4}$	$91\frac{3}{8}$	$731.00
Deco	$10\frac{3}{4}$	$9\frac{3}{8}$	$66\frac{5}{8}$	$533.00
Solid	$7\frac{2}{5}$	$8\frac{3}{5}$	$63\frac{16}{25}$	$509.12
Modern	$10\frac{3}{5}$	$9\frac{1}{2}$	$100\frac{7}{10}$	$805.60

Classic = $\dfrac{17}{2} \times \dfrac{43}{4} = 91\dfrac{3}{8}$ sq ft × $8
= $731.00

Deco = $\dfrac{43}{4} \times \dfrac{75}{8} = \dfrac{3225}{32} = 100\dfrac{25}{32}$
= 100.781 × 8 = $806.25

Solid = $\dfrac{37}{5} \times \dfrac{43}{5} = 63.64$ sq ft × 8
= $509.12

Modern = $\dfrac{53}{5} \times \dfrac{19}{2} = 100.7 \times 8 = $805.60

The Deco rug is the most expensive. It costs $806.25.

2. The area of the Deco is 100.781 sq ft. Divide that by 9.5 = 10.608 or 10.61 ft long.

3. The product will be $\dfrac{1}{100}$ if the last fraction written in the pattern is $\dfrac{1}{100}$. The 99 in the previous fraction's denominator will cross-cancel with the 99 in the last fraction's numerator and you will be left with $\dfrac{1}{100}$.

MODULE 4 Multiplying and Dividing Decimals

LESSON 4-1

Practice and Problem Solving: A/B

1.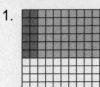

2.

3. 3.96

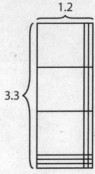

4. 8.61

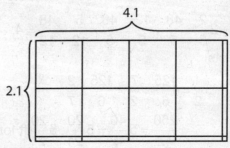

5. 0.02

6. 5.4

7. 0.24

8. 4.64

9. 0.615

10. 0.6432

11. 14.6797

12. 82.8576

13. 17.5 lb

14. $26.25

Practice and Problem Solving: C

1. 1 × 1 or 1; 0.595

2. 3 × 2 or 6; 5.9475

3. 0.5 × 2 or 1; 1.035

4. 4.699 × 1.74 = 8.17626

5. 10 × 5 or 50; 52.74182

6. 5.593 × 19.71 = 110.23803

7. 2 × 4 or 8; 4 × 3 or 12; so, 2.4 × 3.8 < 3.5 × 2.8

8. 6 × 4 or 24; 3 × 7 or 21; so, 6.28 × 3.82 > 3.3 × 6.84

9.

Sector	Map Dimensions (cm)	Map Area (cm²)
A	2.5 × 5.8	14.5
B	3.7 × 2.1	8.88
C	4.7 × 3.5	16.45
D	4.2 × 2.8	11.76

a. Change cm^2 to km^2.

b. The total area is: $14.5 + 7.77 + 16.45 + 11.76 = 50.48$ km^2 .

c. Sectors A, B, and C; Sectors A, B, and D; Sectors A, B, and D; and Sectors B, C and D.

d. The sum of Sectors A, C, and D is 42.71 km^2. Since these sectors have the greatest areas, their sum is maximizes the area studied.

Practice and Problem Solving: D

1. 1.5
2. 3.2
3. 6.3
4. 0.75
5.
6.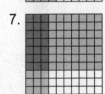
7.
8. 1; 2; 3
9. 3; 1; 4
10. 17.775
11. 5.232

12. a. 3.5 liters × $4.95
    b. $14.85
    c. $2.475 or $2.48
    d. $14.85 + $2.48 = $17.33

Reteach

1. 0.69
2. 0.82
3. 0.05
4. 0.64
5. 0.45
6. 0.84
7. 0.32
8. 0.88
9. 0.16
10. 0.63
11. 0.25
12. 0.18
13. 0.1
14. 0.16
15. 0.09
16. 0.28

Reading Strategies

1.

2. 0.89 + 0.89 + 0.89 + 0.89
3. 0.89 + 0.89 + 0.89 + 0.89 = 3.56
4. 4 × 0.89 or 0.89 × 4
5. 4 × 0.89 = 3.56 or 0.89 × 4 = 3.56

Success for English Learners

1. Add the decimal places in the factors.
2. left
3. Use estimation and compare it to your answer.
3. no; 1 × 3 = 3
4. yes
5. no; 2 × 3 = 6

LESSON 4-2

Practice and Problem Solving: A/B

1.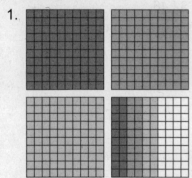

2.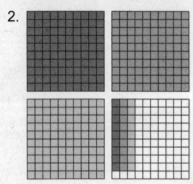

3. 15

4. 13.2

5. 5.44

6. 7

7. 7.5

8. 15

9. About 4; 4.2

10. Between 12 and 18; 14.4

11. About 30; 28

12. About 14; 15

13. 66 images; the exact answer, $66\frac{2}{3}$, means that last image would not be completely captured.

14. About 0.142 centimeters per year (or a little over a millimeter per year).

Practice and Problem Solving: C

1. Estimate: $8 \div 2 = 4$; Exact Quotient: 3.5

2. Estimate: $14 \div 2 = 7$; Exact Quotient: 6.1111111 or 6.11…

3. Estimate: $55 \div 5 = 11$; Exact Quotient: 10.9

4. <

5. >

6. <

7. >

8.

Size	Amount of Liquid	Sale Price	Price per Milliliter
Small	250 milliliters	$4.50	**$0.018 per mL**
Medium	500 milliliters	$9.95	**$0.0199 per mL**
Large	1 liter	$16.95	**$0.01695 per mL**

a. $0.01695 < 0.018 < 0.0199$ or $0.0199 > 0.018 > 0.01695$

b. $\$16.95 + (2 \times \$4.50) = \$25.95$

c. The most expensive way to buy 1,500 mL of the cleaner is to buy three 500 mL bottles, which would be $29.85. The anno given is based on three 1 L bottles, which is 3,000 mL.

Practice and Problem Solving: D

1. 0.7

2. 0.9

3. 0.6

4. 0.8

5. 0.05

6. 0.6

7. 6

8. 7

9. 8

10. 11

11. 2

12. 6

13. $0.48 or 48 cents

14. 0.09 in.

15. 2 months

16. 2 lb

Reteach

1. 0.12

2. 0.13

3. 0.08

4. 300

5. 0.2

6. 0.7

7. 50

8. 0.8

Reading Strategies

1–2.

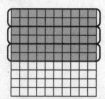

3. 0.20

4. $0.60 \div 3 = 0.20 = 0.2$ or

$3\overline{)0.60} = 0.20 = 0.2$

5–6.

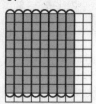

7. 0.09

8. $0.72 \div 8 = 0.9$ or $8\overline{)0.72} = 0.9$

Success for English Learners

1. 3

2. No; 12 divides 36 evenly with no remainder.

3. Answers will vary. Sample answer: How much gas will Sari's car use to travel 332.5 miles? ($332.5 \div 17.5 = 19$) e.g. what is the miles per gallon rate for the total trip?

LESSON 4-3

Practice and Problem Solving: A/B

1. $3.10

2. 3 vans

3. 7 packs

4. 8 pairs

5. $68\frac{4}{5}$ in.; $5\frac{11}{15}$ ft

6. 12 T

7. $3,565

8. Joey; 0.2 points

9. $4\frac{1}{6}$ c

10. $60\frac{1}{2}$ lb

Practice and Problem Solving: C

1. 59 scarves

2. 2 ft

3. $11.09

4. $7.52

5. 11.585 h; 2.317 h; A, C, D

6. 49; $116.13

7. $0.02; $0.068; 397

Practice and Problem Solving: D

1. $\frac{3}{20}$ mi

2. 11 weeks

3. 6 costumes

4. $2.19

5. 27.6 mpg

6. 15 ft

7. $10\frac{1}{2}$ lb

8. $2\frac{1}{2}$ batches

9. 6 costumes

10. $11.76

Reteach

1. divide; 7 tickets

2. multiply; $36.00

3. divide; 10.97 ft

4. divide; 3

Reading Strategies

1. pumpkin's weight of 31.3lb and that there are 3 parts; weight of 1 part; divide; 10.43 lb

2. pumpkin's weight of $22\frac{2}{3}$ lb; $\frac{1}{6}$ of weight;

multiply; $3\frac{7}{9}$ lb

3. pumpkin's weight of $42\frac{1}{3}$ lb and that each

piece will be $2\frac{1}{2}$ lb; number of pieces;

divide; $16\frac{14}{15}$ lb

Success for English Learners

1. You place the decimal point right above the decimal point in the number that is being divided.

2. Multiply the answer by 3, and see if it equals $11.61.

MODULE 4 Challenge

1. Multiply the price of each ingredient by the quantity given, then add.

   Beef: $10.65 × 3.25 = $34.61

   Onion: $2.49 × 0.65 = $1.62

   Potatoes: $3.29 × 0.2 = $0.66;

   Tomatoes: $8.45 × 0.15 = $1.27;

   Asparagus: $4.99 × 0.33 = $1.65;

   Total cost: $34.61 + $1.62 + $0.66 + $1.27 + $1.65 = $39.81.

2. Subtract the price of beef from the original total: $39.81 − $34.61 = $5.20

   Add the price of the chickpeas and lentils. Multiply the price of each ingredient by the quantity given, then add.

   Chickpeas: $2.49 × 2.5 = $6.23; Lentils: $3.59 × 1.75 = $6.28

   The new total price is $5.20 + $6.23 + $6.28 = $17.71

   Divya saves $39.81 − $17.71 = $22.10 by making the vegetarian version of her meal.

3. $3.49 + 2 × $4.99 + 6 × $0.75 = $17.97. She will spend $17.97 on dessert.

MODULE 5 Adding and Subtracting Integers

LESSON 5-1

Practice and Problem Solving: A/B

1. a. 8

   b. negative

   c. −8

2. a. 11

   b. negative

   c. −11

3. −6

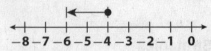

4. −10

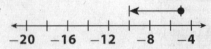

5. −9

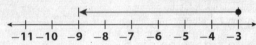

6. −12

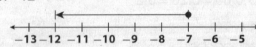

7. −8

8. −9

9. −53

10. −93

11. 224

12. −95

13. −600

14. −1310

15. $-3+(-2)+(-4)=-9$; −9 feet

Practice and Problem Solving: C

1. a. $-42+(-87)+(-29)=-158$

   b. $-57+(-75)+(-38)=-170$

   c. The store had more red apples left over. The store started with the same number of red apples and green apples. It sold more green apples than red apples, so it had more red apples left.

2. a. $-2+(-3)+(-13)=-18$

   b. The hotel guest got off on the 14th floor. The manager started on the 19th floor and rode 2 floors down to the 17th floor when the hotel guest got on. They rode the elevator down 3 floors. $17-3=14$, so the hotel guest got off on the 14th floor.

Practice and Problem Solving: D

1. a. 7

   b. positive

   c. +7

2. a. 10

   b. negative

   c. –10

3. –6

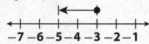

4. –6

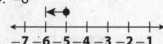

5. –7

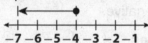

6. –7

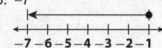

7. –4

8. –8

9. –19

10. –35

11. –$8

Reteach

1. a. positive

   b. $3 + 6 = 9$

   c. 98

2. a. negative

   b. $7 + 1 = 8$

   c. –8

3. a. negative

   b. $5 + 2 = 7$

   c. –7

4. a. positive

   b. $6 + 4 = 10$

   c. 10

5. –13

6. –16

7. 37

8. –41

9. –24

10. 52

Reading Strategies

1. Each counter represents –1.

2. Each counter represents a dollar that Sarah withdrew. The counters make it is easier to see how many dollars Sarah withdrew each day.

3. You can simply count the counters to find the sum.

4. $-3 + (-5) + (-4) + (-1) = -13$

Success for English Learners

1. positive counters

2. because you are adding a negative number

3. Answers will vary. Sample answer: Erica bought stamps three times this week. She bought 5 stamps on Monday, 3 stamps on Wednesday, and 4 stamps on Friday. How many stamps did Erica buy this week? $(5 + 3 + 4 + 12)$

LESSON 5-2

Practice and Problem Solving: A/B

1. –1

2. 1

3. 5

4. –1

5. –1

6. –3

7. –2

8. 4

9. 8

10. 2

11. 43

12. 21

13. –29

14. –10

15. 11°F

16. 3 yards

17. –9 points

18. a. negative

   b. loss of 6, or –6

Practice and Problem Solving: C

1. negative; –10

2. positive; 5

3. negative; –7

4. positive; 5

5. positive; 6

6. positive; 15

7. negative; –1

8. positive; 1

9. the same sign as the integers

10. It is the sign of the integer whose absolute value is greater.

11. –15

12. –24

13. 13

14. –30

15. 0

16. –18

17. –5°F

18. $150

19. Rita; 11 points

Practice and Problem Solving: D

1. –1

2. –7

3. –5

4. –1

5. –1

6. 12

7. 4

8. 8

9. –5

10. –10

11. –6

12. 5°F

13. –22°F

14. –97 ft

15. 17,500 ft

Reteach

1. subtract; the numbers have different signs

2. negative

3. 4

4. –5

5. –1

6. –4

7. 2

8. –5

9. 9

10. –10

11. –16

12. Sample answer: I look at 3 and 9 and see that 9 > 3. Since the sign on 9 is negative, the answer is negative.

Reading Strategies

1. on zero

2. right; 6

3. left; 4

4. 2

5. on zero

6. left; 5

7. left; 3

8. –8

Success for English Learners

1. negative number

2. No, the sum can be positive or negative.

3. negative

4. positive

LESSON 5-3

Practice and Problem Solving: A/B

1. –5

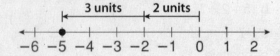

2. 6

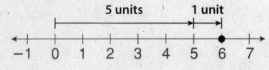

3. –10

4. 5
5. –4
6. 24
7. 0
8. 46
9. –1
10. 42
11. –6
12. –26
13. 30
14. –5
15. –9°C
16. 14°F
17. 4°C
18. 7°C
19. 240°C

Practice and Problem Solving: C

1. 16
2. –22
3. 7
4. 0
5. 29
6. 9
7. –2
8. 0
9. –10
10. when $x < y$
11. when $x > y$
12. 12°F, –2°F
13. Pacific; 2,400 m
14. 11,560; –185; –185 is closer to sea level; 11,375 ft
15. Saturday
16. 3°

Practice and Problem Solving: D

1. –5
2. –4
3. –7
4. –5
5. 6

6. –16
7. 0
8. 1
9. 7
10. 16
11. –11
12. 610°C
13. $13,000
14. 9°F

Reteach

1. a. 5
   b. –1
   c. 20
2. a. negative
   b. 2
   c. –2
3. 40
4. –3
5. –26
6. 0
7. 31
8. –5

Reading Strategies

1. left
2. 7
3. right
4. 3
5. –4
6. right; 2
7. left; 6
8. –4

Success for English Learners

1. positive
2. negative

LESSON 5-4

Practice and Problem Solving: A/B

1. $-2 - 19 + 7 = -14$; 14 feet below the surface of the water
2. $45 - 8 + 53 - 6 = 84$; 84 points

3. 20

4. −27

5. 18

6. 110

7. 52

8. 34

9. <

10. >

11. a. $225 + 75 - 30 = 270$; 270 points

   b. Maya

Practice and Problem Solving: C

1. $-35 - 29 + 7 - 10 = -67$; Jana is 67 ft from the end of the fishing line.

2. a. $500 + 225 - 105 + 445 = 1065$; 1065 ft above the ground

   b. Kirsten is closer to the ground; Gigi's balloon position is $500 + 240 - 120 + 460 = 1080$ ft, which is greater than 1065 ft.

3. a. $20 + 20 + 30 + 30 - 10 - 10 - 10 = 100$; 100 points

   b. David and Jon tied. Jon scored $20 + 20 + 20 + 30 + 30 - 10 - 10 = 100$, or 100 points, which is the same number of points that David scored.

Practice and Problem Solving: D

1. $-2 - 9 + 3 = -8$; 8 ft below the surface of the water

2. $20 - 5 + 10 = 25$; 25 points

3. −1

4. −18

5. 20

6. −9

7. 8

8. 100

9. <

10. >

11. $200 - 30 + 70 = 240$; 240 points

Reteach

1. a. $10 + 5 - 19$

   b. $15 - 19 = -4$

   c. −4

2. a. $14 - 15 - 3$

   b. $14 - 18 = -4$

   c. −4

3. a. $10 - 80 - 6$

   b. $10 - 86 = -76$

   c. −76

4. a. $7 + 13 - 21$

   b. $20 - 21 = -1$

   c. −1

5. a. $13 + 2 - 5 - 6$

   b. $15 - 11 = 4$

   c. 4

6. a. $18 + 6 - 4 - 30$

   b. $24 - 34 = -10$

   c. −10

Reading Strategies

1. +700; above

2. when the balloon rises; rise

3. when the balloon drops; drop

4. $700 - 200 + 500 - 100 = 900$

5. 900 ft above the ground

6. Angelo is higher than where he started because 900 is greater than 700.

Success for English Learners

1. When money is withdrawn, it is taken out of the bank account. So, you subtract.

2. When money is deposited, it is put into the bank account. So, you add.

3. Answers may vary. Sample answer: Jose has $25. He spends $5, and then earns and saves $15. How much money does Jose have at the end? $(25 - 5 + 15 = 35)$

MODULE 5 Challenge

1. Calculate the difficulty using the method shown in the example.

Trail	Mile 1	Mile 2	Mile 3	Mile 4	Mile 5	Total
Breakneck	$100 - (-2) = 102$	$-2 - 100 = -102$	$150 - (-2) = 152$	$-8 - 150 = -158$	$250 - (-8) = 258$	252
Lake Shore	$0 - (-10) = 10$	$6 - 0 = 6$	$55 - 6 = 49$	$-1 - 55 = -56$	$60 - (-1) = 61$	70
Mountain View	$-2 - 40 = -42$	$120 - (-2) = 122$	$35 - 120 = -85$	$200 - 35 = 165$	$180 - 200 = -20$	140

The most difficult trail is Breakneck.

2. The greatest possible value is obtained by filling the boxes as follows.

$-3 \boxed{+} 5 \boxed{-} -4 \boxed{-} -10 \boxed{+} 18 = 34$

MODULE 6 Multiplying and Dividing Integers

LESSON 6-1

Practice and Problem Solving: A/B

1. –80
2. –72
3. 40
4. –39
5. 0
6. –80
7. 189
8. –11
9. –72
10. 80
11. –54
12. 49
13. $4(-6) = -24$; –24 points
14. $5(-3) = -15$; –15°
15. $8(-18) = -144$; $200 + (-144) = 56$; $56
16. $3(-5) = -15$; $8 + (-15) = -7$; –7°
17. $6(-25) = -150$; $325 + (-150) = 175$; $175

Practice and Problem Solving: C

1. –98
2. 120
3. –144
4. 135

5. –24
6. –36
7. 0
8. –1,440
9. 1,176
10. $3(-4) = -12$; $-12 + 9 = -3$; –3 yd
11. $4(-35) = -140$; $-140 + 220 = 80$; $80
12. $3(-50) = -150$; $-125 + (-150) = -275$; –275 ft
13. 1
14. –1
15. 1
16. –1
17. 1
18. negative; positive

Practice and Problem Solving: D

1. –6
2. 0
3. 8
4. –28
5. 12
6. –36
7. –50
8. –18
9. –70
10. 1
11. –12
12. 4
13. $5(-3) = -15$; –15 points
14. $3(-1) = -3$; –3°

15. $2(-4) = -8$; –8 yd

16. $7(-9) = -63$; –$63

17. $5(-5) = -25$; –$25

Reteach

1. –2

2. 18

3. –5

4. 54

5. 44

6. $4(-8) = -32$; –32 points

7. $5(-500) = -2,500$; –2,500 ft

Reading Strategies

1. gaining 10 points

2. losing 17 points

3. left

4. 4

5. left

6. 4

7. left

8. 4

9. The score decreased by 12.

10. –12 points

11. –16 points

Success for English Learners

1. –20

2. 3

3. $(-20) \times (3)$

4. –$60

5. Sample answer: You know the product will be either 400 or –400. It will be 400 because both factors are negative, so the product is positive.

6. Yes. The product of both will be negative because there is one positive factor and one negative factor. Since $4 \times 8 = 32$, each product will be –32.

LESSON 6-2

Practice and Problem Solving: A/B

1. –12

2. 19

3. –3

4. –4

5. 11

6. –8.75

7. 5

8. –10

9. –1

10. $32 \div (-4)$

11. $\dfrac{-30}{6} + (-8)$

12. $12 \div (-3) + (-14)4$

13. $\$3,000 \div 40 = \$75$; $\$75 - \$40 = \$35$

14. a. $-240 \div (-15) = 16$; 16 weeks

b. $20 \times -\$15 = \$300$; $\$300 - \$240 = \$60$

Practice and Problem Solving: C

1. –16

2. 2

3. $3\dfrac{2}{3}$

4. +2 produces +2; +3 produces +6.

5. +2 produces +2.

6. None of the integers from –3 to 3 produces a positive, even integer.

7. +1 produces +2.

8. $-16 \div 4 = -4$; –4 points for each event

9. a. 58°F; 70°F – (6 yd)(2°F/yd) = 70°F – 12°F = 58°F; from 6 yd to 15 yd deep, the temperature is constant, so at 10 yd deep, the temperature is 58°F.

b. 73°F; 50 ft = $16\dfrac{2}{3}$ yd below the surface; at 15 yd below the surface, the temperature is 58°F. But, from 15 yd to 20 yd the temperature increases 3°F per ft. $16\dfrac{2}{3}$ yd is $16\dfrac{2}{3} - 15$ or $1\dfrac{2}{3}$ yd, which is 5 ft, so the temperature there is 58°F + (5 ft)(3°F/ft) or 58°F + 15°F = 73°F.

c. 70°F – (6 yd)(2°F/yd) + (5)(3 ft)(3°F) = 103°F at the spring source

Practice and Problem Solving: D

1. 5

2. –9

3. –4

4. >

5. <

6. =

7. $-45 \div 5 = -9$

8. $\dfrac{55}{-11} = -5$

9. $-38 \div 19 = -2$

10. $-4 \div -2 = 2$

11. $-24 \div 4 = -6$; On average, each investor lost 6%.

12. $-760 \div 4 = -190$; On average, the temperature dropped 190°/h.

13. $-5{,}100 \div 3 = -1{,}700$; On average, the car's value decreased –$1,700/yr.

Reteach

1. right; negative; negative

2. left; negative; positive

3. left; positive; negative

4.

Divisor	Dividend	Quotient
+	+	+
–	+	–
+	–	–
–	–	+

Reading Strategies

1. 3,600 km; 225 kmh; 16 hours

2. 35 degrees; 7 hours; 5 degrees per hour

3. 1,600 liters; 2-liters/bottle; 800 bottles

4. Answers will vary. Sample answers: "102 divided by negative 6." "Negative 6 goes into 102 how many times?."

5. Answers will vary. Sample answers: "The opposite of 17 divided into negative 221." "Negative 221 divided by negative 17."

Success for English Learners

1. $\dfrac{-210}{70} = -3$

2. $300\overline{)-4200} = -14$

3. $-50 \div 10 = -5$

4. $27\overline{)54} = 2$

5. +; 1

6. –; –32

7. –; –4

8. +; 5

LESSON 6-3

Practice and Problem Solving: A/B

1. 14

2. –16

3. –27

4. 15

5. –29

6. –40

7. >

8. >

9. $15(2 - 5) = -45$; $45 less

10. $(-12) + (-11) + (-8) = -31$; falls by 31 ft

11. $5(3) + 2(-12) = -9$; 9-yd loss

12. $7(-3) + (-12) + 5 = -28$; $28 less

Practice and Problem Solving: C

1. +10

2. –18

3. +104

4. –28

5. $8(-2 + 9 + 6)$

6. gained $68

7. $4(-45) + 112 = -68$; 68 ft lower

8. $17(5) + 5(-2) + 8 = 83$; She got an 83.

9. $3(-20) + 2(-12) + (-42) + 57 - 15 = -84$; $84 less

10. a. Positive, because there is an even number of negative factors.

    b. 2,880

Practice and Problem Solving: D

1. $15 + (-12)$; 3

2. $15 + 18$; 33

3. $-7 + 23$; 16

4. $52 + (-5)$; 47

5. $(-50) + (-112) + (-46) = -208$; He has $208 less.

6. $8 + (-4) + 7 + 3 + (-11) = 3$; They had a 3-yd gain.

7. $4(-2) + 2(-1) + 3 = -7$; She had $7 less.

8. $3(-4) + 4(-2) = -20$; The water was 20 in. lower.

Reteach

1. multiplication

2. addition

3. division

4. addition

5. multiplication

6. division

7. multiplication

8. subtraction

9. -1

10. -31

11. -31

12. 33

13. -62

14. -48

Reading Strategies

1. paid; gave; $4(-3) + 7 = -12 + 7 = -5$; $5 less

2. below; $-48 \div 4 = -12$; 12 feet below the surface

3. lost; gained; $3(-5) + 32 = -15 + 32 = 17$; gained 17 yards

Success for English Learners

1. 39

2. -5

3. 6

4. a. Sample answer: Tom bought 3 DVDs for $20 each. He had a coupon for $5 off one DVD. After his purchase, what is the change in the amount of money Tom has?

   b. $-3(20) + 5 = -60 + 5 = -55$; Tom has $55 less now.

MODULE 6 Challenge

1. Sample answer:

   $81 \div (-9) + (-4) - 17 + (4)(3) + 1$

   $-9 + (-4) - 17 + 12 + 1$

   $-13 - 17 + 12 + 1$

   $-30 + 12 + 1$

   $-18 + 1$

   -17

2. Sample answer: Play with 2–4 players. Shuffle the integer cards and deal them out. Place the operations card face-up on the table. One player starts making an expression by placing one card on the table. The next player can choose an operation card and an integer card from his/her hand and extend the expression. Each player does the same until the cards are gone or one player wins. To win, a player makes the expression equal to 0.

3. Sample answer:

   First find multiplication and division signs and do these operations first.

   1. Multiply $(-4)(7) = -28$. The product is negative because one of the factors is negative.

      $(-8) + (-3) + (-28) \div 14 + 9\,(-2)$

   2. Divide $(-28) \div 14 = -2$. The quotient is negative because the dividend is negative and the divisor is positive.

      $(-8) + (-3) + (-2) + 9\,(-2)$

   3. Multiply $(9)(-2) = -18$. Same reason as step 1.

      $(-8) + (-3) + (-2) + (-18)$

   Now go back and add and subtract from left to right.

   4. $(-8) + (-3) = (-11)$ because you are adding two negative numbers.

      $(-11) + (-2) + (-18)$

   5. $(-11) + (-2) = (-13)$, for the same reason. $(-13) + (-18)$

   6. $(-13) + (-18) = (-31)$

MODULE 7 Representing Ratios and Rates

LESSON 7-1

Practice and Problem Solving: A/B

1. 9 to 12; 9:12; $\dfrac{9}{12}$

2. 8 to 16; 8:16; $\dfrac{8}{16}$

3. 9 to 10; 9:10; $\dfrac{9}{10}$

4. 10 to 12; 10:12; $\dfrac{10}{12}$

5. 12 to 9; 12:9; $\dfrac{12}{9}$

6. Answers may vary. Sample answers:
$\dfrac{8}{6}, \dfrac{16}{12}, \dfrac{32}{24}$

7. Answers may vary. Sample answers: $\dfrac{6}{7}$,
$\dfrac{18}{21}, \dfrac{24}{28}$

8. Answers may vary. Sample answers: $\dfrac{2}{3}$,
$\dfrac{8}{12}, \dfrac{12}{18}$

9. Answers may vary. Sample answers:
6 to 8, 9 to 12, 12 to 16

10. Answers may vary. Sample answers: $\dfrac{10}{14}$,
$\dfrac{15}{21}, \dfrac{12}{18}$

11. Answers may vary. Sample answers: $\dfrac{18}{4}$,
$\dfrac{27}{6}, \dfrac{36}{8}$

12. a. 48
   b. 36

Practice and Problem Solving: C

Answers will vary. Check students' work.

Practice and Problem Solving: D

1. 1 circle patch to 3 square patches; 1 to 3

2. 3; 3

3. 3; 12

4. 5 to 1; 5:1; $\dfrac{5}{1}$

5. 1 to 4; 1:4; $\dfrac{1}{4}$

6. 4 to 5; 4:5; $\dfrac{4}{5}$

7. Answers may vary. Sample answers: $\dfrac{4}{6}$,
$\dfrac{6}{9}, \dfrac{8}{12}$

8. Answers may vary. Sample answers: $\dfrac{6}{8}$,
$\dfrac{9}{12}, \dfrac{12}{16}$

9. Answers may vary. Sample answers: $\dfrac{2}{12}$,
$\dfrac{3}{18}, \dfrac{4}{24}$

Reteach

1. 31 to 365

2. 3 to 4

3. Sample answer: 2:3; 4:6. 6:9

4. Sample answer: 4:5, 8:10, 12:15

5. Sample answer: 10:12, 15:18, 20:24

6. Sample answer: 5:7, 15:21, 20:28

Reading Strategies

1. $\dfrac{3}{4}$; 3 to 4; 3:4

2. 8 miles in 2 hours

3. $\dfrac{8}{2}$; 8 to 2; 8:2

4. both compare two quantities

Success for English Learners

1. 15; multiply

2. Sample answer: Multiply $\frac{5}{2}$ by $\frac{3}{3}$ or any representation of 1.

LESSON 7-2

Practice and Problem Solving: A/B

1. 45 mph

2. 95 calories per apple

3. $0.46 per oz

4 a. $0.25 per oz

   b. $0.19 per oz

5. quart

6. Both are the same unit rate.

7. a. $0.19 per oz

   b. $0.16 per oz

   c. the 36-oz box

8. a. 7.5 pages per h

   b. $2.67 per page

Practice and Problem Solving: C

1. 45 mph; 52.9 mph; Ali

2. 95 calories per apple; 62 calories per apple; Oranges

3. $4.95 per lb; $4.69 per lb; Hamburger

4. a. $0.77 per oz

   b. $0.62 per oz

   c. $0.27 per oz

5. An ounce of paint from a quart costs about three times as much as an ounce from a gallon.

6. 4 times larger

7. a. $5.53 per in.

   b. $7.53 per in.

8. a. $21.00

   b. $3.53 per ft^2

   c. 47.6 ft^2

Practice and Problem Solving: D

1. 25 mi per day

2. 4 emails per min

3. $0.04 per oz

4. a. $0.25

b. $0.26

5. economy

6. economy

7. a. $0.50 per oz

   b. $1.00 per oz

8. a. $200 per day

   b. $75.00 per room

   c. 16 rooms

Reteach

1. $315 \div 15 = 21$ peanuts a minute

2. $81 \div 9 = 9$ texts per minute

3. $56 \div 2 = 28$ pages per hour

4. 6 oz: $0.90 \div 6 = 0.15$, 10 oz: $1.10 \div 10 = 0.11$; 16 oz: $1.44 \div 16 = 0.09$; The 16-oz can is the best buy.

5. $2.24 \div 16 = 0.14$; $3.60 \div 20 = 0.18$; $2.56 \div 16 = 0.16$; whole wheat

Reading Strategies

1. $1.25 per lb

2. $1.05 per lb

3. small

4. extra large

5. It has the lowest unit price.

6. Flora

7. Jose

8. Flora

Success for English Learners

1. Divide 300 by 5.2 to find the unit rate.

2. No, sometimes the unit price of a smaller size is less.

3. No, sometimes you might not need that much or it might get stale before you can finish it.

4. Sample answer: Bags of apples in three different sizes are on sale at the store. The large 10-lb bag costs $15, the medium 5-lb bag costs $10, and the small 2-lb bag costs $4.50. Which is the best buy? (The large 10-lb bag has the lowest unit price at $1.50 per pound.)

LESSON 7-3

Practice and Problem Solving: A/B

1.
sugar	3	6	12	18	30
milk	2	4	8	12	20

2. Eve's

3. No, the ratios are not the same. 5 to 7 is not equivalent to 15 to 17.

4. $22.50

5. 110 mi

6. a. $\frac{2}{20}$ or $\frac{1}{10}$

   b. $\frac{3}{23}$

   c. Cafe A: 5; Cafe B: 6

   d. Cafe B

7. The ratios are the same. The unit ratio is $15.00 each.

8. Bud's

9. Divide the top term by the bottom term for each rate. If the quotients are the same, the rates are equivalent.

Practice and Problem Solving: C

1.
water molecule	2	5	10	20
hydrogen atoms	4	10	20	40
oxygen atoms	2	5	10	20

2. The numbers of atoms of hydrogen and oxygen would be equal.

3. 15H, 5N

4. 5 students, 2 adults

5. 72 mi

6. My Sky

7. Appliance Store; $2.50 per lamp

8. a. Ric's

   b. Found the total number of cups in each mixture. Wrote a ratio of cups of chocolate over total cups. Simplified and compared ratios.

Practice and Problem Solving: D

1.
Club soda	2	4	8	10	20
juice	5	10	20	25	50

2. Erin

3. No, the rates are not the same. 22 to 15 is not equivalent to 5 to 10.

4. $42

5. 28 mi

6. The sports store sells the better bargain.

7. Perfect Poultry

8. Write the ratios as fractions. Find a common denominator and compare the numerators

Reteach

1. $\frac{2}{3}, \frac{4}{6}, \frac{6}{9}, \boxed{\frac{8}{12}}, \frac{10}{15} \ldots; \frac{3}{4}, \frac{6}{8}, \boxed{\frac{9}{12}} \ldots;$

   $\frac{8}{12}, < \frac{9}{12}$

2. $\frac{4}{5}, \frac{8}{10}, \frac{12}{15}, \frac{16}{20}, \frac{20}{25}, \boxed{\frac{28}{35}} \ldots; \frac{3}{7}, \frac{6}{14},$

   $\frac{9}{21}, \frac{9}{21}, \frac{12}{28}, \frac{15}{35} \ldots; \frac{28}{35}, > \boxed{\frac{15}{35}}$

3. Jack: $\frac{3}{5}, \frac{6}{10}, \frac{9}{15}, \frac{12}{20}, \frac{15}{25}, \boxed{\frac{18}{30}} \ldots;$

   Evan: $\frac{4}{6}, \frac{8}{12}, \frac{12}{18}, \frac{16}{24}, \frac{20}{30} \ldots; \boxed{\frac{20}{30}} >$

   $\frac{18}{30}$; Evans oatmeal is thicker (has more oats).

Reading Strategies

1. Veggie

2. Greens

3. Greens

4. No, it could come from Greens Salad Bar and you have 9 cups of greens or from Veggie Salad Bar and you have only 4 cups of greens.

5. a. 18 cups

   b. 8 cups

Success for English Learners

1. 18 sit ups
2. 10 sit ups
3. 9 sit ups
4. Sample answer: table because it is easier to draw; number line because you can see the relationship better.

MODULE 7 Challenge

1. Arabella: $\dfrac{7,229 \text{ ft}}{561 \text{ s}} \cdot \dfrac{1 \text{ mi}}{5,280 \text{ ft}} \cdot \dfrac{3,600 \text{ s}}{1 \text{ h}}$

= 8.786 mi/h

Bettina: first convert 13 min, 12 s to
$13 \times 60 + 12 = 792$ s

$\dfrac{3,425 \text{ yd}}{792 \text{ s}} \cdot \dfrac{1 \text{ mi}}{1,760 \text{ yd}} \cdot \dfrac{3,600 \text{ s}}{1 \text{ h}} = 8.846$ mi/h

Chandra: $\dfrac{8,214 \text{ ft}}{0.195 \text{ h}} \cdot \dfrac{1 \text{ mi}}{5,280 \text{ ft}} = 7.978$ mi/h

Divya: $\dfrac{1.62 \text{ mi}}{732 \text{ s}} \cdot \dfrac{3,600 \text{ s}}{1 \text{ h}} = 7.967$ miles/h

2. Bettina ran the fastest. Divya ran the slowest.

3. Answers will vary. Sample answer: It is helpful to convert to the same units so that the rates can be compared easily.

4. The first place finisher Bettina would finish in $\dfrac{3.1}{8.846} = 0.3504$ h, or $0.3504 \times 60 = 21.026$ min.

The last place finisher Divya would finish in $\dfrac{3.1}{7.967} = 0.3891$ h, or $0.3891 \times 60 = 23.346$ min.

$23.346 - 21.026 = 2.32$ minutes will elapse.

MODULE 8 Applying Ratios and Rates

LESSON 8-1

Practice and Problem Solving: A/B

1.

Months	1	2	5	17	32
Movies	6	12	30	102	192

Multiplicative relationship; months × 6 = movies;

ordered pairs: (1, 6), (2, 12), (5, 30), (17, 102), (32, 192).

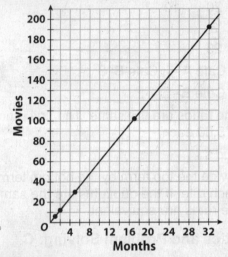

2.

New cats	1	2	3	4	5
Movies	4	5	6	7	8

Additive relationship; new cats + 3 = total cats;

ordered pairs: (1, 4), (2, 5), (3, 6), (4, 7), (5, 8)

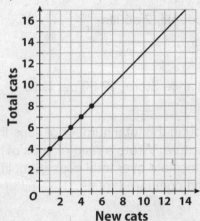

Practice and Problem Solving: C

1. a.

A	1	2	3	4	5
B	5	6	7	8	9

A	1	2	3	4	5
B	5	10	15	20	25

b. Additive relationship: he graph does not start at the origin and the line isn't very steep. Multiplicative relationship: The graph starts at the origin and the line is steeper than the other line.

c. Additive: Ed has 4 RC cars and he buys some more.

Multiplicative: Ed buys 5 RC cars every month.

2. Sample answer:

Additive: Marc has 8 silver dollars now and plans to buy some more.

Multiplicative: Kiira works out at a health club 3 times each week.

Buys	1	2	3	4	5
Total	9	10	11	12	13

Weeks	1	2	3	4	5
Visits	3	6	9	12	15

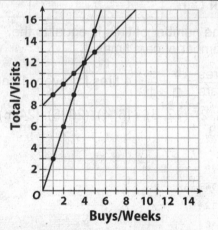

Practice and Problem Solving: D

1.

Pairs of shoes bought	1	2	3	4	5
Total pairs of shoes	7	8	9	10	11

The total pairs of shoes is equal to the number of pairs bought plus 6.

2.

Weeks	1	2	3	4	5
Number of practices	4	8	12	16	20

The number of practices equals the number of weeks times 4.

3. a. It is a multiplicative relationship because it starts at the origin and the line is steep.

b. It is an additive relationship because it does not start at the origin and the line isn't very steep.

Reteach

1. Additive; $A + 5 = B$

2. Multiplicative; $A \times 2 = B$

3. Multiplicative; $A \times 4 = B$

Reading Strategies

1.

Tables	1	2	3	4	5
Chairs	6	12	18	24	30

Tables times 6 = chairs; multiplicative

2.

Number of dogs	1	2	3	4	5
Total number of pets	4	5	6	7	8

Dogs plus 3 = total number of pets; additive

3.

Number of guests	1	2	3	5	8
Total number people served	5	6	7	9	12

Guests served plus 4 = total number of people served; additive

4.

Number of books	1	2	3	6	13
Number of pages	204	408	612	1,224	2,652

Number of books times 204 = number of pages; multiplicative

Success for English Learners

1. Additive; $A + 4 = B$

2. Multiplicative; $A \times 7 = B$

3. Multiplicative; $A \times 3.5 = B$

4. Additive; $A + 2.8 = B$

5. Sample answers:

a.

A	1	2	3	4	5
B	2	3	4	5	6

$A + 1 = B$

b.

A	1	2	3	4	5
B	2	4	6	8	10

$A \times 2 = B$

LESSON 8-2

Practice and Problem Solving: A/B

1. $\dfrac{\text{ounces of water}}{\text{packets of flavoring}} =$

$\dfrac{24 \text{ oz}}{2 \text{ packets}} = \dfrac{12 \text{ oz}}{1 \text{ packet}} =$

12 oz of water per packet

2.

Packets of Flavoring	2	5	7	10	12
Ounces of Water	24	60	84	120	144

3.

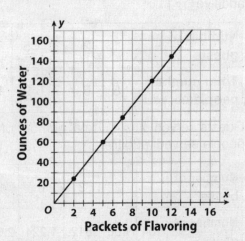

4. 276 oz

5. Yes. You can add half a packet of flavoring to 114 oz of water.

6. $\dfrac{24}{2} = \dfrac{36}{3} = \dfrac{66}{5.5} = \dfrac{108}{9} = \dfrac{180}{15}$

7. It is a multiplicative relationship because the number of packets is multiplied by 12 oz. The line of the graph begins at the origin and is steep.

Practice and Problem Solving: C

1. Sample answer:

A	2	5	7	8	10
B	6	15	21	24	30

2. $\dfrac{A}{B} = \dfrac{2}{6} = \dfrac{1}{3}$. For each 1 A, there will be 3 Bs.

3. Sample answer: An amusement park provides seating on rides in the ratio of 6 children's seats for every 2 adult seats.

4. Multiplicative; Each adult seat is multiplied by 3 to find the number of children's seats.

5. No, because it is unlikely an amusement park would have half a child's seat or half an adult seat.

Practice and Problem Solving: D

1.

Number of Tires	8	12	16	20	24	28
Number of Cars	2	3	4	5	6	7

2. The number of tires is equal to the number of cars times 4.

3. $\dfrac{\text{tires}}{\text{cars}} = \dfrac{8}{2} = \dfrac{4}{1} = 4$ tires for every 1 car

4. (8, 2), (12, 3), (16, 4), (20, 5), (24, 6), (28, 7)

5.

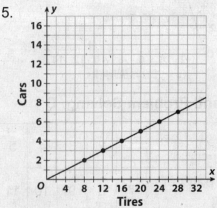

6. $\dfrac{8}{2} = \dfrac{12}{3} = \dfrac{16}{4} = \dfrac{20}{5} = \dfrac{40}{10}$

Reteach

A	6	9	12	15	18	21	24
B	2	3	4	5	6	7	8

2. Sample answer: $\dfrac{6}{2} = \dfrac{3}{1}$, $\dfrac{9}{3} = \dfrac{3}{1}$, $\dfrac{18}{6} = \dfrac{3}{1}$,

$\dfrac{24}{8} = \dfrac{3}{1}$

3. $\dfrac{3}{1}$; $\dfrac{69}{23}$

4. 189; $\dfrac{189}{63}$

Reading Strategies

1. Cost to pounds: ($4.50, 3), ($7.50, 5), ($10.50, 7), ($13.50, 9), ($16.50, 11)

   Pounds to cost: (3, $4.50), (5, $7.50), (7, $10.50), (9, $13.50), (11, $16.50)

2. 1 to $1.50; $1.50

3. Flour to baking soda: (6, 3), (8, 4), (10, 5), (12, 6), (18, 9), (24, 12)

   Baking soda to flour: (3,6), (4,8), (5,10), (6,12), (9,18) (12, 24)

4. 1 tsp of baking soda to 2 c of flour.

Success for English Learners

1. The cost would be on the top of the ratio and the ounces would be on the bottom of the ratio.

2. The ounces would be on the y-axis and the cost would be on the x-axis. The line would be steeper.

3. Sample answer:

Gas (gal)	4	5	6	7	8
Miles	128	160	192	224	256

   Ordered pairs: (4, 128), (5, 160), (6, 192), (7, 224), (8, 256)

LESSON 8-3

Practice and Problem Solving: A/B

1. 16

2. 15

3. 9

4. 60

5. 9 in.

6. 12 cm

7. 16

8. $3.08

9. a. 10 mi

   b. 6 in.

   c. 3 in.

10. 1.5 in.

Practice and Problem Solving: C

1. 5

2. 50

3. 28.8

4. 5.8

5. 9 in.

6. 12 in.

7. $6.71

8 a. 0.67 mi/min

   b. Sinead

   c. 363 mi; $40.2 \times 2.5 = 100.5$. $100.5 + 150 + 112.5 = 363$

9. 2.25 cm

Practice and Problem Solving: D

1. 8

2. 8

3. 20

4. 33

5. $\dfrac{8}{11} = \dfrac{x}{33}$, $x = 24$; The width should be 24 in.

6. 7.5 cm

7. 200 mi

8. $16.00

9. a. 9 mi.

   b. 5 in.

   c. 1 in. = 1.5 mi

10. 1.3 in.

Reteach

1. $3.06

2. $4.47

3. 6 in.

Reading Strategies

1. a. $0.35
   b. $0.33
   c. $0.30
2. $1.98
3. $2.40
4. $1.20
5. a. $22.60
   b. $113.0
6. a. 9.33 mph
   b. 18.67 mi
7. Jeff

Success for English Learners

1. Yes, $\frac{24}{3} = \frac{8}{1}$. 8 ft² per hour is the unit rate. 8 (unit rate) × 9 h = 72 ft² per 9 h.

2. No, not a proportion; $\frac{4.50}{18} \neq \frac{9.00}{30}$; 2 × 4.50 = 9.00, but 2 × 18 ≠ 30

LESSON 8-4

Practice and Problem Solving: A/B

1. 48 in.
2. $1\frac{1}{2}$ gal
3. 5,000 m
4. 2 kg
5. 20c; $\frac{4 \text{ cups}}{1 \text{ quart}}$
6. 6m; $\frac{1m}{100 \text{ cm}}$
7. 5,280 ft
8. 700 m
9.

Dowel	in.	ft	yd
A	36	3	1
B	66	$5\frac{1}{2}$	$1\frac{5}{6}$
C	90	$7\frac{1}{2}$	$2\frac{1}{2}$

10. a. 44 in.; $3\frac{2}{3}$ ft
    b. $25\frac{1}{2}$ in.; $2\frac{1}{8}$ ft

11. Multiply 3 × 36 and 2 × 12 and add the products.

Practice and Problem Solving: C

1. 54 in.
2. 0.375 ft
3. 5.43 m
4. 5,100 m; 510,000 cm
5. 26 c
6. 390 cm
7. 5,280 ft; 1,760 yd
8. 7.36 m
9.

Chain	yd	ft	in.
gold	$3\frac{1}{2}$	$10\frac{1}{2}$	126
silver	$4\frac{1}{6}$	12.5	150
bronze	$4\frac{1}{9}$	$12\frac{2}{3}$	148

10. a. 50 cm by 50 cm
    b. 2,500 cm²
    c. No, a square meter is 100 cm × 100 cm – 10,000 cm².

Practice and Problem Solving: D

1. 4 ft
2. 8 qt
3. 3 km
4. 1.5 kg
5. 28 c; 4 cups
6. 5 m; $\frac{1}{100}$ cm
7. 15,840 ft
8. 900 m

9.

Trim	In.	Ft.	Yd.
A	24	2	$\frac{2}{3}$
B	216	18	6

a. Use the board to see how many inches long the rug is. Divide the number of inches by 12 to find feet.

b. 36 in.; 3 ft

11. Multiply 4 × 100 and add 20.

Reteach

1.

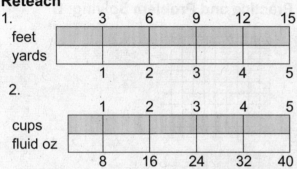

3. Sample answers: No, doubling, tripling, quadrupling 5,280 is difficult. Yes, you would double, triple, quadruple 5,280.

Reading Strategies

1. a. 12

   b. $\frac{1}{12}$

2. a. multiply by 12

   b. divide by 12

3. You could show 1 meter and 100 centimeters, 2 meters and 200 centimeters, 3 meters and 300 centimeters and so on.

4. Sample answer:

customary

yd	1	2	3	4
ft	3	6	9	12

Relationship: 1 yd to 3 ft

metric

kg	1	2	3
g	1,000	2,000	3,000

Relationship: 1 kg to 1,000 g

Success for English Learners

1. 198 in.

2. 12.5 yd

MODULE 8 Challenge

1. There are 6 cars in the first section, 12 cars in the second section and 18 cars in the third section.

2. Answers will vary. Sample answer: One way is to move 6 cars from the third section to the first section. Then there will be 12 cars in each section and the ratio will be 1 : 1 : 1.

3. No. To have the ratio of 1: 2: 3 the total number of cars must be a multiple of 6. 80 is not a multiple of 6.

4. If 18 cars are added to the third section there would be 6 cars in the first section, 12 cars in the second section and 36 cars in the third section. The new ratio would be 1 : 2 : 6.

MODULE 9 Percents

LESSON 9-1

Practice and Problem Solving: A/B

1. $\frac{3}{10}$; 0.3

2. $\frac{21}{50}$; 0.42

3. $\frac{9}{50}$; 0.18

4. $\frac{7}{20}$; 0.35

5. $\frac{1}{1}$ or 1

6. $\frac{29}{100}$; 0.29

7. $\frac{14}{25}$; 0.56

8. $\frac{2}{3}$; 0.67

9. $\frac{1}{4}$; 0.25

10. 3%

11. 92%

12. 18%

13. 40%

14. 92%

15. 70%

16. 40%

17. 64 students

18. black: 20%; $\frac{1}{5}$; 0.2

    navy: 25%; $\frac{1}{4}$; 0.25

    brown: 35%; $\frac{7}{20}$; 0.35

    other: 20%; $\frac{1}{5}$; 0.2

Practice and Problem Solving: C

1. $\frac{9}{200}$; 0.045

2. $1\frac{19}{100}$; 1.19

3. $\frac{2}{1}$; 2

4. $\frac{7}{1,000}$, 0.007

5. $3\frac{7}{100}$; 3.07

6. $\frac{11}{200}$; 0.055

7. 7.143%

8. 0.75%

9. 0.54%

10. Use more than one grid. For 217% you would use 3 grids, shading in 2 completely and shading 17 squares on the third.

11. Divide a small square on the grid into tenths and shade 7 of them.

12. blue: 30%; $\frac{3}{10}$; 0.3

    green: 25%; $\frac{1}{4}$; 0.25

    red: 15%; $\frac{3}{20}$; 0.15

    white: 30%; $\frac{3}{10}$; 0.3

13. 1 h

14. Add the values 25 + 10 + 10 + 3 = 48, 48% of a dollar.

Practice and Problem Solving: D

1.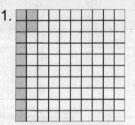

2.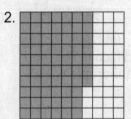

3. 50% = $\frac{50}{100}$ = $\frac{1}{2}$; 50 hundredths = 0.50

4. $\frac{1}{100}$; 0.01

5. $\frac{11}{100}$; 0.11

6. $\frac{1}{10}$; 0.1

7. $\frac{99}{100}$; 0.99

8. $\frac{17}{100}$; 0.17

9. $\frac{73}{100}$; 0.73

10. $\frac{47}{100}$; 0.47

11. $\frac{23}{200}$; 0.115

12. $\frac{1}{10} = \frac{10}{100} = 10\%$

13. 60%

14. 2%

15. 50%

16. 70%

17. 97%

18. 10%

Reteach

1. $\frac{43}{100}$

2. $\frac{18}{25}$

3. $\frac{22}{25}$

4. $\frac{7}{20}$

5. 0.64

6. 0.92

7. 0.73

8. 0.33

Reading Strategies

1. 20 to 100

2. 20%

3. 80 to 100

4. 80%

Success for English Learners

1. 0.37; $\frac{37}{100}$

   0.06; $\frac{6}{100}$ or $\frac{3}{50}$

2. Answers will vary, but should reflect that it depends on the situation and numbers and operations involved.

LESSON 9-2

Practice and Problem Solving: A/B

1. 14

2. 11

3. 7.5

4. 162

5. 60

6. 198

7. 7

8. 570

9. 495

10. 70

11. 96

12. 18

13. 13.6

14. 23.1

15. 0.77

16. 475

17. more than 1.8 billion

18. Asia

19. about 1.2 billion

20. about 1.2 billion

21. about 0.3 in.

Practice and Problem Solving: C

1. less than; 25% is equivalent to $\frac{25}{100}$ or $\frac{1}{4}$, a fraction less than 1 A number multiplied by a fraction less than 1 gives a product less than the original number.

2. greater than; 220% is equivalent to $\frac{220}{100}$ or $2\frac{1}{5}$, a mixed number greater than 1. Multiplying a number by a mixed number gives a product greater than the original number.

3. equal; 100% is equivalent to $\frac{100}{100}$ or 1. A number times 1 equals itself.

4. a.$27.36; b. $26.60; c. In a., you find 80% of the original price and then find 90% of the new price so you are finding 72% of the original price. In b., you are finding 70% of the original price.

5. 6,932,164

6. a. 11%; $550

   b. $600

   c. insurance

Practice and Problem Solving: D

1. 15
2. $\frac{1}{4}$; 16
3. 3
4. 8
5. 128
6. 6
7. 435
8. 70
9. 125
10. $36
11. 19.24 cm
12. $24.08
13. $15.12
14. $15.12
15. A discount of 16% is the same as 84% of the original price.

Reteach

1. 41%
2. 23%
3. 37.5%
4. First divided 100 by 8 to get 12.5. Then multiplied 3 and 8 by 12.5 to get

$$\frac{3 \times 12.5}{8 \times 12.5} = \frac{37.5}{100}$$

5. Accept all reasonable answers. A good answer might include looking at numbers involved and then choosing which to use.

Reading Strategies

1. 0.35
2. Remove the percent sign. Move the decimal point two places to the left.
3. Multiply the decimal times the number.
4. 0.10
5. 6
6. 12
7. 18
8. 24
9. The answers are multiples of 6.
10. Since 30% is three times as great as 10%, I could multiply 25 by 3 to get 75.

Success for English Learners

1. 12.6
2. 75% is 75 hundredths or $\frac{75}{100}$
3. You can find the percent of a number by using a proportion as in Problem 1 or by changing the percent to a decimal and multiplying as in Problem 2.

LESSON 9-3

Practice and Problem Solving: A/B

1. 40
2. 60
3. $1.35
4. 6
5. 9 text messages
6. 300 people
7. 6.5%
8. 600 people
9. 4,200 people
10. 149 people
11. Yes, Sahil is correct; Possible answer: He knew that 30% is 3 times 10%, so he just multiplied 45 by 3.

Practice and Problem Solving: C

1. $255
2. $62.53
3. 15 red tiles
4. $32.07
5. 50 min
6. 30 min
7. 200 min or 3 h 20 min
8. Check student's work.

Practice and Problem Solving: D

1. 1.8 billion
2. 59%; Asia, 59%
3. 15 mg
4. 1,225 students; 588 boys
5. $35.10

Reteach

1. a. 14;

   b. 25;

   c. x;

   d. $\dfrac{x}{100} = \dfrac{14}{25}$; $25x = 1{,}400$; $x = 56$;

   Answer: 56% of 25 is 14.

2. a. 16;

   b. x;

   c. 80;

   d. $\dfrac{16}{x} = \dfrac{80}{100}$; $80x = 1{,}600$; $x = 20$;

   Answer: 80% of 20 is 16.

3. 55%

4. 40

5. 300%

6. 140

Reading Strategies

1. •

2. =

3. n

4. $5 = 25\% \bullet n$

5. $40 = n \bullet 160$

Success for English Learners

1. $191.56

2. $1,440

3. $51.84

MODULE 9 Challenge

1. 20% of 30% of 400 is $0.2 \times 0.3 \times 400 = 24$.

   24 is $\dfrac{24}{45} = 53\dfrac{1}{3}\%$ of 45.

2. Kevin completed $0.4(120) + 0.3(170) + 0.1(90) = 108$ pages

   Dashawn completed $0.5(120) + 0.2(170) + 0.3(90) = 121$ pages

3. Whole milk has $8 \times 9 = 72$ fat calories and 150 total calories. $\dfrac{72}{150} = 48\%$ of the calories are from fat.

   An egg has $6 \times 9 = 54$ fat calories and 80 total calories. $\dfrac{54}{80} = 67.5\%$ of the calories are from fat.

   A hamburger has $15 \times 9 = 135$ fat calories and 220 total calories. $\dfrac{135}{220} = 61.4\%$ of the calories are from fat.

   A slice of pizza has $3 \times 9 = 27$ fat calories and 160 total calories $\dfrac{27}{160} = 16.875\%$ of the calories are from fat.

3. 40% of 300 is $0.4(300) = 120$. The maximum number fat calories is 120. Since there are 9 calories per fat gram, the maximum grams of fat is $\dfrac{120}{9} = 13.3$ g.

UNIT 4: Expressions, Equations, and Relationships

MODULE 10 Generating Equivalent Numerical Expressions

LESSON 10-1

Practice and Problem Solving: A/B

1. 2^4; 16
2. -3^3; -27
3. $\left(\dfrac{3}{5}\right)^2$; $\dfrac{9}{25}$
4. -10^2; 100
5. $\left(\dfrac{-1}{6}\right)^4$; $\dfrac{1}{1,296}$
6. $(0.5)^3$; 0.125
7. 1.728
8. $\dfrac{1}{256}$
9. 64
10. 64
11. 1,000,000 cubic millimeters; 100 or 10^2 millimeters
12. $\left(\dfrac{3}{5}\right)^3$; $\dfrac{3}{5}$ volt
13. <
14. =
15. >
16. $81 = 9^2 = 3^4 = 81^1$

Practice and Problem Solving: C

1. $-3^5 = (-3)^5 = -243$
2. $\left(\dfrac{2}{3}\right)^3 = \dfrac{8}{27}$; $\left(\dfrac{2}{3}\right)^1 = \dfrac{2}{3} = \dfrac{18}{27}$; $\dfrac{8}{27} < \dfrac{18}{27}$
3. $(0.72)^7 > (-7.2)^7$ because $(0.72)^7 > 0$ and $(-7.2)^7 < 0$.
4. a. 4^3 lamps
   b. 4 lamps high, 4 lamps deep, and 4 lamps wide

c. 2^3 lamps
d. $4^3 \div 2^3 = 8$

5. $\left(\dfrac{2}{3}\right)^4 = \dfrac{64}{81}$; $\left(\dfrac{3}{2}\right)^4 = \dfrac{81}{64}$; $\left(\dfrac{2}{3}\right)^4 \times \left(\dfrac{3}{2}\right)^4 = \dfrac{64}{81} \times \dfrac{81}{64} = 1$

6. $(-0.5)^3 = -0.125$; $(-2)^3 = -8$;
   $(-0.5)^3 \times (-2)^3 = -0.125 \times -8 = 1$

7. $\left(\dfrac{5}{7}\right)^2$

8. $(-0.25)^3$ or $\left(-\dfrac{1}{4}\right)^3$

9. $\left(\dfrac{10}{3}\right)^6$

Practice and Problem Solving: D

1. 2, 7
2. $\dfrac{5}{6}$, 4
3. -5, 10
4. 10; 10; 10; 10; 10^4
5. $\dfrac{2}{3}$; $\dfrac{2}{3}$; $\dfrac{2}{3}$; $\left(\dfrac{2}{3}\right)^3$
6. -4; -4; -4; $(-4)^3$
7. $(-2) \times (-2)$
8. $0.25 \times 0.25 \times 0.25$
9. $\dfrac{1}{9} \times \dfrac{1}{9} \times \dfrac{1}{9}$
10. 10^3
11. $3^3 = 27$ baseball cards; $4^3 = 64$ football cards
12. 4,096 mi

Reteach

1. $\left(\dfrac{1}{20}\right)^4$
2. 8^2
3. $(7.5)^3$
4. $(-0.4)^1$

5. $-\dfrac{1}{8}$

6. 2.48832

7. 729

8. $\dfrac{16}{9}$

Reading Strategies

1. The opposite of two to the fifth power

2. The opposite of two is a factor five times:
$(-2) \times (-2) \times (-2) \times (-2) \times (-2)$

3. $(-2)^5 = -32$

4. Three fifths to the fourth power

5. $\dfrac{3}{5} \times \dfrac{3}{5} \times \dfrac{3}{5} \times \dfrac{3}{5}$

6. No; $\left(\dfrac{3}{5}\right)^4 = \dfrac{81}{625}$, but 4 times $\dfrac{3}{5}$ is $\dfrac{12}{5}$ or $\dfrac{1,500}{625}$

Success for English Learners

1. 2

2. 7

3. Four to the third power

4. Two to the seventh power

5. a. 7^3

   b. 3

   c. 7

6. a. 5^6

   b. 5

   c. 6

LESSON 10-2

Practice and Problem Solving: A/B

1. Answers may vary. Sample answers:

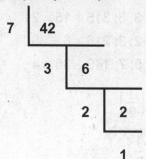

$36 = 3^2 \times 2^2$

2. Answers may vary. Sample answers:

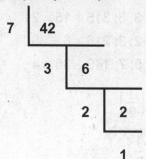

$42 = 7 \cdot 3 \cdot 2$

3. Answers may vary. Sample answers:

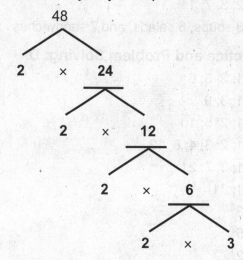

$48 = 24 \times 2$

4. Answers may vary. Sample answers:

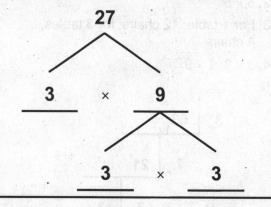

$27 = 3 \cdot 3 \cdot 3 = 3^3$

5. $2^2 \times 11$

6. 5^3

7. 5×17

8. 3×13

Practice and Problem Solving: C

1. 21; 15; 3; 5; $315 \div 15 = 21$
2. 18; 12; 2; 3; $216 \div 6 = 36$
3. 10; 14; 5; 7; $140 \div 35 = 4$
4. $\left(\dfrac{1}{5}\right)^2 \times \left(\dfrac{1}{2}\right)^2$
5. $\left(\dfrac{1}{2}\right)^3 \times \dfrac{1}{3}$
6. 2, 3
7. 3, 5, 7
8. 2, 3, 7, 11
9. 3 soups, 6 salads, and 7 sandwiches

Practice and Problem Solving: D

1. 1; 2; 3; 6
2. 1; 3; 9
3. 1; 2; 5; 10
4. 1; 2; 3; 4; 6; 12
5. 1; 3; 7; 21
6. 1; 31
7. 3^2
8. 5^2
9. 2^3
10. 2×7
11. $2^2 \times 3$
12. 3×5
13. For 1 table, 12 chairs; for 3 tables, 4 chairs
14. 3×3; 1×9
15.

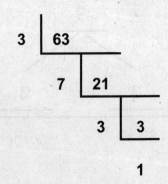

$63 = 3^2 \times 7$

Reteach

1. $1 \cdot 28$, $2 \cdot 14$, $4 \cdot 7$; 1, 2, 4, 7, 14, 28
2. $1 \cdot 15$, $3 \cdot 5$; 1, 3, 5, 15
3. $1 \cdot 36$, $2 \cdot 18$, $3 \cdot 12$, $4 \cdot 9$, $6 \cdot 6$; 1, 2, 3, 4, 6, 9, 18, 36
4. $1 \cdot 29$; 1, 29
5. $2^2 \cdot 7$
6. $3^2 \cdot 5$
7. $5^2 \cdot 2$
8. $2^3 \cdot 3^2$

Reading Strategies

1. $360 = 2^3 \times 3^2 \times 5$

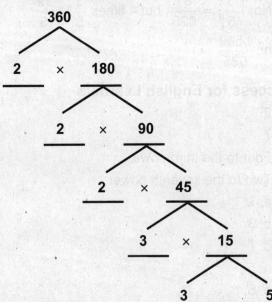

2. $378 = 2 \times 3^3 \times 7$

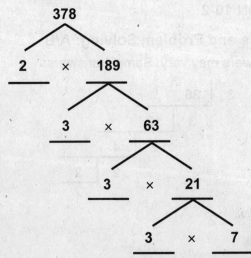

Success for English Learners

1. $24 = 3 \cdot 2 \cdot 2 \cdot 2$ or $\cdot 3 \cdot 2^3$

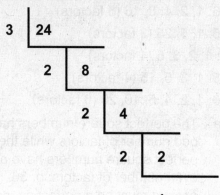

2. $45 = 3 \cdot 3 \cdot 5$ or $\cdot 3^2 \cdot 5$

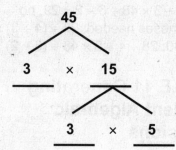

LESSON 10-3

Practice and Problem Solving: A/B

1. Multiplication
2. Division
3. Addition
4. Finding a power, exponent
5. Subtraction
6. Finding a power, exponent
7. G
8. F
9. H
10. A
11. C
12. E
13. D
14. B
15. $3 \times 4 + 0.95$
16. $(240 + 360) \div 100$

Practice and Problem Solving: C

1. Answers will vary. Sample answer: −, +

2. Answers will vary. Sample answer: −, ×

3. Answers will vary. Sample answer: ×, −

4. $\frac{5}{4}$

5. 5

6. $\frac{7}{6}$

7. Undefined

8. $\frac{2}{3}$

9. $\frac{1}{6}$

10. 8; 9

11. 15; 16

12. $x^2 + (x − 4)^2 = 80$; $2x^2 − 8x + 16 = 80$, or $x^2 − 4x − 32 = 0$. By trial and error, the legs are 4 and 8.

13. $b^2 + (2b)^2 = 100$; $5b^2 = 100$; $b^2 = 20$

14. $b^2 + (b − 5)^2 = 2b^2 − 10b + 25 = c^2$. Students might use numbers instead of b to come up with the general pattern.

Practice and Problem Solving: D

1. multiplication
2. division
3. exponent
4. addition
5. E
6. D
7. F
8. A
9. B
10. C
11. a. $2 \times 13 + 3$
    b. $29
12. Answers will vary. Sample answer: $(2 \times 4) + 8 = 16$
13. Answers will vary. Sample answer: $12 \div 2 − 3 = 3$

Reteach

1. 20; 140; 134
2. 46; 460; 463

3. 30; 40; 33

4. 14

5. 46

6. 97

7. 18

8. 5

9. 35

10. Answers will vary. Sample answer:
$3^2 + (4 \times 5) - 5^2 = 4$

Reading Strategies

1. $(9 \div 3) = 3$; $3^2 = 9$; $9 \times 5 = 45$; $45 + 4 = 49$;
$49 - 1 = 48$

2. $(3 \times 2) = 6$; $5^2 = 25$; $8 \div 2 = 4$; $6 + 5^2 = 31$;
$31 - 4 = 27$

3. 40

4. 7

Success for English Learners

1. Answers will vary. Sample answer: (1) In
the problem shown, multiplication is done
before addition. (2) In the problem, the
prices of the types of beads are different,
so the number of each bead has to be
multiplied by its price.

2. Answers will vary. Sample answer: If the
price of each bead is the same, you can
then add the number of beads and then
multiply by the price.

Product	Number of Zeros in Product	Product as Powers
$100 \times 1,000$ $= 100,000$	5	$10^2 \times 10^3 = 10^5$
$10 \times 100,000$ $= 1,000,000$	6	$10^1 \times 10^5 = 10^6$
$1,000 \times 10$ $= 10,000$	4	$10^3 \times 10^1 = 10^4$

MODULE 10 Challenge

To find the product of two powers of 10,
$10^a \times 10^b$, find the sum of the exponents,
$a + b$. The answer is a power of 10 with
the sum as the exponent, 10^{a+b}.

2. The factors of the numbers are as follows:

9: 1, 3, 9 (3 factors)

16: 1, 2, 4, 8, 16 (5 factors)

25: 1, 5, 25 (3 factors)

6: 1, 2, 3, 6 (4 factors)

15: 1, 3, 5, 15 (4 factors)

20: 1, 2, 4, 5, 10, 20 (6 factors)

a. The perfect square numbers have an
odd number of factors while the non
perfect square numbers have an
even number of factors; b. 36. (The
answer must be a perfect square, so
count the factors of perfect square
numbers.)

3. $28 \div 4 + 3 \times 48 \div 6 - 2 = 29$, no
parentheses needed; $28 \div (4 + 3) \times 48 \div 6$
$- 2 = 30$; $28 \div 4 + 3 \times 48 \div (6 - 2) = 43$

MODULE 11 Generating Equivalent Algebraic Expressions

LESSON 11-1

Practice and Problem Solving: A/B

1. $9 + r$

2. $m \div 4$

3. $5n$

4. $25 \cdot 3$

5. $3 + n$

6. $r \div 8$

7. $7m$

8. $48 - 13$

9. $18 \div 3$

10. $t - 189$

11. $w + 253$

12. Sample answer: the sum of t and 23; 23
more than t

13. Sample answer: n less than 45; 45 minus n

14. Possible answer: $2y - 3$

Practice and Problem Solving: C

1. $2(100) + 60$

2. $t - 25 + 17$ or $t - 8$

3. $44 + 4p$

4. $3a + 4b + 5c$

5. $n + n + n + n$ or $4n$

6. $n \cdot n$ or n^2

7. Sample answer: $3a + 2b + 3c + 3$

8. Sample answer: Josef worked 24 hours on the day shift for d dollars per hour and 8 hours on the night shift for n dollars per hour.

Practice and Problem Solving: D

1. A
2. B
3. B
4. C
5. B
6. A
7. C
8. D
9. B
10. A
11. B
12. C
13. x represents the number of beads Nicole lost.
14. x represents the number of shirts Wilhelm bought.

Reteach

1. Sample answer: When finding the difference in two amounts, you subtract.
2. Since each state gets the same number of senators, you multiply the number of states by the number of senators.
3. $n + 3$
4. $c \div 8$

Reading Strategies

1. Sample answer: 8 less than t
2. Sample answer: n divided by 6
3. Sample answer: the product of 4 and w
4. Sample answer: 8 more than z
5. Sample answer: 9 times m
6. $p + 12$
7. $i - 7$
8. $r \div 3$

9. $z - 1$
10. $19y$

Success for English Learners

1. $m + 5$
2. $18 \div 2$
3. $t - 7$
4. $4r$
5. $x - 9$
6. $21 \div 7$

Sample answers are given for 7–12.

7. 2 less than a
8. the product of 8 and 6
9. p divided by 8
10. the sum of v and 10

LESSON 11-2

Practice and Problem Solving: A/B

1. 12
2. 15
3. 13
4. 54
5. 59
6. 13
7. 27
8. 90
9.

p	$2(13 - p)$
2	22
3	20
4	18

10.

v	w	$3v + w$
4	2	14
6	3	21
8	4	28

11.

x	y	$x^2 \div y$
2	1	4
6	2	18
8	4	16

12. $12.96

13. 345 mph

14. $55

Practice and Problem Solving: C

1.

r	$3.14 \bullet r^2$
2	12.56
3	28.26
4	50.24

2.

z	a	$2z - a$
−4	2	−10
0	2	−2
4	2	6

3.

x	y	$10x^2 \div (y + 1)$
2	1	20
−1	3	2.5
−4	4	32

4. No, with 120 gallons of water, her pickup weighs 6,278.2 pounds.

5. 4.5 mm^2

6. Grayson multiplied 4×3 before squaring 3.

7. Emily added 2 to 36 when she should have multiplied 2 and −2 and then added −4 to 36.

8. Pat substituted 2 for y instead of −2.

9. $4x^2 + 2y = 4(3)^2 + 2(-2)$

   $= 36 + 2(-2)$

   $= 36 + (-4)$

   $= 32$

Practice and Problem Solving: D

1. $3 \times 2 + 4^2$

   $3 \times 2 + 16$

   $6 + 16$

   22

2. $2 \times (5 + 3)$

   2×8

   16

3. $8 + 8 \div 2 \times 4$

   $8 + 4 \times 4$

   $8 + 16$

   24

4.

w	$6(3 + w)$
2	30
3	36
4	42

5.

c	$2c + 7$
4	15
6	19
8	23

6.

w	$w^2 - 3$
2	1
3	6
4	13

7. 60

Reteach

1. 10

2. 6; 2

3. 15; 10

4. 3; 9; 18

5. 5; 13

6. 42

7. 9

8. 7

9. 21

10. 0

Reading Strategies

1. $(5 + 14) - 3^2$;

   $(5 + 14) - 9$;

   $19 - 9$;

   There is no multiplication or division;

   10

2. $10^2 - 2(3 \cdot 4 + 6)$;

$100 - 2(12 + 6)$;

$100 - 2 \cdot 18$;

$100 - 36$;

64

Success for English Learners

1.

r	2(3 + r)
2	10
3	12
4	14

2.

c	t	2c + t
4	2	10
6	3	15
8	4	20

3.

w	k	$w^2 - k$
2	1	3
5	2	23
8	3	61

LESSON 11-3

Practice and Problem Solving: A/B

1. Commutative Property
2. Associative Property
3. Distributive Property
4. Subtraction
5. $2r + n^2 + 7 - 2n$
6. $3w + 7$
7. $c^2 + 4c - 3$
8. $z^3 + z^2 + 5z - 3$
9. $6c + 4d - 6$
10. $20a - 2b - 1$
11. $40x$
12. $10x + 16y + 14$
13. Sample answer: sides of $2x + y$, $3x$, and $7x - y$, $P = 12x$

Practice and Problem Solving: C

1. $8a + a^2 - 10$
2. $v - 6w$
3. $-2c^2 + 4c$
4. $z^3 + 5z + 8z^2 + 7$
5. $6c + 4d - 12$
6. $9a + 6b + 3c - 2$
7. $4x - 1.6$
8. $10x - 2y$
9. $6n + 4(2n) = 14n$
10. $1.5n + 1.25n + 2 = 2.75n + 2$

Practice and Problem Solving: D

1. $5a$ and $2a$; b and $2b$; 43 and 4
2. n, $5n$, and $2n$; $2m$ and $6m$
3. $2g$, $3g$, and g
4. $7x^2$ and $3x^2$; x and $3x$, 2 and 3
5. $r + 5n^2 + 7 - 2n$
6. $v + w + 10$
7. $6c^2 + c$
8. $4z + 3e + 5$
9. $6d + 4c$
10. $12a$
11. C
12. D

Reteach

1. 8
2. 3
3. 1
4. 14
5. $10x$
6. $2m$
7. $12y$
8. $11t$
9. $4b + 6$
10. $6a + 4$
11. $6n - 3c$
12. $10d + e$

Reading Strategies

1. 5
2. because the exponents are different
3. 6
4. $5a^2 + a^2 + 6b - 3b - 2 + 4c$
5. $6a^2 + 3b - 2 + 4c$

Success for English Learners

1. No, because the exponents are not the same.
2. No, because the variables are not the same.
3. Yes, $9a^3$
4. 1

MODULE 11 Challenge

1. equilateral triangle; 10.83 cm^2
2. square; 25 cm^2
3. regular pentagon; 43.01 cm^2
4. regular hexagon; 64.95 cm^2
5. regular octagon; 120.71 cm^2
6. regular decagon; 192.36 cm^2
7. tetrahedron; $s^2\sqrt{3}$
8. cube; $6s^2$
9. octahedron; $2s^2\sqrt{3}$
10. dodecahedron; $3s^2\sqrt{25 + 10\sqrt{5}}$
11. icosahedron; $5s^2\sqrt{3}$

MODULE 12 Equations and Relationships

LESSON 12-1

Practice and Problem Solving: A/B

1. yes
2. no
3. no
4. no
5. yes
6. yes
7. yes
8. yes

9. B
10. D
11. Sample equation: $6x = 72$
12. Sample equation: $(6)(5) = (10)(3)(w)$
13. Sample equation: $x - 13°F = 35°F$; $x = 48°F$
14. Sample equation: $\$16x = \$20$; $x = \$1.25$
15. Sample problem: Twenty-four people were divided evenly into y teams. There were 3 people on each team. Determine whether there were 8 teams or 6 teams.

   Answer: There were 8 teams.

Practice and Problem Solving: C

1. A
2. C
3. D
4. B
5. Sample equation: $7(10 + x) = 112$
6. Sample equation: $y = 11 + \frac{1}{3}(15)$; $y = 16$;

   sea cow = 16
7. Sample equation: $22 = \frac{112}{4} - 6$
8. Sample equation: $4x = 80 + 40$; $x = 30$
9. Sample equation: $\frac{24}{x} + 3 = 6$

Practice and Problem Solving: D

1. yes
2. no
3. no
4. yes
5. yes
6. yes
7. A
8. B
9. B
10. C
11. A
12. B
13. (1) $5 + (3)$1 + Other bill = $13; $5 + $3 + x = $13; x + $5; The other bill must be a $5 bill.

Reteach

1. yes
2. no
3. no
4. yes
5. yes
6. no
7. yes
8. yes
9. no

Reading Strategies

1. yes
2. no
3. yes
4. yes
5. yes
6. no
7. no
8. Sample equation: $2 \cdot 13 = 15 + 11$
9. Sample answer: $2 \cdot 13 = 15 + y$; $y = 11$

Success for English Learners

1. Because when the variable in the equation is replaced with 61, it does not make a true statement.
2. Substitute 65 for a and check to see if the equation is true.
3. Sample answer: Andrea is given $82 to buy fruit for the class picnic. She spends some of the money on apples and $23 on bananas. Determine whether she spent $61 or $59 on apples.

LESSON 12-2

Practice and Problem Solving: A/B

1. $r = 4$

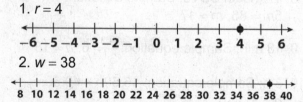

2. $w = 38$

3. $m = \dfrac{5}{8}$

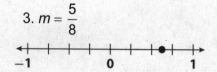

4. $t = -4$

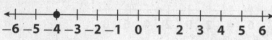

5. $x + 139 = 180$
6. $x = 41°$
7. $x + 18 = 90$
8. $x = 72°$
9. $x = 5$; Sample answer. John has some CDs. If he buys 3 more CDs, he will have 8 CDs. How many CDs did he start with? John started with 5 CDs.

Practice and Problem Solving: C

1. 3.4
2. $\dfrac{7}{9}$
3. $5\dfrac{1}{2}$
4. 17.19
5. -4
6. -40
7. $x + 22 = 90$
8. $x = 68°$
9. Sample answer: $u - 22 = 13$; $u = 35$; Kayla's uncle is 35 years old.
10. Sample answer: $38.95 - 22.50 = g$; $g = 16.45$; Gavin will save $16.45.
11. Sample answer: $s - 10\dfrac{1}{2} = 37\dfrac{1}{2}$; $s = 48$; The board Sierra started with was 48 inches long.
12. $x = 7$; Sample answer: Andy ran 4.65 kilometers. Pam said that if she had run 2.35 fewer kilometers, she would have run as far as Andy. How far did Pam run? Answer: Pam ran 7 kilometers.

Practice and Problem Solving: D

1. $r = 6$

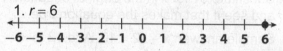

2. $w = -1$

3. $m = 3$

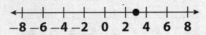

4. $t = 5$

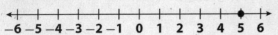

5. $x + 100 = 180$

6. $x = 80°$

7. $23 + n = 40$

8. 17

9. $x = 7$; Sample answer. Joan has some pencils. If she gives away 5 pencils, she will have 2 pencils left. How many pencils did Joan start with? She started with 7 pencils.

Reteach

1. 8
2. 9
3. 5
4. 9
5. 6
6. 8

Reading Strategies

1. left
2. add 21
3. add 21
4. 53
5. right
6. add 25
7. add 25
8. 37

Success for English Learners

1. Because the surfer's height, h, plus 14 inches is equal to the height of the surfboard.

2. Substitute 57 for x in the original equation and see if that makes the equation true.

3. Sample answer: $x - 12 = 10$. Add 12 to both sides. $x = 22$

LESSON 12-3

Practice and Problem Solving: A/B

1. $e = 6$

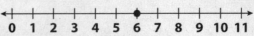

2. $w = 10$

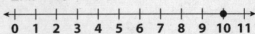

3. $m = \frac{1}{4}$

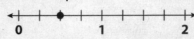

4. $k = 10$

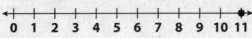

5. Sample answer: $8x = 72$

6. $x = 9$; 9 m

7. $\frac{a}{3} = 9$; $a = 27$; 27 pictures

8. $x = 20$; Sample answer: Toni earns $9 an hour for running errands. Last week, Toni earned $180 by running errands. How many hours did Toni run errands last week? 20 hours

Practice and Problem Solving: C

1. 0.7
2. 27
3. $\frac{1}{2}$
4. 75
5. 20
6. $\frac{4}{3}$ or $1\frac{1}{3}$

7. $A = 144$ in^2 $P = 4s$; $48 = 4s$; $s = 12$. $A = s^2$; $A = 12^2 = 144$

8. 17 model SUVs; Sample equation: $5m = 85$; $m = 17$

9. 18 min; Sample equation: $\frac{n}{3} = 6$; $n = 18$

10. 3 h; Sample equation: $16.50b = 49.50$; $b = 3$

11. $n = 25$; Sample answer: Maria used 12.5 meters of material to make doll clothes for a charity project. Each piece of clothing used 0.5 meter of material. How many pieces of clothing did Maria make? She made 25 pieces of clothing.

Practice and Problem Solving: D

1. $\dfrac{e}{2}$ m = 4

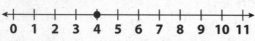

2. $a = 8$

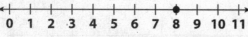

3. $s = 4$

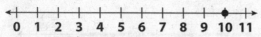

4. $u = 10$

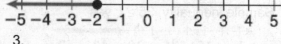

5. Area—60 ft^2; length—12 ft

6. Sample answer: $60 = 12w$

7. 5

8. Jim's garden is 5 feet wide.

Reteach

1. $n = 3$; $3 \cdot 3 = 9$✓

2. $n = 8$; $8 \div 2 = 4$✓

Reading Strategies

1. Divide by 3; $\dfrac{3r}{3} = \dfrac{24}{3}$; $r = 8$; $3 \cdot 8 = 24$✓

2. Multiply by 8; $\dfrac{b \cdot 8}{8}$

   $= 16 \cdot 8$; $b = 128$; $\dfrac{128}{8} = 16$ ✓

Success for English Learners

1. Substitute 8 for m. Check whether that equation is true. $4 \cdot 8 = 32$✓

2. $\dfrac{n}{3} = 2$; $\dfrac{n \cdot 3}{3} = 2 \cdot 3$; $n = 6$; $6 \div 3 = 2$✓

3. $5t = 20$; $\dfrac{5t}{5} = \dfrac{20}{5}$; $t = 4$; $5 \cdot 4 = 20$✓

MODULE 12 Challenge

1. $4{,}700 = 94w$; $w = 50$ ft; $P = 2 \cdot 94 + 2 \cdot 50$; $P = 288$ feet

2. $8{,}250 = 75l$; $l = 110$ m; $P = 2 \cdot 75 + 2 \cdot 110$; $P = 370$ meters

3. $1{,}586 = 26l$; $l = 61$ m; $P = 2 \cdot 26 + 2 \cdot 61$; $P = 174$ meters

4. $8{,}100 = 90w$; $w = 90$ ft; $P = 2 \cdot 90 + 2 \cdot 90$ (or $4 \cdot 90$); $P = 360$ feet

MODULE 13 Inequalities and Relationships

LESSON 13-1

Practice and Problem Solving: A/B

1.

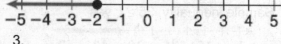

2.

3.

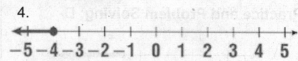

Possible check: $1 \geq 0$ is true

4.

Possible check: $-5 \leq -4$ is true

5.

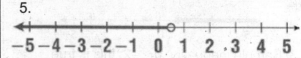

Possible check: $1 < 1.5$ is true

6. Sample inequality: $1 + x < 5$

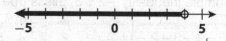

7. Sample inequality: $3 < y - 2$

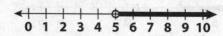

8. Sample inequality: $t \geq 10$

9. Sample inequality: $b \le 3$

10. Sample inequality: $x \ge -2$

11. Sample inequality: $x < -2$

Practice and Problem Solving: C

1. $-1, 0, 4\frac{1}{4}$

2. $-3.5, -1, 0$

3. Sample check: $4 \ge 1$

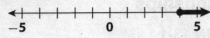

4. Sample check: $-4 \le 0.5$

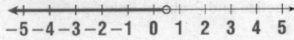

5. Sample check: $-2 < 1 - 3$

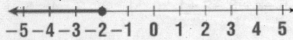

6. Sample inequality: $35 \ge t$; yes

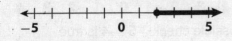

7. Sample inequality: $m \le 35$

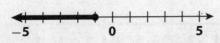

Practice and Problem Solving: D

1.

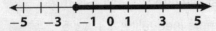

2.

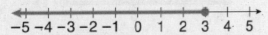

3. Sample inequality: $0 \ge -2$; this is true

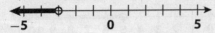

4. Sample inequality: $-2 \le 3$; this is true

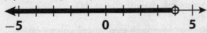

5. Sample inequality: $-4 < -3$; this is true

6. Sample inequality: $x < 4$

Reteach

7. Sample inequality: $-1 > y$

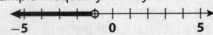

8. Sample inequality: $t > 0$

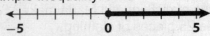

9. Sample inequality: $m > 2$

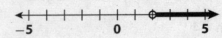

Reteach

1.

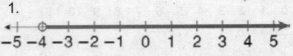

2.

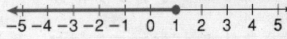

3.

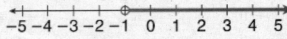

4.

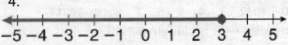

5. Sample inequality: $2 + 3 < y$

6. Sample inequality: $y + 2 \ge 6$

Reading Strategies

1. An inequality is a comparison of two unequal values.

2. The symbol $<$ means less than and the symbol $\le$ means less than or equal to.

3. The symbol $>$ means greater than and the symbol $\ge$ means greater than or equal to.

4. Sample inequality: $x \le 30$

5. 28 is a solution to the inequality because $28 \le 30$ is true.

Success for English Learners

1. yes; $4 \le 4$ is true

2. no, $-2 > -2$ is not true

3. solid circle; the inequality $\ge$ means it can be equal to or greater than

4.

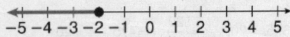

LESSON 13-2

Practice and Problem Solving: A/B

1. $11 > n$

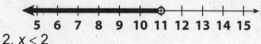

2. $x < 2$

3. $m \leq 54$

4. $-16 \geq b$

5. $266 \leq p$

6. $c \geq -76$

7. $53 + x \geq 76$; $x \geq 23$; DeShawn needs at least $23 more.

8. $x + 418 \geq 500$; $x \geq 82$; Kristen needs at least 82 points to win.

9. $x + 78 \leq 125$; $x \leq 47$; Abha can invite at most 47 more people.

10. Sample answer: Sacha needs 56 ounces of milk for a recipe. He has a 32 ounce carton. What is the least number of ounces he must buy in order to have enough for his recipe?

    $m + 32 \geq 56$; $m \geq 24$; He needs to at least 24 more ounces of milk.

Practice and Problem Solving: C

1. $\$3,007 + \$3,027 + \$3,690 + x \leq \$12,000$;

   $x \leq \$2,276$

   Meagan can spend at most $2,276 for the month of September.

2. $\$680 + \$572 \leq \$905 + s$; $\$3,347 \leq s$

   Meagan could spend at least $337 on food in September.

3. $\$403 + \$455 + \$461 + \$412 \geq \$214 + \$290 + \$614 + x$; $613 \geq x$

   Meagan can spend at most $613 on entertainment in September.

4. $\$905 + \$500 + \$614 \leq \$1,210 + \$461 + y$

   $\$348 \leq y$

   To meet her goal, she would spend at least $348 less.

5. Sample answer: Meagan wants to spend no more than $1,700 on utilities from June through September. How much can she spend on utilities in September and still meet this goal?

   $\$403 + \$455 + \$461 + u \leq \$1,700$

   $u \leq \$381$

   Meagan could spend up to $381 or less on utilities in September.

Practice and Problem Solving: D

1. $r > 3$

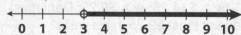

2. $m \leq 3$

3. $x < 3$

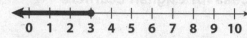

4. $k \geq 3$

5. $a > -5$

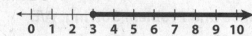

6. $h \leq 12$

7. $v < -8$

8. $y > -21$

9. $44 - 29 < s$ $15 < s$

   An SUV gets at least 15 miles per gallon.

10. $135 + d > 240$ $d > 105$

    Carlos needs to go at least 105 more miles.

Reteach

1. $x > -12$

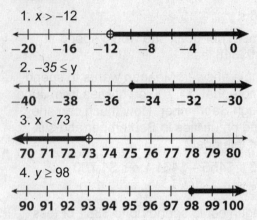

2. $-35 \le y$

3. $x < 73$

4. $y \ge 98$

Reading Strategies

1. $48 + t \le 72$; $t \le 24$; The table can be at most 24 inches.

2. $5 + w \ge \$14.25$; $w \ge \$9.25$; Dani must have at least \$9.25 in his wallet.

Success for English Learners

1. b.

2 c.

3 a.

LESSON 13-3

Practice and Problem Solving: A/B

1. $x > 30$

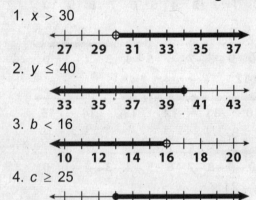

2. $y \le 40$

3. $b < 16$

4. $c \ge 25$

5. $a > 240$

6. $r \le 26$

7. $b < 120$

8. $s \ge 63$ ($15 \times 4.2 = 63$)

9. $6t > 660$, $t > 110$; at least 110 tickets.

10. $3f \ge 87$, $f \ge 261$, at least \$261.

11. $9h > 180$, $h > 20$, more than 20 hours.

12. $6c \le 360$, $c \le 60$, no more than \$60 per chair

Practice and Problem Solving: C

1. $a > 300$

2. $r \le 1.5$

3. $b < 12.2$

4. $s \ge 630$

5. $6t > 660$, $t > 110$; at least 110 tickets must be sold to make a profit. The drama club has already sold 25 tickets. $110 - 25 = 85$, so at least 85 more tickets must be sold.

6. $\frac{f}{3} \ge 80$, $f \ge 240$, so the team must make at least \$240 this year. $\frac{240}{10} = 24$, so the team must sell at least 24 T-shirts. $\frac{80}{5} = 16$, so last year, the team sold 16 hats. $24 - 16 = 8$, so the team will have to sell at least 8 more T-shirts than it sold hats.

7. She gets \$10 in allowance, and $\$190 - \$10 = \$180$, so she only needs to babysit enough hours to make \$180. $9h > 180$, $h > 20$, so she has to babysit more than 20 hours.

8. $6c \le 360$, $c \le 60$, so he can spend no more than \$60 per chair without the coupons. With the coupons, he can spend \$20 more per chair. $60 + 20 = 80$, so he can spend no more than \$80 per chair.

Practice and Problem Solving: D

1. 5; x; 10

2. 5; 5; 2

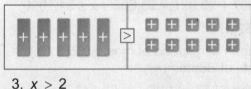

3. $x > 2$

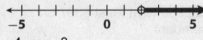

4. $x > 3$

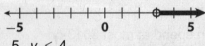

5. $y \le 4$

6. $b < 3$

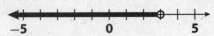

7. $c \geq 4$

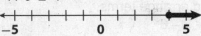

8. $a > 24$

9. $r \leq \dfrac{5}{3}$

10. $b < 4$

11. $s \geq 28$

Reteach

1. 7; remains the same; $<$; $<$
2. 3; remains the same; $\geq$; $\geq$
3. $r \geq 20$
4. $b < 9$
5. $n > 12$
6. $c < 21$
7. $t \leq 26$
8. $y \geq 120$

Reading Strategies

1. multiply
2. 8
3. $x < 40$
4. Sample answers: 37, 38, 39
5. divide
6. 4
7. $y > 3$
8. Sample answers: 4, 5, 6

Success for English Learners

1. It means that the number you found is not included in the answer.
2. You substitute any number from the solution set into the original equation and see if you get a true or false statement.
3. Answers will vary. Sample answer: Carla bought 6 apples and spent more than $12. How much did each apple cost? $6a > 12$, $a > 2$, at least $2.

LESSON 13-4

Practice and Problem Solving: A/B

1. $x \leq 6$

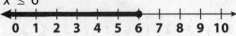

2. $y \geq -8$

3. $b < -5$

4. $c > 3$

5. $x < -\dfrac{1}{4}$

6. $r \leq -0.9$

7. $b < -\dfrac{3}{2}$

8. $a \leq 35$

9. no more than 6 days
10. no more than 16 s
11. at least 12 times

Practice and Problem Solving: C

1. $x < 6$
2. $y \geq \dfrac{2}{3}$
3. $a \geq \dfrac{1}{4}$
4. $b < 1$
5. no more than 9 days
6. no more than 75 s
7. no more than 25 s
8. no more than 3 weeks

Practice and Problem Solving: D

1. $1 < -3$; false; reverse the inequality symbol
2. true; nothing
3. $1 > 2$; false; reverse the inequality symbol
4. false; reverse the inequality symbol
5. $x \leq 4$

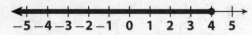

6. $y > -12$

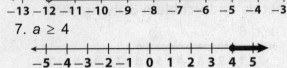

7. $a \geq 4$

8. $b < 2$

9. $a \leq -36$

10. $b \geq -6$

11. $c > 2$

12. $d < 27$

Reteach

1. 8; remains the same; 8, 8, $a < -24$

2. –4; is reversed; –4, –4, $s \leq 9$

3. $r \geq -14$

4. $b < -6$

5. $n < 12$

6. $c < -48$

Reading Strategies

1. To get the x by itself on one side

2. What you do to one side of an equation or inequality, you must do to another.

3. ASK: Did you multiply or divide by a negative number? If yes, reverse the inequality symbol.

4. It would remain the same. You would not reverse it.

Success for English Learners

1. "x is greater than 3."

2. When you multiply or divide by a negative number.

MODULE 13 Challenge

1. The first inequality is solved as usual. The second inequality involves multiplying by a negative number, so the inequality symbol will be reversed.

$\dfrac{x}{3} \geq 2$ $\qquad$ $\dfrac{x}{-3} \geq 2$

$x \geq 6$ $\qquad$ $x \leq -6$

2. Sample answer: $2x + x - 12 + 3x - 6$

Evaluate for $x = 3$. $2(3) + 3 - 12 + 3(3) - 6$

Simplify and arrange terms.

$6 + 3 - 12 + 9 - 6$

Simplify. $6 + 3 + 9 - 12 - 6$

$18 - 18$

0

3. Yes, you can divide both sides by –5, getting $x < 0$. For any negative x, $-5x$ is greater than 0.

4. Predictions will vary.

$x \geq 3$ and $x < -1$ $\qquad$ $x < 3$ and $x \geq -2$

$x \geq 3$ and $x < -1$ $\qquad$ $x < 3$ and $x \geq -2$

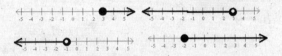

The first pair of inequalities has no common solutions.

The second pair of inequalities has common solutions so that $x \geq -2$ and < 3 or $-2 \leq \hat{\ }x\hat{\ } < 3$. The set of common solutions is where both lines overlap on the number lines.

MODULE 14 Relationships In Two Variables

LESSON 14-1

Practice and Problem Solving: A/B

1. $A(-12, 14)$

2. $B(8, 8)$

3. $C(-12, -4)$

4. $D(0, -14)$

5. $E(14, 0)$

6. $F(0, 0)$

7 –12.

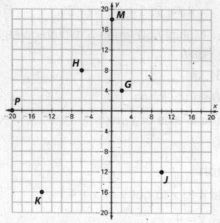

13. Answers will vary. Sample answer: "Go 6 blocks south."

14. Answers will vary. Sample answer: "Go 5 blocks east and 1 block south."

15. Answers will vary. Sample answer: "Go 5 blocks south and 5 blocks west."

Practice and Problem Solving: C

1. Axes labeling may vary. Sample answer:

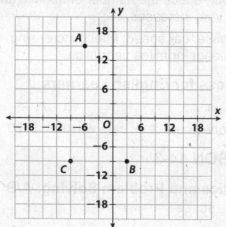

2. Axes labeling may vary. Sample answer:

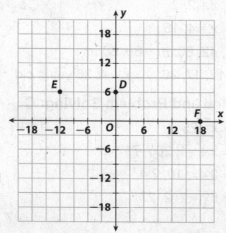

3. Quadrant III; $X(-2, -19)$

4. Quadrant I; $Y(3, 13)$

5. Quadrant IV; $Z(2, -4)$

6. Answers will vary. Sample answer: One of the coordinates of the new point must be 4 or 8. $P(2, 4)$, $Q(2, 8)$, $R(5, 8)$.

7. Answers will vary. Sample answer: One of the coordinates of the new point must be -3 or -4. $S(-3, -5)$, $T(4, -5)$, $U(4, 5)$.s

Practice and Problem Solving: D

1. C

2. C

3. B

4. $A(3, -1)$

5. $B(2, 4)$

6. $C(0, -3)$

7. $D(1, -1)$

Reteach

1. $(-3, +4)$

2. $(+2, -5)$

3. $(+9, +1)$

4. The point $(0, 7)$ is not in a quadrant; it is on the positive y-axis between quadrants I and II.

Reading Strategies

Some answers will vary. Sample answers are given.

1. J

2. r

3. s

4. K

5. Sample answer: L

6. (r, s)

7. Sample answer: M

8. N

Success for English Learners

1. Up or down, if the y-value is non-zero.

2. Quadrants III or IV

3. Yes, unless the x and y-values are equal.

LESSON 14-2

Practice and Problem Solving: A/B

1. m, money; h, hours worked

2. L, large pizza; M, medium pizza

3. Current

4. Light intensity

5. Answers will vary. Sample answer: close to zero.

6. Answers will vary. Sample answer: 1,000; $c = \dfrac{L1}{10}$.

7. y-axis

8. There is no lap time until the driver drives the first lap, $x = 1$.

Practice and Problem Solving: C

1. Speed; number of passengers

2. Answers will vary. Sample answer: the faster the bus goes, the more fuel it uses.

3. Answers will vary. Sample answer: the more passengers the bus carries, the more fuel that is consumed.

4. Answers will vary Sample answer: Students should recognize that the fuel consumption is related to *both* the number of passengers and the bus speed. The three variables interact in a complex way that is not completely clear from or explained by this data.

5. For each increase in the independent variable, the dependent variables changes more for line A than it does for line B, except when the value of the independent variables is zero, in which case the value of line A's dependent variable and line B's dependent variable are the same (22.5 units).

6. For each change in the independent variable, the dependent variable increases by the same amount. However, the value of line B's dependent variable will always be 22.5 units more than the corresponding value of line C's dependent variable.

Practice and Problem Solving: D

1. a. It depends on how long the water has been filling the tank.

b. $50 \div 10 = 100 \div 20 = 150 \div 30 = 200 \div 40 = 250 \div 50 = 5$; 5

c. Multiply 60 times 5, which gives 300 gal/

2. 1.61 km

3. 300 sandwiches

4. vertical axis or y-axis

5. 150

Reteach

1. Add 4 to x to get y or $x + 4 = y$

2. a. $y = 4$

b. $x = -1$

c. $y = 2x$

Reading Strategies

1. Cause: increasing number of families requesting assistance; effect: fewer bottles of drinking water per family.

2. Cause: increasing number of voters per hour; effect: the number of hours it takes to vote increases.

3. Cause: car speed; effect: increasing mileage or miles per gallon.

Success for English Learners

1. 50 in.

2. Money collected; cars washed; $300

LESSON 14-3

Practice and Problem Solving: A/B

1. $y = 7x$; 35

2. $y = x - 5$; 1

3. $y = x \div 2$; 2

4. $y = x + 4$; 15

5. 24, 42, 60; $m = 6d$; 60 mi

6. 6, 12, 17, 36; $y = x - 4$; 36 years old

Practice and Problem Solving: C

1. $y = x^2$; 25

2. $y = x \div -4$; 20, −7

3. $y = 0.4x$; 10, 2.4

4. $y = 5x + 2$; 2, 27

5. F represents °F, C represents °C; 68°F; Yes it is a solution because
$$F = \frac{9}{5}(30) + 32 = 86.$$

6. $C = \frac{5}{9}(F - 32)$; $C = \frac{5}{9}(59 - 32) = 15$, so the temperature is 15°C.

Practice and Problem Solving: D

1. $y = x + 2$
2. $y = x \div 5$
3. $y = 3x$
4. $y = x - 2$
5. 100, 120; C
6. 6, 11, 23; B; 33 years old

Reteach

1. $y = 3x$; $y = 18$
2. $y = x - 3$; $y = 12$
3. 8, 18, 40; $y = 2x$; 40 in.

Reading Strategies

1. 8
2. 24
3. 48
4. y stands for ounces; x stands for cups
5. $y = 16$
6. $y = 8(15)$, So 120 ounces is the same as 15 cups.

Success for English Learners

1. The equation shows the relationship between x and y.
2. To substitute a value means to replace the variable in the equation with the value given for it.
3. $y = 12(5)$, $y = 60$; So Mike has 60 inches of rope.

LESSON 14-4

Practice and Problem Solving: A/B

1. 27, 12, 9, 6, 4, 3
2. radios; hours
3. (0, 24), (2, 22), (4, 20), (6, 18), (8, 16), (10, 14), (12, 12)
4. 2

5. The total number decreases.
6. $n = -2h + 24$
7. Because the total number of radios decreases by 2 every 2 hours.

Practice and Problem Solving: C

1. 27, 12, 9, 6, 3
2. The number of plant fossils counted daily is decreasing.
3. Rate A for Days 1 and 2 is the greatest decrease in fossils counted.
4. −15 fossils counted per day; −3 fossils counted per day; −1 fossil counted per day.

Practice and Problem Solving: D

1. 10, 13; (0, 4), (1, 7), (2, 10), (3, 13); $y = 3x + 4$
2. −8; (0, 0), (1, −4), (2, −8), (4, −16); $y = -4x$
3. 4, 23; (0, 5), (2, 11), (4, 17), (6, 23); $y = 3x + 5$
4. Any three of the ordered pairs (−8, −4), (−4, −2), (4, 2), (8, 2); $y = 0.5x + 0$ or $y = 0.5x$
5. Any three of the ordered pairs (−8, −4), (−4, 0), (0, 4), (4, 8); $y = x + 4$
6. Any three of the ordered pairs (0, 8), (2, 4), (4, 0), (6, −4); $y = -2x + 8$

Reteach

1. $y = 0.5x + 1.5$
2. $y = -\frac{3}{2}x + 6$

Reading Strategies

1. $\frac{7}{5}$
2. $\frac{1}{4}$

Success for English Learners

1. $y = x + 2$
2. $y = 2x - 1$

MODULE 14 Challenge

1. tables and graph

Table 1

°C	°F
10	50
11	52
12	54
13	55
14	57
15	59

Table 2

°C	°F
10	50
11	51.8
12	53.6
13	55.4
14	57.2
15	59

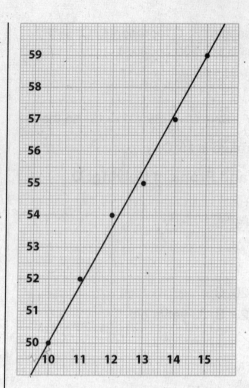

2. Sample answer: The data for Table 2 lie along the straight line because they are computed from the equation. For Table 1, four of the data points are either above or below the line, although they are close to it. The data for Table 1 are approximations because the thermometer can only be read to about the nearest half degree.

UNIT 5: Relationships in Geometry

MODULE 15 Angles, Triangles, and Equations

LESSON 15-1

Practice and Problem Solving: A/B

1. no
2. yes
3. no
4. $2 m + 2 m = 4 m$
5. $4 \text{ in.} + 6 \text{ in.} > 9 \text{ in.}$
6. $5 \text{ mm} + 1 \text{ mm} < 10 \text{ mm}$
7. $\frac{1}{2} + \frac{1}{3} > \frac{1}{5}$; $\frac{1}{2} < \frac{1}{3} + \frac{1}{5}$
8. $0.1 < 0.15 + 0.2$; $0.1 + 0.15 > 0.2$
9. $4 \text{ cm} + 5 \text{ cm} > 6 \text{ cm}$; $4 \text{ cm} + 5 \text{ cm} > 7 \text{ cm}$; $4 \text{ cm} + 6 \text{ cm} > 7 \text{ cm}$; $5 \text{ cm} + 6 \text{ cm} > 7 \text{ cm}$
10. greater; third

Practice and Problem Solving: C

1. 12, 11, 8; 12, 10, 7; 12, 9, 6; 12, 8, 5
2. 12, 8, 11; 12, 8, 10; 12, 8, 9; 12, 8, 7; 12, 8, 6; 12, 8, 5
3. 9, 11, 15; 8, 11, 15; 7, 11, 15; 6, 11, 15; 5, 11, 15
4. No; $5^2 = 25$; $4^2 + 2^2 = 16 + 4 = 20$; $5^2 \neq 4^2 + 2^2$
5. Yes; $(2L)^2 = 4L^2$; $L^2 + (\sqrt{3}\,L)^2 = L^2 + 3L^2 = 4L^2$
6. $60^2 = 30^2 + h^2$; $h = 30\sqrt{3}$ ft
7. $A = 1$, $B = 4$, $C = 3$
8. $A = 5$, $B = 10$, $C = 12$

Practice and Problem Solving: D

1. 6
2. 7
3. 7
4. 8
5. 5
6. 7

7. 9
8. 400 yd

Reteach

1. $A + B = 15$, so $C > 15$; sample answer: 16.
2. $A + \frac{2}{3} > 1\frac{3}{4}$, or $A > 1\frac{1}{12}$; A's only whole number value is 1, since $1\frac{3}{4} > A > 1\frac{1}{12}$.

Reading Strategies

1. 7 inches, 6 inches, and 5 inches are possible lengths.
2. $2.5 + 0.95 = 3.45$, so no triangle is formed with the three lengths.

Success for English Learners

1. Answers will vary; Sample answer: 5 yd, 9 yd, etc.
2. No; $10 + 15 = 25$.

LESSON 15-2

Practice and Problem Solving: A/B

1. $45°$
2. $50°$
3. $30°$
4. $46°$
5. $27°$
6. $37°$
7. $57°$
8. $1°$
9. $45 + b + 3b = 180°$
10. $x + x + 2x = 180°$
11. An equilateral triangle is shown, because all of its sides are equal.
12. $\angle O = 70°$

Practice and Problem Solving: C

1. $57°19'27''$
2. $64°33'25''$

3. $25.6° = 25\dfrac{3°}{5} = 25\dfrac{36°}{60} = 25°36''$

4. $100\dfrac{25}{100} = 10\dfrac{1}{4} = 100\dfrac{15}{60} = 100°15'$

5. $360°$

6. $720°$

7. $900°$

8. The angle measures are $A = 20°$, $B = 100°$, $C = 60°$, $E = 40°$, $F = 80°$, and $G = 60°$.

Practice and Problem Solving: D

1. $125°$; $125°$; $55°$

2. $44°$; $44°$; $136°$

3. $55° + 51°$; $106°$; $74°$

4. $92°$

5. $70°$

6. $54°$

7. $52°$

8. $180 = a + b + \angle C$;
   $\angle C = 180 - (a + b) = 180 - a - b$.

9. $180 = x + 4x + \angle C$ or $\angle C = 180 - 5x$

10. $180 = 90 + x + (90 - x)$ or $\angle C - 90 - x$

Reteach

1. scalene triangle

2. scalene right triangle

3. isosceles triangle

4. The 30° and 50° angles are acute angles; the 100° angle is an obtuse angle.

5. The 45° angle is an acute angle, and the 90° angle is a right angle. The angle marked with a question mark has to be an acute angle, too, since its measure is 45°, too.

Reading Strategies

1. $30 + 30 + ? = 180°$; $? = 180 - 60 = 120$; $120°$

2. $90 + 14 + ? = 180°$; $? = 180 - 104 = 76$; $76°$

3. The angles are all equal, so each angle is 60°.

Success for English Learners

1. To find the measure of the unknown angle.

2. No; $90 + 100$ is 190, which is more than 180.

3. They must add up to 90 degrees.

LESSON 15-3

Practice and Problem Solving: A/B

1. $68°$

2. $60°$

3. $62°$

4. $68°$

5. They are equal.

6. $56°$

7. shortest: x, second: $2x$, third: $3x$;
   $P = x + 2x + 3x = 6x$; longest side $= 3x$
   The longest side is one half of the perimeter.

8. Side DF, since it is the longest side.

9. The sum of the measures of angles Y and Z is greater than the measure of angle X since 180 degree less the sum of the measures of angles Y and Z equals the measure of angle X.

10. Sometimes, e.g. a triangle with angles of 155°, 20°, and 5°.

11. Never, since an isosceles triangle has two equal sides and all of the sides in a scalene triangle are unequal.

12. Sometimes, e.g. a 45°–45°–90° right triangle is the only isosceles right triangle.

Practice and Problem Solving: C

1. The measure of angle B would have to increase to 60°.

2. The measures of sides AB and BC would increase. The measure of angle A would increase. The measures of angle C and side AC would stay the same.

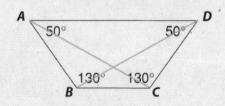

Only the common side for each pair of triangles formed is the same. For $\triangle ABC$ and $\triangle DCA$ that is AC. For $\triangle ADB$ and $\triangle BDC$ that is BD.

4. They are in different triangles. Angles opposite equal sides in the same triangle are equal.

5. In $\triangle ADC$, the triangle with the 50° angles, the sum of the other two angles is 130°. In $\triangle ABC$, the triangle with the 180° angle, the sum of the other two angles is 50°.

Practice and Problem Solving: D

1. 75°
2. 30°
3. *JK*
4. *KL*
5. right, scalene
6. equilateral
7. scalene
8. isosceles, right

Reteach

1. Since angle *X* has a measure greater than 90°, neither of the other two angles can be greater than 90°. Therefore, angle *X* is the largest angle and the side opposite it is the longest side.

2. If the side opposite angle *L* is the longest side, then angle *L* is the largest angle, which means that the other two angles are equal and less than angle *L*. It also means that the other two sides are equal and less than the side opposite angle *L*.

Reading Strategies

1. Answers and art will vary, but the distance *AC* will be greater than *AB* but less than *BC*.

2. No. The restrictions that *AC* point "northwest" and connect points *A* and *C* restrict *AC*'s length between that of *AB* and *BC* if a triangle is to be formed.

Success for English Learners

1. *B; AC*
2. 12

MODULE 15 Challenge

1. Equilateral; it has three congruent sides.

2. An isosceles triangle; sides *BE* and *CE* are corresponding parts of congruent triangles *CDE* and *ABE*.

3. 90°; the angles are complementary, since they form a right angle of the square.

4. 60°; it is one of three congruent angles in an equilateral triangle.

5. 30°; it is the complement of angle *ADE*.

6. 90°; the angles are complementary, since they form a right angle of the square.

7. Yes; since *CD* and *DE* are congruent, the angles opposite them are equal, so $x + x + 30 = 180$, which gives $x = 75°$. Since angles *CDE* and *BCE* are complementary, the measure of angle *BCE* is $90 - 75$ or 15°.

MODULE 16 Areas and volume equations

LESSON 16-1

Practice and Problem Solving: A/B

1. 288 ft^2
2. 45 m^2
3. 34 in^2
4. 8 ft^2
5. 27 cm^2
6. 108 in^2
7. 1,200 in^2
8. 84 cm^2
9. 240 ft^2

Practice and Problem Solving: C

1. 38 m^2
2. 60.2 in^2
3. 47.6 cm^2
4. 144 ft^2
5. 26 in^2
6. 36.75 ft^2
7. 0.56 yd^2
8. 686 cm^2
9. 243 in^2

Practice and Problem Solving: D

1. 60 m²
2. 32 in²
3. 39 cm²
4. 30 yd²
5. 40 ft²
6. 27 cm²
7. 4,500 cm²
8. 75 in²
9. 25 yd²

Reteach

1. 96 m²
2. 48 ft²
3. 12 yd²
4. 27.5 m²

Reading Strategies

1. Use the formula $A = bh$.
2. Substitute 10 for b; Substitute 4 for h.
3. 40 cm²
4. Use the formula $\frac{1}{2}h(b_1 + b_2)$.
5. Substitute 4 for h, 6 for b_1, and 8 for b_2. Add the lengths of the bases.
6. 28 in²

Success for English Learners

1. No, the lengths of the bases get added together before any other operation is completed. The order in which you add the lengths of the bases will not change the sum of the bases.
2. Separate the trapezoid into two triangles and a rectangle. Find the area of each part and add the areas together.
3. 26 cm²

LESSON 16-2

Practice and Problem Solving: A/B

1. 20 cm²
2. 25 in²
3. 50 yd²
4. 7 ft²
5. 20 ft²

6. 1.5 in²
7. 6 ft²
8. 26 in²

Practice and Problem Solving: C

1. 17.55 yd²
2. $8\frac{7}{16}$ ft²
3. 5 m²
4. 8 in²
5. You could change all the areas to one unit, say square inches, by dividing square yards by 36 × 36 and square feet by 12 × 12. Then you could add the areas.
6. 18.7 cm²
7. $\frac{9}{10}$ in²
8. 23.25 cm²
9. 8.4 in.

Practice and Problem Solving: D

1. 1.5 cm²
2. 14 in²
3. 16 m²
4. 35 ft²
5. 36 cm²
6. 48 in²
7. 28 ft²
8. 84 ft²
9. 600 yd²

Reteach

1. 12 cm²
2. 6 ft²
3. 15 m²
4. 9 mm²
5. 14 yd²
6. 20 in²

Reading Strategies

1. Use the formula $A = \frac{1}{2}bh$.
2. Substitute 10 for b; Substitute 4 for h.
3. 20 in²

4. 54 m^2

5. 4.5 ft^2

6. Use the same formula but substitute for area and base in the second and third steps. Then solve for the height.

Success for English Learners

1. No, as long as both sides (base and height) meet at a right angle.

2. because of the Associative Property of Multiplication.

3. 16 ft^2

LESSON 16-3

Practice and Problem Solving: A/B

1. $600 = \frac{1}{2}b(20)$; The base is 60 ft.

2. $1{,}224 = \frac{1}{2}h\left(70\frac{1}{2} + 65\frac{1}{2}\right)$; The base of the countertop is 18 in.

3. The width of the tabletop 3 ft.

4. The base is 30 cm.

5. The width of the door is 9 ft.

Practice and Problem Solving: C

1. 56 front frames

2. $77.97

3. 20 cm and 5 cm

4. 225 yd

5. 120 triangular pieces

Practice and Problem Solving: D

1. 5 in.

2. $525 = \frac{1}{2}h(30 + 40)$; 15 ft

3. 14 in.

4. 20 in.

5. 5 cm

6. 3 ft

Reteach

1. 10 m

2. 18 cm

3. 8 in.

4. 2 yd

5. 8 mm

Reading Strategies

1. 5 in.

2. 6 cm.

Success for English Learners

1. Write the formula for the area of the figure.

2. Substitute in known variables and solve for the missing variable.

LESSON 16-4

Practice and Problem Solving: A/B

1. 1,800 ft^3

2. 6,800 yd^3

3. 270 cm^3

4. 216 in^3

5. 15 ft^3

6. 3 cm

7. 6 in.

8. 8 in.

Practice and Problem Solving: C

1. 0.48 m^3

2. $98\frac{9}{32}$ ft^3

3. 2,274.885 cm^3

4. $35\frac{55}{64}$ ft^3

5. yes

6. 1,600 ft^3

7. 2.5 in.

8. $3,024

9. 1,797.12 in^3 ; 1.04 ft^3

Practice and Problem Solving: D

1. 24 ft^3

2. 960 yd^3

3. 120 in^3

4. 160 m^3

5. 90

6. 4 in.

7. 3 ft

8. 6 cm

Reteach

1. 16 ft³
2. 30 m³
3. 90 cm³
4. 1,000 yd³
5. 27 mm³
6. 120 in³

Reading Strategies

1. 4
2. 3
3. 12
4. 4
5. 3
6. 12
7. 24
8. 24 cubic units
9. Sample answer: 3 layers of 12 blocks each; 36 blocks or cubic units in all

Success for English Learners

1. Multiply the length times the width times the height.
2. Volume is measured in cubic units whereas area is measured in square units.

MODULE 16 Challenge

1. 12 and 28 square units
2. 40 square units
3. Answers may vary, depending on how the triangles are drawn inside ABFG.

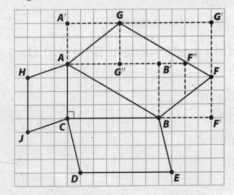

As shown, the triangles and the trapezoid inside ABFG have a total Area of about $36\frac{1}{2}$ square units. The area of the large rectangle A'G'F'C is 77 square units; the triangles AA'G, GG'F, ABC, and BFF' have areas of 6, 6, 14, and 14 square units for a total of 40 square units, which gives an area for ABFG of 37 square units. The area of ABFG is about 37 square units, so there is a small difference between the areas of ABFG and the sum of the areas of ACHJ and BCDE.

4. The measure of AB is $\sqrt{65}$ units.

5. Answers will vary, but students should infer that the area of ABFG may not be a whole number like 37 because at least one of the two quantities used to compute the area is irrational. Students might also question whether the sum of the areas of the smaller parallelograms equals the area of the larger parallelogram.

UNIT 6: Measurements and Data

MODULE 17 Displaying, Analyzing, and Summarizing Data

LESSON 17-1

Practice and Problem Solving: A/B

1. 5
2. 74 in.
3. 73 in.
4. No; both describe the heights equally well.
5. Mean: 49 °F, Median: 50°F
6. Mean: 87.5, Median: 88
7. Mean: 69 beats/min, Median: 69 beats/min
8. a. Mean: 53.75 min, Median: 54 min

   b. No; either the mean or median can be used since they are so close in value.

   c. Mean: 58 min, Median: 56 min

   d. Yes; the median better describes the data. The mean is too high since only two of the 9 times are greater than 58 minutes.

Practice and Problem Solving: C

1. Mean: 6.8 in., Median: 6.45 in.
2. Mean: $185, Median: $190.50
3. Mean: 17.6 calendars, Median: 14.5 calendars
4. Mean: 7 km, Median: 5.5 km
5. Sample answer: The median best describes the data set because it is closer than the mean to the number of kilometers that Clara ran the majority of the days.
6. 15
7. 16
8. Answers will vary. Sample answer: 12, 10, 18, 20, 14. The mean is 14.8 and the median is 14. Both measures can be used to describe the data.

Practice and Problem Solving: D

1. a. 48

   b. $\frac{48}{6} = 8$; 8 m

2. a. 6, 7, 7, 8, 9, 11

   b. 7 and 8; $\frac{7+8}{2} = \frac{15}{2} = 7.5$; 7.5 m

3. 6
4. Mean: 20 points, Median: 22 points
5. Median; Sample answer: The median is closer to more of the data values than the mean.

Reteach

1. $11
2. 21 students
3. Yes; 7 + 8 = 15, 12 + 13 = 25, and 4 + 11 = 15. So, the sum of the data values is 15 + 15 + 25 + 15 = 70.

Reading Strategies

1. close together
2. Mean: 100, Median: 98
3. No; both measures describe the scores equally well.
4. spread out
5. Mean: 102, Median: 94
6. Yes; the median is closer to most of the data values.
7. Answers may vary. Sample answer: The mean and median fall in the center of the data when graphed on a number line.

Success for English Learners

1. The data values are written in increasing order from least value to greatest value.
2. Find the mean of the middle two values.

LESSON 17-2

Practice and Problem Solving: A/B

1. 61, 61, 62, 64, 64, 66, 69, 69, 70, 72, 73, 74, 78, 78
2. 69
3. 64
4. 73
5.

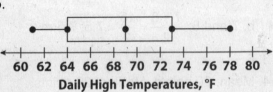

Daily High Temperatures, °F

6. 9
7. 17
8. Class A: 15, 18, 18, 20, 23, 28, 30, 33, 33, 34, 38, 40

   Class B: 18, 20, 24, 26, 26, 27, 28, 28, 29, 29, 29, 30
9. Class: A: median: 29; range: 25; IQR: 14.5

   Class: B: median: 27.5; range: 12; IQR: 4
10. Sample answer: The box plot for Class A would be longer than that of Class B. The box portion for Class A will be more than 3 times as long as that for Class B.

Practice and Problem Solving: C

1. Put the data in order; 40, 40, 41, 42, 42, 42, 43, 43, 43, 44, 47, 47 48, 48, 48, 48, 48, 49, 50, 50
2. median: 45.5; range: 10; IQR: 6
3.

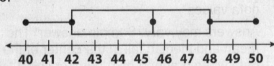

4.

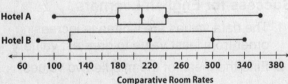

Comparative Room Rates

5. Hotel B
6. Hotel B
7. Sample answer: The interquartile range is smaller for Hotel A than for Hotel B, so Hotel A's room rates are more predictable

Practice and Problem Solving: D

1. 6, 8, 10, 12, 12, 15, 15, 20
2. 12
3. 9
4. 15
5.

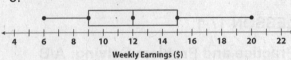

Weekly Earnings ($)

6. 6
7. 14
8. Juan: 1, 2, 2, 3, 4, 4, 6, 6, 8

   Mia: 2, 2, 2, 4, 5, 5, 6, 6, 6
9. Mia
10. Juan
11. Neither, they are both the same, 4.

Reteach

1. 6, 8, 10, 10, 12, 14, 15, 15, 20
2. least value: 6; greatest value: 20
3. median: 12
4. lower quartile: 9; upper quartile: 15
5.

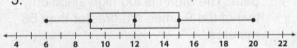

Reading Strategies

1. the middle half of the data
2. The whiskers extend from both ends of the box to the least and greatest values.
3. It divides the set of data in half.
4. least value; lower quartile
5. upper quartile; greatest value
6. median; upper quartile

Success for English Learners

	Median	Least Value	Greatest Value	Lower Quartile	Upper Quartile
1. Box Plot *B*	45.5	40	50	42	48
2. Box Plot *C*	46	42	50	45	47

3. Box Plot *C*

LESSON 17-3

Practice and Problem Solving: A/B

1. statistical; Sample answer: miles

2. not statistical

3.

People in Our Homes

4. mean:4.2; median: 4; range: 9

5. The spread is from 2 to 11, 11 appears to be an outlier. There is a cluster from 2 to 7 with a peak at 4. The distribution is not symmetric.

6. 11; The outlier raises the mean by 0.3 and increases the spread by 4. It does not change the median.

7. Check student's work.

Practice and Problem Solving: C

1.

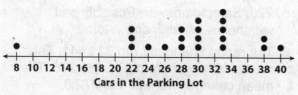

Cars in the Parking Lot

2. mean: 29; median: 30; range: 32

3. The spread is from 8 to 40, 8 appears to be an outlier. There is a cluster from 28 to 33 with a peak at 33. The distribution is not symmetric.

4. 8; The outlier lowers the mean by 1 and increases the spread by 14. It does not change the median.

5–8. Check student's work.

Practice and Problem Solving: D

1.

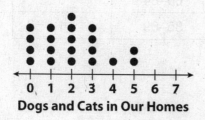

Dogs and Cats in Our Homes

2. mean: 2; median: 2; range: 5

3. B. not symmetric

4.

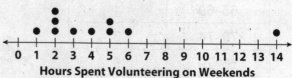

Hours Spent Volunteering on Weekends

5. mean: 4.4; median: 3.5; range: 13

6. A. symmetric

7. an outlier

Reteach

1.

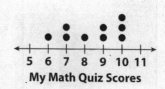

My Math Quiz Scores

2. 14

3. 12.2

4. 12

Reading Strategies

1. The range is 8. The spread of the data is from 0 to 8 with 8 being an outlier.

2. The mean is 2.1 and the median is 2.

3. Sample answer: There are about the same number of dots on each side of the center of the range.

Success for English Learners

1. The spread of the data is 1 to 7, which is a range of 6.

2. 4.1

3. 4

4. There are more dots on one side of the center of the range than on the other side.

LESSON 17-4

Practice and Problem Solving: A/B

1.

Players' Heights

Stem	Leaves
6	5
7	1 2 2 6 7 8 9 9 9
8	0 0 0 0 1 1 2 2 7

2.

Players' Heights	
Heights (in.)	Frequency
65–69	1
70–74	3
75–79	6
80–84	8
85–89	1

3.

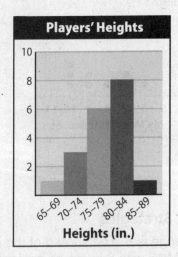

4. a. 22

  b. 79

  c. 80

5. Sample answer: The average height of players is about 78 inches. Explanations will vary.

Practice and Problem Solving: C

1.

Students in School

Stem	Leaves
22	0
23	
24	
25	2 3 4 5 6
26	0 6
27	5 7 8 9 9
28	0 1 2 5 7 8
29	3

2.

Students in School	
Number	Frequency
220–239	1
240–259	5
260–279	7
280–299	7

3.

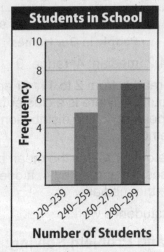

4. range: 73, median: 277.5; mean: 270

5. 220; Sample answer: Possibly bad weather, such as a snowstorm.

6. The range changes from 73 to 41. The median changes from 277.5 to 278. The mean changes from 270 to 272.6.

Practice and Problem Solving: D

1.

Players' Heights	
Heights (in.)	Frequency
60–64	2
65–69	2
70–74	4
75–79	7
80–84	0
85–89	1

2.

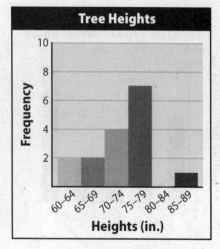

Tree Heights

3.

Tree Heights

Stem	Leaves
6	1 4 5 8
7	0 0 3 4 5 5 5 7 7 9 9
8	6

4. 25

5. 74.5

6. 73

7. range

8. Check students' work. Sample answer: Trees for sale ranging from 61 in. to 86 in.

Reteach

1. Sample answer: Both use frequency intervals of 10. The shape of the bars of the histogram is about the same as the shape of the leaves on the stem-and-leaf plot.

2. Sample answer: The stem-and-leaf plot lets you see the individual data values while the histogram only allows you to see the data grouped in intervals.

3. stem-and-leaf plot

4. 33.5

Reading Strategies

1. Sample answer: The ordered list, stem-and-leaf plot, and dot plot make it easy to identify the median, range, and mean. The mean and the range cannot be found using the frequency table and histogram.

2. Sample answer: When comparing data sets, the line plot makes the comparison easiest. If you need to know the individual values in a data set, a frequency table or a histogram is not the best choice.

Success for English Learners

1. the stem-and-leaf plot because it gives individual values, so you can find the median and the mean

2. Most of the high temperatures are less than 80.

LESSON 17-5

Practice and Problem Solving: A/B

1.

Favorite Birds

blue jay   cardinal   eagle   robin   swan

2. cardinal and eagle

3.

Favorite Type of Summer Olympic Sport					
Sport	athletics	cycling	fencing	Gymnast-tics	swimming
Relative frequency	$\frac{10}{50} = $ 20%	$\frac{5}{50} = $ 10%	$\frac{5}{50} = $ 10%	$\frac{20}{50} = $ 40%	$\frac{10}{50} = $ 20%

4.

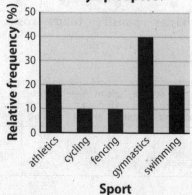

Favorite Type of Summer Olympic Sport

5. gymnastics

6–8. Check students' work.

Practice and Problem Solving: C

1–2. Check students' answers.

3.

Favorite Even Number					
Number	0	2	4	6	8
Relative frequency	$\frac{50}{200}$ $= 25\%$	$\frac{30}{200}$ $= 15\%$	$\frac{40}{200}$ $= 20\%$	$\frac{30}{200}$ $= 15\%$	$\frac{50}{200}$ $= 25\%$

4.

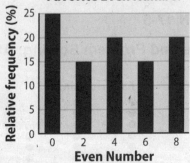

Favorite Even Number

5. 0 and 8

6. The mean and median cannot be found because the numbers 0, 2, 4, 6, and 8 are categorical data, similar to red, yellow, and blue.

7. 60 dolls

8. 100 more games than puzzles

Practice and Problem Solving: D

1.

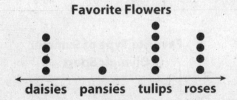

Favorite Flowers

daisies   pansies   tulips   roses

2. tulips

3.

Favorite Type of Water Sport					
Sport	boating	fishing	skiing	surfing	swimming
relative frequency	$\frac{25}{100}$ $= 25\%$	$\frac{20}{100}$ $= 20\%$	$\frac{5}{100}$ $= 5\%$	$\frac{10}{100}$ $= 10\%$	$\frac{40}{100} = 40\%$

4.

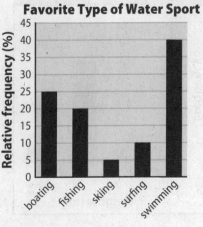

Favorite Type of Water Sport

5. swimming

6. Sample answer: Arrange them from greatest to least frequency: swimming, boating, fishing, surfing, skiing.

Reteach

1.

Our Favorite Season				
Season	Spring	Summer	Fall	Winter
relative frequency	$\frac{12}{50}$ $= 24\%$	$\frac{22}{50}$ $= 44\%$	$\frac{6}{50}$ $= 12\%$	$\frac{10}{50}$ $= 20\%$

Reading Strategies

1.

Activity Night Survey Results				
Activity	Swimming	Volley ball	Skating	Bowling
Relative frequency	$\frac{12}{30} = 40\%$	$\frac{10}{30}$ $= 33.3\%$	$\frac{3}{30}$ $= 10\%$	$\frac{5}{30}$ $= 16.7\%$

Success for English Learners

1. walk

2. 16% because 100% − 84% = 16%

MODULE 17 Challenge

1. 24

2. $Q1 < V1 < M$

3. $21 < V2 < Q1$

4. $V1 > 21$

5. Q1 = 45; M = 66; Q3 = 72; MAX = 84

6. Answers will vary, except for 21 and 84. Other points should include five data points between 21 and 45; six data points each in the intervals between 45 and 66 and between 66 and 72; five data points between 72 and 84.

Sample answer: from 21 to Q1: 21, 24, 27, 30, 33, and 42; from Q1 to M, 48, 51, 54, 57, 60, and 63; from M to Q3, 67, 68, 69, 70, 70, and 71; from Q3 to and including 84, 75, 76, 78, 79, 81, and 84

7. Using the sample data, the stem-and-leaf plot is shown.

8	1 4
7	0 0 1 5 6 8 9
6	0 3 7 8 9
5	1 4 7
4	2 8
3	0 3
2	1 4 7

MODULE 18 Becoming a Knowledgeable Consumer and Investor

LESSON 18-1

Practice and Problem Solving: A/B

1. First State Bank: $10
2. National Bank: $12.50
3. Third City Bank:$12
4. Sample answer: How close you live to the bank. What the days and times are that the bank is open.

5-6.

Check Number	Date	Transaction	Deposit		Withdrawal		Balance	
		Beginning balance					$140	00
123	5/5	Bruns' Bowling Alley			$16	63	$123	37
	5/8	Debit—Z-Store			$20	55	$102	82
	5/14	ATM withdrawal			$40	00	$62	82
	5/14	ATM fee			$2	00	$60	82
	5/15	Deposit	$93	00			$153	82

Practice and Problem Solving: C

1. $8
2. $12.50
3. $9
4. Accept reasonable answers.

5.

Check Number	Date	Transaction	Deposit		Withdrawal		Balance	
		Beginning balance					$208	04
123	5/5	Gloria's Grill			$18	45	$189	59
	5/8	Debit—Stan's Shop			$39	45	$150	14
	5/14	ATM withdrawal			$20	00	$130	14
	5/14	ATM fee			$1	50	$128	64
	5/15	Deposit	$108	50			$237	14

Practice and Problem Solving: D

1. Third City Bank
2. National Bank
3. First State Bank
4. Sample answer: You use your debit card and the ATM machine frequently.

5-6.

Check Number	Date	Transaction	Deposit		Withdrawal		Balance	
		Beginning balance					$200	00
123	5/5	Al's Flower Shop			$30	00	$170	00
	5/8	Debit—Carla's Shop			$20	00	$150	00
	5/14	ATM withdrawal			$30	00	$120	00
	5/14	ATM fee			$1	00	$119	00
	5/15	Deposit	$40	00			$159	00

Reteach

1.

Check Number	Date	Transaction	Deposit		Withdrawal		Balance	
		Beginning balance					$85	00
140	6/1	CP Mart			25	00	$60	00
	6/5	ATM			20	00	$40	00
	6/5	ATM fee			1	50	$38	50
	6/15	Deposit	50	00			$88	50

Reading Strategies

1-2.

	How you use your account	Compare costs of checks	Compare debit cards	Com-pare ATM fees	Do location and hours matter?	Which bank is best? Why?
1.	You write 2 checks a month, use the debit and ATM card every week. Mail in checks to deposit.	Bank B is better	Bank A is better	Bank B is better IF I use their ATM	It depends on how often I need to use the ATM.	Accept reasonable answers.
2.	You write 2 checks a month, use the debit card 10 times a month, use the ATM once a week. You deposit cash you earn twice a week.	Bank B is better	Bank A is better	Bank B is better IF I use their ATM	Yes, I need to deposit cash. Bank A is better.	Accept reasonable answers.

3. Sample answer: A debit card is better because I have the money and don't want to pay interest, although if I pay my credit card balance in full every month, I won't pay interest.

4. Sample answer: A credit card is better because I need the gift immediately and don't have the money to pay for it in my bank account.

Success for English Learners

1. Sample answer: By using the debit card, I won't have to pay interest.

2.

Check #	Date	Transaction	Deposit		Withdrawal		Balance	
		Beginning balance					$65	00
140	6/1	Betty's Bakery			12	50	$52	50
	6/5	ATM			20	00	$32	50
	6/5	ATM fee			1	75	$30	75
	6/15	Deposit	30	00			$60	75

LESSON 18-2

Practice and Problem Solving: A/B

1. a. 580
   b. 660
2. will help
3. will not help
4. will not help
5. a. $12,288
   b. $10,752
   c. $1,536
6. Sample answers: having a high balance; not making payments on time.
7. Sample answers: You want to be sure the information is accurate. If there are errors, you should contact the credit reporting company to see how you can get the errors corrected.

Practice and Problem Solving: C

1. a. Sample answer: Take a small loan from a bank and make payments on time.
   b. Sample answer: Keep the balance on credit cards low, make all payments on time.
2. a. $345
   b. $420
   c. $2,016

3. a. $303,480
   b. $343,440
   c. $39,960

Practice and Problem Solving: D

1. a. poor credit rating
   b. excellent credit rating
2. will not help
3. will not help
4. will help
5. a. $11,040
   b. $13,440
   c. $2,400
6. Sample answers: keeping the balance low, making payments on time.

Reteach

1. will not help
2. will help
3. will not help
4. will help
5. 660
6. 580

Reading Strategies

1. $408
2. $405

Success for English Learners

1. will not help
2. will help
3. will help
4. 550
5. 700

LESSON 18-3

Practice and Problem Solving: A/B

1. work-study, savings
2. loan
3. scholarship, grant
4. yes; 70% of 9,000 = $6,300; $6,300 + $3,000 =$9,300; $9,300 > $9,000
5. $3,100; $6,600 − ($2,000 + $1,500) = $3,100
6. no; tuition cost for 4 years: 4 × $7,200 = $28,800; savings: $100 × 12 months × 18 years = $21,600
7. $1,000; 60% of $5,000 = $3,000; $3,000 + $1,000 = $4,000; $5,000 − $4,000 = $1,000
8. Sample answer: live at home; find several students to share an apartment with
9. Sample answers: using ebooks or buying used books
10. Sample answers: do not have a car on campus; use generic products when possible

Practice and Problem Solving: C

1. $250
2. $23,000
3. $3,380
4. $15,400; $61,600
5. $15,000
6. $5,600
7. $1,400
8. Sample answer: Some expenses may increase over the four years.

Practice and Problem Solving: D

1. B
2. A
3. C

4. $600; 80% of 8,000 = $6,400; $6,400 + $1,000 = $7,400; $8,000 − $7,400 = $600
5. No, he needs $500 more.; 9,000 − $5,500 = $3,500; $3,500 − $3,000 = $500
6. $2,100; $8,600 − ($4,000 + $2,500) = $2,100
7. $1,000; 60% of $5,000 = $3,000; $3,000 + $1,000 = $4,000; $5,000 − $4,000 = $1,000
8. Sample answer: live at home; find several students to share an apartment with
9. Sample answers: use ebooks or buy used books

Reteach

1. $600
2. No, she needs $1,000 more.
3. $2,600
4. The problem cannot be solved without more information. For instance, if the tuition is $9,000, then books cost $2,000 and she does not have enough money. But, if tuition is $10,000, then books cost $1,000 and she does have enough money.

Reading Strategies

1. S
2. E
3. S
4. S
5. E
6. S
7. $400
8. no; $4,800
9. Income: grant: $5,000, savings: $590; loan: $3,000
10. Expenses: room and board: $1,000; tuition: $8,200; books and fees: $700; spending money: $900
11. No, She needs $2,210 more.

Success for English Learners

1. E
2. E
3. S

4. S

5. E

6. S

LESSON 18-4

Practice and Problem Solving: A/B

1. Accept reasonable answers.

2. Registered nurse: $1,940,700;
   Nursing aide: $720,300;
   Home health care worker: 605,100

3. Accept reasonable answers.

4. Architect: $2,176,500;
   Auto body repair: $1,127,400;
   Grounds maintenance: 712,200

Practice and Problem Solving: C

1. Accept reasonable answers.

2. Accountant/Auditor: $1,850,700;
   Middle-School Teacher: 1,558,800;
   Librarian: 1,635,000

3. Check students' work.

4 Check students' work.

Practice and Problem Solving: D

1. $1,132,200

2. $910,800

3. Accept reasonable answers.

4. Accept reasonable answers.

5. Bank manager: $3,117,300;
   Teller: $723,000;
   Bank examiner: 2,248,200

Reteach

1. Accept reasonable answers.

2. Customer service representative:
   $913,800; Police dispatcher: $1,061,100;
   Receptionist: $757,200

Reading Strategies

1. sales and related occupations

2. architecture and engineering occupations
   and community and social service
   occupations

3. healthcare support occupations

4. farming, fishing, and forestry occupations

5. healthcare support occupations and sales
   and related occupations

6. Accept reasonable answers.

Success for English Learners

Accept reasonable answers.

MODULE 18 Challenge

1. $10

2. $192

3. $18,400

4. $1,558,800

5. $13.00

6. $299

7. $6,000

8. $1,447,500